OXFORD MONOGRAPHS IN INTERNATIONAL LAW

Geographical Change and the Law of the Sea

OXFORD MONOGRAPHS IN INTERNATIONAL LAW

The aim of this series is to publish important and original pieces of research on all aspects of international law. Topics that are given particular prominence are those which, while of interest to the academic lawyer, also have important bearing on issues which touch the actual conduct of international relations. Nonetheless the series is wide in scope and includes monographs on the history and philosophical foundations of international law.

RECENT TITLES IN THE SERIES

Statehood and the State-Like in International Law
Rowan Nicholson

Confronting the Shadow State
Henri Decœur

Irresolvable Norm Conflicts in International Law
The Concept of a Legal Dilemma
Valentin Jeutner

Institutionalizing State Responsibility
Global Security and UN Organs
Vincent-Joël Proulx

Geographical Change and the Law of the Sea

KATE PURCELL

OXFORD
UNIVERSITY PRESS

OXFORD
UNIVERSITY PRESS

Great Clarendon Street, Oxford, OX2 6DP,
United Kingdom

Oxford University Press is a department of the University of Oxford.
It furthers the University's objective of excellence in research, scholarship,
and education by publishing worldwide. Oxford is a registered trade mark of
Oxford University Press in the UK and in certain other countries

First Edition published in 2019

Impression: 1

Published in the United States of America by Oxford University Press
198 Madison Avenue, New York, NY 10016, United States of America

British Library Cataloguing in Publication Data
Data available

Library of Congress Control Number: 2019947718

ISBN 978–0–19–874364–4

Printed and bound by
CPI Group (UK) Ltd, Croydon, CR0 4YY

Oh! Blessed rage for order, pale Ramon,
The maker's rage to order words of the sea,
Words of the fragrant portals, dimly-starred,
And of ourselves and of our origins,
In ghostlier demarcations, keener sounds.

Wallace Stevens,
'The Idea of Order at Key West' (1936)

General Editor's Preface

In *The Structure of Scientific Revolutions*, Thomas S. Kuhn famously posited a historical account of scientific progress in which the gradual evolution of received explanatory models is punctuated by moments of rupture in which the data is radically recast and a starkly different conceptual paradigm established. While Kuhn had his critics, explanatory and normative models differ, and international law is unlikely ever to have its Copernicus, Darwin or Einstein (although it has its occasional Bohr), Kate Purcell's *Geographical Change and the Law of the Sea* hints at the overthrow of our current understanding of the impact on maritime jurisdiction under the law of the sea not just of climate change but also of the more general susceptibility of coastal geography to incremental or violent alteration, including by way of falling sea levels, erosion, deltaic sedimentation, accretion, avulsion, and reclamation.

Dr Purcell maintains, contrary to the presently-dominant 'ambulatory' thesis, that the geographical limits and boundaries of a coastal state's sovereign rights over the appurtenant sea and seabed, once established, do not synchronously track the subsequent retreat or advance over time of its coastline or the subsequent disappearance or appearance within its territorial sea of low-tide elevations. Nor, she further submits, does subsequent coastal change give rise to an obligation on the part of the coastal state to adjust the baselines from which its established maritime zonal limits are measured, although, with the exception of the continental shelf, a coastal state is entitled to redraw its zonal limits to take seaward advantage of coastal change. Dr Purcell similarly argues, again against the current flow, that neither the generation of maritime zones by geographically-defined features such as islands and rocks nor a state's qualification as an archipelagic state and its associated entitlement to archipelagic waters is affected by geographical changes such as inundation consequent upon rising sea levels. More fundamentally, she challenges the assumption, which implicitly underpins the 'ambulatory' thesis and its cognates, that the legal conditions for maritime space, maritime limits and maritime boundaries require satisfaction on a continuing basis. To support her original claims, Dr Purcell creatively combines technical black-letter lawyering with insights gleaned from geographical and, more specifically, cartographical concepts and techniques. Her comparison with aspects of the law on territorial boundaries is enlightening. Her insistence on coastal geography as a construct as much as a physical fact and her like take, *mutatis mutandis*, on nautical charting are inspired.

Geographical Change and the Law of the Sea promises not only to make a significant contribution to the literature on the law of the sea but also to provide food for thought for government legal advisors wrestling with these issues.

RO'K, CR
Milan and Oxford
October 2019

Contents

Table of Cases

INTERNATIONAL CASES AND AWARDS

Domestic Cases

Treaties and Related Documents

DOMESTIC LEGISLATION AND RELATED DOCUMENTS

CLCS SUBMISSIONS AND COMMUNICATIONS

List of Abbreviations

ABA	American Bar Association
ABLOS	IOC, IHO, IAG Advisory Board on the Law of the Sea
Ad Hoc SeabedCommittee Report (1968)	Report of the Ad Hoc Committee to Study the Peaceful Uses of the Sea-bed (1968) 23 UNGAOR, Doc. A/7230.
AFDI	*Annuaire Français de Droit International*
AHR	*The American Historical Review*
AJIL	*American Journal of International Law*
AR5	IPCC, *Fifth Assessment Report* (IPCC, 2014)
ASDI	*Annuaire Suisse De Droit International*
ASIL Proceedings	*Proceedings of the American Society of International Law*
BYIL	*British Yearbook of International Law*
CCLR	*Carbon & Climate Law Review*
CLCS	Commission on the Limits of the Continental Shelf
CLCS Guidelines	CLCS, *Scientific and Technical Guidelines* (1999)
CLJ	*Cambridge Law Journal*
CSC	Convention on the Continental Shelf (1958)
CUP	Cambridge University Press
Digest of US Practice	*Digest of United States Practice in International Law*
EEZ	exclusive economic zone
EFZ	exclusive fisheries zones
EJIL	*European Journal of International Law*
ELQ	*Ecology Law Quarterly*
EPL	*Environmental Policy and Law*
FAO	*United Nations Food and Agriculture Organization*
FNI	Fridtjof Nansen Institute
GYIL	*German Yearbook of International Law*
Harvard Research	Harvard Research in International Law
HJIL	*Heidelberg Journal of International Law*
IAEA	International Atomic Energy Agency
IBRU	International Boundaries Research Unit (Durham University)
IBWC	International Boundary and Water Commission, United States and Mexico
IBWC Minutes	Minutes of the US–Mexico International Boundary and Water Commission, <https://www.ibwc.gov/Treaties_Minutes>.
ICJ	International Court of Justice
ICLQ	*International and Comparative Law Quarterly*
IDI	Institut de Droit International

IHB	International Hydrographic Bureau
IHO	International Hydrographic Organization
IJMCL	*The International Journal of Marine and Coastal Law*
ICLR	*International Community Law Review*
ILA	International Law Association
ILA-BC	International Law Association's Baselines Committee
ILC	International Law Commission
ILC Ybk 1951/I, ILC Ybk 1952/II etc.	Yearbooks of the International Law Commission, <http://untreaty.un.org/ilc/publications/yearbooks/yearbooks.htm>
ILM	*International Legal Materials*
IMCO	Inter-Governmental Maritime Consultative Organization
IOC UNESCO	Intergovernmental Oceanographic Commission of UNESCO
IPCC	Intergovernmental Panel on Climate Change
IPCC WGII	IPCC Working Group II
ISA	International Seabed Authority
ISNT	Informal Single Negotiating Text
ITLOS	International Tribunal for the Law of the Sea
JAIL	*Japanese Annual of International Law*
JCR	*Journal of Coastal Research*
JIDS	*Journal of International Dispute Settlement*
LAT	lowest astronomical tide
LIS	*Limits in the Seas*
LLW	lowest low water
LOS Bulletin	*Law of the Sea Bulletin*
LOSC	Law of the Sea Conference
LRIL	*London Review of International Law*
LTE	low-tide elevation
M	nautical mile
MCRM (2014)	*Maritime Claims Reference Manual* (2014), <https://www.jag.navy.mil/organization/code_10_mcrm.htm>
MIM	Maritime Institute of Malaysia
MLW	mean low water
MLWN	mean low water neap
MLWS	mean low water springs
MPEPIL Online	R Wolfrum (ed), *Max Planck Encyclopedia of Public International Law* (OUP, online edition), <https://opil.ouplaw.com/home/EPIL>
MUP	Manchester University Press
NILR	*Netherlands International Law Review*
NOAA	US National Oceanic and Atmospheric Administration
NYIL	*Netherlands Yearbook of International Law*
OAU	Organization of African Unity
ODIL	*Ocean Development & International Law*
OED	*Oxford English Dictionary*
OUP	Oxford University Press

PCIJ	Permanent Court of International Justice
Platzöder (1983/IV), (1984/V)	Platzöder, R. (ed.), *Third United Nations Conference on the Law of the Sea: Documents* (Oceana) (Vol IV, 1983), (Vol V, 1984)
RGDIP	*Revue Générale de Droit International Public*
Rosenne (1975/I), Rosenne (1975/II) etc.	S Rosenne (ed), *League of Nations Conference for the Codification of International Law (1930)*, Vols 1-4 (Oceana Publications, 1975)
RSNT	Revised Single Negotiating Text
Seabed Committee Report (1970)	Report of the Committee on the Peaceful Uses of the Sea-bed and the Ocean Floor beyond the Limits of National Jurisdiction (1970) 25 UN GAOR Supp. 21, UN Doc. A/8021
Seabed Committee Report (1971)	Report of the Committee on the Peaceful Uses of the Sea-bed and the Ocean Floor beyond the Limits of National Jurisdiction (1971) 26 UN GAOR Supp. 21, UN Doc. A/8421
Seabed Committee Report (1972)	Report of the Committee on the Peaceful Uses of the Sea-bed and the Ocean Floor beyond the Limits of National Jurisdiction (1972) 27 UN GAOR Supp. 21, UN Doc. A/8721
Seabed Committee Report (1973)	Report of the Committee on the Peaceful Uses of the Sea-bed and the Ocean Floor beyond the Limits of National Jurisdiction (1973) 28 UNGAOR, Supp. 21, UN Doc. A/9021, Volumes 1–6
SLR	*Stanford Law Review*
TSB	territorial sea baseline
TSC	Convention on the Territorial Sea and Contiguous Zone (1958)
UCP	University of Chicago Press
UJIEL	*Utrecht Journal of International and European Law*
UN Baselines Study (1989)	UN Office for Ocean Affairs and the Law of the Sea, *Baselines: An Examination of the Relevant Provisions of the United Nations Convention on the Law of the Sea* (UN Publications, 1989)
UNCLOS	United Nations Convention on the Law of the Sea (1982)
UNCLOS I: I, UNCLOS I: II, UNCLOS I: III etc.	UNCLOS I Official Records, Volumes I to VII, <http://untreaty.un.org/cod/diplomaticconferences/lawofthesea-1958/lawofthesea-1958.html>.
UNCLOS II: I, UNCLOS II: II	UNCLOS II Official Records, Volumes I and II, <http://untreaty.un.org/cod/diplomaticconferences/lawofthesea-1960/lawofthesea-1960.html>.
UNCLOS III: I, UNCLOS III: II, UNCLOS III: III etc.	UNCLOS III Official Records, Volumes I to XVI, <http://untreaty.un.org/cod/diplomaticconferences/lawofthesea-1982/lawofthesea-1982.html>.

UNDOALOS	United Nations Division for Ocean Affairs and the Law of the Sea
UNEP	UN Environment Programme
UNESCO	UN Educational Scientific and Cultural Organization
UNGA	United Nations General Assembly
UNOLA	UN Office of Legal Affairs
UNSWLRS	*University of New South Wales Law Research Series*
US DoD	US Department of Defense
US DOS	US Department of State
US DOS Bulletin	*US Department of State Bulletin*
US GPO	US Government Publishing Office
US NIMA	US National Imagery and Mapping Agency
USC	United States Code
VCLT	Vienna Convention on the Law of Treaties (1969)
Virginia Commentary	MH Nordquist (ed), *United Nations Convention on the Law of the Sea 1982: A Commentary*, vols 1–7 (Martinus Nijhoff)
VJIL	*Virginia Journal of International Law*
WHO	World Health Organization
WMO	World Meteorological Organization
YUP	Yale University Press

Introduction

The Legal Terrain

I. Introduction

This study considers the implications of geographical change for maritime jurisdiction under the law of the sea. It examines this issue in connection with entitlement to maritime space, unilaterally established maritime limits (baselines and the outer limits of maritime zones), and international maritime boundaries.[1] The question of the implications of geographical change for maritime jurisdiction has taken on a new urgency in view of the present and projected impacts of climate change on the coastal and marine environment. Yet the first proposition of this book and its point of departure is that this question should not be exclusively associated with climate change.

Rising sea levels and more frequent and extreme weather events will increasingly alter coastal geography and threaten the habitability of territory.[2] There is a tendency in the existing scholarship to emphasize the unprecedented and, as such, unanticipated character of these developments. More specifically, it has been emphasized that States negotiating the 1982 United Nations Convention on the Law of the Sea (UNCLOS) and the experts involved in this process 'did not anticipate that there could be a significant global regression of coastlines'.[3] This has encouraged the conclusion that the law relating to maritime jurisdiction is ill equipped to respond to this phenomenon and may even exacerbate its harms.[4]

An initial difficulty with this line of reasoning is that it neglects the extent to which the law has been developed in the context of a general awareness if not specialist knowledge of both the natural variability of coastal geography and the

[1] The basic distinction between limits and boundaries was succinctly expressed in *Guinea/Guinea Bissau* (1985), 277: 'a limit indicates the extent of a domain, whereas the role of a boundary is to separate two States.' This is how the two terms are used in the law of the sea treaties, though their use in other contexts does not always respect this distinction and other factors may have to be considered to determine the meaning of the term used: ibid.

[2] IPCC Working Group II (IPCC WGII), 'Climate Change 2014: Impacts, Adaptation, and Vulnerability', AR5, Chs 5, 28, 29.

[3] David Caron's emphasis on this point in an early and influential article is repeated in much of the subsequent literature. See D Caron, 'When Law Makes Climate Change Worse: Rethinking Baselines in Light of a Changing Sea Level' (1990) 17 *ELQ* 621, 636.

[4] Ibid, 621–53. The many works adopting this same line of reasoning are noted in the following chapters.

Geographical Change and the Law of the Sea. Kate Purcell, Oxford University Press (2019). © Kate Purcell.
DOI: 10.1093/oso/9780198743644.001.0001

impact of extreme weather events on this environment. This study argues that climate-related change is properly located within a broader category of geographical change affecting coastal and maritime features that condition entitlement to particular maritime zones or play a role in the construction and description of maritime limits and boundaries. It challenges the dominant theory emerging from narrower studies of the implications of climate-related change for maritime limits: the 'ambulatory thesis'. According to this thesis, maritime baselines and the zonal limits measured from them as a general rule either shift synchronously with a changing coastline or such change entails an obligation on the part of the coastal State to adjust them.

The ambulatory thesis has parallels in commentary on the implications of climate-related change for entitlement to maritime space—that is, entitlement in respect of a particular piece of coastal territory to a territorial sea and other maritime zones, which maritime limits and boundaries more precisely delimit. It has been suggested that certain types of geographical change affecting an island (especially inundation associated with rising sea levels) may result in the loss of entitlement to an exclusive economic zone (EEZ) and continental shelf or the loss of all entitlement to maritime space in respect of that feature.[5] Similar reasoning has encouraged the conclusion that geographical change may prevent a State from continuing to measure the limits of its territorial sea from low-tide elevations (LTEs) within the territorial sea generated by the mainland or an island.[6] It has also been suggested that geographical change might jeopardize the right to 'draw straight archipelagic baselines' enclosing 'archipelagic waters', which depends upon qualification as an 'archipelagic State'.[7]

The existing scholarship has been less inclined to consider subsequent geographical change a threat to the stability and finality of agreements, arbitral awards, and judicial decisions establishing an international maritime boundary or the stability and finality of the boundaries so established. It has nevertheless been suggested that a boundary defined simply as the median line may shift with coastal change or the relocation of baselines thought to be necessitated by coastal change.[8]

This book challenges the foregoing account of the implications of geographical change for entitlement to maritime space, unilaterally established maritime limits,

[5] See e.g. D Anderson, 'Some Aspects of the Regime of Islands in the Law of the Sea' (2017) 32 *IJMCL* 316, 324; JI Charney, 'Rocks that Cannot Sustain Human Habitation' (1999) 93 (4) *AJIL* 863, 867–8; A Soons, 'The Effects of a Rising Sea Level on Maritime Limits and Boundaries' (1990) 37 *NILR* 207, 217–19. Soons argues that the permanence of the limits of the continental shelf means that entitlement to this zone will exceptionally continue 'while the object which generated these sovereign rights no longer exists'—an analysis challenged in Chapter 9.

[6] TSC Art 11; UNCLOS Art 13; ILA-BC, Final Report (2012), 3; International Law Association (ILA) Sea Level Rise Committee, Conference Report (2018), 10. The difference between (a) the right to measure territorial sea limits from an LTE within the territorial sea of the mainland or an island and (b) the use of LTEs in a system of straight or archipelagic baselines is clarified in Chapter 1.

[7] UNCLOS Arts 46, 47; ILA Sea Level Rise Committee, Conference Report (2018), 10.

[8] See e.g. Soons, 'The Effects of a Rising Sea Level', 226–9.

and international maritime boundaries. It argues that neither loss of entitlement to maritime space nor changes to maritime limits are a necessary consequence of geographical change according to the existing law. It seeks to complicate and refine the conclusions that have been drawn with respect to the implications of geographical change for international maritime boundaries.

It is illuminating to examine in detail both the explicit and implicit reasoning underpinning claims that geographical change will extinguish entitlement to maritime space and necessitate the relocation of most maritime limits and some maritime boundaries. This reasoning entails a misunderstanding of the role of geography in the law relating to maritime jurisdiction. It also fails to adequately track the connections between different elements of the law, obscuring its overall consistency.

There are, of course, relevant legal differences between entitlement to maritime space and its delimitation. There are also important legal differences between the unilateral and interstate delimitation of maritime space—most obviously the importance of agreement in the latter case.[9] However, there is also continuity in the role of geography across the law relating to maritime jurisdiction. Crucially, there is a principled consistency in the way in which the role of geography relates to a broader principle of stability. A central objective of this book is to draw out the content of the principle of stability expressed in the relationship between geography and maritime jurisdiction and to consider how it informs the legal consequences of geographical change.

II. Climate Change and the Law of the Sea: A Novel Problem?

The juridical significance of geographical change is suggested by 'a legal order for the seas and oceans' that refers to physical and human geography in connection with entitlement to maritime space and its spatial organization. Yet apart from the introduction of Article 7(2) relating to straight baselines on deltaic coasts, the implications of geographical change for maritime limits are not expressly addressed in the otherwise comprehensive 1982 Convention on the Law of the Sea. Nor does UNCLOS expressly address the implications of geographical change for either rights to maritime space or international maritime boundaries. Of the four law of the sea treaties concluded in 1958, only the CSC alludes to the possibility of coastal geography changing over time, and only in connection with a boundary delimiting the shelf between opposite or adjacent States.[10]

[9] As Thirlway notes, boundaries established by a court or tribunal are also 'agreed' insofar as 'the parties have agreed that the line that the judicial body pronounces shall be accepted':H Thirlway, 'The Law and Procedure of the International Court of Justice 1960-1989: Supplement, 2007: Parts Four, Five and Six' (2007) 78 *BYIL* 17, 116, fn 395.

[10] CSC Art 6(3).

The 'silence' of the TSC, CSC, and UNCLOS regarding the implications of coastal change for maritime jurisdiction appears to have been of little concern to either States or scholars before the late 1980s, when scientific accounts of the present and projected impacts of climate change on coastal geography began to sound more loudly in the political sphere.[11] Commentators identifying that silence as a political and legal problem at this time and since have been impressed by the novelty of climate change as a phenomenon. Beginning with the observation that climate-related change is unprecedented, their commentary tends to emphasize that it is also, as such, unanticipated by the law relating to maritime jurisdiction. This has encouraged the conclusion that the law as it stands is ill equipped to respond. Indeed, most commentators take the view that the existing law exacerbates the harms of climate change, principally by providing for maritime limits that depend upon the location of the low-water line and other features that are vulnerable to rising seas, such as LTEs and islands. This diagnosis is the crux of the 'ambulatory thesis,' which—although it has been subject to little, if any, critical scrutiny—is accepted by many scholars as an accurate account of the implications of climate-related change for maritime limits.

Before investigating the more specific grounds for the ambulatory thesis expressly advanced or implicitly relied upon by its proponents, it is worth reconsidering the assumptions underpinning this overall approach to the question of the implications of climate-related change for maritime jurisdiction. It is true that climate change has only relatively recently been recognized as a matter of concern for international law. Yet it is important to recall that the law relating to maritime jurisdiction has been developed in the context of an awareness and even specialist knowledge of both the natural variability of coastal geography and the prospect of extreme weather events (e.g. storms, cyclones) resulting in geographical change.

The dynamism of the coastal and marine environment was neither unknown nor in doubt during negotiations at the Third United Nations Conference on the Law of the Sea (UNCLOS III) or, for that matter, at UNCLOS II in 1960, UNCLOS I in 1958, or the 1930 Hague Codification Conference—the latter process producing drafts with considerable subsequent influence on the law of the sea treaties, particularly in relation to baselines. Indeed, the preparatory bodies for the law of the sea conferences (where applicable) and participating governments were advised by geographers, cartographers, and hydrographers with expert knowledge of coastal variability and its mechanisms.[12]

Coastal change of various types and degrees was referred to during the first and third law of the sea conferences, and not only in connection with deltas. Of particular note is the United Kingdom's emphasis in 1958 on the variability of both the

[11] B Bolin, *A History of the Science and Politics of Climate Change: The Role of the Intergovernmental Panel on Climate Change* (CUP, 2007), 19–52.

[12] The Seabed Committee acting as a preparatory body for UNCLOS III (1973–1982), like the Ad Hoc Committee preceding it, was responsible for considering scientific and technical as well as legal and economic dimensions of the matters in its mandate: see UNGA Res 2340 (XXII) (18 December 1967); UNGA Res 2467 A (XXIII) (21 December 1968); UNGA Res 2574 B (XXIV) (15 December

low- and high-water lines—a fact undisputed by other States, though they do not appear to have thought it necessary to include specific provisions securing maritime limits against subsequent coastal change.[13] State practice informing the law relating to maritime jurisdiction must also be situated in the context of a general awareness of coastal variability. The justifications advanced for claims to maritime space and efforts to define maritime jurisdiction more precisely have referred in some detail to naval, navigational, fisheries, and, later, seabed mining practices, suggesting the influence of a relatively expert knowledge of the physical characteristics of the oceans and coasts.

While subject to regional and local variations in pace, extent, and to a lesser degree, character, geographical change is a feature of coastal and marine environments globally. States were aware of this as they developed a body of law investing coastal geography with a central significance and function in connection with maritime jurisdiction, including a key role in the construction and description of the baselines used to locate limits and boundaries by measurements of distance. This would appear to have implications for the way in which the question of the consequences of climate-related change for maritime jurisdiction should be approached.[14]

In the first place, the inability of the existing law to address the issue of climate-related coastal change—or its ill-adaptedness, inadequacy, or exacerbation of harms in this context—should not be presupposed. There is no reason to assume

1969); UNGA Res 2750 C (XXV) (17 December 1970). Specialized agencies of the UN and other intergovernmental organizations including UNESCO's Intergovernmental Oceanographic Commission (IOC), the Food and Agriculture Organization (FAO) and its Fisheries Committee, the World Health Organization (WHO), the Inter-Governmental Maritime Consultative Organization (IMCO), the World Meteorological Organization (WMO), and the International Atomic Energy Agency (IAEA) were encouraged to assist the Committee in this regard: UNGA Res 2340 (XXII) (18 December 1967); UNGA Res 2467 A (XXIII) (21 December 1968); UNGA Res 2574 B (XXIV) (15 December 1969); UNGA Res 2750 C (XXV) (17 December 1970); Seabed Committee Report (1973/I), 5. UNCLOS II lacked a formal preparatory process, though there was 'considerable diplomatic activity' leading up to the Conference: *Virginia Commentary*, vol 1, 29, 30. On scientific and technical advice received by the International Law Commission (ILC) prior to the 1958 Law of the Sea Conference (LOSC), see esp ILC Ybk 1953/II, 76-9. The Preparatory Committee for the Hague Codification Conference received assistance from 'various international scientific societies and study groups' but did not formally consult technical organs of the League of Nations: Rosenne (1975/I), xvii, xxi. Most State delegations at the three law of the sea conferences included technical experts: see lists of delegations UNCLOS I: II, xiii; UNCLOS II: I, xiii; UNCLOS III, A/CONF.62/INF 1-17, *Inventory of Papers of the UN Conferences on LOS*). Documents relating to scientific and technical matters were circulated at UNCLOS I, II, and III. At the Hague Conference, Sub-Committee II of the Second Committee (Territorial Waters) made use of a 'small Committee of Experts, presided over by a Dutch Vice-Admiral, to assist it in defining certain technical terms': Rosenne (1975/I), xxxiii.

---

[13] UNCLOS I: VI, 91–5. See Chapter 5.

[14] Even where it has been recognized that coastal variability is a broader phenomenon, the fact that this would have been generally known during the development of the law has not been taken into account: see e.g. Prescott and Schofield, who note that the low-water line will vary over time even in the absence of sea-level rise associated with a changing climate, but do not take the further step of considering whether the ordinary variability of the coastal environment might bear upon the question of whether baselines are ambulatory as a matter of law: V Prescott, C Schofield, *Maritime Political Boundaries of the World* (2nd edn, Martinus Nijhoff, 2005), 100.

that the law as it stands has nothing to say about the implications of climate-related change for maritime jurisdiction or that its application to this 'unprecedented' phenomenon will be detrimental to the stability of the 'legal order of the seas and oceans' secured by UNCLOS.[15] This follows from the fact that the existing law provides no basis for differentiating between the impacts of climate change and other forms of geographical change of potential significance for maritime jurisdiction.

The impacts of climate change on coastal areas, including small islands, are predicted to be widespread and severe. They may be further distinguished from at least some other forms of coastal change by virtue of their anthropogenic causes. These features of climate-related change may warrant special treatment in other legal contexts. However, once it is recognized that the law relating to maritime jurisdiction was not developed in ignorance of the phenomenon of coastal change and that, as discussed below, the 'silence' of the treaties on this issue was not based on the belief that such change was insubstantial (and *de minimis non curat lex*), it also appears that there is no basis in the existing law for setting climate-related change apart from other types of geographical change. Whether climate-related change *should* be treated as legally equivalent to other types of geographical change in this context is a separate question. Yet only a proper understanding of the way in which the existing law addresses geographical change generally will allow an assessment of whether special rules or practices relating to climate-related change are required. Thus far a focus on the 'novel' problem of climate change has encouraged scholars to concentrate their energies on devising 'solutions' that amend, supplement, or replace the existing law before it has been adequately analysed.

It is necessary to bring the question of the implications of coastal change for maritime jurisdiction back to the law as it currently stands. This book responds to the existing law by locating climate-related change within a broader category of geographical change of potential relevance to a coastal State's entitlement to maritime space and the construction and subsistence of its maritime limits and boundaries. While the general case of geographical change informs the particular case of climate-related change, this analysis has a wider application. Geographical change raises questions in connection with maritime jurisdiction beyond the context of climate change.

III. Geographical Change and the Law of the Sea: An Overview

While this book investigates the implications of geographical change for entitlement to maritime space, maritime limits, and international maritime boundaries, it pays particular attention to the case of maritime limits. The theory of ambulatory

[15] UNCLOS, Preamble.

maritime limits has had a pervasive influence on recent thinking about geographical change in the law of the sea, informing analyses of its implications for entitlement to maritime space and maritime boundaries. This book examines and challenges the ambulatory thesis as it relates to maritime limits as well as the extension of its assumptions and arguments regarding the significance of geographical change for maritime jurisdiction more broadly. It seeks to clarify both parallels and points of difference in the law as it relates to entitlement to maritime space, maritime limits, and maritime boundaries.

The book begins by examining the role of geography in the law relating to maritime jurisdiction—a legally and logically prior step to an investigation of the implications of geographical change in this context. Chapter 1 draws out the symbolic and functional role of geography in the law of the sea, which is connected to the grounding of entitlement to maritime space in the possession of territorial sovereignty over coastal land. The role of geography in the law relating to maritime jurisdiction is heavily mediated by a focus on State interests in the sea and the objective of securing a stable division of rights and obligations that responds to and regulates these interests. While geography plays a key role in securing the stability of this legal order, this does not mean that the stability of maritime limits and boundaries depends upon a geographic referent, still less upon ongoing correspondence with any such referent.

In commentary considering the implications of climate change for maritime jurisdiction, there has been little if any analysis of the relationship between the objectives of the law and the role of geography therein. This has contributed to unwarranted inferences being drawn from the text of the law of the sea treaties. Chapter 2 introduces David Caron's influential argument that Articles 7(2) and 76(9) of UNCLOS 'negatively imply' that baselines and the zonal limits measured from them are, as a general rule, ambulatory. Chapters 3 and 4 interrogate this claim, providing a detailed analysis of the treaty law, its drafting history, and related State practice. This analysis shows that the ambulatory theory of maritime limits cannot reasonably be inferred from these provisions. Articles 7(2) and 76(9) remain consistent with a broader concern to secure a stable legal order for the seas and oceans, and help to clarify what stability is understood to require in this context.

Chapter 5 investigates what, if anything, the law of the sea treaties have to say about the implications of geographical change for interstate maritime boundaries. It draws attention to a provision strangely neglected by proponents of the ambulatory thesis. Article 6(3) of the CSC appears to reflect a belief that baselines following the low-water line will be ambulatory, responding with measures to ensure that the location of a boundary in the continental shelf will be fixed. A closer examination of this provision and its drafting history in context shows that it cannot stand as evidence of a common understanding that baselines are ambulatory or that boundaries defined by reference to baselines require specific measures in order to be fixed. There is equally no support for such an understanding in UNCLOS.

Chapter 6 argues that the question of the implications of geographical change for international boundaries is properly answered by an interpretation of the boundary treaty, award, or decision in the particular case. Emphasizing the difference between the finality of the agreements or decisions establishing a boundary and the question of whether the boundary they establish is ambulatory, it seeks to clarify the legal principles and presumptions informing the latter enquiry. Chapter 6 explains how and why the implications of geographical change for international boundaries may vary, examining both maritime and land boundaries in this regard. It interrogates and qualifies the familiar claim that a 'rule of accretion' governs geographical change in the case of river boundaries, which has been drawn on analogically in some versions of the ambulatory thesis. The principle of stability has an important bearing upon an assessment of the implications of geographical change for interstate boundaries, though this principle does not straightforwardly privilege fixity over change.

Chapter 7 looks at debates over whether the charted or 'actual' low-water line constitutes the normal baseline in commentary considering the implications of climate-related coastal change for maritime jurisdiction. It suggests that there has been some conflation of legal lines with the geographical objects by reference to which they are constructed or described. This seems to have encouraged the attribution of the natural variability of features of the coastal environment to both cartographic constructs and legal limits. Chapter 7 revisits the text and drafting history of UNCLOS and the 1958 Conventions to explain why the identification of natural objects and qualities with either or both cartographic and legal constructs misunderstands the role of charted geographical features in the law.

Chapter 8 further examines the relationship between cartography and the role of geography in the law. This chapter explores a line of reasoning that has not been developed in the existing literature, though it is of clear relevance to the question of the implications of geographical change for maritime jurisdiction. The role of nautical charts in delimitation suggests the relevance of the practice of regularly updating such charts to increase their accuracy and respond to coastal change. Chapter 8 asks whether this implies an obligation to adjust maritime limits or boundaries accordingly. It concludes that this is not the case. Examining the legal relevance of the accuracy and currency of geographical information, it explains why new charts and other evidence of either inaccuracy in the geographical information relied upon for delimitation or subsequent geographical change will not invalidate or require the revision of established limits and boundaries.

Chapter 9 considers what may be the most influential assumption underlying the ambulatory thesis—a belief that the conditions set out in the baselines provisions require satisfaction on a continuing basis. The same assumption is at work in claims that geographical change will precipitate a loss of entitlement to maritime space where such entitlement appertains to a feature defined in geographical terms—e.g. an island or archipelago. This (implicit) line of reasoning raises broad questions relating to intertemporality, which Max Huber's distinction between the creation and subsistence of rights helps to both clarify and answer.[16] There are important differences between the law governing the *creation* of entitlement to maritime space and the *construction* of maritime limits and boundaries on the one hand and the law governing the *continuing existence* of entitlement and established limits and boundaries on the other. While geography plays a key role in conditioning claims to maritime space and the construction of maritime limits and boundaries, the law does not leave established rights and legal limits vulnerable to the vicissitudes of nature.

The Conclusion brings together the results of the preceding analyses in an account of the limited legal significance of geographical change for maritime jurisdiction. It considers some final instances of State practice that may appear to support the ambulatory thesis. It is demonstrated that while the relevant practice is not unlawful, it does not show that maritime limits must be adjusted in response to geographical change under international law.

In the course of critiquing the arguments and assumptions of the ambulatory thesis, this book develops a positive case for the conclusion that, while the coastal State is in most cases entitled to redraw established maritime limits, geographical change does not trigger a legal obligation to do so. It clarifies the circumstances in which an international maritime boundary may change with changes to the coast or other geographical features. It also examines the circumstances in which such change may warrant the termination of a boundary agreement, the revision of a boundary award, or a finding that a boundary agreement or award is invalid or null. Finally, it shows that entitlement to maritime space in general or in respect of particular features will not be lost simply by virtue of subsequent geographical change. While loss of entitlement to maritime space will accompany the loss of territorial sovereignty, the latter depends substantially on the intentions of the State concerned and may not be brought about by geographical change alone. While claims to maritime space in respect of an island or archipelago require the satisfaction of partly geographical conditions, the retention of established rights in circumstances of geographical change remains consistent with the object and purpose of the law in this regard.

Though the focus of this book is geographical change in the law of the sea, its detailed examination of this issue illuminates the content and significance of a general principle of stability with broader application to boundaries and territorial situations. This is illustrated by both the comparative treatment of land boundaries and a brief consideration of the question of the implications of loss of habitable land and large-scale population displacement for continuing territorial sovereignty and statehood. These matters may intersect as a matter of law and fact with the question of the implications of geographical change for maritime jurisdiction.

[16] *Island of Palmas* (1928).

1

Geography in the Law of the Sea

I. Introduction

A clear understanding of the implications of geographical change for maritime jurisdiction depends in the first instance upon a clear understanding of the role of geography in the law relating to maritime jurisdiction. While the significance of geography in this context is often noted, its role is not always well understood. This is most apparent in commentary on the baselines provisions of the law of the sea treaties, where it is sometimes suggested that geography has or should have a highly determinative role in the construction of baselines and that it has or should have such a role in order to guard against the excesses of the coastal State.[1] The characterization of geographical factors as 'objective' considerations to be preferred over 'subjective' considerations in both unilateral and bilateral delimitation may be premised on the same assumptions. This distinction between 'objective' and 'subjective' considerations fails to recognize how far the geographical (and non-geographical) factors that the law identifies as relevant to claims to maritime space and their delimitation are defined in a manner that facilitates both regularity and flexibility.

Insofar as objectivity suggests that neutral 'facts' may be determinative and subjectivity suggests unfettered discretion, regularity and flexibility are more useful concepts for understanding the law relating to coastal State jurisdiction at sea. An effect of regularity is, of course, predictability, which is of particular importance in cases of interstate delimitation by a court or tribunal.[2] Yet regularity and predictability follow from a principled responsiveness to particular circumstances and

[1] This reasoning is particularly prominent in US scholarship and underpins that State's policy of protesting 'excessive' baselines. For the US understanding of the baselines provisions see its Commentary on UNCLOS (1995) 34 ILM 1400, 1400–6. Roach and Smith have developed an 'annotation' of the official US position 'to provide the rationale for those views': JA Roach, RW Smith, 'Straight Baselines: The Need for a Universally Applied Norm' (2000) 31 *ODIL* 47–80. For similar reasoning in scholarship, see RD Hodgson, LM Alexander, 'Towards an Objective Analysis of Special Circumstances: Bays, Rivers, Coastal and Oceanic Archipelagos and Atolls' (1972) 13 *Law of the Sea Institute University of Rhode Island Occasional Paper* 1; J Peter Bernhardt et al, *Standard Guidelines for Evaluating Straight Baselines* (US Office of Ocean Law and Policy, 1987) (these Guidelines do 'not necessarily constitute an official position of the United States Government' though the approach they recommend is largely followed by the United States in its practice); and WM Reisman, GS Westerman, *Straight Baselines in International Maritime Boundary Delimitation* (Macmillan, 1992).

[2] As Jennings has said, '[n]o reasonable litigant expects the decision of a court to be predictable; but the range of considerations used for a decision and the procedures for their application, should certainly be predictable': R Jennings, 'Equity and Equitable Principles' (1986) 42 *ASDI* 27, 38.

Geographical Change and the Law of the Sea. Kate Purcell, Oxford University Press (2019). © Kate Purcell.
DOI: 10.1093/oso/9780198743644.001.0001

do not require objective facts to 'dictate' particular results—an arrangement which may well produce impractical and inequitable results.

The idea that geography is an objective fact with a determinative effect on the construction of baselines and zonal limits seems to have encouraged the conclusion that maritime limits are in most cases ambulatory—shifting with changes to the coast. Similar assumptions regarding the objectivity and determinacy of geography have encouraged the conclusion that certain types of geographical change must result in the loss of entitlement to maritime space—for instance, where an island is submerged by rising seas.

It is interesting that the role of geography in the delimitation of maritime space between States is not generally thought to indicate the ambulatory character of the resulting boundary, though Soons has suggested that a boundary defined simply as a median line may be fluid.[3] It is more often assumed that a broader principle supporting the stability of international boundaries prevents maritime boundaries changing with the coast. Yet the principle of stability does not operate to fix boundaries that would otherwise be ambulatory.[4] The fact that geography plays a key role in the construction and description of international maritime boundaries *without* implying a boundary that shifts with subsequent geographical change is rather a clue to the significance of geography in the law relating to maritime jurisdiction more broadly.

The role of geography in the law relating to entitlement to maritime space and the delimitation of maritime limits and boundaries follows from and is shaped by the law's vision of national maritime jurisdiction as an appropriate extension of sovereignty or sovereign rights consistent with the 'natural' interests of a State in possession of the coast. This vision draws on natural law ideas about what is 'necessary' and 'just' as well as State practice.[5] It continues to underpin the more specific rules and principles composing the modern law of the sea. The law does not require specific proof of the relevant interests to establish the coastal State's entitlement to maritime space. The principle that entitlement to maritime space follows from the possession of territorial sovereignty over coastal land nevertheless reflects the understanding that such maritime space is 'appurtenant' to coastal territory both in the sense of being 'a thing that belongs to another, a "belonging"; a minor property, right, or privilege, belonging to another more important, and

[3] Soons, 'The Effects of a Rising Sea Level', 226–9. As Chapter 6 clarifies, Soons' argument is not based on the role of geography in delimitation but a problematic interpretation of the intentions underlying the definition of a boundary in this way.

[4] See Chapter 6.

[5] An interesting discussion of the relationship between natural law and customary law can be found in A Orakhelashvili, 'Natural Law and Customary Law' (2008) 68 *HJIL* 69, esp 106–9 on 'inherent and fundamental rules'. However, Orakhelashvili's conclusion that '[t]he argument of natural law or social necessity has no play in explaining the emergence of substantive rules of customary law' may give too much weight to what is in some cases little more than a positivist gloss emphasizing State consent to rules otherwise based on reasoning from 'natural necessity': see ibid, 110.

passing in possession with it; an appendage' and '[a] thing which *naturally and fitly* forms a subordinate part of, or belongs to, a whole system; a contributory adjunct, an accessory'.[6]

It is through the filter of the same lens that the geography of the coast appears legally relevant—though not all coastal geography. The law picks out a limited number of ideal-typical geographical circumstances which are given a role in delimitation and, in a limited number of cases, further condition entitlement to maritime space. These geographical circumstances have a symbolic and functional value. The law deems particular geographical circumstances to be relevant and relevant in a particular way based on their symbolic and practical relationship with the State's interests in and uses of the sea and its resources—again not any and all interests, but those picked out as properly protected and regulated by international law. Referring to common elements of a cartographic representation of the coast allows for the regular and relatively simple spatial specification of maritime jurisdiction in a manner facilitating the observance and enforcement of this particular ordering of rights and responsibilities at sea.

II. Entitlement to Maritime Space

The coastal State's entitlement to maritime space follows from its possession of territorial sovereignty over coastal land. This has been described as the 'principle of appurtenance' and its rationale is suggested by the richly allusive maxim 'the land dominates the sea'. This maxim captures the idea that entitlement to maritime space is 'natural' and 'appropriate' given territorial sovereignty over coastal land.

The role of geography in the law of the sea is closely related to this key principle of appurtenance. The idea that 'the land dominates the sea' already blurs legal and geographical concepts and categories. In this formulation, 'land' signifies territorial sovereignty but also a particular (coastal) terrain. The verb 'dominates' suggests rule or control as well as predominance in a landscape (though it is worth noting that the idea that land rather than sea is predominant in a landscape involving both depends upon a culturally and historically specific privileging of the 'terrestrial'). These terms suggest a particular understanding of the sea as a secondary space for legal regulation based on authority established quite literally on other grounds.

According to the principle of appurtenance, the coastal State's entitlement to maritime space—whether subject to its full territorial sovereignty or in which it possesses certain exclusive sovereign rights—is an automatic consequence of its territorial sovereignty over coastal land. As a general rule, no other conditions must be satisfied to establish this entitlement, though specific rules govern the

[6] 'appurtenance', n 1 and 2, *OED Online*, accessed 22 March 2017, emphasis added.

question of its spatial extent. In a small number of specified circumstances, however, entitlement to particular maritime zones depends upon the satisfaction of additional conditions.

The chief example is entitlement to an exclusive economic zone (EEZ) and continental shelf in respect of an island, which is precluded in the case of '[r]ocks which cannot sustain human habitation or economic life of their own'.[7] The rules allowing an archipelagic State to establish archipelagic baselines can also be understood to specify conditions for entitlement to archipelagic waters. Unlike UNCLOS Article 121 regarding islands, the provisions on archipelagos are formulated as rules relating to the construction of baselines. There remains an important distinction between the question of whether a State is entitled to use archipelagic baselines to enclose archipelagic waters and the location of those baselines.

There are aspects of the law relating to the delimitation of maritime space that suggest specific conditions might govern entitlement in other cases—namely, in the case of the continental shelf beyond 200 nautical miles (M) and low-tide elevations (LTEs) within the territorial sea of the mainland or an island. In these two cases, however, the law is properly understood to be concerned with the *extent* of entitlement to the continental shelf and territorial sea where such entitlement is already established.

A. Distinguishing Entitlement from Extent

Article 76 of UNCLOS defines the continental shelf as extending 200M from the baselines of the territorial sea or 'to the outer edge of the continental margin' where it lies beyond this distance (and within other distance-based constraints). This has encouraged the view that the basis of entitlement to the shelf beyond 200M differs from the basis of entitlement within this distance. This confuses the dual definition of the limits of the shelf with the legal basis of entitlement to this maritime zone. It is inconsistent with the unified character of the continental shelf in international law as a single maritime zone.

The confusion here can be traced to the judgment of the International Court in *Libya/Malta* (1985), where the shift to a distance-based definition of the limits of the shelf under both customary international law (associated with the development of the concept of the EEZ) and UNCLOS was misinterpreted as a shift in the legal basis of entitlement to the continental shelf—specifically, a move away

[7] UNCLOS Art 121(3). The International Court considers Article 121 as a whole to be part of customary international law: *Nicaragua v Colombia* (2012), 51. Interestingly, the judgment suggested that the customary status of paragraph 3 follows from its consistency with customary law relating to the EEZ.

from a geophysical notion of natural prolongation to distance as the basic criterion for coastal State rights to the shelf, at least within 200M.[8] Several commentators have subsequently claimed that physical characteristics of the seabed constitute the basis for entitlement to the shelf beyond 200M,[9] though this view has not been endorsed by any international court or tribunal.[10] In fact, neither distance nor seabed geomorphology constitute the legal basis for entitlement to the continental shelf, which—like entitlement to other maritime zones—depends on the possession of territorial sovereignty over coastal land. The definition of the outer limits of most maritime zones by distance *responds* to the legal basis of entitlement but should not be mistaken for it.

As discussed below, the possibility of establishing the outer limits of the continental shelf further seaward where the 'outer edge of the continental margin' lies beyond 200M responds to both the coastal State's interest in exploiting the resources of the physical continental shelf and the interests of States generally in preserving an area of the seabed as the 'common heritage of mankind'. The law makes use of aspects of seabed geomorphology in the definition of limits intended to both realize and constrain the extension of coastal State jurisdiction in the seabed beyond 200M. It does not, however, identify seabed geomorphology or the location of the outer edge of the continental margin beyond 200M as the legal basis for entitlement to this maritime zone.

It follows from UNCLOS Article 76 that a coastal State will only be allowed to locate the limits of the continental shelf beyond 200M from its baselines if the outer edge of the continental margin can be established beyond this distance. This is properly understood as a question of extent rather than entitlement. As such (notwithstanding the doubts expressed by the tribunal in *Barbados v Trinidad and Tobago*[11]), the term 'extended' continental shelf aptly describes the area of shelf

8 *Libya/Malta* (1985), 33–8.

9 See e.g. D Colson, 'The Delimitation of the Outer Continental Shelf between Neighboring States' (2003) 97 (1) *AJIL* 91, 92, 102; S Fietta, R Cleverly, *A Practitioner's Guide to Maritime Boundary Delimitation* (OUP, 2016), 19, 610–11; K Baumert, 'The Outer Limits of the Continental Shelf under Customary International Law' (2018) 111 (4) *AJIL* 827, 832.

10 There have so far been only three decisions involving the delimitation of the shelf beyond 200M—*Bangladesh/Myanmar* (2012); *Bangladesh v India* (2014); and *Ghana/ Côte d'Ivoire* (2017). Pending cases before the ICJ include *Nicaragua v Colombia* and *Somalia v Kenya*. Article 76 has been referred to in order to determine the extent of entitlement to the continental shelf—extent matters in the delimitation context because of the need to determine whether there is overlap. Yet the decisions to date reflect an understanding that the basis of entitlement is territorial sovereignty over coastal land. This accounts for the role of the coastal configuration in delimitation beyond 200M and the irrelevance of geomorphological features of the seabed. The same understanding is apparent in cases involving the delimitation of the continental shelf within 200M. The Tribunal in *Barbados/Trinidad and Tobago* did echo the erroneous account of a shift from natural prolongation to distance as the basis for entitlement to the shelf in *Libya/Malta* (1985): *Barbados/Trinidad and Tobago* (2006), 69. The delimitation was nevertheless based on the understanding that 'it is the coast that is the basis of entitlement over maritime areas': *Barbados/Trinidad and Tobago* (2006), 72.

11 *Barbados v Trinidad and Tobago* (2006), 165, fn 4.

beyond 200M: it captures the notion of the *same thing* being further extended. It is sometimes said that where the continental margin does not extend beyond 200M the coastal State is not entitled to an extended continental shelf. More accurately, the coastal State is in these circumstances not entitled to establish the limits of the shelf beyond 200M.

Article 11 of the Convention on the Territorial Sea and Contiguous Zone (TSC) and Article 13 of UNCLOS must be understood in a similar way. These articles provide that when an LTE is located within the territorial sea of the mainland or an island, the low-water line on that elevation 'may be used as the baseline for measuring the breadth of the territorial sea'. This rule should not be confused with the more limited possibility of using LTEs as basepoints in a system of straight baselines under TSC Article 4(3) and UNCLOS Article 7(4). The application of TSC Article 11 or UNCLOS Article 13 will result in an extension of the outer limits of the territorial sea in which the LTE is located. It will not affect the outer limits of other maritime zones, which will, conversely, be affected by the use of straight baselines taking LTEs into account.

Article 11 of the TSC and Article 13 of UNCLOS may appear to provide for entitlement to a territorial sea in respect of a particular feature subject to particular conditions. They define an LTE in a manner akin to the definition of an island as 'a naturally formed area of land which is surrounded by and above water at low tide but submerged at high tide'. The second paragraph of these provisions clarifies that '[w]here a low-tide elevation is wholly situated at a distance exceeding the breadth of the territorial sea from the mainland or an island, it has no territorial sea of its own'. This could be taken to confirm that the first paragraph sets out the circumstances in which an LTE *does* have a territorial sea of its own. However, the drafting history indicates that the ILC and States participating in the 1958 Law of the Sea Conference (LOSC) were concerned to emphasize that the provision 'did not give drying rocks and drying shoals a territorial sea of their own but extended the territorial sea of the mainland off which they lay'.[12] The express specification that LTEs beyond the territorial sea of the mainland or an island would not have a 'territorial sea of [their] own' was intended to point up the difference between (a) adjusting 'the limit of the territorial sea ... [to] make allowance for the presence of ... drying rocks and ... show bulges accordingly', and (b) granting such features entitlement to a territorial sea in their own right, which would bring into question the legitimacy of any restriction on the capacity of such features to generate a territorial sea based on their proximity to an island or mainland coast.[13]

[12] ILC Ybk 1955/I, 218. See also ILC Ybk 1954/I, 96; ILC Ybk 1956/II, 270; UNCLOS I: III, 186.
[13] ILC Ybk 1956/II, 270–1.

B. Islands

Article 121(3) of UNCLOS is properly understood to set out additional conditions for entitlement to an EEZ and continental shelf in respect of an island. UNCLOS Article 121(1), like TSC Article 10(1), defines an island as 'a naturally formed area of land, surrounded by water, which is above water at high tide'. The TSC recognized that islands, like mainland coastal territory, generated entitlement to a territorial sea.[14] The Convention on the Continental Shelf (CSC) recognized that islands, like mainland coastal territory, generated entitlement to a continental shelf.[15] Under UNCLOS Article 121(3), however, '[r]ocks which cannot sustain human habitation or economic life of their own' will not generate entitlement to either an EEZ (a maritime zone post-dating the 1958 Conventions) or continental shelf.

The effect of UNCLOS Article 121(3) is to make entitlement to an EEZ and continental shelf in respect of an island dependent upon the satisfaction of certain criteria—namely, the island's capacity to 'sustain human habitation or economic life of [its] own'. It has been debated whether the term 'rocks' further limits the application of Article 121(3) to features that are 'rocks' in the 'ordinary sense' of the word, which has been associated with a geological definition referring to 'a hard mass of the solid part of the earth's crust'.[16] This definition would exclude features composed of other materials such as sand or coral.

In the *South China Sea Arbitration* (2016), the Tribunal rejected the view that 'the use of the word "rock" … [limits] the provision to features composed of solid rock' or otherwise distinguishable on the basis of 'geological or geomorphological characteristics'.[17] This conclusion must be considered correct. As the Tribunal observed, 'rocks are a category of island' within Article 121.[18] Article 121(3) of the UNCLOS is the final paragraph in a provision addressing 'the regime of islands'. It follows both the general definition of an island in Article 121(1) and the statement of a general rule that islands are entitled to the same maritime zones as mainland coastal territory in Article 121(2). Article 121(3) clearly sets out an exception to this general rule.[19]

More can be said about the meaning of the term 'rocks' in this clause, though the Tribunal did not consider it necessary to do so in the *South China Sea Arbitration*. An interpretation of Article 121(3) according to the recognized principles governing such a task supports the conclusion that the term 'rocks' is used to describe islands which 'cannot sustain human habitation or economic life of their own'. This

[14] TSC Art 10(2).
[15] CSC Art 1(b).
[16] V Prescott, C Schofield, *The Maritime Political Boundaries of the World* (2nd edn, Martinus Nijhoff, 2005), 61–75. Cf B Kwiatkowska, A Soons, 'Entitlement to Maritime Areas of Rocks Which Cannot Sustain Human Habitation or Economic Life of Their Own' (1990) 21 *NYIL* 139, 150–3.
[17] *South China Sea Arbitration*, 205–6, 227.
[18] Ibid, 206.
[19] Ibid, 175.

reading does not, as Prescott and Schofield allege, put 'the cart before the horse'.[20] Rather the idea that Article 121(3) involves any sort of horse and cart relationship between the expression 'rocks' and the remainder of the provision cannot be accepted. To argue otherwise is to assume that the expression 'rocks' signifies a separate and initial test to be applied to insular features before the question of whether they are capable[21] of 'sustain[ing] human habitation or economic life of their own' can be considered. However, the mere fact that the provision begins with the term 'rocks' does not warrant such an approach—though the fact that the term 'rocks' is used at all remains significant, as is the fact that this expression is not elsewhere defined.

Prescott and Schofield are critical of Kolb's suggestion that an intention to restrict Article 121(3) to 'rocks' in a geological sense would have been indicated by the explicit definition of the term in this way.[22] They suggest that '[i]t could be argued with greater force that if the term "rocks" was a codeword to include islets, sandbanks and barren islands, then it should have so been defined'.[23] What is missed here is the fact that the term 'rocks' *is* defined in UNCLOS—which should hardly be surprising given the care taken to legally define other maritime features granted a role in connection with maritime jurisdiction. The term 'rocks' is defined by Article 121(3). Rather than inserting a term of uncertain meaning into the Convention, this provision defines a subcategory of islands as 'rocks' on the basis that they 'cannot sustain human habitation or economic life of their own'.

What is most significant about Article 121(3) for present purposes—and, indeed, further supports the conclusion that the foregoing is an accurate reading of the term 'rocks'—is its consistency with the overall approach to entitlement to national maritime jurisdiction in the law of the sea. Denying an EEZ and continental shelf to a subcategory of islands on the grounds that they 'cannot sustain human habitation or economic life of their own' is consistent with the broad rationale for entitlement to maritime space, while also responding to concerns associated with recognition of entitlement to a 200M EEZ in international law and a new interest in preserving the seabed beyond national jurisdiction as 'the common heritage of mankind'.

The conditions for entitlement to an EEZ and continental shelf identified in Article 121(3) refer to circumstances understood to clearly establish and justify the coastal State's interest in the sovereign rights in the sea secured by these maritime zones—namely, the existence of a local population or local economy that would benefit from such rights. This is consistent with the idea that the jurisdiction of the State in marine areas off its coasts is appropriate in view of a 'natural interest'

20 Prescott and Schofield, *Maritime Political Boundaries of the World*, 76.

21 As the Tribunal held in the *South China Sea Arbitration*, '[t]he use of the word "cannot" in Article 121(3) indicates a concept of capacity': *South China Sea Arbitration*, 206.

22 Prescott and Schofield, *Maritime Political Boundaries of the World*, 74.

23 Ibid.

in these areas for security and resource exploitation purposes. Of course, human habitation or the capacity to sustain independent economic life is not a precondition for entitlement to maritime space in respect of a mainland coast. It remains significant that the law directly conditions entitlement to an EEZ and continental shelf in this manner only in the case of islands.

The text and drafting history of Article 121(3) supports the conclusion that the provision was partly a response to the new concept of an EEZ. States sought to restrict entitlement to this zone by reference to the considerations understood to justify it—namely, a special economic interest in the conservation, development and use of the resources of waters adjacent to its territorial sea, which Latin American States in particular claimed was necessary 'to promote the maximum development of their economies and to raise the standard of living of their people'.[24] The restriction on entitlement to a continental shelf in respect of an island was a response to the new concern to restrict national maritime jurisdiction in the seabed to ensure that resources beyond the continental shelf, at the time believed to be of significant value, could be reserved for exploitation for the common benefit of mankind.

Article 121(3) makes entitlement to an EEZ and continental shelf conditional upon a particular combination of geographical and non-geographical circumstances. These restrictive conditions apply only to islands, defined as 'a naturally formed area of land, surrounded by water, which is above water at high tide'. This definition of an island can itself be understood as a precondition for entitlement to maritime space,[25] but the main purpose of Articles 121(1) and (2) is to clarify that an island is entitled to the same complement of maritime zones as a mainland coast (subject to the Article 121(3) exception). The specification of a 'naturally formed area' of land was intended to exclude claims to maritime space in respect of artificial islands or, as the United States put it when introducing this language at the 1958 LOSC, the 'artificial placement of land' as 'a means of extension of the territorial sea'.[26]

UNCLOS Article 60 sets out a parallel rule in respect of artificial islands in the EEZ, the presence of which 'does not affect the delimitation of the territorial sea, the exclusive economic zone or the continental shelf'.[27] Reading the first two paragraphs of Article 121 together, however, it seems reasonable to conclude that some forms of artificially reinforcing or reclaiming land that was, prior to such activities, a naturally formed area of land above water at high tide, should not disqualify that feature as an island. This argument is elaborated in Chapter 9, which also considers

[24] Montevideo Declaration (1970). The preamble begins by '[r]ecognizing that there exists a geographic, economic and social link between the sea, the land, and its inhabitant, Man, which confers on the coastal peoples legitimate priority in the utilization of the natural resources provided by their marine environment'. See further SN Nandan, The EEZ: A Historical Perspective' in UNFAO, *Essays in Memory of Jean Carroz: The Law and the Sea* (FAO, 1987).

[25] See further Chapter 9.

[26] UNCLOS I: III, 242–3. See also *South China Sea Arbitration* (2016), 217–18.

[27] UNCLOS Art 60(8).

the legal implications of 'artificial' measures to ensure the continuing capacity of an island to 'sustain economic life or human habitation of [its] own'.

C. Archipelagos

Under UNCLOS Part IV, an 'archipelagic State' is permitted to 'draw straight archipelagic baselines joining the outermost points of the outermost islands and drying reefs' of the archipelagos that 'constitute' it. The waters within these baselines (other than those enclosed as internal waters) have the status of archipelagic waters, in respect of which the coastal State possesses full sovereignty. The rules governing 'archipelagic baselines' refer to geography in a manner consistent with the law governing baselines generally, discussed below. Yet the definition of an 'archipelagic State' in Article 46 also conditions entitlement to archipelagic waters.

Article 46(a) defines an 'archipelagic State' as 'a State constituted wholly by one or more archipelagos' which 'may include other islands'. This is somewhat contradictory insofar as the possession of 'other islands' presumably means that the State is not 'constituted wholly by one or more archipelagos'. It has been suggested that this formulation may allow larger island States with relatively minor offshore archipelagos to benefit from the use of archipelagic baselines, while this option will not be open to States that share a continental landmass as well as possessing territorial sovereignty over mid-ocean archipelagos.[28] Such an interpretation cannot be accepted. The text and drafting history clearly indicate that the provision was intended to limit the use of archipelagic baselines to circumstances where the State is in a significant sense *constituted* by one or more archipelagos—if not wholly, then it would still seem substantially.

The point here is not that 'dependent archipelagos' (i.e. both 'archipelagos which form part of a continental State' and archipelagos belonging to an island State that cannot be considered to be 'constituted' by those archipelagos[29]) should be treated in the same way as archipelagos constituting a State under the law of the sea.[30] Rather, the law makes clear that the special approach is warranted by the fact that the archipelago is the defining feature of the State.[31] The allowance for 'other islands' in Article 46(a) is best understood as an express acknowledgment that such features may be 'included' in the State's territory without detracting from the essential character of that State as 'archipelagic'.

The drafting history confirms this interpretation. At UNCLOS III, Indonesia, the Philippines, Mauritius, and Fiji amended their earlier proposal to the Seabed

[28] J Crawford, *Brownlie's Principles of Public International Law* (8th edn, OUP, 2012), 264.
[29] S Kopela, *Dependent Archipelagos in the Law of the Sea* (Martinus Nijhoff, 2013), 5–6.
[30] For this argument, see Kopela, *Dependent Archipelagos*, esp Ch 6.
[31] UNCLOS Art 46(a).

Committee to replace the definition of an archipelagic State as 'a State constituted wholly *or mainly* by one or more archipelagos'[32] with its definition as a State 'constituted wholly by one or more archipelagos' and possibly including 'other islands'.[33] Indonesia explained that this change was intended 'to emphasize that an archipelagic State must be wholly detached from a continent and must consist wholly of islands'.[34] The point, to be clear, was not that a large island State with a minor archipelago could be considered an archipelagic State. Rather, the amendment was intended to clarify that the archipelago must be the defining feature of the State.

The regime of 'archipelagic States' is consistent with the general idea that the coastal State is entitled to maritime space as an appurtenance of its land territory. It is simply recognized that the constitution of a State by one or more archipelagos, defined as 'a group of islands, including parts of islands, interconnecting waters and other natural features which are so closely interrelated that such islands, waters and other natural features form an intrinsic geographical, economic and political entity, or which historically have been regarded as such', justifies entitlement to the waters within these archipelagos. This is properly understood as a question of entitlement and not merely delimitation, even if the rules governing the construction of archipelagic baselines may spatially restrict the sea areas that can be enclosed as archipelagic waters.

III. Baselines

The baselines provisions of the TSC and UNCLOS take coastal geography into account in several ways. The different types of baseline provided by law respond to the wide range of geographical circumstances across the world's coastlines or, more precisely, generalizations about these variations allowing their categorization as broad types. These broad types—a 'deeply indented' coast or the presence of fringing islands,[35] a 'river [that] flows directly to the sea',[36] bays '[constituting] more than a mere curvature of the coast',[37] and a State 'constituted wholly by one or more archipelagos'[38]—function as conditions precedent for the establishment of certain types of baseline—straight baselines, closing lines, and archipelagic baselines, respectively. The absence of the specified geographical circumstances will

32 Seabed Committee Report (1973/V), unpaginated, emphasis added.
33 UNCLOS III: III, 226.
34 UNCLOS III: II, 260.
35 UNCLOS Art 7(1).
36 UNCLOS Art 9.
37 UNCLOS Art 10.
38 UNCLOS Arts 46, 47.

preclude the application of the particular type of baseline, while their presence in most cases permits rather than requires its use.

The role of geography in the baselines provisions is not confined to the question of the type of baseline that may be used. Geographical circumstances also play a role in the construction of baselines of various types. In some cases, the connection between coastal geography and the legal line is formulated in broad terms—for example, the requirement that straight baselines follow 'the general direction of the coast'.[39] More precise criteria, such as a maximum length for archipelagic baseline segments and closing lines as well as geometrical constructions such as the 'semicircle test' for juridical (as opposed to historic) bays, are applied to geographical objects. Notably, exact figures featuring in the baselines provisions identify outer constraints (e.g. maximum distances) measured from points that are broadly defined (e.g. the 'natural entrance points' of a bay) though subject to specification by the coastal State in the act of delimitation.

A. Geography, Cartography, and the Law

There is a correspondence between the geographical features relevant to safe navigation and the geographical features playing a role in the construction of baselines. This is not accidental but follows from the fact that the spatial organization of maritime jurisdiction in the law of sea makes use of the representation of geography in nautical charts. Geographical facts are mediated by cartography (together with the disciplines from which cartographers draw information) and the law, both of which are selective in the elements they identify as relevant. While the law makes use of a cartographical representation of the coasts and oceans, its concern with geography differs from that of the cartographer.

Preparing and maintaining nautical charts does not require the most objective and comprehensive description of physical geography possible. Experts involved in surveying and charting a coast focus on factors bearing upon navigation and navigational safety in particular. More comprehensive studies of coastal geography may be drawn on selectively. The cartographer understands that '[t]o avoid hiding critical information in a fog of detail, the map [or chart] must offer a selective, incomplete view of reality'.[40] In the case of nautical charts, the requirements of safe navigation guide decisions regarding which facts should be represented and at what level of detail. Features representing a threat to safe navigation are given special prominence. For the cartographer, the chief function of nautical charts points

[39] UNCLOS Art 7(3).

[40] M Monmonier, *How to Lie with Maps* (2nd edn, UCP, 1991), 1; C Jacob, *The Sovereign Map: Theoretical Approaches in Cartography throughout History* (UCP, 2006), 21–33, Ch 2; C Carleton, C Schofield, 'Developments in the Technical Determination of Maritime Space: Charts, Datums, Baselines, Maritime Zones and Limits' (2001) 3 *Maritime Briefing* 1, 15.

to the relevance of geographical change—current facts are of immediate concern to the mariner. Navigational safety remains the basis for selectivity regarding which changes are taken into account in the process of updating charts.

The law governing the construction of baselines makes substantial use of the cartographical view of the coast. The abstract and generalized geographical types that condition the use of different types of baseline and play a role in their construction are derived from the nautical chart. A number of baselines are expressly defined by reference to charted geographical features or other common elements of nautical charts. The 'normal baseline' is described as 'the low-water line along the coast as marked on large-scale charts officially recognized by the coastal State'.[41] In the case of atolls or islands with fringing reefs, the baseline 'is the seaward low-water line of the reef, as shown by the appropriate symbol on charts officially recognized by the coastal State'.[42]

Legal limits that track charted lines are partly a matter of convenience. Taking the low-water line as the baseline makes it relatively easy both for the coastal State to establish its maritime limits and for other parties to respect them. The same practical advantages account for the use of charted geographical features as basepoints in systems of straight or archipelagic baselines and termini for closing lines. This is not to say that nautical charts speak for themselves. Rather, charts officially recognized by the coastal State and used to construct or depict maritime baselines and zonal limits play an important role as expressions of the will of that State.

The cartographer's concern with the accurate representation of current geographical facts necessary to ensure safe navigation does not have a clear parallel in the law relating to the delimitation of maritime space. As subsequent chapters will elaborate, the law may be less concerned with the accuracy and currency of geographical information than the relatively simple and expedient division of maritime space in order to manage competing interests in the sea. While there may be some role for investigations into the accuracy and currency of charts at the time of delimitation, this does not indicate that baselines should be adjusted in response to subsequent coastal change.[43]

The law makes use of cartographic representations of coastal geography to establish a spatial distribution of the maritime jurisdiction of States that partly responds to the particular interests and practices associated with particular geographical configurations (e.g. bays and archipelagos). More generally, baselines are constructed as a representation of the 'coastal front' from which maritime jurisdiction projects. The 'legal coast' in this regard is not identical to the physical coast. The law ignores many aspects of the physical geography of the coast and also allows sea areas to be included within baselines.

[41] UNCLOS Art 5.
[42] UNCLOS Art 6.
[43] See Chapter 8.

Baselines that depart from the low-water line are partly justified on the basis that the sea areas they enclose 'are sufficiently closely linked to the land domain to be subject to the regime of internal waters'.[44] This rationale is translated into a condition for the use of straight baselines in UNCLOS Article 7(3) but also underpins the approach taken to closing lines. While archipelagic baselines do not enclose internal waters,[45] the rules governing their construction also respond to the notion that the waters they enclose are closely linked to the land domain (though this fact alone does not justify the archipelagic State's entitlement to archipelagic waters).[46]

Baselines that reflect 'the general direction of the coast' but do not follow all its 'sinuosities' are further valued as a means of simplifying the line of a complex coast. This facilitates the relatively efficient establishment of clearly ascertainable and thus observable maritime limits. The importance of this 'boundary rationalization function' has nevertheless been overstated by Reisman and Westerman, who suggest that the use of straight baselines should be constrained by reference to the objective of simplifying zonal limits.[47] It is important to recognize that the coastal State's interest in and use of various types of baseline has always been associated with its interest in extending national maritime jurisdiction. This interest has not been 'covert'[48] but carefully justified by reasoning consistent with the overall approach to maritime jurisdiction in the law of the sea. The same reasoning accounts for the way in which this extension of coastal State jurisdiction is constrained.

Straight baselines and closing lines as well as archipelagic baselines are intended to enclose areas in which there is a close relationship between land and sea—a function of both geographical circumstances and other considerations relating to State interests in and uses of the sea that the law recognizes as legitimate. The rules governing the construction of baselines seek to protect internal and archipelagic waters in light of this special relationship between land and sea. Yet the law is also concerned with maritime space beyond the baseline. It takes the 'legal coast' to be located at the seaward limit of the area in which land and sea have such a relationship, providing for the measurement of the territorial sea and other maritime zones defined by distance from this point.

The baselines provisions respond to a concept of the 'coastal front' that considers coastal geography in conjunction with certain security-based, economic, social, political, or historical interests in the sea that the law recognizes as warranting

[44] *Anglo-Norwegian Fisheries* (1951), 133.

[45] Closing lines may still be used to delimit internal waters within archipelagic baselines: UNCLOS Art 50.

[46] States advocating a special regime of archipelagic waters drew on the reasoning of the Court in *Anglo-Norwegian Fisheries* regarding the use of straight baselines along a coastal archipelago, as well as the terms of TSC Art 4, which substantially reflect this decision. Yet they also made clear that it was the constitution of the State by archipelagos that justified this more substantial extension of its sovereignty at sea: see Statement of 'Archipelagic Principles', Seabed Committee Report (1973/III), 1–2; draft articles, Seabed Committee Report (1973/V), unpaginated; draft articles, UNCLOS III: III, 226.

[47] Reisman and Westerman, *Straight Baselines*.

[48] Cf ibid, 198–9.

protection as well as requiring regulation and limitation.[49] The seaward extension of zonal limits is not merely incidental to recognition of the special character of waters enclosed by baselines. This is a deliberate consequence of the law on baselines justified by reference to the central principle that 'the land dominates the sea and it dominates it by the intermediary of the coastal front'.[50]

The law on baselines gives effect to the concept of the coastal front through a selective and evaluative use of the cartographic representation of the coast to allow the spatial specification of the coastal State's entitlement to maritime space. Certain elements are picked out as legally relevant by reference to both (a) the broader justification of entitlement to maritime space as 'natural' and 'appropriate' in view of the State's legitimate interests in the seas off its coasts, and (b) practical considerations, which are not extra-legal but bound up with the objective of securing an effective and stable division of maritime space.

B. Latitude in the Baselines Provisions

In *Anglo-Norwegian Fisheries*, the Court emphasized 'the latitude necessary in order [for the coastal State] to be able to adapt its delimitation to practical needs and local requirements'.[51] The difference between such 'latitude' and unfettered discretion shapes the Court's account of the law in this seminal judgment. The baselines provisions of both the TSC and UNCLOS also give effect to this important distinction. Latitude is an essential feature of the law on baselines and the law relating to maritime delimitation more broadly.

Latitude in the relevant sense refers to 'the range within which anything may vary'.[52] The lawful delimitation of maritime space by the coastal State admits a good deal of variation. The broad range of possibilities it encompasses remains, like any 'range', marked by similarities and defined by its limits.

The role of geography in the baselines provisions is not in tension with such 'latitude' but rather facilitates it. The rules relating to the construction of baselines respond to local geographical circumstances but restrict consideration to a limited set of such circumstances defined in a general way. The law provides for a regular response to these circumstances. This is consistent with the basic equality of coastal States in terms of their interests and corresponding rights in the sea. Yet it is also consistent with the idea that the delimitation of maritime space—as

[49] Notably, the fact that baselines are intended to represent the 'coastal front' does not mean that they constitute the coastal front. A court or tribunal tasked with delimiting a maritime boundary between States may construe the coastal front in a different manner.

[50] P Weil, *The Law of Maritime Delimitation—Reflections* (Grotius Publications, 1989), 51 (emphasis removed).

[51] *Anglo-Norwegian Fisheries* (1951), 133.

[52] See 'latitude', n I (2) (b), *OED Online*, accessed 8 January 2017.

entitlement generated by territorial sovereignty over coastal land and theorized in spatial terms as a projection from the 'coastal front'—should respond to features of the particular 'coastal front' each State happens to have.

The baselines provisions still admit a considerable degree of discretion on the part of the coastal State in their application. This operates at more than one level and is, of course, constrained by the law. The freedom of States to choose whether or not they will employ particular types of baseline where the conditions precedent for their use obtain—e.g. straight baselines on a deeply indented coast—is an obvious example. However, the law also privileges (without treating as unimpeachable) the coastal State's assessment of the relevant features of its coast and its application of the baselines provisions thereto. This dimension of the law warrants some emphasis.

The baselines provisions largely conform to what some scholars take to be a general description of rules *qua* rules: they set out legal directives which include 'a statement of fact (often in conditional form) and ... a statement of the consequences that will or may follow upon the existence of that fact'.[53] Rules having these two component parts can differ in the degree to and manner in which they determine particular outcomes. This will depend on several factors relating to both the relevant facts and the legal consequences associated with them. In the first place, there may be differences in the degree to which an assessment of the relevant facts involves evaluation. Notably, a rule is not necessarily less determinate or indeterminate to the degree that it admits the evaluation of facts. It may either or both direct the process of evaluation and give determinative weight to the evaluation actually arrived at by a particular agent. In the second place, the consequences of identifying certain facts or arriving at certain evaluations of those facts may necessitate rather than exclude further discretionary acts—for instance, by enlivening certain options rather than specifying a particular result. The existence of particular facts may also indicate that certain principles should be taken into account. Principles tend to be less conclusive than rules, though, as Hart argues, this is 'a matter of degree'.[54]

The baselines provisions both guide and privilege an evaluation of the facts by the coastal State. They admit interpretive practices attentive to the relative weight of different factors or considerations. These attributes, moreover, are the result of conscious consideration and reconsideration at different times and in different places—the 1930 Hague Conference, proceedings before the International Court of Justice (ICJ) in the *Anglo-Norwegian Fisheries Case*, and the First and Third Conferences on the Law of the Sea in particular.

This dimension of the law is not always appreciated, with the result that the scope for and appropriate form of critique of State practice is misjudged. Particular

[53] LM Friedman, 'Legal Rules and the Process of Social Change' (1967) 19 *SLR* 786, 786–7.
[54] See HLA Hart, *The Concept of Law* (2nd edn, Clarendon, 1994), 259–63.

baselines constructed by particular States are sometimes challenged as 'unlawful' or 'excessive' based on an interpretation of the baselines provisions that takes them to straightforwardly link objective facts with clear and concrete consequences.[55] Specifically, geographical facts are sometimes taken to 'dictate' the location of the baseline—though it should be noted that this reading is more often advanced by commentators in their individual capacity than States at the level of diplomacy.

C. The 'Dictates' of Geographical Realities

The somewhat surprising authority cited in support of the idea that geography determines the location of baselines with a high degree of specificity is the judgment in *Anglo-Norwegian Fisheries*, or more precisely, the Court's observation that the 'solution' in that case was 'dictated by geographic realities'.[56] This idea, however, is at odds with both this particular statement in context and the judgment as a whole. In the first instance, it ignores the fact that the 'solution' in question was that 'the outer line of the "skjaergaard" . . . must be taken into account in delimiting the belt of Norwegian territorial waters'.[57] This was considered to follow from the fact that 'the mainland is bordered in its western sector by the "skjaergaard", which constitutes a whole with the mainland'.[58] This 'geographical reality' was in considerable part constituted by non-geographical considerations, including the use and significance of the area to the coastal State. The Court emphasized that 'countless arms of the sea, straits, channels and mere waterways serve as a means of communication for the local population which inhabits the islands as it does the mainland'.[59] It also noted that the 'fishing grounds' in this area, 'known to Norwegian fisherman and exploited by them from time immemorial', provided a livelihood for 'the inhabitants of the coastal zone'.[60]

In its judgment, the Court accords these social facts legal significance. Coastal geography both partly explains them and serves as a convenient expression of interconnectedness in extra-geographical ways. In *Anglo-Norwegian Fisheries*, the Court was satisfied that Norway's method of straight baselines was an appropriate adaptation of existing approaches to the delimitation of the territorial sea. Norway's baselines, which connected the outermost points of the *skjaergaard*, were approved as expressing the legally significant line of the coast—the 'dividing line between

[55] The USA has an official policy of making such protests: see US Department of State (DOS), *Limits in the Seas* (*LIS*); US Department of Defense (DoD), *Maritime Claims Reference Manual* (*MCRM*) (2014).

[56] *Anglo-Norwegian Fisheries* (1951), 128. See e.g. Hodgson and Alexander, 'Towards an Objective Analysis of Special Circumstances', esp 38, 40.

[57] *Anglo-Norwegian Fisheries* (1951), 128.

[58] Ibid.

[59] Ibid, 127.

[60] Ibid, 127–8.

land and sea'.[61] It was not solely the coastal configuration that 'dictated' this 'solution' but the human interests and uses associated with these geographical facts. The Court accepted that this combination of geographical and non-geographical circumstances meant that the outer line of the *skjaergaard* was also the point from which the territorial sea, as an appurtenance of national maritime space to coastal territory, should properly begin.

The solution dictated by the geographical realities of Norway's coast was not the establishment of a particular baseline fully determined by the facts. It was a flexible approach to the construction of baselines with considerable scope for the exercise of discretion by the coastal State. The baselines provisions of the TSC and UNCLOS also provide for such an approach, though, like the decision in *Anglo-Norwegian Fisheries*, they identify constraints that allow the validity of established limits to be assessed under international law.[62]

D. Ambiguity and Adaptability

The baselines provisions have attracted criticism on the grounds that their formulation admits discretion and undermines determinacy. This charge may initially appear antithetical to challenges to particular baselines that take the applicable rules to be highly determinate and determinative. In fact, it shares a common root. The objection is in both cases based on the belief that the law aims at determinacy of a particular type and degree. The first type of criticism identifies the recalcitrance of States as the problem, relying on the existing law to challenge particular baselines. Criticism of the law itself tends to focus on the ambiguity of the text. Here the law is considered deficient because it fails to achieve the conclusiveness to which it is thought to aspire.

At the 1958 LOSC, several States criticized the 'ambiguity' of certain phrases included in the ILC's draft articles. A number of the formulations subject to criticism were taken directly from the 1951 judgment in *Anglo-Norwegian Fisheries*. It is clear from the examples cited, which include '[s]uch expressions as "where circumstances necessitate", "to any appreciable extent", "sufficiently closely linked", "adequate grounds", "reasonable measures", [and] "unjustifiable interference"',[63] that the concern was not that uncertainty would prevent their application. The issue was rather the scope for subjective assessment.

Resolving ambiguity to identify '*the* meaning' of a provision remains a basic tenet of the law governing the interpretation of treaties.[64] Yet there is a difference

[61] Ibid.
[62] Ibid, 132–3.
[63] UNCLOS I: III, 69.
[64] Vienna Convention on the Law of Treaties Art 32(1)(a) (emphasis added).

between ambiguity and flexibility: amenability to more than one interpretation may be a virtue. There is a further difference between (a) circumstances in which it is intended that multiple actors should apply a detailed rule in precisely the same way, and (b) circumstances in which it is intended that each actor authorized to effect a particular task is to do so with due regard to local circumstances and subject to broader legal standards. Unilateral maritime delimitation is the latter category of case. It is primarily for the coastal State to interpret and apply the law to establish its maritime limits. Provided its interpretation is reasonable,[65] the fact that there may be other reasonable interpretations is immaterial. This is why the Court in *Anglo-Norwegian Fisheries* deferred to reasonable assessments of the situation by the coastal State. It did not identify strict and determinate rules that could be applied to objective facts to determine if Norway's baselines were the proper result. Instead, it held that unilateral delimitation by the coastal State must conform to broadly framed standards.

In response to charges of ambiguity at the 1958 LOSC, the ILC's Special Rapporteur François agreed with India that 'it was inevitable that expressions supporting subjective assessments should be introduced' and that the courts were the appropriate place for their interpretation in contentious cases.[66] In the Commission's view, 'a codification of international law [could] no more do without these expressions than ... national law'.[67] The interpretation of such expressions by the coastal State and an assessment of the reasonableness of those interpretations by a court or tribunal are different but related exercises. The Court in *Anglo-Norwegian Fisheries* concluded that while there were no 'rules having the technically precise character alleged by the UK', there were 'certain criteria which, though not necessarily precise, can provide courts with an adequate basis for their decisions, which can be adapted to the diverse facts in question'.[68] The Court asked whether the baselines established by Norway 'conform' to or 'depart ... to any considerable extent' from these criteria.[69]

In *Anglo-Norwegian Fisheries*, the 'ambiguity' of notions such as the 'general direction of the coast' was not considered a problem. The Court described this idea as both 'devoid of any mathematical precision' and a valuable safeguard against

[65] On reasonableness as a principle in international law, see O Corten, 'Reasonableness in International Law', MPEPIL Online, accessed 24 April 2018. See also D Anderson, 'The Principle of Reasonableness in the Law of the Sea' in Hestermeyer et al (eds), *Co-Existence, Cooperation and Solidarity: Liber Amicorum Rüdiger Wolfrum*, vol 1 (Martinus Nijhoff, 2012) 657–70. As Anderson notes, the principle of reasonableness is reflected in UNCLOS Art 300, which provides that 'States parties shall fulfil in good faith the obligations assumed under this Convention and shall exercise the rights, jurisdiction and freedoms recognized in this Convention in a manner which would not constitute an abuse of right': ibid, 667.

[66] UNCLOS I: III, 69; India's comments in UNCLOS I: VI, 12, 99. See also statement by Alvarez Aybar (Dominican Republic): UNCLOS I: VI, 9.

[67] UNCLOS I: III, 69.

[68] *Anglo-Norwegian Fisheries* (1951), 132–3.

[69] Ibid, 140–3. For the criteria, see ibid, 132–9.

cases of 'manifest abuse'.[70] Rather than mathematical imprecision being an objection to its use, it was considered a virtue in light of the general principle that 'a State must be allowed the latitude necessary in order to be able to adapt its delimitation to practical needs and local requirements'.[71] This may be compared with the view of the Committee of Experts reporting to the ILC in 1953, which was in agreement that,

> Dans plusieurs cas … il sera impossible d'établir une « direction générale de la côte », et il a pris acte que tout effort en ce sens entraîne des questions comme celle de l'échelle de la carte à employer dans ce but et la décision quelque peu arbitraire sur l'étendue de la côte à utiliser dans la recherche de la « direction générale ».[72]

This is an apt illustration of the difference between a technical concern with precision and the aims of the law. The ILC and States at the 1958 LOSC were concerned with the risks of ambiguity and the value of objectivity from a legal perspective. They sought to develop a set of provisions governing unilateral maritime delimitation that were clear, simple, and applied equally to all States while responding to a diversity of facts and ensuring adaptability to local conditions. It was eventually agreed that the Court's 'ambiguous' formulations contributed to these ends.

The rule that '[t]he drawing of straight baselines must not depart to any appreciable extent from the general direction of the coast' is an excellent example of this.[73] As noted in the 1989 UN Baselines Study, this rule is not concerned with 'the distance between the mainland and the straight baseline; it deals solely with the congruence of two bearings'.[74] Indeed, while 'congruence' admits a range of possibilities, it may be a more strenuous standard than that indicated by the law. The negatively formulated rule is intended to prevent a 'divergence between the baseline and the land formations' that amounts to a 'distortion of the general direction of the … coast'.[75]

The flexibility of the baselines provisions is further illustrated by the possibility of justifying a straight baseline that *does* distort the general direction of the coast on other grounds. In *Anglo-Norwegian Fisheries*, the Court found that *even if* a baseline across the Lopphavet basin were 'too pronounced' a deviation from the general direction of the coast, it could be justified on the basis of a 'very ancient and peaceful usage' of the waters 'founded on the vital needs of the population'.[76]

[70] Ibid, 142.
[71] Ibid, 133.
[72] ILC Ybk 1953/II, 78.
[73] TSC Art 4(2); UNCLOS Art 7(3). See also UNCLOS Art 47(3), which provides that the drawing of archipelagic baselines 'shall not depart to any appreciable extent from the general configuration of the archipelago'.
[74] UN Baselines Study, ix.
[75] *Anglo-Norwegian Fisheries* (1951), 142.
[76] Ibid.

Though it referred in this context to Norway's claim to 'historic title' and 'the survival of traditional rights', these comments must be interpreted in light of an earlier clarification that the Norwegian notion of 'historic title' was not an assertion of 'exceptional rights'.[77] Rather than '[claiming] areas of the sea which the general law would deny',[78] Norway 'invoke[d] history, together with other factors, to justify the way in which it applies the general law'.[79] The baseline across Lopphavet was justified on the basis of what the Court elsewhere described as 'economic interests peculiar to the region concerned, the reality and the importance of which are clearly evidenced by a long usage'.[80] The law of the sea treaties also recognize that such interests may inform the determination of 'particular baselines' where conditions precedent for the use of a system of straight baselines (a deeply indented or island-fringed coast) already apply.[81]

Notwithstanding the charges of ambiguity leading up to and at the 1958 LOSC, many of the formulations from the judgment in *Anglo-Norwegian Fisheries* were directly reproduced in the TSC. After a short-lived resurgence of such complaints in the discussions of the Seabed Committee,[82] the same expressions were retained in UNCLOS. Those adjustments and additions that were made cannot be attributed to a concern with vagueness or indeterminacy. Indeed, most were motivated by a concern to ensure greater fidelity to the 1951 judgment. UNCLOS Article 7(4), for example, was amended to provide for the use of LTEs not bearing a lighthouse or similar installation as basepoints in a system of straight baselines 'where the drawing of baselines to and from such elevations has received general international recognition'.[83] It is important to recognize that this provision, like the provision regarding 'economic interests peculiar to the region concerned', does not introduce purely 'subjective' considerations into the delimitation process. The importance of certain local interests and practices is acknowledged, but the law also insists upon '[clear evidence] by a long usage' and 'general international recognition'—matters clearly amenable to assessment by a court or another State.

It is nevertheless clear that challenges to the lawfulness of established baselines will only be justified in genuinely contentious cases. Where such a dispute comes

77 Ibid, 133.
78 Ibid.
79 Ibid.
80 Ibid.
81 TSC Art 4(4); UNCLOS Art 7(5).
82 Seabed Committee Report (1973/I), 49.
83 This change accommodated the fact that the Court had upheld the lawfulness of straight baselines making use of LTEs without a lighthouse or similar installation: *Virginia Commentary*/II, 102–3. At UNCLOS III, Norway (with Canada, Chile, Iceland, India, Indonesia, Mauritius, Mexico, and New Zealand) had suggested removing any restriction on the use of LTEs as basepoints for straight baselines: UNCLOS III: III, 81. Norway made a similar proposal at the 1958 LOSC, though this was rejected: UNCLOS I: II, 62–3, 118. The Main Trends Paper and Informal Single Negotiating Text (ISNT) at UNCLOS retained the reference to lighthouses or similar installations but incorporated the possibility of using LTEs as basepoints where 'States have historically and consistently' done so (UNCLOS III: III, 110) or this practice has 'received international recognition' (UNCLOS III: IV, 153).

before a court, the proper question is whether the unilateral delimitation by the coastal State was consistent with the broad standards provided by law. It would be inappropriate to give a restrictive interpretation of treaty provisions that are designed to maximize flexibility.[84] It would be equally misplaced to test established baselines by directly applying the rules for construction to the facts rather than assessing the reasonableness of the State's decisions.[85]

In practice, there have been relatively few formal objections to established baselines. Most examples involve States with vested interests as neighbours or distant water fishing nations. Only the United States has a general policy of protesting what it considers 'excessive maritime claims'.[86] There have been no international judicial proceedings on this particular issue, though baselines have been challenged in the context of international maritime delimitation cases.[87] The ICJ has refrained from assessing unilaterally established baselines by reference to the standards set out in the baselines provisions in this context. This is entirely appropriate, as the role of baselines in interstate delimitation is in important respects distinct from their role in unilateral maritime delimitation.[88]

E. Determinacy through Decision

Critics of the alleged ambiguity and indeterminacy of the existing law tend to pay insufficient attention to the way in which both adaptability and determinacy are achieved by specifying *who* is authorized to evaluate particular circumstances and make decisions on this basis—namely, the coastal State. Of course, the law guides this process and constrains the adaptations that may reasonably be made. It is nevertheless the coastal State which is exclusively responsible for establishing baselines within these broad parameters. In any given case, there may be multiple possible lines, all of which are in conformity with the law. The law authorizes the coastal State to make decisions that are deliberately underdetermined by the rules in order to allow flexibility and adaptability. It is the fact of the coastal State's authoritative decision that brings determinacy. The baselines that a State has established can only be challenged if they are inconsistent with broadly framed standards. This restricts the scope for legal challenges, supporting the stability of established maritime limits.

[84] Cf Reisman and Westerman, *Straight Baselines*, 75–6.

[85] The concept of 'reasonableness' is used by the Court to assess Norway's baselines in *Anglo-Norwegian Fisheries* (1951), 129, 142.

[86] See Reisman and Westerman, *Straight Baselines*, 190; US DOS, 'United States Responses to Excessive Maritime Claims' (1992) 112 *LIS* 1; US DoD, *MCRM* (2014).

[87] The expense of such proceedings relative to potential gains and losses may partly explain this fact.

[88] See Section V below.

It must be emphasized that the claim here is not that the authority of the coastal State for unilateral delimitation as well as the 'latitude' it is afforded in this exercise mean that the lawfulness of its maritime limits cannot be challenged by interested parties. The baselines provisions are both directed towards the coastal State and formulated in a way that allows their application to be scrutinized by other States. It remains important to recognize that these provisions do not set out 'objective' rules that would 'determine' the same result—that is, the same baseline—whether they are applied by the coastal State, another State, or, indeed, a mariner at sea. This means that an evaluation of the lawfulness of established baselines must be sensitive to the fact that the law admits a range of possibilities. It must also be recognized that it does so for good reason—to allow a flexible adaptation to local circumstances. Many of the proposals by critics to make the rules less 'ambiguous' and more 'objective' would erode if not eliminate this valuable quality. They would also be likely to encourage challenges to the lawfulness of limits established by other States. This may undermine the stability that the law seeks to achieve by organizing States' rights and obligations in the sea along spatial as well as functional lines.

IV. Zonal Limits

Most zonal limits are defined by distance from the baseline. As noted above, the role of distance here responds to the principle of appurtenance—the grounding of entitlement to maritime space in the possession of territorial sovereignty over coastal land. Limits defined by measurements of distance from the baseline are consistent with the concept of national maritime jurisdiction as a projection from the 'legal coast' or 'coastal front'.

Both the TSC and UNCLOS indicate that the limits of the territorial sea are to be constructed by 'an envelope of arcs' swung from prominent points along the legal coast represented by the baseline.[89] The same approach is understood to apply to the construction of other maritime limits defined by distance from the baseline: the law provides that these limits should not 'exceed' or 'extend beyond' specified distances from the baselines from which the breadth of the territorial sea is measured.[90] A line parallel to straight or archipelagic baselines will also meet this requirement.

When the arcs of circles method is applied only salient points on the baseline are taken into account in the construction of maritime limits. As such, these limits not only simplify but to a considerable degree depart from the 'actual coastal configuration'.[91] This is consistent with the way in which coastal geography is generally taken into account in the law governing unilateral maritime delimitation (and the

[89] TSC Art 6; UNCLOS Art 4.
[90] UNCLOS Arts 3, 33(2), 57, 76(5), and (6).
[91] Cf Reisman and Westerman, *Straight Baselines*, 199.

law relating to maritime jurisdiction more broadly). Limits constructed using the arcs of circles method depart from the detail of the geographical configuration of the coast but remain consistent with the notion that the coastal State's maritime jurisdiction is a projection from the coastal front.

In the case of the continental shelf, the outer limit may be established 200M from the baseline or by reference to 'the outer edge of the continental margin' where this extends beyond 200M.[92] The role of geomorphology in the establishment of limits beyond 200M deserves special attention. An examination of Article 76 and its history shows that this is in some respects similar to the role of geography in the construction of baselines. Yet there are also important differences—some of which may have encouraged the erroneous view that entitlement to the continental shelf beyond 200M has a different legal basis to entitlement within this distance. In fact, it is the significance of the limits of the continental shelf as the limits of the international seabed area that accounts for the relevant features.

UNCLOS Article 76, like the baselines provisions, is selective in its identification of natural features for use in the construction of legal limits. The 'Irish formula' adopted in Article 76 identifies the 'foot of the slope' as a key point of reference, defining this more precisely as 'the point of maximum change in the gradient at its base'.[93] This 'feature' had already been identified (albeit not with the greatest accuracy) and represented as a line on charts available at the time the provision was being drafted.[94] Rather than providing for a limit tracking seabed geomorphology directly, Article 76 sets out exercises in geometry to be applied to measures of specified aspects of seabed geomorphology.[95] Distances are specified as outer constraints rather than strict requirements.[96] There is also some scope for discretion in the location of the 'foot of the continental slope', which may vary according to the type of evidence used and whether there is (a) more than one substantial change in its gradient or (b) a region rather than a point of maximum change.[97]

Locating the geomorphological features of the seabed identified in the legal definition of the 'outer edge of the continental margin' and applying the specified metric criteria to them remains a more data-intensive and technical exercise than the construction of baselines by reference to the charted coast. It is also more onerous than the establishment of limits defined by distance through the construction of an 'envelope of arcs'. Uniquely, a State intending to establish the limits of the

92 UNCLOS Art 76.

93 UNCLOS Art 76(4).

94 At UNCLOS III, the fourth edition and several pages of the fifth edition of the General Bathymetric Chart of the Oceans were available. Participants were provided with the *World Ocean Floor Physiographic Diagram*, though the Secretariat later expressed concern that '[t]his Diagram ... used only a part of the total slope data now available and furthermore has inherent positional inaccuracies': UNCLOS III: XI, 122.

95 UNCLOS Art 76(4).

96 UNCLOS Art 76(4), (5).

97 IOC/IHO 'Study of the Implications of Preparing Large-scale Maps for the Third United Nations Conference on the Law of the Sea': UNCLOS III: XI, 121–2.

shelf beyond 200M is required to submit 'particulars of such limits ... along with supporting scientific and technical data' to the Commission on the Limits of the Continental Shelf (CLCS)—an autonomous body composed of 'experts in the field of geology, geophysics or hydrography'.[98] Article 76(8) provides that 'the limits of the shelf established by a coastal State on the basis of [the] recommendations [of the CLCS] shall be final and binding'. Annex II indicates that the coastal State must 'make a revised or new submission' to the CLCS if it disagrees with that body's recommendations.[99]

Crucially, these procedural requirements and the more technical definition of the limits of the continental shelf beyond 200M do not support the conclusion that the legal basis of entitlement is the physical existence of an extended continental shelf. It is rather the significance of the outer limits of the continental shelf as the limits of the international seabed area that accounts for these features of the legal regime. The definition of the limits of the shelf beyond 200M was intended to facilitate but also regulate and restrain the extension of coastal State jurisdiction in the seabed. The more technical treatment of geomorphological features in the definition of the limits of the shelf beyond 200M and the role of the CLCS in reviewing and making recommendations regarding these limits serves to constrain the extension of national jurisdiction and facilitate the establishment of a clearly defined and permanent boundary with the international seabed area.

Allowing the coastal State to establish the limits of the continental shelf beyond 200M where the outer edge of the continental margin exceeds this distance was a political compromise. It does not amount to an endorsement of any natural right supervening on the physical facts. At UNCLOS III it was agreed that the coastal State should be allowed to exploit the resources of the continental margin beyond 200M. This was because the coastal State was recognized as having a special interest in and capacity for the exploitation of these resources. It was also agreed that (a) this extension of jurisdiction should be subject to clearly defined and permanent limits; (b) a revenue-sharing scheme should apply to any exploitation beyond 200M; and (c) States should not have the same discretion to withhold their consent to marine scientific research projects of another State or international organization in the continental shelf beyond 200M as they do within this distance.[100] These elements of the law reflect an effort to balance the interests of the coastal State with the interests of the international community in the seabed. They do not treat the physical continental shelf as a 'natural' extension of the coastal State's territory.

The role of the CLCS in relation to the establishment of the outer limits of the extended shelf is thought by some commentators to amount to a departure from

[98] UNCLOS Art 76(8), Annex II.
[99] UNCLOS Annex II, Art 8.
[100] UNCLOS Art 246(6). This point of difference is emphasized by J Mossop, *The Continental Shelf beyond 200 Nautical Miles: Rights and Responsibilities* (OUP, 2016), 3, 164.

the law's otherwise clear emphasis on the exclusive authority and responsibility of the coastal State for establishing baselines and maritime limits. Cook and Carleton, for example, believe that 'the ultimate arbiter in terms of claims is the Commission, which is composed entirely of scientists', concluding that '[t]he intention is that science alone should be the deciding factor'.[101]

In this regard, it should not be forgotten that the coastal State remains responsible for establishing the limits of the shelf beyond 200M—the CLCS is only authorized to provide 'recommendations'. It remains significant that only those limits 'established on the basis of' the recommendations of the CLCS will be 'final and binding'.[102] It is also significant that '[i]n the case of disagreement by the coastal State with the recommendations of the Commission', the coastal State is required to 'within a reasonable time, make a revised or new submission to the Commission'.[103]

It is clear that the limits of the continental shelf beyond 200M will not be considered lawful and opposable to other States unless they are established 'on the basis of' the Commission's recommendations. At the same time, it is not the case that either the CLCS or 'science' itself 'determines' the limits of the shelf beyond 200M.[104] The role of the CLCS under UNCLOS responds to the concern that States might (a) establish the limits of the shelf beyond 200M where this is not justified by the law or (b) establish the limits of the shelf beyond 200M further seaward than the law permits. States were concerned to protect the 'common heritage of mankind' in the international seabed area against extensions of national jurisdiction in the seabed that were not properly authorized by the law. They were also concerned to limit the potential for disputes regarding established limits, which were to be 'final and binding'. An important function of the CLCS's recommendations is to invest the limits that are established with legitimacy as well as finality.[105] The overarching objective is the timely and permanent establishment of the outer limits of the continental shelf, which was considered necessary in view of their function as the limits of the international seabed area.

V. Maritime Boundaries

Geography plays a role in the delimitation of maritime boundaries between States at several stages and in several ways. As Evans has observed, 'geographical factors have always dominated delimitation' and '[a]lmost all methods advocated are

[101] P Cook, C Carleton (eds), *Continental Shelf Limits: The Scientific and Legal Interface* (OUP, 2000), 3, 6.

[102] UNCLOS Art 76(8).

[103] UNCLOS Annex II, Art 8.

[104] Cf Cook and Carleton, *Continental Shelf Limits*, 6.

[105] This legitimizing function is emphasized in TL McDorman, 'The Role of the Commission on the Limits of the Continental Shelf: A Technical Body in a Political World' (2002) 17 *IJMCL* 301, 308.

consequential upon geography'.[106] This is a key feature of the law of delimitation developed in the context of third-party adjudication and arbitration. It is also a common feature of delimitation by direct agreement between States.

The priority of agreement in interstate delimitation means that States negotiating a maritime boundary are not bound to limit their considerations to factors that a court or tribunal might identify as legally relevant.[107] This does not mean that the law has no bearing upon delimitation by negotiation. Under UNCLOS and customary law, the delimitation of the EEZ and continental shelf must be 'effected by agreement on the basis of international law, as referred to in Article 38 of the [ICJ] Statute . . . , in order to achieve an equitable solution'.[108] The law provides that, in the absence of agreement, the delimitation of the territorial sea will be governed by the 'equidistance-special circumstances' rule set out in TSC Article 12 and UNCLOS Article 15, which also has customary status.[109] A parallel rule applies to the delimitation of the continental shelf under Article 6 of the CSC.[110]

While these provisions apply where States cannot reach agreement, this does not mean that they are only relevant where the failure of negotiations leads to third-party delimitation. The 'default' rule may influence negotiations directly.[111] More generally, States may refer to the principles and methods applied by courts and tribunals in the delimitation context to make a case for the equitable character of a proposed delimitation. As Oude Elferink notes, '[g]rounding one's position in terms of international law does not mean that the other party will necessarily accept it'.[112] Yet a negotiating position grounded in law may have particular weight where the failure to reach agreement may in any case result in delimitation by a court or tribunal.

While there may be no record of the method used to produce a negotiated boundary, the results show that States make substantial use of the equidistance method[113] and other geometrical methods based upon the configuration of the coasts and their relationship.[114] Geographical circumstances may also be the basis for adjustments to an equidistance line, though State practice is inconsistent

[106] M Evans, *Relevant Circumstances and Maritime Delimitation* (OUP, 1989), 119.

[107] See *Libya/Malta* (1985), 40.

[108] UNCLOS Arts 74, 83.

[109] *Qatar v Bahrain* (2001), 94.

[110] Where the States in question are also parties to UNCLOS, the latter instrument prevails: UNCLOS Art 311(1). Article 6 of the CSC does not have customary status. If the State is not party to either the CSC or UNCLOS, the rule in UNCLOS will apply as custom.

[111] See D Anderson, 'Negotiating Maritime Boundary Agreements: A Personal View' in Lagoni and Vignes (eds), *Maritime Delimitation* (Martinus Nijhoff, 2006) 121–41.

[112] AG Oude Elferink, 'International Law and Negotiated and Adjudicated Maritime Boundaries: A Complex Relationship' (2015) 58 *GYIL* 232, 248.

[113] See Y Tanaka, *Predictability and Flexibility in the Law of Maritime Delimitation* (Hart, 2006), 133–6. The effect, however, has not been to elevate this method to the status of a rule.

[114] L Legault, B Hankey, 'Method, Oppositeness and Adjacency, and Proportionality in Maritime Boundary Delimitation' in Charney and Alexander (eds), *International Maritime Boundaries* (ASIL, 1993) 203–41.

regarding both the factors taken into account and their effect on the boundary.[115] The approach to maritime delimitation by courts and tribunals is more consistent. This is unsurprising in view of the requirements for objectivity and predictability associated with the judicial and arbitral functions.

The delimitation of a maritime boundary by a court or tribunal usually involves a number of considerations relating to geography. In the first instance, identifying the 'relevant area' for delimitation depends upon an identification of the 'relevant coasts'. It is necessary to consider the configuration of the coasts and their position relative to one another in order to determine whether and where there is an overlap between the maritime entitlements of the two States necessitating delimitation. The projection of maritime entitlements into an area of overlap constitutes the 'relevant area' for the purposes of delimitation.[116] It is worth noting that a court or tribunal may refer to the definition of the limits of the shelf beyond 200M in UNCLOS Article 76 in this context, but this is not premised on an understanding that the provision indicates the *basis for entitlement* to the continental shelf beyond this distance. Rather, *extent* matters in the delimitation context because it is necessary to establish whether and where the maritime jurisdiction of neighbouring States overlaps.[117]

Coastal configuration is also a key consideration in determining the appropriate method of delimitation. In the case of the territorial sea, the parties may agree to use a boundary that departs from the equidistance or median line, whether this is a consequence of the adjustment of an equidistance line or the application of another method of delimitation.[118] In the absence of such agreement, the use of a method other than equidistance must be justified on the basis of either historic title or 'special circumstances', as must any adjustment of the equidistance line.[119] In the case of the delimitation of the EEZ and continental shelf, the choice of method need only be justified as consistent with an 'equitable solution'.

The construction of an equidistance or median line as a provisional first step in the delimitation of the EEZ and continental shelf is increasingly common, though this does not mean that equidistance applies as a rule in this context.[120] Courts

[115] Tanaka, *Predictability and Flexibility*, Ch VII.

[116] *Nicaragua v Colombia* (2012), 683.

[117] See Section II (A) above, esp note 10.

[118] TSC Art 12, UNCLOS Art 15.

[119] TSC Art 12, UNCLOS Art 15. As noted above, the ICJ has recognized these provisions constitute customary international law: *Qatar v Bahrain* (2001), 94.

[120] In the *Black Sea Case*, the Court asserted that '[s]o far as delimitation between adjacent coasts is concerned, an equidistance line will be drawn unless there are compelling reasons that make this unfeasible in the particular case': *Black Sea Case* (2009), 101. This is clearly a high bar for justifying a departure from the equidistance method; it appears more strenuous than the requirement to justify departures from the equidistance line as 'necessary by reason of historic title or other special circumstances' in the delimitation of the territorial sea. Even more boldly, the Court asserted that the provisional boundary between opposite coasts '*will be* the median line' and did not acknowledge any basis for departing from this line: ibid. These aspects of the decision cannot be considered consistent with the law on delimitation. Neither the prior nor subsequent jurisprudence privileges the equidistance

and tribunals have largely taken care to assess the 'appropriateness' of applying an equidistance-relevant circumstances approach to the delimitation of these maritime zones—particularly where the parties have not agreed to employ this method.[121] It is by reference to the central concept of equitableness in maritime delimitation with its particular connection to geographical circumstances that this assessment of 'appropriateness' has been made.[122]

Methods other than equidistance may be appropriate in the geographical circumstances. For example, a bisector method of construction may be considered appropriate due to the concavity or convexity of the coast.[123] Where the coasts of two adjacent States form a straight line, it may be appropriate to construct the boundary as a perpendicular.[124] Other geographical factors, such as the complexity of the coastline or the presence of islands, may inform the choice of method and its application. As Evans explains, '[e]quidistance is normally calculated from baselines drawn from, and reflecting, the coasts', while '[p]erpendiculars and bisectors are normally a function of the general direction of the coast'.[125]

The equidistance method requires the selection of basepoints, an exercise which again refers to 'the physical geography of the relevant coasts'.[126] This generally means the coastal configuration represented on charts, though in some cases disagreement between the parties as to whether a chart accurately represents coastal geography at the time of delimitation has led to other evidence of contemporary geographical circumstances playing a role.[127] In the case of the delimitation of the territorial sea under the TSC and UNCLOS and the continental shelf under the

method to this degree. The Court has since clarified that 'it will not be appropriate in every case to begin with a provisional equidistance/median line': *Nicaragua v Colombia* (2012), 696.

[121] *Nicaragua v Colombia* (2012), 696–8; *Bangladesh/Myanmar* (2012), 74–6; *Bangladesh v India* (2014), 97–100; *Ghana/Cote d'Ivoire* (2017), 82–93. In *Costa Rica v Nicaragua*, the Court seems to have skipped over the question of the appropriateness of constructing a provisional equidistance line due to the parties' agreement on the use of this method: *Costa Rica v Nicaragua* (2018), 53–4, 71. In *Peru v Chile*, Peru had requested the application of the equidistance method, while Chile advanced no arguments in this regard as it claimed the entire area had already been delimited by agreement: *Peru v Chile* (2014), 66.

[122] *Nicaragua v Colombia* (2012), 696–8; *Bangladesh/Myanmar* (2012), 74–6; *Bangladesh v India* (2014), 97–100; *Ghana/Côte d'Ivoire* (2017), 82–93.

[123] This was an important consideration in *Nicaragua v Honduras* (2007), 742.

[124] This was identified as the ideal circumstance for delimitation by a perpendicular in the *Gulf of Maine Case* (at 320); in that case, however, these circumstances did not obtain, though the Chamber delimited the third segment of the boundary by a line perpendicular to a closing line across the Gulf: *Gulf of Maine Case* (1984), 337–8. It insisted in this regard that such a line continued to reflect the 'particular characteristics of [the parties'] coasts': *Gulf of Maine Case* (1984), 338. See also *Guinea/Guinea-Bissau*, where the tribunal unusually considered the configuration of the West African coast more broadly: *Guinea/Guinea-Bissau* (1985), 189–90.

[125] Evans, *Relevant Circumstances*, 119.

[126] *Black Sea Case* (2009), 105–10.

[127] Chapter 8 examines whether the law requires accuracy and currency in charts and other geographical information relied upon for delimitation. It considers how this bears upon the implications of subsequent geographical change for maritime limits and boundaries.

CSC, it is specified that basepoints are to be located 'on the baselines from which the breadth of the territorial seas of each of the two States is measured'.[128] These are, of course, baselines constructed on the basis of rules and principles that also refer to a range of geographical circumstances. In the case of the delimitation of the territorial sea and the delimitation of the continental shelf under the CSC, the decision to use alternative basepoints should be justified on the basis of 'historic title or other special circumstances'.[129] No such justification is necessary in the delimitation of the EEZ and continental shelf, where there is no obligation to use established basepoints.

The jurisprudence has made clear that 'determining the baseline for the purpose of measuring the breadth of the continental shelf and the [EEZ] and ... identifying base points for drawing an equidistance/median line for the purpose of delimiting the continental shelf and the exclusive economic zone between adjacent/opposite States are two different issues'.[130] Determining whether certain basepoints are 'appropriate' for the purposes of delimitation is an exercise that refers back to the central notion that the coastal State's entitlement to maritime space projects from the 'coastal front'. It is appropriate, as such, to refer to 'the physical geography of the coasts' with 'particular attention being paid to those protuberant coastal points situated nearest to the area to [be] delimited'.[131] Yet, as distinct from unilateral delimitation, it is not just the coastal configuration of one State but the relationship of the coasts of two or more States that must be considered. This means that certain geographical circumstances that generate entitlement to maritime space may be given only partial 'effect' or denied any effect on a median line or another boundary.

The geographical circumstances of third States may also be taken into account to ensure that the delimitation at hand does not prejudice their rights. Somewhat unusually, the Tribunal in *Guinea/Guinea-Bissau* further considered what would be required for 'the delimitation between the two Guineas to be suitable for equitable integration into the existing delimitations of the West African region, as well as into future delimitations which would be reasonable to imagine from a consideration of equitable principles and the most likely assumptions'.[132] The Tribunal may have gone too far in its speculation regarding a future boundary between Guinea and Sierra Leone.[133] Its focus on the configuration of the coast and the importance of ensuring that the maritime area projecting from the coastal front of a given State is not 'cut off' remains consistent with the way in which the principle of appurtenance and its relationship with delimitation have been understood in the case law.

[128] TSC Art 12; UNCLOS Art 15; CSC Art 6.
[129] TSC Art 12; UNCLOS Art 15; CSC Art 6.
[130] *Black Sea Case* (2009), 108.
[131] Ibid, 101, 106, 108.
[132] *Guinea/Guinea-Bissau* (1985), 189.
[133] See M Aquarone, 'The 1985 Guinea/Guinea-Bissau Maritime Boundary Case and its Implications' (1995) 26 (4) *ODIL* 413, 426.

The 'relevant circumstances' taken to warrant the adjustment of a provisional equidistance line or a line constructed on the basis of another method are again chiefly geographical.[134] This is also true of the 'special' circumstances that might warrant the use of basepoints other than those 'from which the breadth of the territorial sea ... is measured', the application of a method other than equidistance, or the adjustment of a provisional equidistance line in the delimitation of the territorial sea and, where the CSC applies, the continental shelf. The '(dis)proportionality check' ordinarily applied by courts and tribunals as the final stage of the delimitation process seeks to assess whether there is 'any marked disproportion between the ratio of the respective coastal lengths and the ratio between the relevant maritime area of each State by reference to the delimitation line'.[135]

The delimitation of maritime boundaries is heavily informed by the principle that the land dominates the sea and does so through 'the intermediary of the coastal front'.[136] It is this principle that underpins the somewhat idiosyncratic concept of equitableness in the law of maritime delimitation. Equity is not here a matter of modifying legal norms in the interests of justice. The law itself admits a considerable degree of flexibility in the delimitation of maritime boundaries. Such flexibility is built in and not a consequence of modification by reference to other principles. Instead, equity in the law of the sea is concerned with a particular notion of what is 'just' or 'appropriate'. What is distinctive about this notion of equity is the way it connects ideas about what is 'just' or 'appropriate' with coastal geography.

The law relating to maritime jurisdiction is at a fundamental level concerned with giving the coastal State its 'due'. The notion of what is 'due' to a State in terms of maritime jurisdiction is grounded in certain historically contingent ideas about the natural interests and rights of a State with land territory that meets the sea. In particular, the sovereign State *qua* sovereign State is understood to have economic and security interests in the sea off its coasts. Coastal geography is given a symbolic and practical role in securing these interests. The 'natural' appurtenance of maritime space to the coastal State is given symbolic expression in the role of geographical circumstances in the construction of maritime limits and boundaries and the additional conditions for entitlement to certain maritime zones.

Making use of a limited set of ideal-typical geographical circumstances to both justify and serve as spatial points in the construction of legal lines also practically facilitates the relatively regular delimitation of maritime space notwithstanding the diversity of coasts globally. It can be understood to reflect the principle of the equality of States, though the notion of equitableness in maritime delimitation does not require or recommend as a matter of legal principle an equal division of maritime space between two States. The law provides that coastal States are

[134] Evans, *Relevant Circumstances*, 119–59.
[135] *Black Sea Case* (2009), 103.
[136] Weil, *The Law of Maritime Delimitation*, 51.

equally entitled to sovereignty and sovereign rights in the waters off their coasts by virtue of their territorial sovereignty over these land areas. The extent of that entitlement—its spatial specification—is determined by reference to the particular combination and configuration of generalized geographical types picked out as legally relevant by the law. In the case of interstate delimitation, a boundary that reflects the projection of jurisdiction from these 'legal coasts' as far as possible will be considered equitable.

VI. Conclusion

The role of geography in the law relating to maritime jurisdiction is both symbolic and functional. The law identifies the possession of territorial sovereignty over coastal land as a juridical fact that automatically generates entitlement to national maritime jurisdiction. This arrangement is based upon the idea that the coastal State's interest in certain maritime activities off its coasts is 'natural' and 'appropriate'. The same idea accounts for the character of coastal State jurisdiction beyond the territorial sea as a bundle of functionally defined exclusive sovereign rights. The regulation of the rights of the coastal State with respect to the passage of foreign vessels through its territorial waters and the specification of certain duties applying to the coastal State across the different zones of national maritime jurisdiction (such as duties to protect and preserve the marine environment) can be understood to mark the limits of the coastal State's legitimate interests in this regard as well as responding to the interests of other States in the sea.[137]

Where additional conditions for entitlement to certain maritime zones apply, geographical requirements are tied to the use and significance of coastal territory by and for the coastal State. It is thus only a State 'constituted' by archipelagos, further defined as 'group[s] of islands, including parts of islands, interconnecting waters and other natural features which are so closely interrelated that such islands, waters and other natural features form an intrinsic geographical, economic and political entity, or which historically have been regarded as such', that is entitled to archipelagic waters.[138] An island must be capable of sustaining 'human habitation

[137] Of course, the coastal State also benefits from the protection of the marine and coastal environment and the law recognizes its *right* to take measures directed towards this end: see e.g. UNCLOS Arts 21, 56. The *duties* in UNCLOS Part XII nevertheless place limits on the coastal State's pursuit of economic or security interests in response to a broader interest in environmental protection. Notably, the concern with environmental protection remains to a large extent anthropocentric, responding to the value of the environment for humans, whose interests are also viewed through a lens primarily focused on the State. The notion of legitimacy here refers back to the notion of what is 'just' and 'appropriate' given territorial sovereignty over coastal land and, in a similar manner, a notion of what is 'just' and 'appropriate' in terms of the interests and activities of seafaring States (including land-locked States) and States generally. This reasoning underpins the law; it is not suggested that character of these rights and restrictions *as law* depends on an assessment of their legitimacy in any particular case.

[138] UNCLOS Art 46.

or economic life of [its] own' to generate entitlement to an EEZ and continental shelf.[139] The restrictions on entitlement to archipelagic waters and entitlement to an EEZ and continental shelf in the case of an island again indicate the limits of what the law recognizes as the legitimate interests of the coastal State as well as responding to the interests of other States in the sea and seabed.

The role of geography in the construction of maritime limits and boundaries gives symbolic expression to the idea that coastal territory is the basis for national maritime jurisdiction, which projects from the 'legal coast'. The interests and activities of the coastal State have been taken into account in the identification and definition of geographical circumstances playing a role in the construction of the legal coast. These interests and activities may occasionally play a direct role in delimitation—for example, where the location of straight baselines is informed by 'economic interests peculiar to the region concerned, the reality and the importance of which are clearly evidenced by long usage'.[140] More commonly, geographical circumstances are referred to directly while their place in the delimitation process symbolically reflects the rationale for coastal State jurisdiction over adjacent seas. This facilitates a regular and reasoned approach to the unilateral delimitation of maritime space by coastal States and the delimitation of maritime boundaries between States (especially by a court or tribunal).

Tying maritime limits and boundaries to the coast—or, in the case of the limits of the continental shelf beyond 200M, seabed geomorphology—places limits on the extension of national maritime jurisdiction by any particular State. However, the role of geography in constraining the maritime claims of the coastal State should not be overstated. The law also allows States to maximize their jurisdiction by providing a framework for justifying the location of the 'dividing line between land and sea' beyond the physical line of the coast. It admits and even reflects a preference for the use of protuberant points on the coast as basepoints in both unilateral and interstate delimitation. This is consistent with the character of entitlement to maritime space as a projection from the coastal front. It also allows the establishment of limits and boundaries that are geometrically simple rather than serpentine—a character facilitating their observance and enforcement in practice.

This type of practical consideration is not extra-legal but bound up with the law's central objective of securing a stable division of maritime space. The role of geography in connection with entitlement to maritime space and its delimitation contributes substantially towards this end. The law responds to and makes (selective) use of the cartographical representation of the coast in nautical charts. The conceptualization of maritime jurisdiction as a just and appropriate appurtenance to coastal territory is already informed by the nautical chart—there is a close relationship between the legal and cartographical imagination in this context. More

[139] UNCLOS Art 121(3).
[140] UNCLOS Art 7(5).

straightforwardly, the law relating to maritime jurisdiction was developed in response to the fact that nautical charts were widely available artefacts already reflecting the division of land territory between States and relied upon by sea users.[141] The law makes use of the geographical circumstances depicted in these charts in part because this facilitates the timely establishment of observable and enforceable limits and boundaries. Though charted geographical circumstances do not independently determine the location of maritime limits, the availability of charts contributes to the reviewability of the limits that are established—an exercise which must remain sensitive to the degree of discretion afforded to the coastal State in the delimitation process.

The schematic treatment of geography in the law of the sea brings a substantial measure of order to unilateral and interstate maritime delimitation. It plays an important part in ensuring the generality of the law. The baselines provisions refer to coastal geography according to ideal types with a view to ensuring that delimitation in the same general circumstances by coastal States around the world is subject to the same broad standards. A similar approach can be identified in the jurisprudence regarding the delimitation of maritime space between neighbouring States.

This is consistent with the equality of coastal States in terms of their interests and corresponding rights in the sea off their shores. It introduces a notion of proportionality as determinative of the proper distribution of those rights. This notion of proportional equality is key to the concept of equity in the law of the sea, the contours of which are brought out most explicitly in the jurisprudence on the delimitation of maritime space between opposite or adjacent States oriented towards an 'equitable solution'. The spatial extent of entitlement to maritime space, and in some cases entitlement to particular maritime zones, is responsive to the presence, absence, or particular combination of a limited number of ideal-typical geographical circumstances. Both unilateral and interstate delimitation respond to the character of the coastal State's jurisdiction as a projection from the 'legal coast'—a construction that makes selective use of the representation of the coast on nautical charts. Coastal geography is filtered through a lens composed of the law's vision of the 'natural' interests of the coastal State in sea areas off its coasts together with practical considerations associated with the objective of securing a stable division of maritime space. It is these considerations that make sense of both the geographical circumstances identified as relevant and the effects that they are given or, in certain circumstances, denied.

[141] See Chapter 7.

2
UNCLOS and the 'Ambulatory Thesis'

I. Introduction

According to the ambulatory thesis, maritime baselines and the zonal limits measured from them as a general rule either shift synchronously with a changing coastline or such change enlivens an obligation on the part of the coastal State to adjust them. While 'ambulatory' is not an entirely satisfactory adjective in this context, it is convenient to defer to existing use. The relevant sense of the word is 'movable';[1] however, proponents of the ambulatory thesis do not claim that baselines and zonal limits are merely capable of movement or being moved. Rather, it is alleged that maritime limits *must* move or be moved in the event of geographical change affecting the low-water line or other features referred to in the baselines provisions. 'Exceptions' to this general rule are understood to apply in the case of straight baselines on deltaic coasts and the outer limits of the continental shelf.

Related and analogous arguments have been made with respect to international maritime boundaries. In particular, it has been suggested that, in some circumstances at least, maritime boundaries based on an 'equidistance' or 'median' line—that is, a line every point of which is equidistant from the nearest points on the baselines of opposite or adjacent States[2]—may shift or otherwise be brought into question by subsequent change in the location or configuration of those baselines. Significantly, this possibility has only been contemplated where baseline change is thought to be a necessary consequence of coastal change.[3] It has not been suggested that the discretionary adjustment of maritime baselines by one of the States concerned might have the same effect. Nor has it been suggested that either optional or obligatory baseline changes prompted by factors other than geographical change might alter established maritime boundaries or affect their legal validity or opposability.

The question of whether maritime limits and boundaries are ambulatory may be distinguished from the question of whether entitlement to maritime space generally or rights to particular maritime zones in respect of particular features might be lost as a consequence of geographical change. Logically, the question of whether maritime limits and boundaries are ambulatory only arises where rights

[1] 'Ambulatory', adj. 3, 4, *OED Online*, accessed 22 March 2017.
[2] See TSC Art 12; CSC Art 6; UNCLOS Art 15.
[3] See e.g. Soons, 'The Effects of a Rising Sea Level', 207.

Geographical Change and the Law of the Sea. Kate Purcell, Oxford University Press (2019). © Kate Purcell.
DOI: 10.1093/oso/9780198743644.001.0001

to maritime space exist. Yet the reasoning that underlies the ambulatory thesis is also at work in claims that certain types of geographical change will result in a loss of entitlement to maritime space.

In view of the influence of the ambulatory thesis on contemporary accounts of the implications of geographical change for maritime jurisdiction, it is appropriate to begin the present enquiry by examining that thesis in the context in which it first seems to have been developed—as a theory relating to the maritime limits unilaterally established by the coastal State. Unilateral maritime delimitation is governed by rules and principles set out in the United Nations Convention on the Law of the Sea (UNCLOS), most of which have either or both a parallel in the 1958 Law of the Sea Conventions (the Convention on the Territorial Sea and Contiguous Zone (TSC) and the Convention on the Continental Shelf (CSC) in particular) and customary status. As such, they will usually apply to States not party to UNCLOS.[4]

The idea that baselines and the zonal limits measured from them are 'ambulatory' is increasingly taken for granted in scholarly literature considering the implications of climate change for maritime jurisdiction. Yet there is no express provision to this effect in the TSC, CSC, or UNCLOS. Many commentators nevertheless take the ambulatory character of baselines and zonal limits to be 'negatively implied' by the positive law. The most influential argument to this effect was made by David Caron in 1990.[5]

II. The 'Ambulatory Thesis' by Negative Implication

In a piece titled 'When Law Makes Climate Change Worse' and clearly concerned to galvanize efforts to prevent or mitigate this effect, Caron claimed that the 'ambulatory' character of maritime limits could be inferred from UNCLOS Articles 7(2) and 76(9). He understood Article 7(2), which provides that straight baselines on a deltaic coast 'shall remain effective' despite 'subsequent regression of the low-water line', to 'fix' or 'freeze' straight baselines in this context.[6] He suggested that UNCLOS '*arguably* also permanently fixes the outer boundary of the continental shelf' through the requirement in Article 76(9) that the coastal State deposit charts and other geodetic data 'permanently describing' these limits.[7] Caron took these provisions to exceptionally secure straight baselines on deltaic coasts and the outer limits of the continental shelf against subsequent coastal regression.[8] The 'negative

[4] Those provisions of UNCLOS without a parallel in the 1958 Conventions or customary international law are noted as relevant below.

[5] Caron, 'When Law Makes Climate Change Worse'.

[6] Ibid, 634.

[7] Ibid, 634–5 (emphasis in original).

[8] Ibid, 634–6.

implication', he argued, was that baselines and zonal limits would otherwise shift with the changes to the coast.[9]

Caron diagnosed 'ambulatory baselines' as an underlying condition becoming malignant in the context of climate change.[10] His prognosis was that this would manifest in the landwards retreat of maritime limits, resource waste through efforts to prevent the coastal change thought to entail this result, and conflict due to uncertainty in the location of legal limits.[11] This analysis has heavily influenced the existing literature on the implications of coastal change for maritime jurisdiction.

Though Caron was not the first scholar to suggest that rising sea levels may affect maritime limits,[12] most subsequent commentators on the issue have affirmed his characterization of baselines, and most zonal limits measured from them, as 'ambulatory'.[13] In some cases, this understanding is underpinned by the (generally implicit) reasoning discussed in Chapters 7 to 9 of this book rather than Caron's (explicit) arguments regarding the 'negative implication' of UNCLOS Articles 7(2)

[9] Ibid.

[10] Ibid, 623, 636–41; see also D Caron, 'Climate Change, Sea Level Rise and the Coming Uncertainty in Oceanic Boundaries: A Proposal to Avoid Conflict' in Hong and Van Dyke (eds), *Maritime Boundary Disputes, Settlement Processes, and the Law of the Sea* (Martinus Nijhoff, 2009) 1, 2, 9–14.

[11] Caron, 'When Law Makes Climate Change Worse', 623, 636–41; Caron, 'Climate Change, Sea Level Rise and the Coming Uncertainty in Oceanic Boundaries', 2, 9–14.

[12] See e.g. LM Alexander, 'Baseline Delimitations and Maritime Boundaries' (1982–83) 23 *VJIL* 503, 535; V Prescott, E Bird, 'The Influence of Rising Sea Levels on Baselines from which National Maritime Claims are Measured and an Assessment of the Possibility of Applying Article 7 (2) of the 1982 Convention on the Law of the Sea to Offset Any Retreat of the Baseline' in *International Boundaries and Boundary Conflict Resolution: Conference Proceedings 1989* (IBRU, 1990) 279.

[13] See e.g. Soons, 'The Effects of a Rising Sea Level'; D Freestone, JS Pethick, 'Sea Level Rise and Maritime Boundaries: International Implications of Impacts and Responses' in Blake (ed), *Maritime Boundaries: World Boundaries*, vol 5 (Routledge, 1994) 73; A Khadem, 'Protecting Maritime Zones from the Effects of Sea Level Rise' [1998] *IBRU Boundary and Security Bulletin* 76; C Schofield, 'Sea Level Rise and Options to Secure Maritime Jurisdictional Claims' (2009) 4 *CCLR* 405; C Schofield, 'Against a Rising Tide: Ambulatory Baselines and Shifting Maritime Limits in the Face of Sea Level Rise' in *Proceedings of International Symposium on Islands and Oceans* (Ocean Policy Research Foundation, 2009) 70; M Hayashi, 'Sea Level Rise and the Law of the Sea: Legal and Policy Options' in *Proceedings of International Symposium on Islands and Oceans* (2009) 78; R Rayfuse, 'W(h)ither Tuvalu? International Law and Disappearing States' (2009) Paper 9 *UNSWLRS* 1; C Schofield, 'Rising Waters, Shrinking States: The Potential Impacts of Sea Level Rise on Claims to Maritime Jurisdiction' (2010) 53 *GYIL* 189; K Houghton et al, 'Maritime Boundaries in a Rising Sea' (2010) 3 *Nature Geoscience* 813; ILA-BC, *Baselines under the International Law of the Sea: Internal Discussion Document* (2010); R Rayfuse, 'International Law and Disappearing States: Utilising Maritime Entitlements to Overcome the Statehood Dilemma' [2010] Paper 52 *UNSWLRS* 1; R Rayfuse, 'International Law and Disappearing States: Maritime Zones and the Criteria for Statehood' (2011) 41 (6) *EPL* 281; ILA-BC, *Baselines under the International Law of the Sea: Final Report* (Sofia Conference, 2012); C Redgwell, 'UNCLOS and Climate Change' (2012) 106 *ASIL Proceedings* 406; C Schofield, A Arsana, 'Climate Change and the Limits of Maritime Jurisdiction' in Warner and Schofield (eds), *Climate Change and the Oceans: Gauging the Legal and Policy Currents in the Asia Pacific and Beyond* (Edward Elgar, 2012) 127; R Rayfuse, 'Climate Change and the Law of the Sea' in Rayfuse and Scott (eds), *International Law in the Era of Climate Change* (Edward Elgar, 2012) 147; A Powers, C Stucko, 'Introducing the Law of the Sea and the Legal Implications of Rising Sea Levels' in Gerrard and Wannier (eds), *Threatened Island Nations: Legal Implications of Rising Seas and a Changing Climate* (CUP, 2013) 123; C Schofield, D Freestone, 'Options to Protect Coastlines and Secure Maritime Jurisdictional Claims in the Face of Global Sea Rise' in Gerrard and Wannier (eds), *Threatened Island Nations* 141; R Rayfuse, 'Sea Level Rise and Maritime Zones: Preserving the Maritime Entitlements of "Disappearing" States' in Gerrard and Wannier (eds), *Threatened Island Nations* 167.

and 76(9). Yet Caron's interpretation of UNCLOS in this respect has been endorsed by a number of scholars. It has also so far gone unchallenged.

III. Conclusion: An Inference from Unsteady Grounds

The simple logical form of Caron's analysis may partly explain why it has been so readily accepted, or at least left undisputed, in subsequent scholarship. Yet insufficient attention has been paid to the premises of his argument, which involve a highly problematic interpretation of the relevant provisions and UNCLOS more broadly.

Caron's characterization of Articles 7(2) and 76(9) as 'fixing' or 'freezing' straight baselines along deltaic coasts and the limits of the shelf, respectively, is an oversimplification that elides at least two important differences between these provisions. Firstly, while Article 7(2) is concerned with unstable coasts, there is nothing in the text of Article 76(9) or its drafting history to suggest that coastal instability or change was a factor bearing upon the requirement that the limits of the shelf be permanently described. Caron claims that participants at UNCLOS III otherwise failing to 'anticipate that there could be a significant regression of coastlines generally' were 'presented with concern over such a possibility' in relation to both deltas and the outer edge of the continental shelf.[14] This, he argues, prompted a decision to 'fix' maritime limits in these circumstances.[15] Yet there is no evidence of any such concern playing a role in connection with Article 76(9) or the development of the law relating to the limits of the shelf more broadly.

The second point of difference between the two provisions is that Article 7(2) refers expressly to the possibility of redrawing established baselines, whereas Article 76(9) expressly excludes the possibility of redrawing the limits of the continental shelf. This important distinction, which helps to illuminate the meaning of each provision by reference to its purpose and effect, is neglected in Caron's generalizations regarding the 'fixing' or 'freezing' of maritime limits.

In order to explore the significance of these points of difference and the broader question they reopen—that is, what, if anything, these provisions have to say about the implications of geographical change for maritime limits—it is necessary to revisit Articles 7(2) and 76(9) in some detail. This is the task of the following two chapters, which examine the ordinary meaning of the terms of these provisions in context and in light of the treaty's object and purpose.[16] As we shall see, Caron's analysis pays insufficient attention to both the immediate context for these

[14] Caron, 'When Law Makes Climate Change Worse', 636; Caron 'Climate Change, Sea Level Rise and the Coming Uncertainty in Oceanic Boundaries', 10.

[15] Caron, 'When Law Makes Climate Change Worse', 636; Caron 'Climate Change, Sea Level Rise and the Coming Uncertainty in Oceanic Boundaries', 10.

[16] Vienna Convention on the Law of Treaties Art 31(1).

clauses—that is, the articles in which they are situated as well as the provisions relating to baselines and zonal limits as a whole—and the 'object and purpose' of UNCLOS. His conclusions are also at odds with 'the preparatory work of the treaty and the circumstances of its conclusion', which may, of course, be drawn on to confirm the ordinary meaning of a treaty provision or determine its meaning where this is inter alia 'ambiguous or obscure'.[17]

A careful examination of Caron's argument shows that it relies on premises that are unsupported by either the text of the relevant provisions or the circumstances of their conclusion. Indeed, revisiting the treaty law suggests that the implications of geographical change for maritime limits are seriously misrepresented by the ambulatory thesis. Rather than implying that baselines and most zonal limits measured from them are ambulatory, the treaty law supports the conclusion that baselines and zonal limits, once established, *may*, with the exception of the limits of the continental shelf, be relocated at the discretion of the coastal State. This exercise remains governed by the rules and principles pertaining to the construction of these legal lines. There is no legal requirement, however, that baselines and zonal limits *must* be adjusted in response to geographical change. An examination of the treaty law both in its specifics and as a whole helps to explain why this is the case.

[17] Ibid, Art 32.

3

Article 7(2) and the Special Case of Deltaic Coasts

I. Introduction

Article 7(2) of the United Nations Convention on the Law of the Sea (UNCLOS) provides that where the low-water line on a highly unstable deltaic coast regresses, 'straight baselines shall remain effective until changed by the coastal State in accordance with this Convention'. This provision clearly identifies circumstances '[w]here the presence of a delta and other natural conditions' make the coastline 'highly unstable' as a special case. In Caron's view, expressly providing for the retention of baselines in this special case implies that they must otherwise shift with the coast.[1] Yet this does not necessarily follow from 'the ordinary meaning to be given to the terms of the treaty in their context and in the light of its object and purpose'.[2]

It was evidently understood that the presence of a delta would make the coastline far more unstable than it would be in other circumstances. Yet Article 7(2) may reasonably be taken to specify that the rapid and dramatic change typical of deltaic coasts, *like* the more gradual and modest change affecting most coasts in most circumstances, would *not* render established baselines ineffective. The implication of this reading would be that baselines of all types, once established, will not shift unless the coastal State elects to redraw them—*even* in circumstances of substantial coastal change.

The present Chapter explores this alternative reading of Article 7(2), comparing it to Caron's understanding of the provision as an exception to a general rule that baselines are ambulatory. It argues that the alternative reading is more consistent with the ordinary meaning of Article 7(2) in context and in light of UNCLOS's object and purpose, though State practice in the application of the treaty does not clearly favour one reading over the other. Turning to the drafting history to confirm the meaning of the treaty, however, reveals a surprising disjunction between (a) the proposals on which Article 7(2) is widely understood to be based, and (b) the meaning and effect of that provision.

[1] Caron, 'When Law Makes Climate Change Worse', 634–6; Caron 'Climate Change, Sea Level Rise and the Coming Uncertainty in Oceanic Boundaries', 9–10.

[2] Vienna Convention on the Law of Treaties (VCLT) Art 31(1).

Geographical Change and the Law of the Sea. Kate Purcell, Oxford University Press (2019). © Kate Purcell.
DOI: 10.1093/oso/9780198743644.001.0001

This does not undermine the alternative reading of Article 7(2), though equally it cannot be considered to confirm it. Rather more interestingly, the drafting history shows that the formulation in Article 7(2) does not in fact reflect a recognized concern with the implications of geographical change for established baselines at all. Instead, Article 7(2) appears to be based on the misunderstanding of a different proposal regarding the special case of deltaic coasts. Of course, this does not mean the provision as adopted has no legal effect. But it does contradict the basic assumption upon which Caron's account of the 'negative implication' of this provision rests—an assumption regarding the intentions underlying Article 7(2). As such, the drafting history supports the conclusion that Article 7(2) does not imply that maritime baselines are ambulatory.

II. Between Text and Implication

Caron's account of the meaning of Article 7(2) is closely linked with his understanding of the motivation for this provision. The idea that Article 7(2) 'negatively implies' that baselines are ordinarily ambulatory has been said to be 'based on [a] textual interpretation' of UNCLOS.[3] Yet Caron himself did not discuss the text of Article 7(2) in any detail. In fact, his account of the 'negative implication' of this provision seems to have informed his understanding of its more immediate meaning, rather than the other way around.

Caron's account of the meaning of Article 7(2) and its alleged 'implication' cannot be derived from the text in the absence of certain assumptions regarding the intentions underlying this provision (and the broader beliefs upon which they were based). The text itself does not justify these assumptions. In this sense, the text may be considered ambiguous; however, Caron's interpretation cannot be considered one among other equally tenable readings of Article 7(2), still less the reading that might be preferred. It is an interpretation which pays insufficient attention to the role played by geography in the baselines provisions generally, which is an important context for Article 7(2). It is also difficult to reconcile with the 'object and purpose' of the treaty in this connection.

Article 7(2) applies where the use of straight baselines has been justified under Article 7(1), which provides that:

> In localities where the coastline is deeply indented and cut into, or if there is a fringe of islands along the coast in its immediate vicinity, the method of straight baselines

[3] Rayfuse, 'W(h)ither Tuvalu', 3; Rayfuse, 'Sea Level Rise and Maritime Zones', 172–3.

> joining appropriate points may be employed in drawing the baseline from which the breadth of the territorial sea is measured.

An unstable deltaic coast must also be 'deeply indented and cut into' or fringed with islands to warrant the use of straight baselines in the first instance. It is occasionally suggested that the circumstances identified in Article 7(2) are a separate basis for entitlement to use straight baselines.[4] This is at odds with the text. Article 7(2) provides that:

> Where because of the presence of a delta and other natural conditions the coastline is highly unstable, the appropriate points may be selected along the furthest seaward extent of the low-water line and, notwithstanding subsequent regression of the low-water line, the straight baselines shall remain effective until changed by the coastal State in accordance with this Convention.

The reference back to 'the appropriate points' mentioned in Article 7(1) indicates that the second paragraph relates to the selection and continuing 'effectiveness' of baselines justified under that first paragraph. The idea that Article 7(2) sets out a separate basis for the use of straight baselines is not generally supported by scholars.[5]

Article 7(2) provides that straight baselines on a coast rendered 'highly unstable' by 'the presence of a delta and other natural conditions' will remain effective 'notwithstanding regression of the low-water line'. Though some commentators have devoted attention to the question of whether the presence of a delta is a necessary precondition for the application of Article 7(2), this question only arises if Article 7(2) is already taken to exceptionally guarantee the effectiveness of straight baselines when coastal change otherwise requires their adjustment.[6] The text makes clear that the provision refers to cases of high coastal instability due to the presence of a delta. Whether this is properly described as a *precondition* for its application depends upon how one interprets the provision as a whole.

Based on the text alone, it is reasonable to conclude that Article 7(2) responds to a concern that 'subsequent regression of the low-water line' on a 'highly unstable' deltaic coast might leave straight baselines established on such a coast 'ineffective'—specifically providing that this will not be the case. Caron emphasized that none of the other provisions on baselines provide for their continued effectiveness 'notwithstanding subsequent regression of the low-water line'.[7] This, however, it is not enough to establish that baselines are generally ambulatory.

[4] See e.g. International Law Association's Baselines Committee (ILA-BC), *Final Report*.

[5] See e.g. R Churchill and V Lowe, *The Law of the Sea* (3rd edn, MUP, 1999), 38; UN Baselines Study (1989), 24.

[6] See Section IV below.

[7] Caron, 'When Law Makes Climate Change Worse', 635.

As noted above, Article 7(2) may reasonably be taken to respond to a concern that the particular character or degree of change affecting a deltaic coast might unusually render baselines ineffective when ordinary coastal variability did not. The provision could be understood to affirm a general rule that baselines are *not* ambulatory in the particular case of highly changeable deltaic coasts. On this reading, Article 7(2) would underscore the importance of this general rule. It would appear that States were so concerned to ensure the stability of maritime limits that they agreed that baselines should remain in place *even* in circumstances where changes to the coastline after their establishment were likely to be substantial.

This reading remains consistent with the principle of effectiveness in treaty interpretation. Expressly affirming the application of a general rule in circumstances where it might be brought into question is as substantial an effect as the identification of an exception to such a rule. It also appears to be more consistent with the 'object and purpose' of UNCLOS, which aims inter alia at a stable division of maritime space.

As discussed in the Introduction to this book, geographical change is an ordinary condition of most coasts around the world, even if it is not always as rapid or extreme as change resulting from the presence of a delta (or climate change). The geographical features or cartographical constructs given a role in maritime delimitation are especially vulnerable to coastal change. Yet it does not follow that established limits must be adjusted to reflect subsequent geographical change. Indeed, the part played by geography in securing stability and equity in the delimitation of maritime space may be undermined if this were the case. At the very least, these objectives indicate that we should not be too hasty to *read in* a requirement to constantly adjust maritime limits to reflect the regularly changing geography of the coast.

The law does not expressly provide for ambulatory baselines and zonal limits or answer the kind of legal questions such a system would be expected to generate (e.g. questions regarding when established limits become unlawful and must be redrawn). This cannot be explained by the flexibility and discretion that the law governing unilateral maritime delimitation affords the coastal State—it would be at odds with the theory that the adjustment of maritime limits in response to coastal change is legally required if it were entirely up to the coastal State to make such adjustments. Certainly it is difficult to see how the alleged obligation could be effectively enforced in these circumstances.

In this regard, it is worth reflecting on the clause 'until changed by the coastal State in accordance with this Convention', which Caron omits from his restatement of what he takes to be the relevant part of Article 7(2) 'negatively implying' the 'ambulatory thesis'.[8] Several commentators who also consider Article 7(2) to

[8] Ibid, 634.

exceptionally guarantee the effectiveness of straight baselines in circumstances of coastal change have suggested that this implies an obligation to adjust the baselines to take the regression of the low-water line into account *at some point*.[9] The idea that Article 7(2) provides for a *temporary* retention of baselines remains consistent with—though it does not prove—the theory that baselines are ordinarily 'ambulatory'. Yet the phrase 'until changed by the coastal State in accordance with this Convention' would be a very oblique way of indicating an *obligation* to change the relevant baselines. It is relevant in this regard that clear language is used to identify the obligations of the coastal State elsewhere in the baselines provisions. The alleged obligation also lacks the specificity necessary for it to be effective. There is no indication of when established baselines must be changed or whether and when unchanged baselines can no longer be relied upon. If the law were generally concerned to ensure that baselines should be 'updated' to reflect changes to the coast and only exceptionally and temporarily guaranteed their effectiveness notwithstanding such change, it would be reasonable to expect some indication of when this exceptional and temporary guarantee could no longer be relied upon. Rather than concluding that Article 7(2) is in this regard poorly formulated and potentially ineffective, this is a further reason to doubt that it implies an obligation to revise baselines at all.

The words 'until changed by the coastal State in accordance with this Convention' in fact have a much more straightforward meaning that is consistent with the baselines provisions and the law relating to maritime jurisdiction as a whole. The baselines provisions generally emphasize the authority and responsibility of the coastal State for establishing its maritime limits in accordance with the law (which has not so far been shown to require their revision in the event of coastal change). By providing that baselines 'remain effective until changed', Article 7(2) can be understood to affirm the control of the coastal State over its baselines, which includes an option to redraw them. The right of the coastal State to redraw its baselines is supported by abundant State practice. States typically revise their maritime limits to take advantage of coastal change allowing the seaward extension of their maritime jurisdiction. This is perfectly lawful, though there is no reason to think that it is *required* by law.

Given that deltas not only retreat but advance (in some cases substantially over relatively short periods of time), it is unsurprising that it should have been thought necessary to specify that while baselines established along a deltaic coast 'remain effective' in the event of coastal regression, they are not fixed once and for all time. The clause 'until changed in accordance with this Convention' specifically recognizes that the coastal State retains the option to redraw straight baselines along a deltaic coast in accordance with the terms of the Convention—a right it

[9] See e.g. J Grote Stoutenberg, *Disappearing Island States in International Law* (Brill, 2015), 132; Soons, 'The Effects of a Rising Sea Level', 220; Churchill and Lowe, *The Law of the Sea*, 38.

possesses with respect to baselines generally. As Chapter 4 will explain, the right (not obligation) of the coastal State to revise maritime limits is exceptionally denied in the case of the limits of the continental shelf. Far from resembling Article 7(2) in this regard, the fact that Article 76 expressly prohibits the coastal State from changing the limits of the continental shelf once established may be a further reason why States were concerned to specify that no such prohibition was intended by Article 7(2).

III. State Practice

There is very little State practice relating directly to Article 7(2) and certainly not enough to establish the agreement of States parties to UNCLOS regarding its interpretation.[10] No State has expressly relied on this provision to retain straight baselines on a deltaic coast, though several States use straight baselines in the vicinity of a delta.[11] In some cases this practice predates UNCLOS. Bangladesh established its baselines in the vicinity of the Ganges-Brahmaputra delta in 1974[12] and has not since revised them to give effect to changes in the configuration of its deltaic coast. Yet the State does not justify the retention of its established baselines on the basis of Article 7(2). Rather—as discussed below—Bangladesh has relied on basepoints located at sea from the outset.

Egypt proclaimed its use of straight baselines in various geographic circumstances in 1951, though it did not specify their location in coordinates until 1990, after it became a party to UNCLOS (though before that treaty entered into force).[13] Despite the rapid erosion of the Nile delta, the baselines established in this area have not subsequently been adjusted.[14] Like Bangladesh, Egypt has not specifically justified the retention of its established baselines on the basis of Article 7(2). Indeed, neither Bangladesh nor Egypt appears to have considered it necessary to justify the retention of established baselines along their dynamic deltaic coasts at all.

There have been some objections to the baseline practices of Bangladesh and Egypt based on an alleged inconsistency with UNCLOS Article 7. India and Myanmar have argued that Bangladesh's use of basepoints established on the basis

[10] VCLT Art 31(3)(b).

[11] It also appears that no State has relied on Article 7(2) as the basis for establishing straight baselines along a deltaic coast, supporting the view that the provision does not identify circumstances justifying the use of straight baselines in the first instance (governed by Article 7(1)). Cf Bangladesh's comments on Article 7(2) in *Bangladesh/Myanmar* (2012) and *Bangladesh v India* (2014), discussed below.

[12] Bangladesh Territorial Waters and Maritime Zones Act 1974 and Notification No LT – I/3/74.

[13] Egypt Decree concerning Territorial Waters (1951) as amended (1958); Egypt Baselines Decree (1990). Unfortunately, the geodetic datum was not specified: D Dzurek, C Schofield, 'Parting the Red Sea: Boundaries, Offshore Resources and Transit' (2001) 3 (2) *IBRU Maritime Briefing* 1, 9–10. Egypt was not a party to the Convention on the Territorial Sea and Contiguous Zone (TSC).

[14] Churchill and Lowe, *The Law of the Sea*, 38.

of depth is at odds with this provision. In this regard, Myanmar has emphasized that Article 7(2) in particular 'specifies in precise and unambiguous terms the fundamental rule that straight baselines may be drawn only from land-point to land-point, and not from sea-point to sea-point' (i.e. 'along the furthest seaward extent of the low-water line').[15] India and Myanmar reiterated these objections in response to Bangladesh's 2011 submission to the Commission on the Limits of the Continental Shelf (CLCS), which made use of the existing baselines.[16] The United States has objected to Egypt's baselines on the grounds that the coast in the relevant area is 'neither deeply indented nor fringed with islands'.[17]

Notably, these objections relate to the lawfulness of the establishment of straight baselines in the first instance. While it is evident that India, Myanmar, and the United States consider the baselines in question to be governed by UNCLOS Article 7, there has been no objection by these States or any other to Bangladesh and Egypt retaining straight baselines despite substantial changes to their deltaic coasts. In the case of Bangladesh, this may be because coastal change has no bearing on the basepoints it has established at sea (though it is possible that depth changes mean that the basepoints established in 1974 are no longer on the 10 fathom line). As far as Egypt is concerned, it is unclear whether the absence of protest follows from the belief that the retention of straight baselines in these circumstances is permitted by Article 7(2) and, if so, whether this permission is understood to be exceptional or consistent with a more general rule admitting the retention of established baselines notwithstanding coastal change. If Article 7(2) *is* understood to justify the continuing effectiveness of Egypt's baselines, then it seems—given the extent of coastal regression in the vicinity of the Nile delta[18]—that the terms 'until changed by the coastal State in accordance with this Convention' have not been understood to signify a duty to revise baselines to take such coastal change into account.

Other States using straight baselines in the vicinity of a delta include Vietnam, Venezuela, Guinea-Bissau, Russia, and Ukraine, as well as the Soviet Union before its dissolution in 1991. Vietnam's baselines in the region of the Mekong delta (established in 1982[19] and reaffirmed in 2012[20]) connect basepoints on islands that are a considerable distance from the coast. These baselines have been subject to protests on the grounds that (a) the islands in question cannot be considered a 'fringe', and (b) the resulting lines depart from the general direction of the coast.[21]

[15] UNCLOS III: XVI, 255.

[16] Bangladesh Submission to CLCS (2011); Myanmar Note Verbale re Bangladesh's Submission (2011); India Note Verbale re Bangladesh's Submission (2011); India Note of 29 October 2009 on India's Submission to CLCS (2009); Myanmar Note of 23 July 2009 on Myanmar's Submission to CLCS (2008).

[17] US DOS, 'Straight Baseline Claims: Albania and Egypt' (1994) 116 *LIS* 1, 9.

[18] A Scheffers, T Browne, 'Egypt—Mediterranean' in Bird (ed), *Encyclopedia of the World's Coastal Landforms* (Springer, 2010) 893–6.

[19] Vietnam Statement on Baseline (1982).

[20] Vietnam Law of the Sea (2012) Art 8.

[21] These were the grounds for objection listed by the USA: see JA Roach, RW Smith, *Excessive Maritime Claims* (3rd edn, Martinus Nijhoff, 2012), 99. France and Singapore have more generally

Whether or not they may be considered unlawful on this basis, they are not located on the 'seaward low-water line' of the deltaic coast and Article 7(2) does not come into play. Vietnam's Red River Delta is located in the Gulf of Tonkin, which Vietnam considers historic waters (a claim which is also disputed).[22] On this basis, Vietnam claims that the straight baseline in this area should be located at 'the opening line of the gulf' and thus beyond the delta.[23]

Venezuela (which is not a party to UNCLOS) encloses the Orinoco delta with a single straight baseline connecting just two basepoints located on the (relatively stable) coast beyond the delta (in the case of point B, on part of the coast of Guyana claimed by Venezuela).[24] There have been objections to Venezuela's account of the legal basis for the use of straight baselines generally[25] as well as this particular baseline.[26] Subsequent coastal change, however, has not been an issue.

Guinea-Bissau uses straight baselines in the vicinity of the Bissagos Archipelago delta, with basepoints located either on fringing islands or, apparently, at sea.[27] Guinea-Bissau maintains that these baselines 'are in no way in contravention of the rules contained in Article 7 of [UNCLOS]',[28] though Senegal considers them 'manifestly contrary to international law'.[29] Again, the question of their retention notwithstanding geographical change has not arisen.

In 1985, the Soviet Union (which had signed but not yet ratified UNCLOS) established straight baselines some 5 nautical miles seaward of the Danube delta, making use of at least one basepoint at sea 'where the State maritime boundary line between the USSR and the Socialist Republic of Romania intersects the line connecting the eastern extremity of the northern entrance pier of the Sulinsky Canal with the eastern islet of the Tsyganki Islands.'[30] The USA objected to these basepoints, focusing on the fact that there was neither a 'deeply indented' coastline

asserted that Vietnam's baselines are at variance with UNCLOS Article 7 (and TSC Art 4): UNDOALOS, *Law of the Sea: Current Developments in State Practice* (UN Publications, 1987), 146 (France); (1987) *LOS Bulletin*, 53 (Singapore). Germany also protested Vietnam's baselines in 1984: Roach and Smith, *Excessive Maritime Claims*, 99, fn 105.

---

22 Vietnam Statement on Baseline (1982). Thailand and France have expressly protested this claim: see UNDOALOS, *Current Developments in State Practice* (1987), 146–8. China has not denied that the Gulf is 'historic waters', though it has objected to Vietnam's claim that a maritime boundary between the two States was established here on the basis of an 1887 treaty between China and France: ibid, 145.

23 Vietnam, Statement on Baseline (1982).

24 Venezuela Presidential Decree (1968). This Decree was issued pursuant to legislation predating the TSC (to which Venezuela is party) and allowing straight baselines '[w]hen circumstances require a special regime because of the configuration of the coastline or the presence of nearby islands, or when the particular interest of a given region so justify': Venezuela Territorial Sea, Continental Shelf, Fishery Protection and Air-Space Act (1956) Art 2.

25 See Roach and Smith, *Excessive Maritime Claims*, 123, fn 139.

26 US DoD, 'Venezuela' in *MCRM* (2014); see also US DOS, 'Straight Baselines: Venezuela' (1970) 21 *LIS* 1, 3.

27 Guinea-Bissau Act No 2/85.

28 Guinea-Bissau Note Verbale (1986) 8 *LOS Bulletin* 1, 23.

29 Senegal Note Verbale: ibid, 24.

30 USSR Declaration 4450 (1985).

nor a fringe of islands in the immediate vicinity of the coast.[31] Though it 'does not necessarily represent an official acceptance ... of the limits claimed', it is interesting to note that the US State Department's analysis of the USSR's baselines recognized that 'the use of geographic features of two states to justify the location of a baseline terminus where the terminus itself is not anchored to a piece of territory' was supported by 'some state practice'.[32] Ukraine now uses the same basepoints in this area.[33] Given their location beyond the deltaic coast, its 'regression' would appear to be irrelevant.

Russia's straight baselines in the vicinity of the Lena delta on its Arctic coast connect basepoints located on a number of small islands on the delta's margins.[34] While this delta is reported to be unstable and subject to erosion in particular, a lack of detailed information about these changes means that it is unclear whether they have affected the features upon which Russia locates its basepoints.[35] These basepoints have remained unchanged since their establishment by the USSR in 1985.

Ultimately, the practice of States using straight baselines in the vicinity of a delta does not help to resolve the question of whether Article 7(2) is properly interpreted as expressing a general rule that baselines are not ambulatory (*even* on a deltaic coast) or an exception to a general rule that they are. In most cases, the straight baselines that have been established in the vicinity of a delta do not depend on basepoints located on the highly unstable low-water line. Only Egypt's baselines in the vicinity of the Nile delta and Russia's baselines in the Lena delta appear to have been originally located 'along the furthest seaward extent of the low-water line' (though in both cases they were established before UNCLOS and Article 7(2) bound the States concerned). While it is unclear whether and to what extent coastal change has affected the areas in which basepoints are located in the Lena delta, it is apparent that Egypt has retained its baselines notwithstanding substantial coastal change. It remains unclear whether it considers this to be exceptionally justified by Article 7(2) or otherwise consistent with the law.

Egypt's retention of its baselines has not been protested by other States. However, it does not follow that they accept this practice as lawful. While the United States

31 US DoD, 'Russian Federation' in *MCRM* (2014); US DOS, 'Continental Shelf Boundary: Turkey-USSR and Straight Baselines USSR (Black Sea)' (1988) 109 *LIS* 1, 8.

32 US DOS, 'Continental Shelf Boundary: Turkey-USSR and Straight Baselines USSR (Black Sea)' (1988) 109 *LIS* 1, 8.

33 Ukraine, List of coordinates defining baselines in the Black Sea (1992).

34 USSR Declaration 4450 (1985).

35 A Selivanov, 'The Arctic Coast of Russia' in Bird, *Encyclopedia of the World's Coastal Landforms*, 823; F Are, E Reimnitz, 'An Overview of the Lena River Delta Setting: Geology, Tectonics, Geomorphology and Hydrology' (2000) 16 (4) *JCR* 1083. See also the activities of the Alaskan Permafrost Laboratory on the Lena River Delta: <http://permafrost.gi.alaska.edu/project/lena-river-delta-various-project-activities>. If there was relevant coastal change subsequent to the establishment of these baselines, it would also have to be shown that Russia was aware of it. Given that the area is poorly surveyed, this seems unlikely.

has taken a particularly active interest in the use of straight baselines by coastal States and protests those it considers 'excessive',[36] other States have been less concerned to scrutinize foreign practice regarding baselines unless there appear to be significant consequences for their own interests. Given that the United States has objected to Egypt's baselines on other grounds, its silence with respect to their retention notwithstanding considerable coastal change is more likely to reflect a belief that this practice is lawful. The United States has not expressly stated whether it considers the retention of baselines following changes to the low-water line on a deltaic coast to be exceptionally justified by Article 7(2) or permissible in any case. Other aspects of US practice discussed later in this book suggest that the former view is more likely.[37] The United States, however, is not a party to UNCLOS and its practice cannot directly contribute to evidence of the agreement of the parties regarding its interpretation. Overall, State practice relating to the use of straight baselines on deltaic coasts where UNCLOS Article 7(2) applies tells us little about how that provision is understood by the parties to the treaty.

IV. The Origins of Article 7(2)

Caron's argument that Article 7(2) 'negatively implies' that baselines are usually ambulatory is not established by an interpretation of the ordinary meaning of the terms of Article 7(2) in their context and in light of the treaty's object and purpose. Nor does such an interpretation support the variations on this theme that take Article 7(2) to indicate an obligation to adjust straight baselines to reflect 'subsequent regression of the low-water line' at some unspecified point. No further support can be found for these readings in State practice. There is no indication that the parties to UNCLOS agree that this provision is properly understood to exceptionally admit the continuing effectiveness of straight baselines on a deltaic coast against the backdrop of a general rule that baselines must be revised in response to coastal change.

To the extent that the meaning of Article 7(2) can still be considered 'ambiguous', or, indeed, to confirm the alternative reading developed above, it is appropriate to refer to the *travaux préparatoires*.[38] It is here that one would expect to find evidence of the beliefs, concerns, and intentions in fact underpinning the development of this provision, which was one of the relatively few amendments to the articles on baselines already incorporated in the TSC. It might also be expected that the drafting history would support one of the two interpretations already

[36] US DOS, 'US Responses to Excessive Maritime Claims'; US DoD, *MCRM* (2014); Reisman and Westerman, *Straight Baselines*, 190.
[37] See the Conclusion to this book.
[38] VCLT Art 32.

discussed—though it must be reiterated that these readings are not otherwise on par (the difficulties with Caron's analysis in terms of its fit with the baselines provisions generally and the overarching objectives of the law relating to maritime jurisdiction remain). In fact, a review of the drafting history further complicates any conclusions that may be drawn regarding what Article 7(2) 'implies' about the consequences of geographical change for maritime baselines. This is because it complicates our understanding of what this provision was intended to achieve.

Somewhat surprisingly, the drafting history does not confirm the correctness of either reading regarding the question of meaning on which they diverge. It does not confirm that Article 7(2) is an exception implying a general rule that baselines are ambulatory. And it does not confirm that Article 7(2) clarifies (and underscores the importance of) a general rule that geographical change will not leave baselines ineffective or necessitate their revision even in cases of substantial coastal change. Significantly, however, an examination of the origins of Article 7(2) does provide further reasons for rejecting Caron's claim that this provision negatively implies that baselines are, as a general rule, ambulatory.

The origins of Article 7(2) are often treated cursorily in the scholarly literature, being generally summed up by the observation that the provision responds to a proposal by Bangladesh, which was concerned with the variability of its deltaic coast.[39] This observation is only partly true and rather misleading. A review of the drafting history shows that the provision adopted as Article 7(2) is in fact at odds with both the nature of Bangladesh's concern regarding the variability of its coast and its proposal on this basis. Some proponents of the ambulatory thesis have treated the drafting history more carefully (including Caron, though the discussion is contained in a footnote).[40] Yet insufficient attention has been paid to the extent to which this history casts doubt upon the idea that Article 7(2) 'negatively implies' that baselines are ambulatory.

The drafting history reveals a discrepancy between the text of Article 7(2) and the proposals upon which it is held to be based. This cannot be ignored. Of course, it is not suggested that an interpretation of the text according to the recognized principles of construction should be revised to give effect to these proposals, which the provision as adopted does not in fact reflect. Rather, what is significant is the absence of *any* indication beyond the text of Article 7(2) that States were concerned that established baselines would become ineffective due to subsequent coastal change.

[39] See, for example, Churchill and Lowe, *The Law of the Sea*, 37–8; V Prescott, 'Indian Ocean Boundaries' in Colson and Smith (eds), *International Maritime Boundaries*, vol 5 (Martinus Nijhoff, 2005) 3457; Grote Stoutenburg, *Disappearing Island States*, 131; T Scovazzi, 'Baselines', MPEPIL Online, accessed 24 November 2015.

[40] Caron, 'When Law Makes Climate Change Worse', 634–5, fn 77. See also S McDonald, V Prescott, 'Baselines along Unstable Coasts: An Interpretation of Article 7(2)' (1989) 8 *Ocean Yearbook* 70; Prescott and Schofield, *Maritime Political Boundaries of the World*, 151–2.

Both Caron's characterization of Article 7(2) as an exception and the suggestion that it might rather represent the rule seek to account for such a concern. Yet Article 7(2) originated in proposals by Bangladesh that were *not concerned with the ongoing effectiveness of established baselines at all*. Instead, Bangladesh sought to secure support for 'a variation of the straight baseline on the depth method to suit its local requirements'.[41]

Bangladesh's first proposal to this effect was included as 'Provision 9' of the Main Trends Working Paper produced by the Second Committee in 1974.[42] While the Committee undertook a second reading of this Paper in 1975, it did not debate 'the major issues' in any detail.[43] Instead, 'small informal working groups representing mainly special interests' were established 'to try to reduce the alternatives and, if possible, to produce a single text'.[44] With this broad mandate, an informal working group on baselines prepared a Blue Paper setting out a series of revised and consolidated provisions on the topic.[45] Among them was a formulation said to 'reflect' Provision 9 of the Main Trends Paper.[46] This clause was adopted without amendment as part of draft Article 6(1) of the first Informal Single Negotiating Text (ISNT) (Part II).[47] In 1976, the text was altered to refer to 'the presence of a delta *and* other natural conditions' instead of 'the presence of a delta *or* other natural conditions'.[48] The same text was adopted as UNCLOS Article 7(2).[49]

It is necessary in view of scholarly arguments on the matter to comment on the significance of this replacement of 'and' with 'or' in the text. While some scholars have suggested that this was an important change, it is crucial to recognize that such an assessment follows from their acceptance of the ambulatory thesis coupled with the belief that its consequences—baselines and zonal limits subject to change with a variable coast—are undesirable. Prescott and Bird have suggested that a 'liberal interpretation' of Article 7(2) might allow its extension to cases of coastal instability where a delta is not present, including cases of climate-related coastal change.[50] Other scholars have thought that this stretches the text too far.[51] The more important point is that this admittedly strained construction is only necessary if Article 7(2) is already understood to exceptionally fix baselines against subsequent coastal change.

[41] Platzöder (1983/IV), 179–82.
[42] Ibid, 14 (15 October 1974).
[43] UNCLOS III: IV, 13.
[44] Ibid.
[45] Baselines C.2/Blue Paper No 4, 9 April 1975 in Platzöder (1983/IV), 126 (Provision 5, para 1).
[46] Ibid, fn 1.
[47] UNCLOS III: IV, 153.
[48] Revised Single Negotiating Text (RSNT)/Part II (1976).
[49] ISNT/Part II (1975).
[50] Prescott and Bird, 'The Influence of Rising Sea Levels', 292–6.
[51] See e.g. C Schofield, B Sas, 'Uncovered and Unstable Coasts: Climate Change and Territorial Sea Baselines in the Arctic' in Lalonde and McDorman (eds), *International Law and Politics of the Arctic Ocean: Essays in Honor of Donat Pharand* (Hotei, 2015) 330.

Where the ambulatory thesis is accepted, the specification of circumstances '[w]here because of the presence of a delta and other natural conditions the coastline is highly unstable' tends to be interpreted as a *limitation* on the application of Article 7(2). There is no evidence that this was the intention.[52] The ordinary meaning of the text of the provision confirms that it is concerned with circumstances where coastal instability is in part or whole due to the presence of a delta. If, however, Article 7(2) is understood as an express statement of the general rule that baselines will remain effective until changed by the coastal State, these terms are not limiting. Rather, on this view, the purpose of Article 7(2) is to make clear that the general rule holds true where deltas together with other natural conditions leave coastlines highly unstable. It is a specification rather than a limitation. As such, it is unnecessary to rely on Article 7(2) to argue that baselines in other circumstances of coastal instability—including circumstances where there is no delta or instability is not attributable to it—will remain unaltered and effective unless and until the coastal State chooses to redraw them. This will be the effect of establishing baselines consistently with the relevant provisions of UNCLOS regardless.

Though Provision 9 of the Main Trends Paper was held to be 'reflected' in ISNT draft Article 6(1), even the briefest comparison shows how far the latter departs from the former. The Bangladeshi proposal reproduced in the Main Trends Paper provided that:

> In localities where no stable low-water line exists along the coast due to continual process of alluvion and sedimentation and where the seas adjacent to the coast are so shallow as to be non-navigable by other than small boats and pertain to the character of inland waters, baselines shall be drawn linking appropriate points on the sea adjacent to the coast not exceeding 10 fathom line.[53]

The relevant part of draft Article 6(1) in the ISNT, which became Article 7(2), states that:

> Where because of the presence of a delta or other natural conditions the coastline is highly unstable, the appropriate points may be selected along the furthest seaward extent of the low-water line and, notwithstanding subsequent regression of the low-water line, such baselines shall remain effective until changed by the coastal State in accordance with the present Convention.

[52] Indeed, as Prescott and Bird point out, it is not clear that the change from 'or' to 'and' was deliberate: Prescott and Bird, 'The Influence of Rising Sea Levels', 294. The amendment was made by the Chairman of the Second Committee, who explained that his revisions were based on formal and informal discussions at the Fourth Session: UNCLOS III: V, 152–4. Yet there is no record of this part of the text being discussed, still less evidence that the amendment was a response to concerns that Article 7(2) should be framed as an exception with limited scope.

[53] Platzöder (1983/IV), 14.

These provisions diverge in a number of important respects. Most significantly, Bangladesh was not concerned that the instability of its deltaic coast would jeopardize the continuing effectiveness of straight baselines established along it. Rather, it sought approval for a variation on the rules relating to straight baselines set out in TSC Article 4 to cover the case of deltaic coasts. Specifically, it proposed that States should be permitted to locate basepoints connecting straight baselines *at sea* up to a stated line of depth off a deltaic coast.

As a variation on the existing law, Bangladesh's proposal drew upon elements already established within it. It was not suggested that the instability of a deltaic coast—its 'continual process of alluvion and sedimentation'—might result in baselines connecting basepoints along it becoming 'ineffective'. Instead, the characteristic fluctuation of deltaic coasts together with the presence of offshore waters 'so shallow as to be non-navigable by other than small boats' was identified as a condition warranting the assimilation of these sea areas to internal waters. It was on this basis that the use of straight baselines connecting basepoints at sea was held to be justified.

Bangladesh emphasized the consistency of the use of basepoints defined by depth along deltaic coasts with considerations of principle accepted by the International Court of Justice (ICJ) in *Anglo-Norwegian Fisheries* and reflected in Article 4 of the TSC. Even before formally presenting the proposal becoming Main Trends Provision 9, Bangladesh had stressed the 'legal relevance' of the 'geographical and hydrographical peculiarities' of certain coasts, including deltaic coasts, to unilateral maritime delimitation.[54] It argued that support for 'straight baselines ... following the depth method' could be found in the ICJ's observation that 'a State must be allowed the latitude necessary to adapt its delimitation to practical needs and local requirements'.[55] In addition to the 'geographical peculiarities' of its deltaic coast, Bangladesh noted that 'a great many of its people ... depended solely on fishing for their livelihood'[56]—a consideration also taken into account by the Court in its assessment of the lawfulness of Norway's baselines.[57]

In a position paper shortly postdating the Main Trends Paper, Bangladesh again emphasized 'the need to take into account the peculiarities of the coasts of littoral states in the matter of employing baselines'.[58] It suggested a reformulation of its initial proposal which integrated the terms of TSC Article 4, providing that in

> [t]he localities where the coast line is deeply indented and cut into or if there is a fringe of islands along the coast in its immediate vicinity or *if the water adjacent to the coast*

[54] UNCLOS III: I, 102; UNCLOS III: II, 109.
[55] UNCLOS III: I, 102.
[56] Ibid.
[57] *Anglo-Norwegian Fisheries* (1951), 127–8.
[58] Platzöder (1983/IV), 179.

> *is marked by continual process of alluvion and sedimentation creating a highly unstable low water line* the method of straight baselines joining appropriate points on the coasts or *on the coastal waters* may be employed in drawing the baseline from which the breadth of the territorial sea is measured.[59]

In this formulation, the fluctuating coast is identified as an alternative basis for the use of straight baselines in the first place, whereas draft article 6(1) and ultimately Article 7(2) relate to the continuing effectiveness of straight baselines where their use is justified on other grounds.[60] Bangladesh's claim was that the 'geographic realities' of its deltaic coast, like the 'geographical realities' of the Norwegian coast, independently justified both the use of straight baselines and the location of basepoints offshore. The constant variation of its low-water line was clearly identified as a factor justifying the use of offshore basepoints. However, this circumstance was not held to be significant because it might result in established baselines becoming ineffective. Rather, it was identified as a special local phenomenon indicating that, similarly to the Norwegian *skjaergaard*, the 'coast of the mainland does not constitute ... a clear dividing line between land and sea'.[61]

Bangladesh does not appear to have considered coastal change a threat to established baselines. Its dissatisfaction with the provision alleged to 'reflect' its original proposal and respond to its concerns is evidenced by the proposals reiterating its claims after the inclusion of draft article 6(1) in the first negotiating text.[62] Significantly, one such proposal suggested the use of baselines connecting basepoints located 'along the furthest seaward extent of submerged sedimentary delta'—a geographical feature also subject to change and not always in a seaward direction.[63] A draft declaration prepared by experts for the member States of the Islamic Conference, taken note of by their Foreign Ministers, and circulated to States at UNCLOS III by the group of Islamic States in 1979, similarly proposed that straight baselines connecting 'appropriate points ... along the farthest seaward extent of submerged sedimentary delta' should be permitted '[w]here most part of a coastline of a State is constituted by a continuous process of sedimentation of fluvial deposit rendering the low-water line highly unstable'.[64] In both cases, this proposal was made without any suggestion that it need also be specified that the

[59] Ibid, 181 (emphasis in the original). The *Virginia Commentary* incorrectly presents this as Bangladesh's original proposal and suggests, also erroneously, that it predated the Main Trends Working Paper: *Virginia Commentary* (1993/II), 97.

[60] The clause was formulated in this way from the outset, even though it was initially included in the same paragraph as the conditions precedent for the use of straight baselines identified in TSC Article 4: ISNT Part II, Draft Art 6(1), UNCLOS III: IV, 153. It was moved to a separate paragraph in RSNT Part II, Draft Art 6(2), UNCLOS III: V, 154.

[61] *Anglo-Norwegian Fisheries* (1951), 127; Platzöder (1983/IV), 179–82.

[62] Platzöder (1983/IV), 389 (1977); Platzöder (1984/V), 11 (1978).

[63] Platzöder (1984/V), 11 (1978); E Bird, *Coastal Geomorphology* (2nd edn, Wiley, 2008), 331.

[64] UNCLOS III: XII, 69. Two representatives of members of the Islamic Conference said that they would like to study the question further but did not indicate why.

baseline would not shift with the delta. The States concerned do not appear to have thought that the movement of the delta would leave baselines ineffective.

It is equally striking that no such concern was expressed in connection with the proposal that baselines should be established on the basis of depth. The basepoints Bangladesh had in fact established at sea in 1974 were (with one exception) located along the ten-fathom depth contour[65]—a line also subject to change with the vertical growth and erosion of the delta (the subaqueous component of which extends to approximately the 80m or 43 fathom isobath in this region).[66] Yet Bangladesh's proposals were not designed to ensure that, once established, these baselines would not change in response to changes in ocean depth. Rather, it sought recognition of the lawfulness of its method of establishing baselines based on depth in the first place. It seems to have been taken for granted that established baselines would remain in place and effective.

Bangladesh continued to advocate a 'depth method' of constructing straight baselines on a deltaic coast throughout UNCLOS III. When it became apparent that Article 7 would be adopted without a clause recognizing the lawfulness of this method, Bangladesh sent a letter to the President of the Conference (circulated to participants as an official document[67]) indicating that, in its view, the provision could not 'preclude the founding of its baseline on depth criteria and bathymetric factors'.[68] Bangladesh claimed that its proposal in this regard had 'received substantial and favourable support from a large number of delegations', which 'in [its] estimate ... still exists'.[69] Its neighbouring States, India and Myanmar, responded with letters indicating that in their view the 'depth method' proposed by Bangladesh had not received the support claimed during proceedings. Both States also pointed to the adoption of Article 7 as evidence that this method was 'not accepted'.[70]

The official records suggest that there was in fact relatively little in the way of either express support for or express opposition to the 'depth method' advocated by Bangladesh at UNCLOS III.[71] The United States seems to have been the only State

[65] Bangladesh Memorial (vol I), 30, in *Bangladesh/Myanmar*.
[66] Bangladesh Reply (vol I), 15, in *Bangladesh v India*.
[67] UNCLOS III: XVI, 246.
[68] Ibid.
[69] Ibid.
[70] UNCLOS III: XVI, 254–5.
[71] The Main Trends Paper was introduced with the caveat that 'inclusion of a provision ... does not necessarily imply that there are no other opinions ... or that all or most delegations agree on the necessity for such a provision': UNCLOS III: III, 109. Vietnam expressed support for Bangladesh's views early on, asserting that the diverse geographical conditions along its own coasts, including the 'heavy alluvial deposits' of the Mekong delta, were the basis for certain 'rights and obligations': UNCLOS III: II, 119. There is no evidence that this claim was later abandoned, though Vietnam did not press for its explicit recognition in the treaty. The report circulated by the group of Islamic States had been 'taken note of' rather than adopted at the Tenth Islamic Conference of Foreign Ministers in 1979 and distributed to member States 'to help them formulate their policies' at UNCLOS III: UNCLOS III: XII, 69. Members of the group do not seem to have made further efforts to secure a provision expressly admitting the location of basepoints 'along the farthest seaward extent of the sedimentary delta'. Neither India nor

other than India and Myanmar that expressly indicated that it could not 'support a system of straight baselines ... which does not use fixed terrestrial (as opposed to maritime) points no further seaward than the appropriate low water mark'[72]—a view it expressed in bilateral discussions with Bangladesh contemporary with but outside the formal sessions of the Conference.[73]

India and Myanmar had a special interest in Bangladesh's practice in this regard. At the time, their maritime boundaries with the State had either not been established or the question of whether they had been was in dispute.[74] As noted above, both States have subsequently reiterated their objections to Bangladesh's baselines. Despite its active policy of protesting what it considers to be 'excessive' or unlawful straight baselines claims, the United States has not. Nor have protests from any other State been forthcoming. Indeed, the subsequent practice of States parties to UNCLOS has not clarified whether or not the use of marine basepoints in unilateral maritime delimitation—that is, their deliberate use in the construction of straight baselines rather than the retention of basepoints originally identified on the coast that are left at sea by subsequent geographical change—is compatible with the 1982 Convention.[75] Some States have used 'floating' basepoints where their system of straight baselines connects to that established by a neighbouring State;[76] however, these basepoints are not defined by depth but located on boundaries between adjacent States.[77] The States relying on these basepoints have not justified their use by reference to coastal geography (although in some cases the boundaries on which they are located may have been constructed by reference to coastal geography).

Myanmar directly objected to Bangladesh's proposals before 1982, though India had suggested that Bangladesh was putting forward a new rule, which '[required] wide acceptance by the international community before it could come into force': UNCLOS III: IX, 73.

---

[72] *Digest of US Practice* (1978), 942–3.

[73] The role of bilateral discussions, agreements, and deals outside the Conference as an important element of the negotiating process is noted in *Virginia Commentary* (1985/I), 57–8.

[74] Bangladesh claimed that a boundary had been established with Myanmar in the territorial sea by Agreed Minutes or practice affirming the line indicated by these Minutes. This claim, which Myanmar disputed, was rejected by the International Tribunal for the Law of the Sea (ITLOS) in 2012: *Bangladesh/ Myanmar* (2012), 25–45.

[75] The question of whether basepoints used to construct an international boundary must be located on land and 'solid land' in particular has received some attention in the jurisprudence and will be discussed in Chapter 6.

[76] For example, Cambodia–Vietnam, Denmark–Germany, Norway–Sweden, and Finland–Sweden. See JRV Prescott, *The Gulf of Thailand* (MIM, 1998), 10; S Bateman, C Schofield, 'State Practice regarding Straight Baselines in East Asia – Legal, Technical and Political Issues in a Changing Environment' (ABLOS Conference, IHB, Monaco, 16–17 October 2008), fn.42; RD Brubaker, 'The Legal Status of the Russian Baselines in the Arctic' (1999) 30 (3) *ODIL* 191, 204–5; V Prescott, 'Straight and Archipelagic Baselines' in Blake (ed), *Maritime Boundaries and Ocean Resources* (Routledge, 1987), 44.

[77] See US DOS, 'Straight Baselines: Denmark' (1978) 19 *LIS* 1, 3, 10; US DOS, 'Straight Baselines: Germany' (1974) 38 *LIS* 1, 4; US DOS, 'Straight Baselines: Sweden' (1972) 47 *LIS* 1, 7; US DOS, 'Straight Baselines: Finland' (1972) 48 *LIS* 1, 8; Cambodia Decree (1982); Vietnam Statement on Baseline (1982); Cambodia–Vietnam Historic Waters Agreement (1982).

Prescott has suggested that, like Bangladesh, Guinea-Bissau has used basepoints at sea in a system of straight baselines where there is no adjacent State.[78] The location of the basepoints to which he refers, however, appears to have been influenced by Guinea-Bissau's maritime boundary dispute with Senegal, which was ongoing at the time of their establishment (1978).[79] Still, Guinea-Bissau has since revised its basepoints in an Act referring to 'the need to establish straight baselines in accordance with [UNCLOS]' and it appears that at least one of the replacement basepoints is again located at sea.[80] Senegal has objected to this system of straight baselines, which Guinea-Bissau maintains is 'in no way in contravention of the rules of international law contained in Article 7'.[81]

The question of whether marine basepoints are consistent with UNCLOS does not directly bear upon the question of whether baselines and the zonal limits measured from them are ambulatory. There is a crucial difference between the establishment of baselines at sea in the first instance and the prospect of subsequent geographical change meaning that basepoints originally located on land are left at sea. It is nevertheless worth noting the consonance between the types of argument advanced by Bangladesh in support of its marine basepoints and the justifications for the use of straight baselines recognized by the treaty law.

Bangladesh has more recently identified the instability of the coast in the vicinity of the Ganges-Brahmaputra delta as an issue bearing upon the delimitation of its maritime boundaries with Myanmar and India in the Bay of Bengal. It is interesting to compare its claims in this context to its approach to the territorial sea baseline in unilateral delimitation.

While Bangladesh has continued to rely on the baselines it established in 1974 to locate its maritime limits, it expressly stated that it would not rely on the same baselines for the delimitation of boundaries with Myanmar and India. This much is unremarkable. Bangladesh was aware that Myanmar and India objected to these baselines and may well have wanted to avoid any authoritative assessment of their lawfulness (though such an assessment would presumably be limited to the question of their appropriateness in the context of interstate delimitation).

As noted in Chapter 1, there is no legal requirement to use baselines established for unilateral delimitation in the interstate delimitation of the EEZ and continental shelf, where the choice of basepoints will refer to 'the physical geography of the relevant coasts'.[82] In *Bangladesh/Myanmar* and *Bangladesh v India*, the same approach was taken to the selection of basepoints for delimiting the territorial

[78] Prescott, 'Straight and Archipelagic Baselines', 44–5.

[79] The basepoints were located along a line mentioned in an 1886 treaty between France and Portugal. Guinea-Bissau later agreed with Senegal that this treaty did not delimit the maritime boundary: see *Guinea-Bissau/Senegal* (1989), 129.

[80] Guinea-Bissau, Act No 2/85.

[81] See Guinea-Bissau and Senegal Notes (1986) 8 *LOS Bulletin* 1, 23–4.

[82] *Black Sea Case* (2009), 51.

sea—a move which should have been specifically justified given the application of UNCLOS Article 15, which refers to 'the baselines from which the breadth of the territorial seas of each of the two States is measured'.[83] What is more remarkable for present purposes is Bangladesh's account of its decision not to rely on its established baselines. In its submissions in both *Bangladesh/Myanmar* and *Bangladesh v India*, Bangladesh stated that

> because its 1974 baselines were drawn along the 10 fathom line, they do not conform to the terms of the later-adopted 1982 Convention. It therefore does not rely on them for purposes of this maritime delimitation ... Instead, for delimitation purposes, it relies only on base points along its coast on the Bay of Bengal, in conformity with UNCLOS.[84]

Notably, Bangladesh continued to insist on the lawfulness of its baselines for the purposes of unilateral maritime delimitation. In this regard, it emphasized that those baselines were established prior to the conclusion of UNCLOS on the basis of 'expert advice from the Commonwealth Secretariat and distinguished international lawyers, including Sir Robert Jennings and Professor DP O'Connell'.[85] As such, it appears to have accepted that baselines established after the conclusion of UNCLOS cannot be located beyond the low-water line. Its argument implies that this prohibition is a consequence of the adoption of Article 7(2).

At UNCLOS III, Bangladesh had insisted that Article 7 'cannot preclude the founding of its baseline on depth criteria and bathymetric factors'.[86] Though its baseline had already been established on this basis (prior to the adoption of UNCLOS), its claim seems to have been that it remained legitimate to establish (not merely retain) baselines constructed on the basis of depth notwithstanding the adoption of Article 7(2). In its 1982 letter to the President of the Conference, Bangladesh cited support for its formulation of a general rule admitting this practice.[87] In *Bangladesh/Myanmar* and *Bangladesh v India*, however, Bangladesh defended the continuing lawfulness of its baselines based on what appears to be an argument from the doctrine of intertemporal law. While this doctrine does bear upon the question of the lawfulness of maritime limits,[88] its application here is problematic.

Bangladesh has suggested that a change in the law altering the conditions for the construction of straight baselines (requiring their location on the low-water line) could not affect the baselines it had lawfully established before that time.

[83] See Chapter 1.
[84] Bangladesh Memorial (vol I), 32, in *Bangladesh/Myanmar*; Bangladesh Memorial (Vol 1), 46, in *Bangladesh v India*.
[85] Bangladesh Memorial (vol I), 32, in *Bangladesh/Myanmar*; Bangladesh Memorial (vol I), 44, in *Bangladesh v India*.
[86] UNCLOS III: XVI, 246.
[87] Ibid.
[88] See Chapter 9.

The difficulty is that the States negotiating UNCLOS clearly intended that established baselines would be brought into line with any agreed alterations to the rules applying to their construction. Significantly, the existence of an obligation to revise established baselines to give effect to changes to the *law* can be clearly distinguished from any obligation to give effect to changes to *geographical facts* referred to at the point at which baselines are established in accordance with the law.[89] This means that if Article 7(2) is properly understood to require that basepoints are located on the low-water line of a deltaic coast rather than at sea (which is not beyond doubt[90]), then Bangladesh would be under an obligation to revise its baselines accordingly.[91]

In *Bangladesh/Myanmar* and *Bangladesh v India*, Bangladesh rather surprisingly claimed that while it 'was unable to persuade the delegates of all other States to sign on to the idea of permitting straight baselines to be drawn from points determined by a depth-based method', it '[succeeded] in obtaining the inclusion of a new subparagraph 7(2) in the 1982 Convention'.[92] Though it now claimed that its marine basepoints were lawful because they were established prior to the adoption of Article 7(2), it also suggested during these proceedings that '[a]s Professors Reisman and Westerman have observed, this compromise provision "in effect, allows baselines to be established offshore, as Bangladesh had urged"'.[93]

The idea that the adoption of Article 7(2) was a success for Bangladesh or constituted a 'compromise' is completely at odds with the record of negotiations at UNCLOS III, where Bangladesh repeatedly pushed to have its very different proposal accepted and, when it was not, downplayed the importance of Article 7(2) (which India and Myanmar referred to as evidence that marine basepoints were not permitted). The idea that Article 7(2) 'in effect, allows baselines to be established offshore, as Bangladesh had urged' is also incorrect. Article 7(2) does not allow the *establishment* of baselines offshore. Instead, the provision recognizes that baselines connecting basepoints that were located along the low-water line at the time of delimitation will remain effective even if subsequent coastal regression leaves those basepoints at sea. Bangladesh's system of straight baselines employed basepoints located at sea *from the outset*. These basepoints were not 'selected along the furthest seaward extent of the low-water line' and then left at sea by subsequent

[89] This distinction is further elaborated in Chapter 9 and the Conclusion to this book

[90] It is not clear that Article 7(2) provides that basepoints along a deltaic coast *must* be located on the low-water line or simply indicates that where they are located on the low-water line they will remain effective notwithstanding its subsequent regression. Article 7(1) refers simply to 'appropriate points' and there is no evidence that Article 7(2) was intended to be more restrictive as far as the selection of basepoints along a deltaic coast was concerned. Article 7(2) could, however, be taken to imply that 'appropriate' basepoints are usually located on the low-water line.

[91] The relevant parallel here is the change in the law regarding the preconditions for claiming an EEZ and continental shelf in respect of an island, discussed in the Conclusion to this book.

[92] Bangladesh Memorial (vol I), 31, in *Bangladesh/Myanmar*; Bangladesh Memorial (vol I), 46, in *Bangladesh v India*.

[93] Ibid.

coastal regression. As such, it appears that Article 7(2), so often described as a response to Bangladesh's concerns, does not apply to Bangladesh's baselines at all.

Significantly, this does not mean that Bangladesh's baselines will become ineffective in the event of geographical change bearing upon the conditions by reference to which they *were* established—i.e. the location of the ten-fathom line. Whether geographical change has this effect depends upon whether the law can be understood to provide that baselines are as a general rule ambulatory. Ultimately, Article 7(2) does not imply that this is the case. Bangladesh's representations in *Bangladesh/Myanmar* and *Bangladesh v India* may have complicated and even weakened that State's claim to the lawfulness of its offshore baselines,[94] but they do not lend support to the ambulatory thesis.

Bangladesh in fact made two claims about Article 7(2) in the aforementioned cases. In the first place, it claimed that Article 7(2) precludes the establishment of straight baselines using basepoints at sea even while it provides that baselines established by reference to basepoints on the low-water line remain lawful if subsequent coastal change leaves those basepoints at sea.[95] This suggests that it now understands Article 7(2) to require that basepoints are established on the low-water line rather than at sea. Bangladesh's second claim was that Article 7(2) independently justifies the use of straight baselines even where the coast is not 'deeply indented' or 'fringed with islands'. Bangladesh's submissions make clear that it considered Article 7(2) to identify coastal instability due to the presence of a delta as a separate and sufficient condition precedent for the use of straight baselines.[96]

It is this last claim that accounts for Bangladesh's suggestion that its proposals at UNCLOS III were 'partially accepted' and reflected in Article 7(2). Despite citing Reisman and Westerman's erroneous account of the effect of Article 7(2), Bangladesh did not ultimately claim that its baselines were justified by that provision (relying instead upon a problematic argument from intertemporal law). However, at UNCLOS III, Bangladesh had argued that an unstable coast should be a separate basis for the use of straight baselines.[97] In *Bangladesh/Myanmar* and

[94] Bangladesh seems to have aimed for strategic ambiguity in its submissions but made some unnecessary concessions. In particular, it seems to have been ill advised to concede that post-Article 7(2) basepoints could only be established (in the first instance) on land: see Bangladesh Memorial (vol I), 45, in *Bangladesh v India*. This opens the way for arguments that the Bangladesh baseline must be brought into line with Article 7(2), where this provision is understood to require (as Bangladesh seems to believe) basepoints on the low-water line.

[95] Bangladesh Memorial (vol I), 31–2, in *Bangladesh/Myanmar*; Bangladesh Memorial (vol I), 45–6, in *Bangladesh v India*; Hearing Transcript Day 1 in *Bangladesh v India*, 117–18.

[96] Bangladesh Memorial (vol I), 22, in *Bangladesh/Myanmar*; Hearing Transcript Day 1 in *Bangladesh v India*, 117–18.

[97] This is particularly obvious in the draft article included in its 1974 position paper, which provides for the use of straight baselines connecting 'appropriate points on the coast or ... coastal waters' in ' localities where the coast line is deeply indented and cut into *or* if there is a fringe of islands along the coast in its immediate vicinity *or* if the water adjacent to the coast is marked by continual process of alluvion and sedimentation creating a highly unstable low water line': Platzöder (1983/IV), 179 (emphasis added).

Bangladesh v India, Bangladesh indicates that, in its view, this is precisely what Article 7(2) does.[98]

This reading of Article 7(2) is not supported by the text, which, as noted above, indicates that this paragraph is subordinate to Article 7(1). Straight baselines cannot be used on a deltaic coast unless it is 'deeply indented' or fringed with islands. Yet it remains significant that this is the interpretation accepted by Bangladesh. The crucial point is that Bangladesh appears to consider the identification of a third and alternative justification for the use of straight baselines to be the main work that Article 7(2) does. At no point has it suggested that the provision is intended to secure baselines against what would otherwise be legally necessary change.

The point of this detailed discussion of Bangladesh's proposals at UNCLOS III and its subsequent views on the meaning and effect of Article 7(2) is that it clearly shows that the provision does not respond to or reflect any concern on the part of Bangladesh that coastal instability would leave straight baselines on a deltaic coast 'ineffective'. Bangladesh proposed that (a) the use of straight baselines should be permitted on 'highly unstable' deltaic coasts whether or not they were deeply indented or fringed with islands, and (b) the use of offshore basepoints defined by depth should also be permitted on unstable deltaic coasts. It justified these proposals on the grounds that it was appropriate to treat the shallow waters at the seaward edge of the changeable delta as 'internal waters' and identify the effective 'coast line' seaward of this area where there was not only a close link but continual interchange between land and sea. Article 7(2) as adopted does not reflect this proposal, even if it might be argued that it does not necessarily preclude the use of marine basepoints for unilateral delimitation.

What, then, can be made of Article 7(2), which clearly is concerned with the continuing 'effectiveness' of straight baselines on a deltaic coast? There are no records of the meetings of the working group producing the Blue Paper on Baselines or the discussions leading to its incorporation in the ISNT. At UNCLOS III, small, informal, and private working groups were part of a deliberate strategy aimed at facilitating negotiations and achieving consensus.[99] The three Committees were advised by the President of the Conference to keep their reports general as '[p]ublic opinion was interested in results, not in how they had been obtained'.[100] The 1975 Statement on the Work of the Second Committee indicates only that there was an informal group working on baselines, that it had three meetings considering provisions 4 to 20 of the Main Trends paper, and that the Bureau prepared a consolidated text '[o]n the basis of the discussion in the group and the work of a small working

[98] Bangladesh Memorial (vol I), 22, in *Bangladesh/Myanmar*; Hearing Transcript Day 1 in *Bangladesh v India*, 117–18.
[99] *Virginia Commentary* (1985/I), 15, 20–1, 104–12.
[100] UNCLOS III: I, 226–9.

group'.[101] It is not clear whether that 'small working group' was part of the baselines group or the Bureau of the Second Committee.

Given the extent to which Article 7(2) varies from the terms of Bangladesh's proposal, the absence of records is unfortunate. As far as the matter is left to speculation, it seems that one of three possible scenarios may account for this result. First, the baselines working group may simply have misinterpreted Bangladesh's concerns, mistakenly believing that they related to the ongoing effectiveness of baselines in the event of changes to the coastline. Secondly, Article 7(2) may have been based on the concerns of another member or members of the baselines working group regarding the implications of coastal change for established baselines. Finally, it may have been considered expedient to formulate a provision that apparently recognized the special character of deltaic coasts but did not recognize the lawfulness of marine basepoints given the sharp disagreement on this point between Bangladesh on the one hand and India and Myanmar on the other.

It is difficult to see how Bangladesh's concerns could have been misunderstood given its repeated efforts to have the provision changed to reflect its very different proposals. Yet such a misunderstanding seems to account for the US response to Bangladesh's request to support its proposals at UNCLOS III: it replied that 'Article 7(2) as currently drafted protects [Bangladesh's] interests' and 'further[s] [its] concerns' (though it did not elaborate on precisely how).[102] To the extent that Article 7(2) continues to be presented as a response to Bangladesh's concerns, such a misunderstanding persists. This is despite the fact that Bangladesh expressly stated at the plenary session concluding UNCLOS III that 'not all [its] hopes have been realized in this Convention' and reiterated its claim that 'the unique geographical circumstances of our coastline and the peculiar conditions associated therewith warrant adequate treatment'.[103] While it initially rejected claims by India and Myanmar that its use of a depth method for constructing straight baselines was incompatible with Article 7(2), Bangladesh clearly did not consider the provision to respond to its concerns.

If suggestions that Article 7(2) responds to Bangladesh's concerns are not in error, they may represent the success of a move to loosely acknowledge Bangladesh's claims to the 'unique geographical circumstances' of its coastline without taking a clear position on that State's claims regarding the lawfulness of marine basepoints—that is, its success in moving the debate beyond the apparently intractable disagreement of interested States. Such a move would be in keeping with the overall approach to negotiations at UNCLOS III and does not imply a calculated effort to undermine Bangladesh's position. Notably, if this does account for the difference between Bangladesh's proposals and the text as adopted, the

[101] UNCLOS III: IV, 196.
[102] *Digest of US Practice* (1978), 942.
[103] UNCLOS III: XVII, 112.

significance of the reference to the continuing effectiveness of baselines on a deltaic coast must still be accounted for. Yet in this regard the drafting history does not add anything to the conclusions admitted by the text. The formulation in Article 7(2) could have been preferred as a non-controversial statement of the continuing effectiveness of established baselines in the particular context of rapid and substantial coastal change. Neither the text nor the drafting history implies that it was understood to exceptionally 'fix' such baselines against coastal change.

The second possibility identified above is that the provision may have been a response to the concerns of another State or States regarding the implications of coastal change for straight baselines. This is rather at odds with both the specific reference to the presence of a delta and the familiar association of the provision with Bangladesh. Moreover, if another State participating in the Baselines Working Group was indeed concerned that coastal change may render straight baselines on a deltaic coast ineffective, there is again no indication that this was based on a belief that baselines were generally ambulatory—the concern being to insulate straight baselines on deltaic coasts from what would otherwise be frequent and substantial changes. It may equally have been understood that baselines were ordinarily fixed unless and until the coastal State decided to revise them—the concern being to specify that established baselines would remain effective even in circumstances of rapid and substantial coastal change due to the presence of a delta.

Once the text becoming Article 7(2) was included in the ISNT, the unusual rules of procedure at UNCLOS III made it difficult to amend. While the ISNT was intended to be an informal basis for discussion and, as such, 'a negotiating and not a negotiated text',[104] a rule that 'silence-means-agreement-with-the-SNT' applied to debate in the Second Committee.[105] As observed in the *Virginia Commentary*, this 'created a presumption in favour of the text', which meant that 'those [States] who wanted certain provisions changed ... had to muster as many other like-minded delegations as they could and orchestrate a chorus of criticism ... in the hope that the Chairman would alter the text'.[106] This approach was maintained throughout proceedings, with negotiations focusing on defined 'hard-core' issues and conducted by smaller (though open) groups comprising 'a nucleus of those countries principally concerned'.[107] The decision whether to amend the text based on the reports of these groups rested with the Chairman of the three Committees and the President of the Conference.[108] These procedures reflected the overall preference for decision by consensus, which was further advanced by rules serving to avoid

[104] *Virginia Commentary* (1985/I), 115–16.
[105] Ibid, 119.
[106] Ibid, 119–20.
[107] UNCLOS III: IX, 6–8. The 'hard-core issues' upon which debate focused from 1978 did not relate directly to the baselines provisions, though, as we shall see, negotiations regarding the definition of the limits of the continental shelf and the delimitation of maritime boundaries (identified as 'hard-core issues') also cast doubt on Caron's claim that baselines are generally ambulatory.
[108] Ibid.

or delay voting on substantive matters[109] together with the 'package deal' approach to negotiations at UNCLOS III.[110] In this context it is perhaps unsurprising that there was no direct response to Bangladesh's repeated proposals regarding a depth method of constructing straight baselines on deltaic coasts, which clearly indicated its dissatisfaction with the provision developed by the Baselines Working Group.

The drafting history ultimately does not clarify the particular beliefs and concerns that account for the formulation in Article 7(2). Yet it does show that Bangladesh—the State whose concerns to which the provision is said to respond—was *not* concerned that established baselines would be rendered ineffective by subsequent coastal change. There is no evidence at all that Bangladesh believed that baselines were ordinarily ambulatory. And there is no evidence that Bangladesh or any other State considered Article 7(2) to exceptionally (whether temporarily or indefinitely) permit the retention of established baselines in circumstances where coastal change would otherwise necessitate their revision.

V. Conclusion

Neither the text nor drafting history establishes that Article 7(2) 'negatively implies' that baselines are generally ambulatory. All that can be established is that the retention of straight baselines on a deltaic coast is expressly permitted 'notwithstanding subsequent regression of the low-water line'. The drafting history suggests that this formulation could have resulted from a misunderstanding of Bangladesh's concerns or responded to a concern genuinely held by another participant in the Baselines Working Group. It could also have been a strategic response to the disagreement of Bangladesh and its neighbouring States on the use of marine basepoints. In any and all of these cases, the fact remains that the drafting history does not establish that Bangladesh or any other State considered coastal change to ordinarily necessitate the revision of baselines. It does not establish that it was considered necessary to clarify that baselines would remain effective *even* in cases of rapid and substantial coastal change on a deltaic coast either. Yet the drafting history is particularly damaging to Caron's account of the 'negative implication' of Article 7(2), which rests so heavily upon the assumption that States were concerned to protect baselines on deltaic coasts against the otherwise inevitable consequences of coastal change.

The alternative reading remains broadly consistent with the baselines provisions as a whole and the object and purpose of the treaty. The drafting history also offers significant if indirect support for this interpretation through its general 'silence' on the implications of geographical change for baselines and zonal limits. This 'silence'

[109] *Virginia Commentary* (1985/I), 99–102.
[110] Ibid, 103–4.

only really registers as such—and as a problem—if it is assumed that baselines must change with the coast. It is reasonable to expect that such a consequential legal effect would be regulated in some detail in the context of a regime clearly concerned to secure a stable division of maritime space. If the ambulatory thesis is not assumed, however, there is no reason to expect the law to expressly address the implications of geographical change for maritime limits. The law's 'silence' supports the conclusion that baselines are not ambulatory. Indeed, it is remarkable that *even* in connection with Article 7(2)—the *only* provision of UNCLOS directly considering the prospect of coastal change in connection with maritime limits —there is no clear evidence of a belief that baselines must change with the coast. What *is* clear is that Article 7(2) does not prove the ambulatory thesis. Caron's argument requires further evidence of the alleged belief on the part of States that maritime limits must, as a matter of law, shift with changes to the coast. This, he suggested, can be found in Article 76(9) or, once again, its 'negative implication'.[111]

[111] Caron, 'When Law Makes Climate Change Worse', 634–5.

4

The Permanent Limits of the Continental Shelf

I. Introduction

Caron's argument regarding Article 76(9) of the United Nations Convention on the Law of the Sea (UNCLOS) takes the same logical form as his argument with respect to Article 7(2). According to Caron, Article 76(9) 'negatively implies' the ambulatory thesis as a consequence of its requirement that '[t]he coastal State ... deposit with the Secretary-General of the United Nations charts and relevant information, including geodetic data, *permanently describing* the outer limits of its continental shelf'.[1] There is no reason to doubt that 'the inclusion of the word "permanent" was intentional'.[2] Yet this 'negatively implies' no more than that zonal limits are ordinarily subject to change. Caron, however, has suggested that the relevant change against which those limits are fixed is geographical change affecting the baseline and, in turn, the limits of the continental shelf. In this regard, he appears to have relied upon Bernard Oxman, quoting the latter's view that

> the inclusion of the word 'permanent,' at least as far as the United States is concerned, likely also reflects earlier recommendations such as that made in an influential 1968 U.S. study which proposed that the outer limit of the continental shelf 'should ... not be subject to change because of subsequent alterations in the coastline or revelations of more detailed surveys.'[3]

The study to which Oxman referred was conducted by a US Commission on 'Marine Science, Engineering and Resources' and published as *Our Nation and the Sea: A Plan for National Action* in 1969.[4] It does not appear to have had any special influence on the work of the Seabed Committee in preparation for the Third Law of the Sea Conference (though the United States was a member of this Committee and the Ad Hoc Seabed Committee preceding it). Nor can it be singled out as

[1] Emphasis added.

[2] See Caron, 'When Law Makes Climate Change Worse', 635; Caron, 'Climate Change, Sea Level Rise and the Coming Uncertainty in Oceanic Boundaries', 10.

[3] Caron, 'When Law Makes Climate Change Worse', 635; Caron, 'Climate Change, Sea Level Rise and the Coming Uncertainty in Oceanic Boundaries', 10. His source is a telephone interview with Oxman on 28 February 1990.

[4] US Commission on Marine Science, Engineering and Resources, *Our Nation and the Sea: A Plan for National Action* (US GPO, 1969).

Geographical Change and the Law of the Sea. Kate Purcell, Oxford University Press (2019).
DOI: 10.1093/oso/9780198743644.001.0001

having any special bearing upon the formulation of Article 76(9) through negotiations at the Conference.

Oxman may nevertheless have been right to suggest that Article 76(9) reflects 'recommendations such as those made' in the *Plan for National Action*.[5] The view that the limits of the shelf 'should not be subject to change' appears to have been widely shared by States at UNCLOS III. Crucially, however, this did not follow from a belief that baselines and thus the zonal limits measured from them would ordinarily shift with coastal change.

While Caron focused on Article 76(9), Article 76(8) provides the first indication that States at UNCLOS III were *not* concerned to secure the limits of the continental shelf against adjustments automatically or necessarily following coastal change. According to this provision, the limits of an extended continental shelf beyond 200 nautical miles (M) 'established by a coastal State on the basis of... recommendations [of the Commission on the Limits of the Continental Shelf (CLCS)] shall be final and binding'. This demonstrates that permanency was also a concern in circumstances where the limits of the shelf do not depend upon a measurement of distance from the baseline. There is nothing to suggest that changes to the geomorphology of the seabed referred to in the legal definition of the outer edge of the continental margin were anticipated. Instead, it is clear that both paragraphs 8 and 9 of Article 76 provide for permanent limits in the case of the continental shelf because it was considered necessary to permanently define what UNCLOS refers to as 'the Area'.[6]

II. Where Depth Admits Exploitation: The Limits of the Shelf in the CSC

The authors of the 1969 US *Plan for National Action*, like members of the Seabed Committee and participants at UNCLOS III, were concerned with 'uncertainties in [the] existing definition of the continental shelf'.[7] Article 1 of the 1958 Convention

[5] Caron, 'When Law Makes Climate Change Worse', 635; Caron, 'Climate Change, Sea Level Rise and the Coming Uncertainty in Oceanic Boundaries, 10. It is interesting to note that the *Plan for National Action* also urged Congress to 'establish a National Seashore Boundary Commission to [inter alia] fix the baselines from which to measure the territorial sea and areas covered by the Submerged Lands Act of 1953'. The authors noted that '[i]t is important, too, that the boundaries be fixed once and for all in terms of geographic coordinates that can be portrayed on maps, rather than in terms of distances from the coasts. This would avoid the problem of baselines changing due to tidal effects, floating islands, migrating sandbars, and the deposit of riverborne sediments': *Plan for National Action*, 62–3. As will be discussed in the Conclusion to this book, the United States does consider baselines and the zonal limits measured from them to be ambulatory. It is argued that its position and practice in this regard—which may be explained (though not justified) by certain domestic developments and has nothing to do with Article 76(9)—is at odds with that of the majority of States. The *Plan for National Action* responds to the US practice of treating baselines as ambulatory but, notably, identifies this as a 'problem'.

[6] UNCLOS Art 1(1).

[7] *Plan for National Action*, 143.

on the Continental Shelf (CSC) defined the continental shelf ('for the purpose of these articles') as

> the seabed and subsoil of the submarine areas adjacent to the coast but outside the area of the territorial sea, to a depth of 200 metres or, beyond that limit, to where the depth of the superjacent waters admits of the exploitation of the natural resources of the said areas

This two-part definition had been developed by the ILC in its preparatory work for the 1958 Conference on the Law of the Sea. In 1951, the Commission had moved from an initial proposal that jurisdiction should extend to the 200-metre depth line[8] to a definition of the shelf as extending to the point where depth admits exploitability.[9] After reverting to a fixed depth criterion in 1953,[10] it settled on this particular conjunction of the mooted alternatives.[11]

A. Depth and Exploitability: A Common Rationale

The exploitability criterion was reintroduced in 1956 by Garcia-Amador, then ILC Chairman, who presented it as an additional and alternative criterion to depth.[12] This proposal was adopted by a majority of the Commission, though not without debate.[13] Some members argued that it was unnecessary to provide for the extension of the limits of the shelf beyond a depth of 200 metres 'since exploitation beyond that limit was improbable in the foreseeable future'.[14] Notably, the exploitability criterion was considered *more* restrictive than the 200-metre depth line insofar as it excluded areas where exploitability was not presently possible.[15] Even when the ILC finalized its draft in 1956, 200 metres was not the depth up to which exploitation was technically possible. This was estimated at a more modest 60 to 70 metres, at least as far as drilling from superjacent waters was concerned.[16] The 200-metre depth line was considered to '[make] sufficient allowance for future technical development'.[17]

Some members of the ILC had also argued that exploitability was too vague and uncertain a criterion on which to base the extension of the exclusive rights

[8] ILC Ybk 1951/II, 102.
[9] Ibid, 141.
[10] ILC Ybk 1953/II, 212.
[11] ILC Ybk 1956/II, 264, 296 (Draft Art 67).
[12] ILC Ybk 1956/I, 131.
[13] Ibid, 131–40.
[14] Ibid, 138 (Edmonds); see also François, ibid, 132.
[15] ILC Ybk 1956/II, 296.
[16] ILC Ybk 1956/I, 135. As discussed in Section II (D) and Section VI, the ILC and States at the 1958 Law of the Sea Conference (LOSC) did not propose to place any limits on the exploitation of the seabed by tunnelling from land. This is expressly noted in Article 7 of the CSC.
[17] ILC Ybk 1956/I, 135.

of the coastal State. Interestingly, 'uncertainty' was primarily held to follow from the fact that 'doubts would always persist as to the actual depth at which it was technically possible to exploit the natural resources of the seabed'.[18] The concern in this regard was that the limits of the shelf may differ and be disputed between States.

Despite these objections, it is notable that supporters of the depth criterion overwhelmingly agreed with advocates of the exploitability criterion that the coastal State should have the exclusive right to exploit the resources of the seabed off its coasts as far as this was technically possible. Although the ILC's shifting position suggests competition between the depth and exploitability-based definitions followed by their reconciliation in the final draft, these two criteria were intimately connected from the outset.

The ILC had contemplated fixing the limit at the 200-metre isobath in its initial draft on the basis that this 'would at present be sufficient for all practical needs'—that is, it would adequately facilitate exploitation.[19] The 200-metre limit was replaced by a more general reference to 'where the depth of the superjacent waters admits of the exploitation of the natural resources of the seabed and subsoil' on the grounds that exploitation at a depth greater than 200 metres might rapidly become practicable. In both formulations and their final amalgamation, depth is considered legally relevant because it bears upon the practical possibility of exploiting submarine resources.

B. Depth and the Geological Continental Shelf

The International Law Commission (ILC) considered the 200-metre depth line an appropriate limit to the continental shelf for other reasons. It was noted that '[t]his depth also coincides with that at which the continental shelf in the geological sense generally comes to an end and the continental slope begins, falling steeply to a great depth'.[20] Yet the Commission also emphasized that

> The mere fact that the existence of a continental shelf in the geological sense might be questioned in regard to submarine areas where the depth of the sea would nevertheless permit of exploitation of the subsoil in the same way as if there were a continental shelf, could not justify the application of a discriminatory legal regime to these regions.[21]

[18] Ibid (François).
[19] ILC Ybk 1956/II, 296.
[20] Ibid.
[21] Ibid, 297.

Defining the limits of the shelf by reference to the 200-metre isobath seems to have been partly intended to placate States who insisted on the relevance of the physical continental shelf while responding to the objections of narrow-shelf States to a definition based on geology or geomorphology. If the depth-based definition responded to certain generalized 'facts' about the geological continental shelf, it did not require the existence of a physical shelf.

Of course, the depth criterion would still give States with broad, shallow shelves an advantage over States with narrow shelves or steeply descending submarine areas close to shore. One justification for the exploitability criterion was that it would avoid or overcome this disadvantage for the latter category of States by guaranteeing the right to exploit the seabed at greater depths. The ameliorative effect may have been overstated given the difficulty of exploiting the seabed at greater depths at the time. Nevertheless, the ILC emphasized that 'exploitation of a submarine area at a depth exceeding 200 metres is not contrary to the present rules, merely because the area is not a continental shelf in the geological sense'.[22]

C. The Relevance of Charts

The drafting history suggests a further reason why the 200-metre isobath was identified as an appropriate limit for the continental shelf. The ILC initially used the concept of exploitability to define the shelf, though the Special Rapporteur had proposed the 200-metre isobath as a limit.[23] Responding to the ILC's draft article in 1952, Gidel observed that

> La profondeur de 200 mètres ou, si l'on préfère, celle analogue mais non identique de 100 brasses se recommande du fait que la courbe isobathe de 200 mètres (ou celle de 100 brasses) figure dès maintenant d'une manière courante sur les cartes marines.[24]

In a monograph on the continental shelf published in the same year, Mouton emphasized the advantages of the 200-metre isobath over a limit based on exploitability on similar grounds, recommending the former as 'une limite parfaitement claire et aisément identifiable, indiquée sur toutes les cartes nautiques'.[25] Waldock had made a similar point at the ILA's 1952 Conference: like Gidel and Mouton, he thought that 'the shelf should be defined by reference to a fixed limit of depth'.[26] Waldock,

[22] Ibid.
[23] Ibid, 296.
[24] G Gidel, *Le plateau continental* (Martinus Nijhoff, 1952), 5, reproduced in ILC Ybk 1953/II, 8.
[25] MW Mouton, *The Continental Shelf* (Martinus Nijhoff, 1952), 40, reproduced in ILC Ybk 1953/II, 9.
[26] ILA, *Report of the Forty-Fifth Conference* (Lucerne 1952) 143, 148.

however, considered the 100-fathom line to have a distinct advantage over the 200-metre line on the grounds that '[i]t is marked on all good nautical charts whereas the 200-metre line is not'.[27] The 100-fathom line was also identified as legally significant by Iceland and the UK in their formal response to the ILC's draft articles in 1952, though Iceland argued that 'à l'heure actuelle, la limite du plateau continental peut être considérée comme établie exactement à une profondeur de 100 brasses', while the UK claimed that 'la pratique des Etats est suffisamment uniforme pour que l'on puisse, a juste titre, fixer cette limite à la profondeur de 100 brasses' whether or not the subjacent seabed could be considered the continental shelf in a geological sense.[28] It is likely that the relevant State practice responded to the fact that this line was charted.

These comments together with criticism that the exploitability criterion 'lacked the necessary precision' seem to have encouraged the Special Rapporteur to introduce a new definition based on a fixed depth.[29] Yet the new text referred to a depth of 200 metres rather than the 100-fathom isobath. Commenting on the ILC's draft in 1956, the UK observed that while it was 'prepared to accept the 200 metre line', it considered that

> the 100 fathom line would be preferable on practical grounds, since this line and not the 200 metre line is the one already marked on most of the ocean charts of those countries that produce charts covering the whole world.

The 100-fathom line was shown on charts prepared by the US Naval Hydrographic Office (responsible at the time for non-domestic surveying and cartography) and the US Coast Survey as well as British Admiralty Charts.[30] The White House press release accompanying the influential Truman Proclamation (which itself made no specific reference to a limit based on depth or any other criterion) asserted that 100 fathoms was the point up to which 'submerged land which is contiguous to the continent ... is considered as the continental shelf'.[31]

The ILC's view was that the 200-metre isobath was so close to the 100-fathom isobath (182.88 metres) that the difference was legally irrelevant. Responding to the UK's proposal to refer to the 100-fathom line, the Special Rapporteur suggested that 'the point be met by a statement in the comment that the Commission had adopted the term "200 metres" as being more comprehensible to those unfamiliar with the marine system of measurement'.[32] He also noted that the Commission

[27] ILC Ybk 1953/II, 9; ILA, *Report of the Forty-Fifth Conference*, 148.
[28] ILC Ybk 1953/II, 7.
[29] Ibid, 5–9, 46.
[30] Records of the Hydrographic Office, 1754–1971, <http://www.archives.gov/research/guide-fed-records/groups/037.html>; Records of the US Coast Survey <https://www.archives.gov/research/guide-fed-records/groups/023.html#23.3.6>.
[31] White House Press Release accompanying Truman Proclamation (1945).
[32] ILC Ybk 1956/I, 141.

'would have no objection to the change if considered advisable for practical reasons', observing that '[t]he difference in depth, amounting to 15 metres, was insignificant'.[33]

In the end, draft Article 67 was adopted to refer to 'a depth of 200 metres (approximately 100 fathoms)'.[34] The bracketed text was dropped at the 1958 Conference.[35] It appears to have been cut without discussion as a minor drafting amendment—a move which met with no objection and may have been encouraged by the fact that participants at the Conference referred almost exclusively to the 200-metre depth line.[36] This amendment does not alter the fact that the 100-fathom depth line was generally considered an approximation of the 200-metre isobath and equally appropriate as the outer limit of the continental shelf. The US delegate Marjorie Whiteman had suggested that a more precise equivalent of 200 metres in fathoms be included but did not make a formal proposal to this effect.[37] There is no evidence that the ILC or States participating in the 1958 LOSC were concerned to strictly enforce the 200-metre depth line over and above the 100-fathom isobath.

Although the fact that the 200-metre or 100-fathom isobath was indicated on charts would facilitate the observance of corresponding legal limits, it appears that most commentators emphasizing this fact did so with a view to the practical benefit for the coastal State. Identifying the legal limit as a line already shown on existing charts was largely a matter of convenience. It obviated the need for new hydrographic surveys and charts and allowed the coastal State to immediately begin or continue exploring and exploiting submarine resources.

A conspicuous difference between UNCLOS I and III in respect of the unilateral delimitation of the continental shelf is the relative lack of concern in 1958 with the precise definition of established limits for the purpose of facilitating observance by other States. Even if the 200-metre or 100-fathom depth line was shown on charts, a general concern to ensure that the limits of the shelf were ascertainable and observable would presumably have been reflected in charting requirements relating to the limits of the shelf based on exploitability. The absence of charting requirements (or any other effort to ensure that the precise location of the limits of the shelf could be determined) may be explained by the fact that there was at the time no competition between the coastal State and foreign States for submarine resources, except where coastal States were proximate neighbours. As the Special Rapporteur observed in the course of explaining the shift from depth to exploitability in his 1953 report,

> Pour la navigation, cette limite, qui n'indique qu'une possibilité théorique, n'a aucune importance pratique. Il va de soi que le navigateur doit tenir compte des

[33] Ibid.
[34] LC Ybk 1956/II, 296.
[35] UNCLOS I: II, 91.
[36] See generally UNCLOS I: IV.
[37] UNCLOS I: VI, 19.

> installations qui ont été érigées dans la mer au-dessus du plateau continental, mais ces installations seront indiquées sur les cartes et elles doivent être munies d'appareils avertisseurs.[38]

Although the Special Rapporteur was responding to criticism on the grounds that 'la proposition de la Commission rend impossible d'indiquer les limites du plateau continental sur les cartes maritimes',[39] States at the 1958 LOSC appear to have agreed that charting was unnecessary, at least where there were no overlapping national claims.

In 1958, there was little if any foreign activity relating to the seabed below the high seas that threatened to encroach upon the submarine areas in which the coastal State possessed exclusive sovereign rights. Indeed, the exploitability criterion effectively excluded this possibility—sovereign rights to explore and exploit any area that was in fact exploitable would appertain to the coastal State. Charting requirements did apply to a boundary dividing the continental shelf between neighbouring States. Yet this followed from the fact that areas of overlap would by definition be exploitable by one or the other State. Similarly, the widespread exercise of the freedoms of the high seas—navigation and fishing in particular—gave the coastal State reason to ensure that the location of the limits of the territorial sea (in which those freedoms were restricted or prohibited in favour of its sovereign rights) were charted and so made known.

D. A Variable Limit

The most significant difference between the 1958 CSC and UNCLOS for present purposes is the fact that, under the earlier instrument, the limits of the shelf could be *varied* by the coastal State. Although changes had to be justified on the basis of developments in technological capacity, there was no objection to change itself.

At the 1958 LOSC, several States expressed misgivings about the 'vagueness' and 'subjectivity' of the exploitability criterion.[40] Yet even when it was considered that the limits of the shelf should in all cases follow the 200-metre depth line, it was anticipated that this number would be revised in response to technological developments allowing seabed exploration and exploitation at greater depths.[41]

[38] ILC Ybk 1953/II, 38.
[39] Ibid.
[40] See e.g. UNCLOS I: VI, 2 (France), 3 (South Africa), 4 (UK), 6 (Greece).
[41] ILC Ybk 1956/II, 296.

Other advocates of a definition based on depth proposed a specification of 550 metres.[42] While some of these States pointed to a memorandum by UNESCO said to indicate that this was also 'the lowest edge of the continental shelf',[43] this geological 'fact' was not generally considered legally relevant. The UNESCO memorandum in question indicated that in certain cases (e.g., 'around the Antarctic' and the Sahul shelf off northern and north-western Australia) 'a depth of two to three hundred fathoms (370 to 555 metres) is ... found before the break of slope which marks the edge of the continental shelf'.[44] It also emphasized the 'great variety' in seabed geomorphology around the world as well as the fact that 'biological, geological, geophysical and hydrographic' knowledge about the shelf was 'very incomplete'.[45] The memorandum concluded by observing that '[n]ature does not lend itself—in fact, it is very far from lending itself—to classification and to definition of strict borderlines as desired by man'.[46]

States advocating a limit at 550 metres seem to have appreciated this much. Their primary concern was to guarantee the exclusive right of the coastal State to exploit the resources of the seabed up to a depth that was both generous and specific—allowing for future technological advances and minimizing the likelihood of disputes.[47] In the end, however, none of the proposals to define the limits of the shelf by a specified depth alone—all of which had been amended to replace 200 metres with 550 metres—were adopted at the 1958 LOSC. A Canadian proposal (reintroduced by Germany) that provided the shelf would extend to either 'the point where a substantial break in grade occurs leading to abyssal ocean depth or, where there is no such substantial break', a depth of 550 metres (as orally amended), was also rejected. Proposals by Korea and Panama to define the shelf by reference to exploitability alone were considered equally unsuitable.[48] Notably, the Panamanian proposal qualified the exploitability criterion by providing that the area would '[exclude] the great depths of the oceanic basins'.[49] Yet the only amendment to the ILC text adopted by the Fourth Committee was a second paragraph proposed by the Philippines, which provided that the definition of the continental shelf also applied to submarine areas around islands.[50]

[42] UNCLOS I: VI, 46 (Canada revised proposal); 46 (Yugoslavia revised proposal), 131 (Netherlands) 132 (UK), 135 (India) (UK and the Netherlands), 136 (Sweden), 138 (UK revised proposal).

[43] Ibid, 36 (UK); 37, 65 (Netherlands).

[44] UNESCO, 'Scientific Considerations Regarding the Continental Shelf' in UNCLOS I: I, 39–46.

[45] Ibid.

[46] Ibid.

[47] States advocating a limit at 550 metres of depth as well as those advocating a definition of the shelf based on exploitability alone expressed concern that disputes might arise if other States were to exploit the seabed just beyond the 200-metre isobath where this was very close to the shore: see e.g. UNCLOS I: VI, 34.

[48] Ibid, 47 (vote), 127 (Panama's proposal). This seems to have been the effect of the Korean proposal (see ibid, 43), though the details are not clear as the text is unfortunately omitted from the annex to the records of the Fourth Committee at UNCLOS I.

[49] Ibid, 127.

[50] Ibid, 47, 133.

At the Plenary Session of the 1958 LOSC, France (supported by the Netherlands and the UK) managed to reopen the question of whether the exploitability criterion should be included in the provision by requesting a separate vote on the words 'or, beyond that limit, to where the depth of the superjacent waters admits of the exploitation of the natural resources of the said areas'.[51] The French delegate had also hoped to reopen the question of whether the 200-metre depth limit should be replaced by a 550-metre depth limit if the exploitability criterion were rejected. This did not eventuate. The exploitability criterion was adopted by forty-eight votes to twenty with two abstentions. The possibility of defining the shelf by reference to the exploitability criterion alone was not revisited. As such, States previously advocating this approach now supported the dual criteria of depth (at 200 metres) and exploitability.

The ILC and States participating in the 1958 LOSC clearly agreed that coastal State jurisdiction over the shelf should be expanded as exploitation at greater depths became practically possible. Not only did the exploitability criterion allow for the extension of coastal State jurisdiction with advances in technological capacity, it was also expressly provided that there should be no legal limitation on the right of States to exploit the seabed by tunnelling from land.[52] Article 7 of the CSC states that '[t]he provisions of these articles shall not prejudice the right of the coastal State to exploit the subsoil by means of tunnelling irrespective of the depth of water above the subsoil'. The reasoning was that tunnelling from land would not entail any interference with high seas freedoms in the superjacent waters.[53]

E. Competing Rights

During their preparatory work for the 1958 LOSC, several members of the ILC had suggested that there may be a conflict between the exclusive rights of the coastal State in the shelf and the freedoms of all States on the high seas. The majority, however, seem to have been satisfied by assurances that the coastal State's rights were limited to the exploration and exploitation of submarine areas and would neither extend to superjacent waters nor interfere unjustifiably with freedoms on the high seas—matters expressly addressed elsewhere.[54] Only Scelle, Pal, and El-Khoury argued that there was a more direct conflict between coastal State rights and high seas freedoms.

These three members of the Commission considered submarine areas of the high seas to be included within it as part of the 'common property' of all States.[55]

[51] UNCLOS I: II, 13.
[52] ILC Ybk 1956/II, 297. UNCLOS I: VI, 47.
[53] ILC Ybk 1956/II, 297; UNCLOS I: VI, 6–7, 17, 35, 42, 44, 65, 67–8.
[54] ILC Ybk 1956/II, Draft Arts 69–72.
[55] ILC Ybk 1951/I, 274 (Scelle); ILC Ybk 1956/I, 133–4, 139 (Pal), 135 (El-Khoury).

Scelle objected to the concept of the continental shelf as a whole on this basis,[56] while Pal and El-Khoury emphasized the importance of a clear limit on the seaward extent of coastal State rights—an objective they argued would be best achieved by a limit based on depth rather than exploitability.[57]

The idea that the seabed was 'common property' had also been advanced by certain members of the International Law Association (ILA). In an influential speech before the French branch in 1949, Lapradelle had proposed vesting authority over the exploitation of submarine areas in an international body (specifically, the United Nations). Calling for recognition of submarine areas as '*res communes omnium*,' he invoked Franklin Roosevelt's emphasis in 1941 on access to the world's resources as an important aspect of post-war reconstruction.[58] In Article 4 of the 1941 Atlantic Charter, Roosevelt and Churchill had affirmed that their countries would 'endeavor, with due respect for their existing obligations, to further the enjoyment by all States, great or small, victor or vanquished, of access, on equal terms, to the trade and to the raw materials of the world which are needed for their economic prosperity'.[59]

Responding to Lapradelle in 1950, the ILA's Special Rapporteur on 'Rights to the Seabed and its Subsoil', Jonkheer Feith, denied that common ownership was a necessary corollary of Roosevelt's view or its expression in the Charter[60]—a point echoed by Professor JW Bingham, then Chair of the ILA's American branch.[61] Feith and his Committee considered the characterization of the seabed and its subsoil as *res communis* to be at odds with emerging State practice, though they strategically suggested that the exploitation of submarine areas by coastal States may nevertheless benefit mankind as a whole.[62] Lapradelle continued to argue that '[l]a communauté de la mer est le principe fondamental qui doit s'appliquer au droit existant et à son développement futur' and that an international body should be responsible for administering what were not sovereign rights to exploit the seabed but the common rights of man.[63] Several other members of the ILA agreed, proposing a variety of new and existing bodies for this task.[64]

In 1952, the ILC's Special Rapporteur François advised the ILA that the Commission's view was that

56 Ibid, 274.

57 ILC Ybk 1956/I, 133 (Pal), 135 (El-Khoury).

58 ILA, *Report of the Forty-Fourth Conference* (Copenhagen 1950), 91.

59 Atlantic Charter (1941).

60 ILA, *Report of the Forty-Fourth Conference*, 91–3.

61 Ibid, 96. Bingham had defended the Truman Proclamations as 'not inconsistent with' international law in JW Bingham, 'The Continental Shelf and the Marginal Belt' (1946) 40 *AJIL* 173, 174, 177–8.

62 Feith also noted that the French Govare Committee did not take up Lapradelle's proposal in their report: ILA, *Report of the Forty-Fourth Conference*, 92.

63 ILA, *Report of the Forty-Fourth Conference*, 102–3. Lapradelle's account of the seas, including territorial waters, as 'le patrimoine de l'humanité' is set out in his much earlier work: A de Lapradelle, 'Le droit de l'État sur la mer territoriale' (1898) *RGDIP* 264.

64 ILA, *Report of the Forty-Fourth Conference*, 103, 104.

> dans les circonstances actuelles cette internationalisation se heurterait à des difficultés d'ordre pratique insurmontables et n'assurerait pas l'exploitation efficace des richesses naturelles qui est nécessaire pour faire face aux besoins de l'humanité. Il existe des plateaux continentaux dans de nombreuses parties du monde; leur exploitation devra être entreprise dans des conditions très diverses et il semble actuellement impossible de compter sur les institutions internationales pour effectuer cette exploitation.[65]

In subsequent ILC debates, only Scelle appears to have been concerned to characterize the resources of the seabed as 'riches ... of which humanity as a whole ought not to be deprived'—a point which he presented alongside the argument that coastal States should not be restricted in their exploitation of those resources by any limit.[66] For Scelle, '[i]t was entirely irrelevant which State laid claim to exercise rights over its continental shelf, since all States were equal before the law. All that was necessary was to establish how submarine resources could be exploited for the benefit of the world community as a whole.'[67]

Scelle spoke of a system whereby concessions would be granted by an international body to 'interested' States, suggesting the coastal State should have no necessary priority. Yet he had no intention of making a formal proposal to this effect, accepting that debate on this issue had closed with his thesis being roundly rejected.[68]

At the 1958 LOSC, several participants in the Fourth Committee claimed that the exploitation of the seabed would be for the common benefit of mankind. Few, however, insisted that all States should be able to participate on an equal basis in the exploitation of all areas of the seabed or share directly in the gains: those that did were given short shrift.[69] Many more States invoked the common benefit of humanity as not only consistent with but the very basis for exclusive national jurisdiction in the seabed.[70] To the extent that any common right was accepted, it was considered (to some extent) divisible.

The 1958 Convention on the High Seas did not include any reference to a freedom to explore or exploit the subsoil of the high seas. The ILC explained that it did not make 'specific mention' of such a freedom on the grounds that 'apart from the case of the exploitation or exploration of the soil or subsoil of a continental shelf ... such exploitation had not yet assumed sufficient practical importance to justify special regulation'.[71] Though this explanation does not deny the existence of a high seas freedom relating to the exploitation of the seabed, it accepts that

[65] ILA, *Report of the Forty-Fifth Conference*, 166.
[66] ILC Ybk 1953/I, 73.
[67] Ibid, 82.
[68] Ibid.
[69] See e.g. the concerns expressed by Japan: UNCLOS I: VI, 14.
[70] See e.g. UNCLOS I: IV, 55 (New Zealand).
[71] ILC Ybk 1956/II, 278.

the 'exploitation or exploration of the soil or subsoil of a continental shelf' is the prerogative of the coastal State. At the 1958 LOSC, there was some debate over whether this should be characterized as a 'sovereign right' or a right of 'jurisdiction and control'.[72] Only Germany seems to have argued that the '[f]reedom to explore or exploit the subsoil of the high seas' included the freedom of all States to exploit the continental shelf beyond the territorial sea.[73] Its informal suggestion that (a) this freedom should be expressly recognized, and (b) the sovereign rights of the coastal State in the seabed should be restricted to the territorial sea, was not well received.[74]

There seems to have been little doubt in the view of the great majority of participants in the 1958 LOSC that the coastal State should be entitled to exploit the seabed as far as it was exploitable. Some States emphasized that this was in the interests of the international community as a whole.[75] This is an argument that the ILC seems to have accepted, though it did not approve associated suggestions that 'the exploitation of the natural resources of submarine areas should be entrusted, not to coastal States, but to agencies of the international community generally'.[76] To the extent that the regime of the continental shelf in the CSC responds to the 'needs of mankind', it does so by providing for the exclusive sovereign rights of the coastal State to exploit the seabed up to the 200-metre isobath or as far as 'the depth of the superjacent waters admits of the exploitation of the natural resources' of the seabed and without any explicit reference to the interests of the international community.

III. The Common Heritage of Mankind

If the possibility of exploiting the deep seabed 'had not yet assumed sufficient practical importance to justify special regulation' in the late 1950s,[77] it assumed such importance in the next decade with the rapid development of seabed mining technologies and research suggesting the value of deep seabed resources, manganese nodules in particular. States at the 1958 LOSC had agreed that coastal State jurisdiction over the seabed should extend as far as the seabed was exploitable. At the same time, their expectations regarding the depths at which exploitation might become technologically possible and economically viable would not have allowed for the possibility that the seabed in its entirety might be carved up between coastal States, or between coastal States with the capacity to exploit its resources. By 1967,

[72] UNCLOS I: VI, 3–6, 13–20, 29, 41–71.
[73] Ibid, 7–8, 125–6.
[74] Ibid, 9–10, 12–13, 17, 19.
[75] See e.g. ibid, 7–8, 31, 71, 125–6 (Germany), 26 (Indonesia), 54–5 (New Zealand), 59 (Greece, Indonesia).
[76] ILC Ybk 1956/II, 296.
[77] ILC Ybk 1956/II, 278.

when the Ad Hoc Seabed Committee was established by a resolution of the UN General Assembly, there was a very real concern that the expandability of the exploitability criterion in step with technological advances might have this effect.

The establishment of the Seabed Committee was prompted by an influential speech by Arvid Pardo of Malta before the United Nations General Assembly (UNGA) in 1967. Pardo called for a resolution recognizing inter alia that 'the seabed and the ocean floor are a common heritage of mankind and should be used and exploited for peaceful purposes and for the exclusive benefit of mankind as a whole'.[78] The driving concern was that 'rapidly developing technology [had made] possible the exploration, occupation and exploitation of the world's seabeds and much of its ocean floor ... leading ... to appropriation for national uses of these areas'.[79] As Pardo emphasized, this entailed 'not only immense prejudice to land-locked countries but also to most of the coastal States that do not have the requisite technical competence to exploit the coastal floor'.[80]

Pardo was not the first to suggest that all mankind had an interest in the resources of the seabed.[81] Yet there was an important difference between his vision of 'the common heritage of mankind' and both earlier accounts of the seabed as *res communes omnium* and claims that national exploitation of the seabed was in the common interest. Pardo urged members of the General Assembly to consider 'whether it might not be wise to establish some form of international jurisdiction and control over the sea-bed and the ocean floor underlying the seas *beyond the limits of present national jurisdiction*'.[82] By associating the notion of the common heritage of mankind with the seabed *beyond* national jurisdiction, he provided a principled basis for pushing back against ever-expanding coastal State claims to the resources of the seabed. Pardo recognized that States had sovereign rights in the continental shelf beyond the limits of the territorial sea, but he denied that those rights could be extended indefinitely.

The idea that the seabed area beyond present national jurisdiction was the 'common heritage of mankind' implied the necessity of clearly defined and permanent limits to coastal State rights in the continental shelf. This vision was more compatible with the existing fact of exclusive coastal jurisdiction over some part of the seabed than the idea that the whole of the seabed (or that part beyond the territorial sea, including the continental shelf) was *res communis*. Moving away from the argument that the seabed as a whole (or beyond the territorial sea) should be

[78] UN Doc A/C.1/PV.1515 & 1516 (1967). See also A Pardo, 'Who Will Control the Seabed?'(1968) 47 *Foreign Affairs* 124.

[79] UN Doc A/C.1/PV.1515 & 1516 (1967).

[80] Ibid.

[81] As noted in Section II (E), arguments to this effect were made inter alia by Lapradelle: ILA, *Report of the Forty-Fourth Conference*, 91; de Lapradelle, 'Le droit de l'État sur la mer territoriale', 264. For an account of similar arguments by other actors in the 1960s, see S Ranganathan, 'Global Commons' (2016) 27 (3) *EJIL* 693, 707–8.

[82] UN Doc A/C.1/PV.1515 (1967) (emphasis added).

exploited for the common benefit of mankind also took the wind out of the sails of claims that granting the coastal State exclusive sovereign rights to the seabed as far as exploitation was possible was the best way of securing that 'common benefit'. Under the CSC, the distinction between the limits of present national jurisdiction in the seabed and submarine areas beyond those limits was no more than a reflection of the technical capacity for exploitation at a particular time. Under UNCLOS, this became a difference in legal character and status. It was now considered imperative to constrain and clearly define the limits of the coastal State's exclusive jurisdiction in the seabed. And it was now considered necessary that those limits should be *permanently* defined rather than subject to adjustment (and seaward extension) in response to technological developments.

The clear priority given to arresting the seaward advance of exclusive sovereign rights to the seabed is evidenced by the call for 'a moratorium or freezing of national claims … beyond the limits of present national jurisdiction' by members of the Ad Hoc Seabed Committee.[83] The result was UN General Assembly Resolution 2754D (XXIV), which in 1969 '[declared] that pending the establishment of [an international regime governing peaceful uses of the seabed] (a) States and persons … are bound to refrain from all activities of exploitation of the resources of the area of the seabed … beyond the limits of national jurisdiction; [and] (b) no claim to any part of that area or its resources shall be recognized'. The terms of the resolution ultimately failed to 'freeze' national claims. As Malta pointed out in the course of explaining its vote against the resolution, this formulation could not prevent the extension of national claims based on the exploitability criterion 'since as soon as an area of the sea-bed becomes technically exploitable it comes automatically under [the State's] national jurisdiction'.[84] Nevertheless, the intention was clearly to suspend any further extension of coastal State rights in the seabed in the interests of preserving an area beyond national jurisdiction.

The UN General Assembly declared the seabed beyond the limits of national jurisdiction 'the common heritage of mankind' in 1970.[85] Under UNCLOS, this is known as the (international seabed) 'Area'. UNCLOS Article 136 provides that '[t]he Area and its resources are the common heritage of mankind', while Article 137 expressly prohibits States from claiming, exercising sovereignty over, or appropriating the Area and its resources and provides that '[a]ll rights in the resources of the Area are vested in mankind as a whole'. Article 140 provides that '[a]ctivities in the Area shall … be carried out for the benefit of mankind as a whole, irrespective of the geographical location of States, whether coastal or land-locked, and taking

[83] Ad Hoc Seabed Committee Report (1968), 49.

[84] UN Doc A/PV.1833 (1969), para 35. The United States makes a similar point at para 9, though it was opposed to any 'retardation' of 'the development of seabed exploitation', presenting national efforts as in the interests of mankind.

[85] UNGA Res 2749 (XXV) of 17 December 1970.

into particular consideration the interests and needs of developing States and of peoples who have not attained full independence or other self-governing status'. An International Seabed Authority was established to act on behalf of 'mankind as a whole' in organizing and controlling activities in the Area and administering its resources.[86]

The identification of the seabed beyond national jurisdiction as the 'common heritage of mankind' was both an expression of the rationale for limiting the expansion of coastal State claims to the seabed and a means of bringing such limitation about. Article 311(6) goes so far as to expressly preclude any amendment or 'agreement in derogation' from the declaration that the international seabed area and its resources are the 'common heritage of mankind'.[87] The 'need for a more precise definition of the sea-bed and the ocean floor underlying the high seas beyond national jurisdiction', identified as a priority from the very first session of the Ad Hoc Seabed Committee in 1968,[88] was also understood to depend upon a more precise definition of the outer limits of the continental shelf.[89]

The mandate of the Ad Hoc Seabed Committee to consider the definition of the limits of the continental shelf was initially doubted by some of its members.[90] With the expansion of both the membership and mandate of the standing Seabed Committee, the question of limits could be considered by all sub-committees in connection with other matters.[91] The Main Committee was responsible for formulating a final recommendation based on the Second Committee's conclusions regarding 'the precise definition of the [A]rea'.[92] It was generally agreed that if the Area was to be defined as the seabed 'beyond the limits of the national jurisdiction', it would be necessary to define the outer limits of the continental shelf more exactly. While in 1958 States concerned with the 'imprecision' of the exploitability criterion had referred to the possibility of disagreement regarding the depth at which the seabed was in fact exploitable, the more pressing concern in the Seabed Committee and at UNCLOS III was that (a) established limits were under the existing law subject to change with advances in technology, and (b) this would by definition result in all exploitable areas of the seabed being brought under national jurisdiction.

[86] UNCLOS Arts 137, 156, 157.

[87] Even the 1994 Agreement relating to Part XI begins by reaffirming that the seabed and subsoil of the Area are the common heritage of mankind. Rather than simply signalling hypocrisy, this points to the amenability of the concept of 'common heritage' to arguments based on 'market principles' as a consequence of the focus on resource exploitation that has shaped it.

[88] Ad Hoc Seabed Committee Report (1968), 48.

[89] Ibid.

[90] Ibid.

[91] Seabed Committee Report (1973/I), 38.

[92] Ibid, 39.

IV. The 200M Limit: UNCLOS and the Turn to Distance

At UNCLOS III, most States agreed that it was necessary to replace the exploitability criterion in the 1958 CSC and many also rejected a depth-based definition of the limits of the shelf (and the 200-metre isobath specifically).[93] Only Chile suggested that the exploitability criterion was part of customary international law,[94] while Mexico recalled that it was 'part of international law' insofar as it was part of the 1958 Convention.[95] The overwhelming majority of States—including those that argued that rights 'acquired' under the 1958 CSC (i.e. on the basis of exploitability) could not now be lost[96]—agreed that the existing definition of the shelf was not sufficiently precise.[97]

At UNCLOS III, the topics under consideration were distributed between three Main Committees corresponding to the three Sub-Committees of the whole established by the Seabed Committee in 1971.[98] At the second session of the Conference in 1974, the First Committee was tasked with considering inter alia the definition and limits of the international seabed area, while the Second Committee was responsible for considering the definition of the outer limits of the continental shelf.[99] It was nevertheless acknowledged that the limits of the Area were in fact the limits of the continental shelf[100] and the First Committee decided to defer discussion of the precise definition of the limits of the Area pending 'the results of the discussion of "limits" as a whole in the Second Committee'.[101]

The Informal Single Negotiating Text (ISNT) prepared by the Chair of the First Committee in 1973 included only a general definition of the Area as 'the sea-bed and ocean floor and subsoil thereof beyond the limits of national jurisdiction'.[102] This definition had been used as a matter of course in the Committee's proceedings.[103] There is no evidence that the issue of the precise limits of the Area was raised again in the First Committee.[104] Its broad, negative definition of the Area was retained in the Revised Informal Negotiating Text of 1976. It was subsequently included in the Informal Composite Negotiating Text prepared in 1977 by the President and the Chairs of the Main Committees, though it was moved to the definition of terms in Article 1 (a change not specifically commented on). Here it remained, becoming Article 1(1)1 of UNCLOS.

93 UNCLOS III: II, 142–69.
94 Ibid, 166.
95 Ibid, 173.
96 Ibid, 142–69; UNCLOS III: III, 117–18.
97 See e.g. UNCLOS III: II, 142–69.
98 UNCLOS III: I, 5.
99 UNCLOS III: III, 59–61.
100 UNCLOS III: I, 220–1.
101 UNCLOS III: II, 53; UNCLOS III: III, 158, fn 8.
102 UNCLOS III: IV, 138 (ISNT, Part I, Art 2).
103 See UNCLOS III: II, 3–91; UNCLOS III: IV, 51–73.
104 At least, this issue is not mentioned in the available records of its work.

UNCLOS' two-part definition of the limits of the shelf by reference to distance from the baseline and 'the outer edge of the continental margin' was intended to place clear and permanent limits on the extent of national jurisdiction in the seabed, preserving an area beyond those limits as 'the common heritage of mankind'. The turn to distance to achieve these ends is particularly noteworthy given Caron's claim that Article 76(9) implies the ambulatory character of baselines and the limits measured from them.

Defining the limits of the shelf (in part) by distance was not an innovation. States had defined their territorial seas by miles from the coast long before the 1930 Hague Conference, where it was thought necessary and desirable to more precisely specify the starting point for such measurements as well as their appropriate extent.[105] The baselines provisions of the 1958 Convention on the Territorial Sea and Contiguous Zone (TSC) permitted the more precise definition of zonal limits through measurements of distance, though a uniform breadth for the territorial sea was not agreed upon until UNCLOS III.[106]

A distance-based definition of the limits of the continental shelf had also been considered leading up to and at the 1958 LOSC. In 1951, ILC members El-Khoury and Yepes made proposals to this effect based on submissions to the ILA's Committee on Rights to the Seabed and its Sub-Soil (1948–54) by the French branch in 1950.[107] A strong majority of the ILC rejected El-Khoury's suggestion that the law should provide for sovereign rights in the seabed up to a minimum distance, as well as the proposal to specify a maximum limit based on distance.[108] Yet a narrow majority accepted Yepes' proposal, which (as amended by El-Khoury and Hsu) provided that

> The rights of control and jurisdiction referred to in the present chapter belong, up to a distance of twenty miles beyond territorial waters, to all the coastal States which do not possess a continental shelf as defined in article 1.[109]

In view of the close vote, persistent criticism by dissenters, and subsequent doubts regarding the wording expressed by supporters, a subcommittee was established to consider the central issue, which was framed as a question of how the case of coastal States with a steeply descending seabed close to their shores should be addressed.[110] The subcommittee agreed unanimously that 'the best way of avoiding any difficulty' was to define the limits of the shelf by reference to exploitability rather than depth—a proposal adopted by the ILC at the time.[111]

[105] See Chapter 7.
[106] TSC Art 24(2) provided, however, for a contiguous zone of 12M.
[107] See ILA, *Report of the Forty-Fourth Conference*, 94 ('Govare Committee').
[108] ILC Ybk 1951/I, 271–3.
[109] Ibid, 299.
[110] Ibid, 299–300.
[111] Ibid, 346.

At the 1958 LOSC, distance was again proposed as a basis for defining the limits of the continental shelf. As a member of the ILA's Committee on Rights to the Seabed between 1951 and 1954, Norway had doubted the necessity of sovereign rights in the seabed beyond the territorial sea but considered that their extent in any case 'ought to be based on distance from the shore'.[112] Other Committee members disagreed, considering a distance criterion 'inappropriate' because it 'ignores whether or not the seabed and subsoil are in fact accessible' (a matter of depth).[113] A depth-based definition was considered more consistent with the character of the rights in question, which were restricted to the exploration and exploitation of submarine resources.[114] Commenting on the ILC's draft articles in 1957, Norway again suggested that 'it might seem preferable to define the zone by a fixed maximum distance from the coast'.[115] It reiterated this proposal at the 1958 LOSC,[116] where several other States commented on the viability and desirability of a distance criterion.

The Canadian delegate listed distance among 'five possible methods of defining the continental shelf'.[117] Despite describing this as a 'simple solution with the obvious advantage of according exactly the same treatment to every country', he dismissed it on the grounds that it bore 'no real relationship to geographical or geological facts or to the realities of the situation with regard to exploitation'.[118] Undeterred by or unaware of this opinion, Guatemala shortly afterwards suggested 'a new concept, which might perhaps be termed the "continental terrace", comprising an area bounded by a line drawn at a given distance from the baseline of the territorial sea of the coastal State'.[119] Yugoslavia proposed an outer limit at the 200m depth line or a distance of 100M, whichever was closest to the coast. It also recommended that narrow shelf States with submarine areas dropping to 200 metres or more within 50M of the baseline should be entitled to a further 50M beyond the 200-metre depth line.[120] Only Brazil expressed support for this proposal[121] and it was not adopted.[122]

A distance-based limit on the right to exploit the *living* resources of the seabed (i.e. sedentary fisheries) was also proposed by Iceland, which sought to secure support for more extensive exclusive fishery rights beyond the territorial sea for States especially dependent upon these resources.[123] Denmark agreed that exclusive

[112] ILA, *Report of the Forty-Sixth Conference* (Edinburgh 1954), 414–15; ILA, *Report of the Forty-Fourth Conference*, 157.
[113] ILA, *Report of the Forty-Sixth Conference*, 438. Distance is not a reliable indicator of depth.
[114] Ibid.
[115] UNCLOS I: I, 96.
[116] UNCLOS I: VI, 5.
[117] Ibid, 30.
[118] Ibid.
[119] Ibid, 31.
[120] Ibid, 32.
[121] Ibid, 36.
[122] Ibid, 46–7.
[123] Ibid, 28, 59.

fishing rights should be extended on this basis; however, it suggested that sedentary fisheries should be included in a separate distance-based fisheries zone, 'limiting the rights of coastal States in respect of the [depth-based] continental shelf to mineral resources only'.[124]

Ultimately, the only use of distance in connection with the continental shelf in the 1958 CSC was to define safety zones around installations, with States deciding to specify a maximum of 500 metres instead of the ILC's reference to 'a reasonable distance'.[125] This limit on the extent of safety zones is retained in UNCLOS subject to exception where another distance is 'authorized by generally accepted international standards or ... recommended by the competent international organization'.[126]

A distance-based definition of the limits of the shelf was among the possibilities discussed by the Seabed Committee, though it did not recommend any particular approach.[127] Such a definition was nevertheless encouraged by developments in State practice between the 1958 LOSC and the conclusion of UNCLOS—in particular, the increasing number of States claiming exclusive fisheries zones (EFZs) or exclusive economic zones (EEZs) beyond the territorial sea, sometimes including submarine areas.[128] These zones, defined by distance, were recognized in customary international law before the conclusion[129] and entry into force[130] of the 1982 Convention.[131] While several States (including members of the Organization of African Unity) suggested that the EEZ might subsume sovereign rights to the continental shelf,[132] it was finally agreed that the law should recognize two separate zones which could coincide or partly overlap where an EEZ was claimed (rights to the continental shelf existing *ipso facto* and *ab initio* and potentially extending beyond the EEZ).[133] It was partly in the interests of harmonization that the continental shelf was redefined in similar terms to the EEZ as an extended zone of functional jurisdiction defined by distance from the baseline.[134]

124 UNCLOS I: VI, 12–13.

125 CSC Art 5(3). The ILC had suggested in its commentary that this distance was 'sufficient for the purpose': ILC Ybk 1956/II, 299.

126 UNCLOS Arts 60(5), 260.

127 Seabed Committee Report (1973/I), 51.

128 In reviewing State practice, it can be difficult to separate claims to an extensive territorial sea from claims to more limited functional jurisdiction beyond the territorial sea comprising exclusive rights to fisheries and in some cases seabed resources as well. Some commentators attempt to present all claims beyond 12M as claims to an EFZ or EEZ and, as such, State practice supporting the customary concept of the EEZ: see e.g. F Orrego Vicuña, *The Exclusive Economic Zone* (CUP, 1989). In fact, the issue of the breadth of the territorial sea and claims to either or both the sea and seabed beyond it were not clearly distinguished. The articulation into separate zones was largely a consequence of negotiations at UNCLOS III.

129 *Tunisia/Libya* (1982) 74.

130 *Libya/Malta* (1985) 33.

131 Churchill and Lowe, *The Law of the Sea*, 161.

132 UNCLOS III: II, 162; UNCLOS III: III, 117 (Working Paper of the Second Committee, 1974: Main Trends).

133 *North Sea Cases* (1969) 22; *Libya/Malta* (1985) 33; UNCLOS Art 56(1)(a), (2), (3).

134 See *Libya/Malta* (1985), 33.

Significantly, States also considered a distance-based definition of the shelf to have the key advantage of detaching or at least further distancing the question of limits from the question of exploitability. Defining the limits of the shelf at 200M removed the possibility of a continual expansion of national claims to the shelf with advances in technology. Allowing the limits of the shelf to be established at the outer edge of the continental margin where it lay beyond 200M and within either 350M from the baseline or 100M from the 2,500 isobath facilitated the seaward extension of jurisdiction for some States but once and for all time. Both parts of the double criterion for establishing the limits of the shelf removed the prospect of further seaward advances. While either part would have sufficed to achieve this objective, their combination balanced the interests of broad shelf States with the interests of both narrow shelf States and, by virtue of a revenue-sharing scheme applying to the continental shelf beyond 200M, States concerned to protect a significant proportion of the seabed for common use and benefit.

Among other difficulties, Caron's interpretation of Article 76 pays insufficient attention to the fact that States considered the distance criterion an answer to their search for a clear and ascertainable limit marking the boundary between the continental shelf and the international seabed area. They did not (a) elect to define the limits of the shelf in a way that would make their location contingent upon the configuration of the variable coast before (b) adding that, in this particular case, established limits would exceptionally be preserved against coastal change. Instead, the distance-based definition was *itself* understood to result in a more stable limit for both the continental shelf and the Area. Of course, limits defined by distance might still be changed by the coastal State if it changed its baselines or (more unusually) specified that its zonal limits would be located at less than the maximum permissible distance from the baseline. Yet the ordinary ability of the coastal State to redraw its baselines and zonal limits is one thing, an obligation to adjust them in response to coastal change another.

Article 76(9) responds directly to the first possibility, forestalling it by providing that the limits of the shelf, whether based on distance or the edge of the continental margin, must be *permanently* described. Article 76(8) emphasizes that the limits of the continental shelf beyond 200M are 'final and binding'. These injunctions are addressed to the coastal State as the agent responsible for establishing the outer limits of the maritime zones to which it is entitled. They exceptionally prohibit the coastal State from redrawing the limits of the shelf once lawfully established. Developed against the backdrop of a regime allowing for the continual revision of the limits of the shelf in response to advances in technology, the purpose of the law in this regard is to ensure the clear and permanent definition of the international seabed area and the preservation of the rights of all States to its resources as the common heritage of mankind.

There is no evidence at all that the 'permanence' of the limits of the shelf reflects a belief that coastal change would otherwise necessitate changes to these limits because it necessitates changes in the location or configuration of the baseline. Indeed, far from 'negatively implying' the ambulatory thesis, Article 76 positively suggests that the States negotiating this provision did *not* understand baselines and zonal limits to move with the coast. If they had, this would presumably have been identified as a drawback to a (partly) distance-based definition of the shelf. At UNCLOS III, there was overwhelming agreement that the limits of the shelf should be clearly and permanently defined and the best means of achieving this was discussed at length. It is significant, then, that there is no mention of the possibility that defining those limits by distance from the baseline might mean that they would have to be adjusted in response to coastal change. A distance-based definition of the continental shelf was understood to be part of the solution to the problem of imprecise and variable limits under the CSC.

V. The Limits of the Continental Shelf beyond 200M

The decision to define the Area negatively by reference to the limits of the continental shelf followed from recognition of the existing rights of the coastal State in this zone.[135] A number of States at UNCLOS III claimed to have 'acquired' rights in the shelf on a variety of grounds. While it was widely agreed that the exploitability criterion had to be replaced, [136] several States argued that they had nevertheless acquired rights under the CSC of which they could not now be deprived.[137] Others argued that they had an inherent entitlement to the continental shelf under customary international law—some referring in this regard to the 'natural prolongation' of their land territory.[138]

In its work on the 'regime of the high seas' between 1950 and 1956, the ILC had been unable to agree on whether there was any existing customary law regarding national rights to the seabed beyond the territorial sea. As a result, agreement could not be reached on the question of whether its draft articles were properly considered the codification or progressive development of the law—a characterization believed, based on a certain interpretation of the ILC Statute, to bear upon its final recommendations to the UNGA.[139] The ILC's 1956 commentary on its draft articles on the continental shelf is appropriately ambiguous, referring to 'a development which, in the opinion of the Commission, can be to the benefit of all mankind' and, as such, should not be 'obstructed' on the basis of its minimal

[135] Seabed Committee Report (1973/I), 51.
[136] UNCLOS III: II, 142–69.
[137] This was a line of argument first raised in the discussions of the Seabed Committee: Seabed Committee Report (1973/I), Annex 1, 38, 51. See further UNCLOS III: II.
[138] See e.g. UNCLOS III: II, 144 (Bangladesh), 145 (Honduras), 147 (Australia), 148 (Republic of Korea) (Spain), 149 (El Salvador), 150 (Argentina), 158 (Ecuador), 163 (Mauritius) (see generally 16th to 20th meetings, Second Committee, 1974).
[139] ILC Ybk 1953/I, 359–60.

interference with freedoms of the high seas.[140] Noting the impossibility of distinguishing between provisions according to whether they codified or 'progressively developed' the law, the Commission concluded that '[i]n these circumstances, in order to give effect to the project as a whole, it will be necessary to have recourse to conventional means'.[141]

States participating in the 1958 LOSC continued to disagree on whether customary law already recognized national rights to the seabed beyond the territorial sea and in what form.[142] In the *North Sea Cases* (1969), the International Court of Justice (ICJ) had found that the first three articles of the CSC relating to the rights of the coastal State in the continental shelf and defining their content and extent 'were then regarded as reflecting, or as crystallizing, received or at least emergent rules of customary international law relative to the continental shelf'.[143] The somewhat suspect basis for this conclusion was that reservations to these provisions were precluded—the Court inferring that Article 6 relating to the delimitation of the shelf between States, in respect of which reservations were permitted, did *not* have customary status.[144]

This reasoning is problematic. While reservations to treaty provisions that also have customary status cannot prevent the parallel rule or principle in custom from binding the State concerned, this does not prevent the formulation of a reservation to the said treaty provision, provided that reservation is consistent with the treaty's object and purpose.[145] Moreover, the express prohibition of reservations in respect of certain provisions is not necessarily indicative of the customary character of those provisions. States may agree to prohibit reservations to any conventional provision, whatever its customary status.[146]

In 1967, the UN General Assembly considered customary law on the limits of the continental shelf to be 'inconclusive'.[147] The suggestion that the CSC created rights which could not be affected by the subsequent development of the law was rejected by most States at UNCLOS III.[148] Yet a number of broad-shelf States also argued that rights to the seabed beyond 200M were recognized in customary international law (and independently of any claim to the superjacent waters). In support of this claim, they invoked the Court's observation in the *North Sea Cases* that 'the rights of the coastal State in respect of the area of continental shelf that constitutes a

[140] ILC Ybk 1956/II, 296.
[141] ILC Ybk 1956/II, 255–6.
[142] UNCLOS I: VI, esp 2–31.
[143] *North Sea Cases* (1969), 39.
[144] Ibid.
[145] *Reservations to the Genocide Convention Advisory Opinion* (1951), 24. See also ILC, 'Guide to Practice on Reservations' (2011), 3.1.5.3, and Commentary, 368.
[146] ILC, 'Guide to Practice on Reservations', 3.1.1 and Commentary, 355.
[147] UNGA Res 2574 A (XXIV) of 15 December 1969.
[148] See e.g. UNCLOS III: II, 151 (Singapore), 174 (Upper Volta), 240 (Sweden).

natural prolongation of its land territory into and under the sea exist, *ipso facto* and *ab initio*, by virtue of its sovereignty over the land'.[149]

Other States objected to the idea that the notion of 'natural prolongation' had customary status, stressing that the expression was not used in the CSC.[150] Indeed, to the extent that 'natural prolongation' was interpreted as a geomorphological concept, it was not only the expression but the content given to it that was new. The ILC and States participating in the 1958 LOSC had consciously departed from a physical concept of the shelf in the legal definition of this zone of functional jurisdiction. While there was certainly State practice showing that claims to the seabed had been made on grounds other than depth and exploitability, there was considerable variation in accounts of both the basis for entitlement and the type of rights involved. 'Natural prolongation' was not always identified with a physical definition of the shelf but also or otherwise associated with distance through ideas of adjacency, appurtenance, and contiguity. Claims based on seabed geomorphology had no particular priority that might suggest emerging custom in this regard, still less an established customary right.

The definition of the shelf finally settled upon in UNCLOS Article 76 was sufficiently extensive to encompass the area in which certain States claimed 'acquired rights' based on either the CSC or various accounts of the content and consequences of a principle of 'natural prolongation'. Yet there was no general consensus that the provision either preserved acquired rights or codified custom. By the time UNCLOS was concluded, the proliferation of unopposed claims to an EFZ or EEZ meant that exclusive sovereign rights to exploit the resources of the seabed up to 200M from the baseline were also recognized in customary international law. This development was parallel to and encouraged by negotiations at UNCLOS III. Though Article 76 also provides that the continental shelf may 'extend beyond [the coastal State's] territorial sea throughout the natural prolongation of its land territory to the outer edge of the continental margin', it was not agreed that this part of the definition had customary status at the time the Convention was concluded. Some States rejecting the claim that seabed geomorphology was already the basis for rights to the continental shelf allowed that it might be granted a role in the new treaty.[151] Significantly, it appears that all States supporting some reference to 'natural prolongation' in the treaty text understood that the concept was not independently determinative of the limits of the shelf, which required further definition.

[149] *North Sea Cases* (1969), 22. See e.g. UNCLOS III: II, 144 (Bangladesh), 145 (Honduras), 147 (Australia), 148 (Republic of Korea) (Spain), 149 (El Salvador), 150 (Argentina), 158 (Ecuador), 163 (Mauritius) (see generally 16th to 20th meetings, Second Committee, 1974).

[150] This was the view of the nine States sponsoring A/CONF.62/L.4 (Canada, Chile, Iceland, India, Indonesia, Mauritius, Mexico, New Zealand, and Norway): UNCLOS III: I, 203. See further UNCLOS III: II, 157 (Sweden), 163 (Mauritius), 165 (Germany).

[151] See e.g. UNCLOS III: II, 154 (Pakistan).

According to UNCLOS Article 76, the coastal State is entitled to sovereign rights in the seabed beyond 200M where 'the outer edge of the continental margin' is located beyond this distance. Yet the limits of the 'extended shelf' are also clearly defined and, once established (based on the recommendations of the CLCS), they are 'final and binding'.[152] There are also distance-based constraints on the ability of the coastal State to extend its sovereign rights to 'the outer edge of the continental margin'. States concerned to protect an international seabed area from national claims based on geomorphology negotiated a maximum limit at 350M from the baseline or 100M from the 2,500-metre depth line where the edge of the continental margin lies beyond this distance.[153]

The definition of the limits of the shelf beyond 200M responds to the concern to clearly and permanently define the limits of the Area in which seabed resources had been recognized as the 'common heritage of mankind'. The role of the CLCS in reviewing and making recommendations regarding the limits of an extended continental shelf is also connected with a concern to restrict and regulate the seaward extension of coastal State jurisdiction in the shelf. There is a time limit on submissions to the CLCS—initially ten years from UNCLOS' entry into force[154] with the start date moved to 13 May 1999 in response to difficulties experienced by developing States given the resources, capacity, and expertise needed to compile a submission.[155] The possibility of further extensions has been discussed and remains under review; however, it is clearly anticipated that there will be a final cut-off for claims to an extended shelf.

Other aspects of the regime governing the extended continental shelf underscore the importance placed upon preserving the 'common heritage of mankind'. Broad shelf States secured support for the extension of sovereign rights beyond 200M by agreeing to a revenue-sharing scheme. UNCLOS Article 82 requires 'payments or contributions in kind' in respect of submarine resource exploitation beyond 200M to be distributed by the International Seabed Authority 'on the basis of equitable sharing criteria, taking into account the interests and needs of developing States, particularly the least developed and the land-locked among them'.[156] This provision was based on a proposal by the US, which presented it 'as a way to reconcile the positions of States which maintained that their rights extended to the edge of the continental margin beyond 200 miles and those that did not wish to see the

[152] UNCLOS Art 76(8).
[153] UNCLOS Art 76(5).
[154] UNCLOS Annex II, Art 4.
[155] This was the date of adoption of the CLCS's *Scientific and Technical Guidelines*: SPLOS/72, 29 May 2001.
[156] This is reminiscent of earlier suggestions that even seabed resources within national jurisdiction were the common heritage of mankind, though the latter concept is now (deliberately) tied exclusively to the Area.

common heritage of mankind diminished by recognizing coastal State jurisdiction beyond 200 miles'.[157]

VI. Unlimited Tunnels: A Vestigial Law

Paragraphs 8 and 9 of UNCLOS Article 76 are elements of a provision more broadly concerned with clearly and permanently defining the limits of the continental shelf as the limits of the Area. There is nevertheless a provision that appears potentially at odds with the objectives of the law in this regard. Article 85 of UNCLOS, like Article 7 of the CSC, provides that Part VI on the continental shelf

> does not prejudice the right of the coastal State to exploit the subsoil by means of tunnelling, irrespective of the depth of water above the subsoil.

The text of this provision already indicates that it was imported wholesale from the CSC. As UNCLOS does not limit the coastal State's right to exploit the seabed on the basis of depth, it is difficult to see what work the phrase 'irrespective of... depth' does in this context. More problematically, the article seems to suggest that exploitation of the seabed by tunnelling is not subject to any limitation at all. This is difficult to reconcile with a regime that is otherwise designed to clearly and permanently limit the sovereign rights of the coastal State in the seabed, preserving an area as the common heritage of mankind.

Article 85 must be interpreted in a manner that is consistent with the broader context of the provision as well as the object and purpose of the treaty.[158] This would appear to preclude a reading of the provision as an exception to the otherwise permanent limits of the continental shelf. It is necessary, then, to consider what meaning Article 85 might otherwise have.

The provision begins by specifying that Part VI of UNCLOS 'does not prejudice the right of the coastal State to exploit the subsoil by means of tunnelling'. This suggests at first glance that the exploitation of the seabed by tunnelling cannot be restricted by the limits of the continental shelf as defined in Article 76. However, this reading pays insufficient attention to the specific reference to the irrelevance of the depth of the superjacent water in this regard. The provision specifies that tunnelling from land is permitted irrespective of depth. It is not clear that it also admits tunnelling from land irrespective of the establishment of permanent limits pursuant to Article 76.

This ambiguity warrants recourse to the drafting history.[159] The tunnelling provision was included in one of the variant sets of articles on the continental

[157] The original proposal provided for revenue sharing beyond the 200M isobath or territorial sea, whichever was further seaward: UNCLOS III: II, 291.

[158] Vienna Convention on the Law of Treaties 1969 (VCLT) Art 31.

[159] VCLT Art 32.

shelf submitted by delegations to the Seabed Committee.[160] It was reproduced as Provision 9 of the Main Trends Paper prepared by the Second Committee in 1974[161] before becoming Article 72 of the ISNT prepared in 1975.[162] The provision was retained throughout negotiations until its adoption as UNCLOS Article 85. Curiously, it does not seem to have been directly discussed at UNCLOS III at all.

As already noted, the ILC and States at the 1958 LOSC had agreed that it was unnecessary to restrict the exploitation of the seabed by tunnelling from land because this did not interfere with high seas freedoms in the superjacent waters. Yet States at UNCLOS III agreed that there should be no exercise or assertion of national jurisdiction in the seabed beyond limits permanently established in accordance with Article 76.[163] There is no evidence that they considered tunnelling from land into the seabed beyond these clearly and permanently defined limits to be exceptionally justified. While it could be speculated that they considered it unlikely that tunnelling could as a practical matter extend this far, there is no evidence of this view either. Nor does the drafting history explain why States should have been concerned to provide that there should be no restrictions on tunnelling based on the depth of superjacent waters.

The silence of the drafting history with respect to the tunnelling provision coupled with the overt concern of States to clearly and permanently define the limits of the continental shelf as the limits of the Area supports the conclusion that Article 85 does not exceptionally allow the exploitation of the seabed beyond the limits defined in Article 76. This negative conclusion is consistent with the broader context of Article 85 and the objectives of the law. Unfortunately, the only positive interpretation of that provision that does not directly contradict the content, aims, and effect of the preceding articles as well as the regime governing the Area also fits poorly with the same. There seems to have been no reason to provide that the coastal State's right to exploit the seabed by tunnelling from land was not limited by depth once the coastal State's right to exploit the seabed was not limited by depth at all. The conclusion that must be drawn is that Article 85 is simply a vestige of the regime governing the continental shelf under the CSC. While the exploitation of the seabed by tunnelling remains a lawful practice under UNCLOS, Article 85 cannot be taken to signify an exception to the clear rule that the limits of the shelf as the limits of the Area should be clearly and permanently defined.

160 Seabed Committee Report (1973/IV), 63.
161 UNCLOS III: III, 119.
162 UNCLOS III: IV, 163.
163 See UNCLOS Art 137 on the legal status of the Area and its resources.

VII. Conclusion: The Limits of the Continental Shelf as the Limits of the 'Area'

Article 76 of UNCLOS defines the limits of the continental shelf in a manner intended to prevent expanding national claims to the seabed. The significance of the limits of the shelf as the limits of the Area is reflected in the requirement under UNCLOS Article 84(2) that charts or coordinates indicating 'the outer limit lines of the continental shelf' are to be deposited with the Secretary-General of the International Seabed Authority. Charts and coordinates 'permanently describing' the outer limits of the shelf must also be deposited with the UN Secretary-General—the depositary for charts and coordinates indicating all other maritime limits.[164] While Article 84 includes the standard requirement that the coastal State shall give due publicity to the limits of the shelf, Article 76(9) unusually provides that the UN Secretary-General shall do the same.

Paragraphs 8 and 9 of Article 76 make clear that once the limits of the shelf are established they cannot be revised. The requirement under Article 76(9) to deposit charts and other information 'permanently describing' the outer limits of the continental shelf operates to prevent States from adjusting that limit at all—whether on the basis of redrawn baselines, new claims regarding submarine geology, or any other grounds.[165] There is no evidence whatsoever that States believed that baselines would necessarily shift with the coast and sought to secure the limits of the continental shelf against such change. It is significant in this regard that Article 76(8) also provides that the limits of the extended shelf, established on the basis of recommendations by the CLCS, 'shall be final and binding'. These limits are ordinarily independent of the baseline[166] and there is no indication that States were concerned that physical changes might affect 'the outer edge of the continental margin'.

There is no reason to think that the outer limits of the shelf would be unstable as a consequence of fluctuations in the low-water line or other coastal change in the absence of UNCLOS Article 76(8) and (9). Once established, zonal limits, like baselines, remain fixed and effective unless and until they are actively changed by the coastal State (where such change is permitted). It is unnecessary to expressly 'fix' baselines or zonal limits, whether temporarily or permanently, to ensure stability in this regard. Stability is achieved by regulating the initial establishment of maritime limits and, where permitted, any subsequent revision of the same. The

[164] UNCLOS Art 76(9).

[165] Notably, a limit already established beyond 200M will, if consistent with the detailed rules set out in Article 76, be located at the outer edge of the continental margin. It could not therefore be substantially adjusted in either direction, landward or seaward, and continue to meet the relevant criteria for construction—though more minor adjustments could be made consistently with these rules. More substantial change could only be effected by the application of an alternative method of delineation permitted by Article 76.

[166] Only the outer constraint of 350M (one of two alternatives) is measured from the baseline: UNCLOS Art 76(5).

redrawing of baselines and zonal limits is subject to the same rules and principles as their initial establishment (unless the law has changed in the interim).

Paragraphs 8 and 9 of Article 76 are not required to reinforce the basic understanding that established zonal limits will remain in place notwithstanding coastal change. Rather, Article 76(9) removes the option ordinarily available to the coastal State to adjust its baselines and the limits measured from them. This means that any baseline adjustment subsequent to the establishment of the limits of the continental shelf will, exceptionally, be denied any effect on those limits where they are defined by distance. Article 76(8) similarly provides that limits established beyond 200M based on seabed geomorphology (and subject to an outer constraint based on distance or a combination of distance and depth) must be established once for all time. In both cases, the aim is not to prevent coastal change from affecting zonal limits but to prevent ever-expanding national claims to the seabed area and its resources. The only 'negative implication' is that the coastal State as a general rule retains the right to relocate the outer limits of other maritime zones, either by changing the baseline or defining limits at less than the maximum distance from the baseline permitted by law.

5

Fluidity in Maritime Boundaries

The Law of the Sea Treaties

I. Introduction

The characterization of baselines and (most) zonal limits measured from them as 'ambulatory' is not usually extended to international maritime boundaries, though it has been suggested—most prominently by Alfred Soons[1]—that a boundary defined as the median line may have this fluid character. More commonly, the stability of boundaries between States is emphasized as a point of contrast with allegedly ambulatory baselines and (some) maritime limits, even if it is proposed that the latter should be rendered similarly stable by securing them against subsequent geographical change (a measure generally understood to require a change in the law).

The assumption that baselines and most maritime limits are ambulatory, challenged above, is not the only problem here. This analysis also obscures important dimensions of the principle of stability in connection with international boundaries both on land and at sea. What is lacking is a clear understanding of when, why, and how geographical change may be legally significant for boundaries between States. A better understanding of this 'when, why, and how' reveals the consistency between the law governing maritime limits and the law relating to international maritime boundaries, which in neither case takes a default position of leaving such legally, politically, and economically significant lines vulnerable to the vagaries of nature. The analysis supporting this conclusion will be further developed in the following chapters, but it is appropriate to begin by considering whether the law of the sea treaties have anything to say about the implications of geographical change for international maritime boundaries.

While the treaty law does not deal explicitly with the implications of geographical change for maritime boundaries, there is a provision in the 1958 Convention on the Continental Shelf (CSC) that demands further attention. Article 6(3) provides that

> [i]n delimiting the boundaries of the continental shelf, any lines which are drawn in accordance with the principles set out in paragraphs 1 and 2 of this article should

[1] Soons, 'The Effects of a Rising Sea Level', 226–7.

Geographical Change and the Law of the Sea. Kate Purcell, Oxford University Press (2019). © Kate Purcell.
DOI: 10.1093/oso/9780198743644.001.0001

> be defined with reference to charts and geographical features as they exist at a particular date, and reference should be made to fixed permanent identifiable points on the land.

Somewhat surprisingly, proponents of the ambulatory thesis have not made mention of this provision. This may be a consequence of a primary focus on maritime limits coupled with the assumption that maritime boundaries are a very different case. Yet it is surely necessary to consider what this provision might imply about the legal consequences of geographical change. It is also necessary to consider the potential significance of the *absence* of parallel provisions in the Convention on the Territorial Sea and Contiguous Zone (TSC) and the United Nations Convention on the Law of the Sea (UNCLOS).

II. Article 6(3) of the CSC

As demonstrated in Chapter 4, the work of the Seabed Committee and the record of negotiations at UNCLOS III do not support Caron's suggestion that Article 76(9) was a response to the threat of geographical change affecting the location of the baseline and thus the zonal limits measured from it. Strangely neglected by Caron and other proponents of the ambulatory thesis, however, is the United Kingdom's response to the 1956 draft article by the International Law Commission (ILC) on the delimitation of the shelf between two or more States[2] and its related proposal for the amendment of this provision at the 1958 Law of the Sea Conference (LOSC).[3] This is particularly surprising given the relevant part of the British proposal was adopted as Article 6(3) of the CSC.[4]

In the ILC's final report to the UN General Assembly in 1956, draft article 72 dealt with the delimitation of the shelf in two separate but similarly worded paragraphs applying to opposite and adjacent States, respectively. Both paragraphs provided that the boundary 'shall be determined by agreement' but went on to specify that 'in the absence of agreement, and unless another boundary line is justified by special circumstances', the boundary would be the median line.[5] At the 1958 LOSC, the UK proposed inter alia the addition of a third paragraph, which provided that

> any lines which are drawn in accordance with the principles set out in paragraphs 1 and 2 of this article shall be defined with reference to charts and geographical

[2] UK Note Verbale, 20 September 1957: UNCLOS I: I, 105. See also UK comments on the same draft articles in the ILC's report on its fifth session in 1953: ILC Ybk 1956/II, 87.

[3] UNCLOS I: VI, 134.

[4] UNCLOS I: VI, 98; UNCLOS I: II, 15.

[5] ILC Ybk 1956/II, 300.

> features as they exist at a particular date, and reference shall be made to fixed permanent identifiable points on the land.[6]

At the request of the US delegate Marjorie Whiteman, the UK replaced the words 'shall be' with 'should be'.[7] The proposed text was adopted without further substantive amendment.[8]

Whiteman's concern to rephrase this part of the proposed text as a recommendation rather than an obligation followed from the fact that the new paragraph had been drafted with a particular type of boundary in mind. The UK had argued and Whiteman had agreed that 'paragraph 3 … would give the *median line*, once established, greater stability'.[9] Yet Whiteman appears to have been concerned that the term 'shall' in this connection might imply that the construction of a median line must play a role in every delimitation and 'she did not feel that States should be bound in advance to reach agreement in a particular way'.[10]

This was a reasonable concern. The UK's proposed third paragraph was an element of a broader proposal which, in its original form, substantially altered the first two paragraphs of the ILC's draft article. The UK had proposed changes that were clearly designed to give priority to the median line in negotiations between States as well as in circumstances where they could not agree on a boundary. In the British view, a median line was 'the fairest method of establishing a sea boundary'[11] and the 'best starting point for negotiations'.[12]

The UK initially proposed that reference to the possibility of using 'another boundary line' where 'justified by special circumstances' should be removed from both paragraphs of the ILC's draft article.[13] It did not deny that special circumstances might warrant a departure from the median line—the British delegate Commander RH Kennedy even identified examples of such circumstances.[14] Yet the UK thought that States negotiating a boundary should be encouraged to adopt the median line.[15] The UK also appears to have thought that special circumstances would only warrant a departure from a median line where States *agreed* that this was necessary. According to the UK proposal, a median line would apply in all circumstances where agreement could not be reached.[16]

The UK subsequently revised its proposal to reinstate the reference to special circumstances, though it seems to have maintained the view that States would have

6 UNCLOS I: VI, 134.
7 Ibid, 96.
8 Ibid, 98.
9 Ibid, 96 (emphasis added).
10 Ibid.
11 Ibid, 93.
12 Ibid, 92–3, 96.
13 Ibid, 92, 134.
14 Ibid, 93.
15 Ibid, 92–3, 96.
16 Ibid, 134.

to agree to any boundary other than the median line. The British delegate Joyce Gutteridge advised the Committee that the UK had 'restored the reference … to "special circumstances" which might lead the States concerned to *agree* to adopt another boundary than the median line'.[17] This gloss does not seem to be consistent with the text or the views of other States seeking to retain the clause. Indeed, the US insisted that the reference to special circumstances should be retained precisely because 'it was impracticable to expect that all special circumstances could be dealt with by agreement'.[18]

The UK's clear preference for a median line as the boundary in the shelf helps to make sense of its proposed third paragraph. The recommendation that boundaries be defined by reference to charts and geographical features 'at a particular date' as well as 'fixed permanent identifiable points on land' (originally framed as a requirement) was prompted by concerns that the UK associated with a median line in particular. Both the original proposal and Article 6 as adopted specify that paragraph 3 applies to 'any lines which are drawn in accordance with the principles set out in paragraphs 1 and 2' on the delimitation of the shelf between opposite and adjacent States. Of course, the first two paragraphs of Article 6 as adopted allow not only for a median line but other boundaries in the shelf established by agreement or on the basis of special circumstances. The UK's proposed third paragraph, however, was submitted together with an amendment to the ILC's draft article that would have privileged the median line.[19]

The UK had identified the variability of the low-water line as a potential problem in connection with the median line prior to the 1958 LOSC. Commenting on the ILC's draft article on the delimitation of the shelf in 1956,[20] it presented its concerns as relating to 'the application of an exact median line'.[21] It suggested that this exercise, 'which is a matter of considerable complexity, would in many instances be open to the objection that the geographical configuration of the coast made it inequitable, and that the base lines (i.e., the low-water mark of the coast) were liable to physical change in the course of time'.[22] On this basis it recommended the application of 'the principle of the median line: that is, an approximate or simplified median line based as closely as circumstances allow on an exact median line and drawn on a specific chart of a specific date.'[23] Notably, the UK at this time made exactly the same comments with respect to the ILC's draft article on the delimitation of the territorial sea between opposite States.[24] With regard to what was then draft article 7 on the delimitation of the continental shelf, the UK proposed the

17 Ibid, 96 (emphasis added).
18 Ibid, 95.
19 Ibid, 134.
20 See ILC Ybk 1953/II, 213 (draft articles); ILC Ybk 1956/II, 87 (UK comments).
21 ILC Ybk 1956/II, 87.
22 Ibid.
23 Ibid.
24 Ibid, 85. For the text of the draft article see ILC Ybk 1955/II, 38.

addition of a new third paragraph providing that '[l]ines shall be marked on the largest scale charts available which are officially recognised'.[25] It did not make a parallel proposal with regard to the draft articles on the delimitation of the territorial sea between opposite and adjacent States because the same text was already included as paragraph two of those provisions.[26]

In 1956, then, the UK's concern that boundaries based on the 'principle of equidistance' in both the continental shelf and the territorial sea should be defined by reference to 'a specific chart of a specific date' was apparently satisfied by the inclusion of a general charting requirement. The nature of this solution clarifies the UK's understanding of the problem, which seems to have been that the liability of the low-water line 'to physical change in the course of time' would make it difficult to identify the location of, and so respect, a median line boundary over time. The UK did not consider the variability of the low-water line to mean that a median line would be ambulatory—indeed, the operative assumption was that such a boundary would ordinarily be fixed.

The ILC's decision to include charting requirements in its draft articles on the delimitation of the territorial sea was also intended to ensure that established boundaries could be identified and respected over time. The Commission does not seem to have considered the variability of the low-water line to imply that a median line boundary—or any other boundary constructed by reference to the coastal configuration—would shift with subsequent geographical change.

The ILC's Special Rapporteur François had recommended the delimitation of the territorial sea between adjacent States by a median line in his first report on the regime of the territorial sea in 1952.[27] Following discussions with the Commission, it was agreed that he should seek both expert advice and further information from governments on their practice before an article to this effect was included in the draft.[28] In 1953, François revised his second report on the regime of the territorial sea to endorse inter alia the recommendation of the Committee of Experts that the delimitation of the territorial sea between *both* opposite and adjacent States should be governed by a general rule of equidistance.[29] The draft article on delimitation between opposite States proposed by the Special Rapporteur further recognized (in accordance with recommendations of the Committee of Experts) that this rule may be departed from where necessary for 'special reasons'.[30] It was also specified—again in the case of opposite States only—that '[l]a ligne devrait

[25] ILC Ybk 1956/II, 86.
[26] See draft Arts 14 and 15 in ILC Ybk 1955/II, 38.
[27] ILC Ybk 1952/II, 38.
[28] See discussion in ILC Ybk 1952/I, 180–6 and ILC Ybk 1956/II, 68. Article 13 was omitted from the original version of the Special Rapporteur's second report of February 1953 pending consultation with experts scheduled for the following month: ILC Ybk 1953/II, 59.
[29] ILC Ybk 1953/II, 77.
[30] Ibid.

être tracée sur les cartes en service à grande échelle, surtout lorsqu'une partie quelconque de l'étendue d'eau est étroite et relativement tortueuse'.[31]

While the Commission postponed further consideration of the regime of the territorial sea until the following session in 1954,[32] it drew on the report of the Committee of Experts in its formulation of a new draft article on the delimitation of the continental shelf between both opposite and adjacent States.[33] (The Committee of Experts expressly noted that it had tried to find formulas for delimiting the territorial sea that were equally applicable to the shelf).[34] The two paragraphs of the ILC's new draft article (later adopted with minor amendments as the first two paragraphs of Article 6 of the CSC) provided that, unless States agreed otherwise, the default boundary would be the median line (or a boundary 'determined by application of the principle of equidistance').[35] The new provision also recognized that a departure from the rule of equidistance may be justified by special circumstances in the case of both opposite and adjacent States.[36] It did not, however, include a charting requirement along the lines of that proposed by the Committee of Experts and endorsed by Special Rapporteur François with respect to the delimitation of the territorial sea between opposite States.

In 1954, the ILC adopted parallel rules for the delimitation of the territorial sea between both opposite and adjacent States. In his third report, Special Rapporteur François had also included a third paragraph in each of these articles providing that '[l]a ligne sera tracée sur les cartes en service à grande échelle'.[37] These paragraphs appear to have been unintentionally omitted in the draft adopted by the Commission in 1954. This is properly identified as a drafting error—in fact, the third paragraph on charting had been unanimously adopted by the Commission during the debate in the case of the draft article on delimitation of the territorial sea between opposite States.[38] Efforts to reformulate the first two paragraphs of the provisions on the delimitation of the territorial sea to align with the provision on the delimitation of the continental shelf (which did not include any reference to charting) seem to have resulted in the unintentional omission of this third paragraph.[39]

The error was rectified in 1955 with the reinstatement of charting requirements in relation to territorial sea boundaries between both opposite and adjacent

31 Ibid, 77, 79.
32 Ibid, 201.
33 Ibid, 213 (draft Art 7).
34 Ibid, 79.
35 Ibid, 213 and commentary, 216. This was a significant shift from its preliminary draft of 1951 which provided that States 'should establish boundaries in the area of the continental shelf by agreement' and that '[f]ailing agreement, the parties are under the obligation to have the boundaries fixed by arbitration': ILC Ybk 1951/II, 145.
36 ILC Ybk 1953/II, 213 and commentary, 216.
37 ILC Ybk 1954/II, 6.
38 ILC Ybk 1954/I, 102–3.
39 Ibid.

States.[40] As the articles on the continental shelf were not reopened for debate by the ILC after their submission to the UN General Assembly in 1953,[41] the absence of a parallel provision with respect to interstate boundaries in the continental shelf was not discussed. In its commentary on its draft articles of 1956, however, the ILC noted that

> There would be certain advantages in having the boundary lines [in the continental shelf] marked on official large-scale charts. But as it is less important to users of such charts to have this information than to know the boundary of the territorial sea, the Commission refrained from imposing any obligation in the matter.[42]

This indicates that, for the ILC, the chief rationale for charting requirements was not securing established boundaries against subsequent alteration as a consequence of changes in either the coast or legal baselines. It was to ensure that sea users were aware of the location of boundaries of significance to their activities.

The final comments of governments on the ILC draft in advance of the 1958 LOSC included a *note verbale* from the UK in which it observed that while '[c]oast lines, and thus the baselines for measuring the width of territorial waters, are liable to alter in the course of time', '[b]oundaries through continental shelves should not be susceptible to any movement depending on nature'.[43] At the 1958 LOSC, Commander Kennedy explained that the UK's proposal regarding the charting of boundaries in the shelf was a response to both the variability of the low-water line and the fact that many charts were out of date and time-consuming to revise.[44] These considerations, he argued, recommended that 'turning points of boundary lines should be related to fixed points on land, such as a church, a beacon, or a lighthouse' and boundaries defined 'with reference to charts and to geographical features as they exist at a particular date'.[45] Kennedy emphasized that 'once a boundary was fixed by agreement, it must be entirely independent of the low-water line', which 'varied from year to year, particularly at the mouths of rivers'.[46] He was not concerned that States might rely on charts that were already out of date, actively recommending the definition of boundaries by reference to currently available charts though 'many of these were extremely old'.[47] He also recommended, however, that 'the States involved should reach agreement on what chart was used,

40 ILC Ybk 1955/II, 51.
41 See ILC Ybk 1953/II, 223; ILC Ybk 1955/I, 10.
42 ILC Ybk 1956/II, 300.
43 UNCLOS I: I, 105.
44 UNCLOS I: VI, 93.
45 UNCLOS I: VI, 93, 134.
46 Ibid.
47 UNCLOS I: VI, 93, 134.

as charts differed considerably, depending on the date on which they were drawn, and those "officially recognized" by the State might not conform in every detail'.[48]

The British proposal was evidently motivated by a concern to ensure that the location of international boundaries in the continental shelf, understood to be fixed at the point of establishment, could be clearly identified over time. Kennedy was particular concerned to pre-empt future disputes between the parties to a boundary agreement regarding its location. It is in this sense that the additional paragraph was understood to contribute to the stability of established boundaries.

Kennedy's comments on the variability of 'the baselines used for measuring the breadth of the territorial sea' are more ambiguous. He describes '[c]oast lines, and thus the baselines for measuring the width of territorial waters' as 'liable to alter in the course of time' and 'susceptible to ... movement depending on nature'— insisting that international boundaries in the continental shelf should not share these characteristics.[49] This may appear to reflect a belief that baselines used for the purposes of unilateral delimitation—the low-water line in particular—are ambulatory, necessitating corresponding changes to maritime limits. However, it is not at all clear that the UK considered coastal change to *require* changes to the location of established maritime baselines and limits.

Kennedy's comments are also consistent with the understanding that the coastal State is entitled—though not obliged—to adjust maritime limits in response to geographical change. Given Kennedy's concern to ensure agreement between States on a clearly identifiable and fixed boundary in the continental shelf, the point of difference being emphasized here may well be the freedom of the coastal State to unilaterally respond to natural changes to the coastline by adjusting established maritime limits. Kennedy was concerned to ensure that the vagaries of nature would not make the location of an established boundary between States in the continental shelf difficult to ascertain or unsettle the parties' agreement on its location.

Britain's proposed third paragraph on the delimitation of the shelf between States provoked little response at the 1958 LOSC. The US delegate thought that 'the amendment would give the median line, once established, greater stability' but did not specify why.[50] She may have agreed that specifying the location of a boundary in this way would facilitate its observance and prevent ongoing disputes over its location.

TheYugoslavian delegate observed that 'while he was not convinced of the usefulness of paragraph 3 of the United Kingdom proposal, he had no objection to the proposal as a whole and would vote in favour of it'.[51]There is no record of his reasons for doubting the utility of the British amendment. In view of

[48] UNCLOS I: VI, 93.
[49] UNCLOS I: I, 105.
[50] UNCLOS I: VI, 95.
[51] Ibid, 92.

the UK's insistence that coastal change over a relatively short time frame could be substantial—a factual claim that was not challenged—it is unlikely that Yugoslavia was simply confident that changes to the low-water line or other coastal features were too insignificant to raise concerns.[52] It is notable that the British emphasis on the high degree of coastal variability did not alter Yugoslavia's evaluation of its proposed amendment as unnecessary though innocuous.

Most States accepted the British amendment without comment. This was presumably due to its broad consistency with the law relating to international boundaries. No State seems to have considered the provision necessary to prevent the movement of international maritime boundaries in the event of coastal change or the updating of maps and charts to show such change. The largely silent assent suggests that States agreed that boundaries in the shelf would ordinarily remain fixed, whether or not they were constructed by reference to the low-water line. It also suggests that most States understood the provision to ensure that the location of such boundaries was clearly agreed upon and could be ascertained over time. It is possible that the Yugoslavian delegate (mis)understood the provision to be directed towards securing boundaries in the shelf against subsequent coastal change. This would make sense of his view that the provision was unnecessary—there being no assumption that such boundaries would otherwise be ambulatory.

It is interesting to compare Britain's concern with the variability of the low-water line with the concerns expressed by several other States regarding the difficulty of identifying the low-water line on certain types of coast. The Iranian delegate, for example, explained his country's preference for the high-water mark given practical difficulties relating to surveying and charting the low-water line where sediment deposit left extensive mudflats exposed at low-tide.[53] His particular concern was that 'it would be almost impossible to identify the low-water line by visual observation or photography', a method understood to be 'more practicable for the high-water mark'.[54] Iran recommended the use of the high-water mark as the baseline for constructing a median line in these circumstances.[55]

The British delegate, Commander Kennedy, reframed the Iranian proposal in line with his own concerns, observing that 'while the high-water line did not move as rapidly as the low-water line, it was nevertheless liable to move, and in certain places ... had moved seaward by several miles in the course of about 50 years'.[56] In response, the Iranian delegate clarified that

52 Ibid, 93–4.

53 Ibid, 92. See also ABLOS, *Manual on Technical Aspects of UNCLOS* (4th edn, IHB, 2006), 24–5.

54 This was a particular concern in the Persian Gulf (presumably the Shatt al-Arab delta). The Iranian delegate did concede that low-water might be determined 'by calculation from the high-water mark and time measurements' but remained concerned that 'there were many areas where no tide measurements had been made and where it might be necessary to define a boundary line for the continental shelf in the near future.': UNCLOS I: VI, 92.

55 Ibid.

56 Kennedy dismissed Iran's proposal on this basis. UNCLOS I: VI, 92. The misunderstanding may have been encouraged by the delegate for the Netherlands, who enquired 'whether the thought

> whereas the United Kingdom proposal was intended to prevent any subsequent fluctuation of the boundary once it had been defined, the purpose of the Iranian amendment was to permit some measure of relaxation of the general rule followed in delimiting the boundary to the extent of referring to the high-water mark rather than the low-water mark where an exceptional geographical configuration or other circumstances might justify such a departure.[57]

This is not an accurate account of the intention underlying the UK proposal, which was not designed to 'prevent any subsequent fluctuation of the boundary' but to ensure that its location, once established, could be ascertained over time. It nevertheless clarifies that Iran's concern with the variability of the low-water line was not due to any belief that a boundary measured therefrom would be ambulatory.

Iran's proposal was concerned with practicality in the establishment of baselines used to construct maritime limits and boundaries. The ILC had shared this concern. It had dismissed, for example, South Africa's suggestion that 'in certain cases the seaward edge of the surf should be taken as the point of departure in measuring the breadth of the territorial sea' on the grounds that it 'could not be given practical effect.'[58] Special Rapporteur François observed that

> it would be most impracticable to try and measure the territorial sea from the 'surf line' because the surf line was very much dependent on atmospheric conditions. In his own country, the Netherlands, the surf line was very near the coast with calm seas, but extended to several hundred metres when there was wind, and even further in case of storm.[59]

Variability, in this case due to local weather conditions, was considered problematic not because it might affect the baseline and the limits of the territorial sea once established but due to the difficulty of identifying '*the* surf line' in order to establish the baseline in the first place.

It is worth noting that the British proposal adopted as CSC Article 6(3) came from Commander Kennedy, a former member of the British Navy and an expert in hydrography serving as Naval Assistant in the British Hydrographic Department at the time of the Conference.[60] Kennedy was expert adviser to the UK in the *Anglo-Norwegian Fisheries* dispute and a member of the Expert Committee consulted

underlying both [the UK and Iranian] proposals was that the low-water mark was not necessarily stable, but might shift as a result of sedimentation': ibid. It is interesting that instability due to sedimentation rather than coastal retreat was again the primary concern.

57 UNCLOS I: VI, 94.
58 ILC Ybk 1956/II, 24.
59 ILC Ybk 1955/I, 196.
60 Hansard, HC (series 5) vol 582, col 1187 (19 February 1958).

by Special Rapporteur François in 1953. He prepared a 'geographical and hydrographical study of straits' at the request of the UN Secretariat for circulation to participants in the 1958 LOSC.[61] He was also responsible for an influential paper describing the construction of equidistance lines between opposite and adjacent States presented by the UK to the Conference.[62] As a 'widely respected expert on maritime boundary delimitation', Kennedy played a part in the negotiation of several maritime boundaries by the UK, and his work in this regard featured in at least two later disputes.[63]

Kennedy's valuable contribution in each context was as a technical expert—a hydrographer acutely aware of the changeability of the coastline and a retired Navy Commander acutely aware of the concerns and requirements of the mariner. This background makes sense of his efforts to ensure that the location of boundaries in the continental shelf would be clearly defined and assented to by neighbouring States as well as being identifiable and observable over time. Kennedy's emphasis upon the importance of stable maritime boundaries in this regard was and remains entirely consistent with the law and politics of international boundary-making at the time and since. Far from implying that a median line boundary will ordinarily be ambulatory, Article 6(3) of the CSC as adopted clearly reflects an understanding that maritime boundaries, including a median line, will not be ambulatory unless expressly provided.

III. From the CSC to UNCLOS

It remains significant that those elements of Article 6(3) requiring reference to 'charts and geographical features as they exist at a particular date, and ... fixed permanent identifiable points on the land' were not retained in the provisions relating to the interstate delimitation of the continental shelf in UNCLOS. Nor were they reproduced in any other provision relating to the delimitation of maritime space between opposite or adjacent States.

UNCLOS Article 83 provides that the'delimitation of the continental shelf between States with opposite or adjacent coasts shall be effected by agreement on the basis of international law ... in order to achieve an equitable solution'. A parallel

[61] UNCLOS I: I, 114.

[62] RH Kennedy, 'Brief Remarks on Median Lines and Lines of Equidistance and the Methods Used in their Construction', provided by the UK delegation to the first United Nations Law of the Sea Conference, 2 April 1958; S Ferrero et al, 'An Algorithm for the Unambiguous Determination of the Equidistant Boundary Line Between Two (or More) Coastlines' (2009) 1 *Applied Geomatics* 49, 49–50.

[63] The equidistance line constructed by Kennedy and included in a 1961 draft treaty between British Guiana and Surinam (Dutch Guiana) played a role in *Guyana v Suriname* (2007): see *British Draft Treaty—British Guiana/Surinam Boundary* (1961) in Guyana Memorial, Annex 90. The Boggs-Kennedy report of 16 November 1948 on maritime delimitation in the Gulf played a role in *Qatar v Bahrain* (2001): see esp Qatar Memorial (Merits), 234, and Annex IV, 123.

provision governs the delimitation of the exclusive economic zone (EEZ) between States.[64] The 1975 Informal Single Negotiating Text (ISNT) had echoed CSC Article 6(3) in connection with both the delimitation of the continental shelf and the delimitation of the EEZ, providing that 'any lines which are drawn in accordance with the provisions of this article should be defined with reference to charts and geographical features as they exist at a particular date, and reference should be made to fixed permanent identifiable points on the land'.[65] The Revised Single Negotiating Text (RSNT) replaced this text with a requirement to identify delimitation lines on charts or by lists of coordinates, which were to be given due publicity and deposited with the UN Secretary-General and, in the case of boundaries in the shelf, the Secretary-General of the International Seabed Authority.[66] These provisions were adopted as UNCLOS Articles 75 and 84.[67]

This reformulation of the charting requirements was based on a Canadian proposal,[68] but the 1958 TSC had already provided that '[t]he line of delimitation between the territorial seas of two States lying opposite to each other or adjacent to each other shall be marked on large-scale charts officially recognized by the coastal States'.[69] This language was reproduced as draft Article 13(2) of the ISNT at UNCLOS III.

The obligation to mark boundaries in the territorial sea on large-scale charts was intended inter alia to ensure due publicity. In the RSNT, this charting requirement was moved to a separate article providing more broadly that straight baselines, closing lines, lines delimiting roadsteads, and interstate boundaries in the territorial sea must be 'shown on charts of a scale or scales adequate for determining them' or '[a]lternatively, a list of geographical co-ordinates of points, specifying the geodetic datum, may be substituted'.[70] It was also provided that 'the coastal State shall give due publicity to such charts or lists of geographical co-ordinates and shall deposit a copy of each such chart or list with the Secretary-General of the United Nations'.[71] Both the reference to coordinates and the express deposit and due publicity requirements seem to have been inspired by the Blue Paper prepared by the informal working group on baselines in 1974 (though that Paper did not directly comment on interstate boundaries in the territorial sea).[72] The RSNT harmonized

64 UNCLOS Art 74.
65 UNCLOS III: IV, 162–3.
66 RSNT, draft Articles 63, 72 in UNCLOS III: V, 164–5.
67 Ibid.
68 Platzöder (1983/IV), 316.
69 TSC Art 12(2).
70 RSNT, Art 15(1) in UNCLOS III: V, 155–6.
71 RSNT, Art 15(2) in UNCLOS III: V, 156.
72 Baselines C.2/Blue Paper No 4, 9 April 1975 in Platzöder (1983/IV), 126–8. Deposit and due publicity requirements were provided in each of the baselines provisions. The provision on straight baselines referred to the use of coordinates, though as supplementary information rather than a substitute for charted lines.

the charting and due publicity obligations applying to boundaries in the territorial sea, the EEZ, and the continental shelf.[73]

There is no reason to think that it was considered unnecessary to refer to 'charts and geographical features as they exist at a particular date, and ... fixed permanent identifiable points on the land' because of the shift from a default median line in the CSC to delimitation aimed at an 'equitable solution' in UNCLOS. Article 83 does not require an equidistance-special circumstances approach to the delimitation of the shelf; however, a median line may still play a role in or constitute an 'equitable solution'. There is equally no evidence that the terms used in Article 6(3) were dropped to make room for the possibility of establishing an ambulatory boundary, though, as we shall see in the following chapter, this option is not excluded by the law (which is not to say that a median line boundary will *necessarily* be ambulatory).

It seems that the fluidity or otherwise of international maritime boundaries wasn't a live issue at UNCLOS III. This is not surprising—the matter was already clearly and adequately addressed by established rules and principles of international law supporting the stability of international boundaries.[74] In this context, it is most likely that the measures in CSC Article 6(3) that provoked so little reaction at the 1958 LOSC were simply considered unnecessary. As the text of UNCLOS itself makes clear, the charting requirements applying to international boundaries in the territorial sea, EEZ, and continental shelf reflect a concern to ensure that States and sea users can '[ascertain] their position'.[75] They do not operate to fix boundaries that would otherwise be ambulatory.

At the 1958 LOSC, Britain did not seek to amend the charting requirements relating to boundaries in the territorial sea to echo its proposed third paragraph on the delimitation of the continental shelf. Yet the UK did not claim that boundaries in the shelf had any special qualities or significance meaning that special care should be taken to ensure that their location could be identified over time. Nor did it suggest that boundaries in the shelf required express assurance that, once established, their location would remain fixed. The UK did not raise the same concerns regarding the variability of the low-water line in connection with the unilaterally established limits of the shelf, though this may be explained by the fact that these limits were not at the time defined by distance from the baseline but rather depth or exploitability.[76] It remains striking that where unilaterally established limits *were* defined relative to the baseline (i.e. the limits of the territorial sea and contiguous zone) neither the UK nor any other State participating in the 1958 LOSC raised concerns regarding instability due to fluctuations of the

[73] RSNT Arts 15, 63, 72 in UNCLOS III: V, 155–6, 164–5.
[74] These rules and principles are discussed in Chapter 6.
[75] See UNCLOS Arts 16, 74, 85.
[76] CSC 1958 Art 1.

low-water line or other types of coastal change. Indeed, other than the introduction of Article 7(2) at UNCLOS III—which at least suggests the possibility that such a concern was raised during informal discussions of the Baselines Working Group—there is no indication that the implications of geographical change for unilaterally established maritime limits were discussed at any one of the three law of the sea conferences.

IV. Conclusion

A review of CSC Article 6(3) and its drafting history shows that this provision was developed with a view to ensuring that the location of boundaries constructed by the equidistance method in particular—that is, a median or equidistance line—could be clearly identified and so respected over time. Significantly, this does not mean that a boundary constructed or defined in this way was generally understood to be ambulatory. Article 6(3) did not exceptionally fix interstate boundaries in the continental shelf against subsequent geographical change. Instead, it expressly specified techniques to ensure that the original location of a median or equidistance line could continue to be identified notwithstanding changes to the physical coast or updates to charts.

It is important to recognize that the reasons that account for the permanence of the unilaterally established limits of the continental shelf under UNCLOS do not apply to interstate boundaries in the continental shelf. As elaborated in Chapter 4, UNCLOS Article 76 responds to the need for clearly defined and permanent limits between national jurisdiction in the seabed and the common heritage of mankind in the 'Area'. Where the continental shelf is delimited between States, the boundary in question will not also delimit the 'Area'. Any stability guaranteed by law in this case can be distinguished from the permanence considered necessary for the limits of the shelf where they also serve as the limits of the 'Area'.

Article 6(3) of the CSC reflects a concern to ensure the stability of maritime boundaries generally. It remains significant that no similar provision was included in the otherwise almost identical rules governing the delimitation of the territorial sea under both the TSC and UNCLOS or the provisions on the delimitation of the EEZ and continental shelf in the 1982 Convention. But this cannot be taken to signify an understanding that the maritime boundaries governed by these provisions will necessarily be ambulatory—even if they are defined as a median or equidistance line. Instead, it reflects the fact that ordinary charting requirements were considered sufficient to ensure that the location of an established maritime boundary could be observed over time. The fact that a parallel provision to CSC Article 6(3) was considered unnecessary confirms that States at both the 1958 LOSC and UNCLOS III understood Article 6(3) to be concerned with ensuring that a boundary could be accurately located over time. They did not consider CSC

Article 6(3) to secure maritime boundaries in the shelf against change due to subsequent fluctuations in the low-water line.

As noted above, the idea that a boundary described as a median line may be ambulatory has been advanced by Soons and picked up by other commentators considering the implications of climate-related change for maritime jurisdiction. While Soons does not base this argument on the text of the law of the sea treaties, revisiting the treaty law provides insight into the legal considerations bearing upon a determination of the implications of geographical change for maritime boundaries. In short, it supports the conclusion that a median line boundary is not necessarily ambulatory. By providing for the identification of its location over time despite coastal change, the law indicates that such a boundary was generally understood to be fixed. As Chapter 6 will illustrate, this conclusion is supported by the jurisprudence of international courts and tribunals regarding both land and maritime boundaries—though it remains possible to establish ambulatory boundaries of all types, including those defined as the median line.

There is another element of the treaty law that bears upon the question of whether and when an international maritime boundary may be ambulatory. The 1958 TSC and CSC prioritize delimitation by agreement between neighbouring States, in the absence of which they provide for delimitation by equidistance unless another boundary is justified by 'special circumstances'.[77] UNCLOS Article 15 sets out a parallel provision with respect to the delimitation of the territorial sea. UNCLOS Articles 74 and 83 provide simply that the delimitation of the EEZ and continental shelf (in practice often by a single maritime boundary, at least up to 200M) 'shall be effected by agreement on the basis of international law, as referred to in Article 38 of the [ICJ] Statute … in order to achieve an equitable solution'. Articles 74 and 83 also expressly provide that '[w]here there is an agreement in force between the States concerned, questions relating to the delimitation of the exclusive economic zone/continental shelf shall be determined in accordance with the provisions of that agreement'.

The treaty law clearly reflects the importance of agreement in interstate delimitation, which is otherwise well established. The International Court of Justice has characterized the requirement to delimit overlapping entitlement to maritime space by agreement as a principle of international law.[78] In this regard, it is worth bearing in mind that delimitation by arbitral award or judicial decision is also delimitation by agreement—as Thirlway has observed, the resulting boundaries are also 'agreed' insofar as 'the parties have agreed that the line that the judicial body pronounces shall be accepted'.[79]

[77] TSC Art 12; CSC Art 6.
[78] *Gulf of Maine Case* (1984), 291–2.
[79] Thirlway, 'The Law and Procedure of the ICJ 1960–1989: Supplement, 2007', 116, fn 395.

The role of agreement in the establishment of international boundaries bears upon the question of the implications of geographical change in this context. As the following chapter will demonstrate, the answer to this question does not depend upon a general rule. It is a question of what the States concerned have agreed to in a particular treaty, award, or judicial decision, or through their practice. Certain principles and presumptions inform a determination of whether States have agreed to an ambulatory or fixed boundary. As we shall see, the law admits both possibilities but indicates that an ambulatory character should not be presumed—particularly in the case of interstate boundaries at sea.

6

Principles and Presumptions in an Assessment of Boundary Fluidity

I. Introduction

Scholars considering the implications of climate change for maritime limits have also pointed to some possible implications for established maritime boundaries. Caron, for instance, has suggested that '[e]ven though states generally have a great interest in upholding the sanctity of ... [maritime boundary] agreements, it is entirely plausible that a state might argue that circumstances had changed in that the parties had not foreseen ... a rise in sea level'.[1] It has elsewhere been stressed that 'boundary treaties have a privileged status in the international law of treaties and are not subject to change even in the case of "subsequent fundamental change of circumstances"'.[2] The prospect of rising seas warranting the termination of or withdrawal from a boundary agreement due to 'impossibility of performance' has also been considered (and rejected) by Soons.[3]

Somewhat surprisingly, there has been little consideration of the logically prior question of whether and when a maritime boundary might shift in response to geographical change—though the answer must surely inform an assessment of whether such change can be grounds for terminating or withdrawing from a boundary treaty.[4] Soons' arguments regarding the fluidity of a boundary defined as a simple median or equidistance line represent a notable exception. Yet the law does not support his ready assumption that '[t]he States concerned have

[1] Caron, 'When Law Makes Climate Change Worse', 621, 641; Caron 'Climate Change, Sea Level Rise and the Coming Uncertainty in Oceanic Boundaries', 1, 13–14. Houghton et al similarly begin by asserting that '[s]ea level rise may ... profoundly affect ... maritime delimitations between states with opposite or adjacent coasts": Houghton et al, 'Maritime Boundaries in a Rising Sea', 813. Nevertheless, they also appear to recognize that the existing boundaries would have to be *renegotiated* to take into account 'new geographic realities'. The authors flag the possibility that this may be resisted and that an agreement may persist despite 'rendering the concept of equidistance historical (or fictional) rather than factual': ibid, 813–14. Both Caron and Houghton et al limit their discussion to what States 'might argue' and do not consider in detail which arguments might stand up as a matter of law.

[2] Schofield, 'Sea Level Rise and Options to Secure Maritime Jurisdictional Claims', 409–10. See also Soons, 'The Effects of a Rising Sea Level', 228; Prescott and Bird, 'The Influence of Rising Sea Levels on Baselines', 297; Rayfuse, 'International Law and Disappearing States', 5; Freestone and Pethick, 'Sea Level Rise and Maritime Boundaries', 77–8; Hayashi, 'Sea Level Rise and the Law of the Sea', 81.

[3] Soons, 'The Effects of a Rising Sea Level', 228.

[4] See Chapter 9. An earlier version of the author's views on this question can be found in K Purcell, 'Maritime Jurisdiction in a Changing Climate' in Gerrard and Kuh (eds), *The Law of Adaptation to Climate Change: US and International Aspects* (ABA, 2012) 731, 755–9.

Geographical Change and the Law of the Sea. Kate Purcell, Oxford University Press (2019). © Kate Purcell.
DOI: 10.1093/oso/9780198743644.001.0001

deliberately opted for a (potentially) fluctuating boundary line'.[5] Nor are the rules governing termination of or withdrawal from a boundary agreement a sufficient basis for the conclusion that all other maritime boundaries are 'fixed'.[6]

The question of whether a maritime boundary is 'fixed' or 'ambulatory' must be determined on a case-by-case basis. This is an exercise in interpretation governed by legal principles and presumptions that, significantly, have some parallel in the law relating to maritime limits. The content and consequences of these principles and presumptions require clarification. An examination of the considerations that inform a determination of whether an established boundary is 'fixed' or 'ambulatory' illuminates the way in which the law more generally manages stability and change in relation to boundaries of international significance. As we shall see, the law does not prohibit the establishment of an ambulatory maritime boundary but it does indicate that a fluid character should not be presumed. Understanding the legal rules and principles that account for this approach casts further light upon the principled basis for a system in which the coastal State is permitted to adjust maritime limits (other than the limits of the shelf) in response to geographical change but by no means required to do so.

II. Ambulatory International Boundaries: An Exercise in Interpretation

Under international law, boundaries between States must be established by their agreement. This is true of both land and maritime boundaries. The context for the priority given to agreement is inter alia international law's particular understanding and privileging of stability in an order of formally equal territorial States.[7] This context both illuminates and is illuminated by the more circumscribed role of agreement where the principle *uti possidetis juris* effects the transformation of former administrative divisions into international boundaries for newly independent States.[8] A boundary established in this way can still be modified by

[5] Soons, 'The Effects of a Rising Sea Level', 227.

[6] Ibid, 228.

[7] This is not to say that this vision of international order is unproblematic or in fact ensures equality between States. The *uti possidetis* principle points to the capacity of international law to entrench inequality in the same moment it asserts the formal equality of States.

[8] This principle is not limited in its application to land boundaries: a colonial administrative boundary in the sea may be inherited as a maritime boundary by operation of the principle *uti possidetis juris*: see: *Guinea-Bissau/Senegal* (1989), 36–7; M Shaw, The Heritage of States: The Principle of Uti Possidetis Juris Today' (1996) 67 *BYIL* 75, 127; M Kohen, Lecture on Uti Possidetis and Maritime Delimitations, UN Audiovisual Library of International Law, <http://legal.un.org/avl/ls/Kohen_BD.html>. It will, of course, be necessary to prove that there was an existing boundary to be preserved under this principle. On the difficulty of establishing the existence and location of colonial administrative maritime boundaries, see S Lalonde, 'The Role of the Uti Possidetis Juris Principle in the Resolution of Maritime Boundary Disputes' in Chinkin and Baetens (eds), *Sovereignty, Statehood and State Responsibility: Essays in Honour of James Crawford* (CUP, 2015) 248–72.

agreement, though the legal privileging of former administrative divisions may influence negotiations and raise the already high bar for determining that a new boundary has been established by tacit agreement.

For present purposes, it is important to recognize that the question of whether a *uti possidetis* boundary is ambulatory or not must be answered in the same way as the question of whether any established boundary is ambulatory. Where the principle *uti possidetis juris* applies, the answer will depend on the definition of the relevant administrative boundaries as well as the subsequent practice of the States who inherit them. The '"photograph" of the territorial situation' at the 'moment' of independence may '[freeze] the territorial title',[9] but it does not fix a boundary that was at that moment 'ambulatory'. In such a case, an ambulatory rather than fixed boundary will be preserved.

The role of agreement as the basis for the establishment of international boundaries is clearly recognized and reflected in the law of the sea treaties. As noted in the previous chapter, the delimitation of a maritime boundary by a third party is also properly understood as a means of establishing a boundary by agreement. The rules and principles applying to the interpretation of a treaty and the interpretation of an arbitral award or judicial decision are not entirely identical.[10] Common to both, however, is a concern to determine what was intended by the parties or the decision-maker. In both cases the law privileges what is sometimes distinguished as the 'objective' or 'declared' intention rather than 'subjective intention'.[11] This is chiefly evidenced by the text of the agreement, decision, or award and any associated maps or charts (the status of which may vary).[12] To determine the implications of subsequent geographical change for the established boundary, it is necessary to determine precisely what the parties can be understood to have agreed in this regard. Where a boundary has been established by tacit agreement, State practice will necessarily play a central role. The subsequent practice of States may also evidence their common understanding of the meaning of a boundary treaty.[13] In the case of a decision by a court or tribunal, the subsequent practice of the parties cannot help to illuminate the intention of the judges or arbitrator[14] but may be relevant as evidence of the parties' understanding and acceptance (or otherwise) of the decision

[9] *Burkina Faso/Mali* (1986), 568.

[10] *Encuentro/Palena* (1966), 174; *Laguna del Desierto* (1994), 25.

[11] See O Dörr, 'Article 31, General Rule of Interpretation' in Dörr and Schmalenbach (eds), *Vienna Convention on the Law of Treaties: A Commentary* (Springer, 2018) 560–1; J Sorel, V Eveno, 'Article 31, General Rule of Interpretation' in Corten and Klein (eds), *The Vienna Conventions on the Law of Treaties: A Commentary*, vol 1 (OUP, 2011) 804, 809, 812–17, 829.

[12] Dörr, 'Article 31, General Rule of Interpretation', 560–1; Sorel and Eveno, 'Article 31, General Rule of Interpretation', 809, 812–17, 829; A Alvarez-Jimenez, 'The International Court of Justice's Use of the Vienna Convention in the Interpretation of Boundary Agreements: 2000–10' (2012) 3 (2) *JIDS* 409–43; KH Kaikobad, *Interpretation and Revision of International Boundary Agreements* (CUP, 2007), Chs 5 and 6.

[13] Vienna Convention on the Law of Treaties (VCLT) Art 31(3)(b).

[14] See *Temple Case* (1962), 307; *Encuentro/Palena* (1966), 174; *Laguna del Desierto* (1994), 25.

or award. The parties' understanding of an award or decision in this sense cannot alter its meaning (short of a new agreement) and refusal to accept an award or decision does not mean a State will no longer be legally bound by the same. However, these considerations may be relevant, for example, to questions of estoppel in subsequent disputes.

The possibility that geographical change may be legally significant for maritime boundaries between States is suggested by the role of geographical circumstances in their construction and description. The construction of a maritime boundary will be substantially based on the geographical circumstances obtaining at the time of delimitation or, at least, the relevant geographical circumstances depicted in recognized charts.[15] As already noted, it is widely agreed that, as a general rule, the location of international maritime boundaries once established remains fixed. An ambulatory maritime boundary may still be established by the terms of a boundary agreement or award.

Soons has suggested that a fluid character may follow from the simple definition of a boundary as the median line, distinguishing this type of agreement from one specifying the location of the particular median line in a more detailed way at the time of delimitation.[16] Soons cites the 1980 Convention between France and Tonga on the Delimitation of Economic Zones as an example of the first type of agreement, which he acknowledges to be rare.[17] This example does not in fact support Soons' point; instead, it illustrates the importance of clearly establishing what the parties have agreed in the particular case.

The 1980 Convention does not merely define the boundary as the median line. It indicates that this line is to be more precisely defined. Article 3 provides that

> (a) The two Governments shall, as soon as possible, draw up the appropriate cartographic documents by mutual consent.
> (b) These documents shall be drawn up taking into account available cartographic and geodetic data.
> (c) The necessary technical corrections to bring these data up to date may be made subsequently by exchange of letters.

Paragraph (c) is interesting insofar as it may appear to suggest that the boundary was intended to be ambulatory. However, read in context as a follow up to the injunction to draw up the relevant documents 'as soon as possible' 'taking into account *available* cartographic and geodetic data', the provision may be better understood to admit the rectification of any inaccuracies in charts that were not up to date at the time of agreement. Moreover, even if the terms of the treaty *could*

[15] On the question of whether delimitation must be based on facts on the ground or charts, see Chapter 7.
[16] Soons, 'The Effects of a Rising Sea Level', 226–7.
[17] Ibid, 226, fn 78.

be understood to leave open the option of adjusting the boundary in response to subsequent geographical change, these provisions clearly indicate that any changes require the consent of both parties. If an ambulatory boundary is established, this is not, as Soons would have it, by virtue of the definition of the boundary as the median line but by virtue of this express provision for the future updating of geographical information through an exchange of letters.

The definition of a maritime boundary as a median line cannot be considered sufficient evidence of the fact that '[t]he States concerned have deliberately opted for a (potentially) fluctuating boundary line'.[18] There are many reasons why States may choose to define the boundary as a median line—this is a relatively simple and expedient way of establishing a boundary that broadly reflects and respects the coastal projections of two States. This does not mean that the States in question have agreed that the boundary will shift in the event of subsequent geographical change affecting their coasts.

The law requires further evidence that the agreement, award, or decision in question establishes a fluid boundary. The text and context of the particular agreement matters here but so too does the object and purpose of boundary treaties generally. As the International Court of Justice (ICJ) has observed, '[i]n general, when two countries establish a frontier between them, one of the primary objects is to achieve stability and finality'.[19] An ambulatory boundary may be consistent with these goals, but this would ordinarily require some specification of the type of geographical change that is considered relevant and when and how it is to be taken into account. Such details would themselves serve as evidence that the parties have agreed to an ambulatory boundary. The subsequent practice of the parties may also inform an assessment of whether a treaty establishes an ambulatory boundary.[20]

An established international boundary cannot ordinarily be altered by a unilateral act, unless the boundary agreement or award expressly provides for this. As such, the unilateral adjustment of maritime baselines and zonal limits by the coastal State will not ordinarily have consequences for the location of an established maritime boundary. In State practice, the unilateral adjustment of baselines does not usually result in the relocation of international boundaries, even when the former baselines played a role in delimitation.[21] Nor has the revision of baselines prompted either calls to renegotiate existing boundaries or challenges to their lawfulness. There is no reason to treat unilateral changes to baselines used to locate zonal limits *in response to coastal change* as exceptionally impacting established

[18] Ibid, 227.
[19] *Temple Case* (1962), 34.
[20] Such practice will be taken into account where it constitutes 'subsequent practice in the application of the treaty which establishes the agreement of the parties regarding its interpretation': VCLT Art 31(3).
[21] Tanaka, *Predictability and Flexibility*, 231.

international boundaries—that is, as compared with unilateral baseline changes in other circumstances. This would be true even if adjustments to those baselines in response to geographical change were required by the law (and it has been argued here that they are not).

It is useful to reflect on the circumstances in which ambulatory international boundaries *have* clearly been established to understand both the rationale for such an arrangement and the conditions that make it practicable. It is important to bear in mind here that the broader context for the establishment of international boundaries is an international legal order which privileges stability in the spatial organization of jurisdiction.

It may make sense for a boundary to shift with a river where the States concerned consider direct access to that river from their territories of greater importance than a fixed division of land territory. In comparison, it is difficult to see how a median line dividing maritime space that shifts as coasts shift or baselines are redrawn would be an advantage for either of the neighbouring States—particularly given that coastal change and, for that matter, unilateral baseline adjustments are difficult to predict with any accuracy. Even in the case of river boundaries, moreover, the aforementioned prioritization of interests will not always apply. Crucially, there can be no presumption that an international boundary will change with a river used to define it or with certain types of change affecting that river.

Textbook descriptions of the law relating to international boundaries often refer to the accretion/avulsion distinction according to which a river boundary will shift with gradual and imperceptible changes in the location of the river (accretion) but remain fixed where a river changes its course more suddenly and dramatically (avulsion). It is a mistake to treat this as a general rule applying to river boundaries in international law. The accretion/avulsion distinction is instead one possible outcome of legal reasoning about what the parties to a boundary treaty can be understood to have agreed, which will be informed by the 'object and purpose' of such a treaty more broadly. It is this process of interpretation that takes priority. The only principle that applies generally to an assessment of the implications of geographical change pertains to stability—a notion that does not mandate either fixity or change in international boundaries but may nevertheless inform the interpretation of boundary agreements, decisions, and awards.

The claim that the simple definition of a maritime boundary as a median line implies its ambulatory character and the associated idea that maritime boundaries are otherwise 'fixed' appear to depend in part upon analogical reasoning from the case of river boundaries. Among other problems, this involves a misunderstanding of the legal rules and principles applying to river boundaries. As such, it misdescribes the sense in which these two cases are in fact analogous. This obscures the broader consistency of the law as it relates to international boundaries of all types. It also obscures the principled consistency of the law of the sea as it relates to both maritime limits and international maritime boundaries.

III. River Boundaries and the Accretion/ Avulsion Distinction

The idea that international river boundaries are subject to a 'rule of accretion' that distinguishes the implications of gradual and imperceptible change (accretion) from sudden and more dramatic change (avulsion) routinely features in recitals of the law on this topic. This alleged 'rule', however, is rarely applied in practice. The notion that international river boundaries shift with accretion seems to have been imbued with an air of settled authority in significant part due to its association and, in some cases, conflation with accretion as a clearly established mode of acquiring territory in international law. The influence of private law analogies drawn from Roman and common law relating to river boundaries in the writings of 'eminent jurists' has also contributed to the belief that this is a rule with a well-established pedigree.[22] Yet it should not be forgotten that the 'teachings of the most highly qualified publicists' are a 'subsidiary means for the determination of rules of law'.[23] State practice and the emphasis on the stability of boundaries in international law cast doubt on the existence of a 'rule of accretion' and the 'accretion/avulsion' distinction it entails. It appears, at the very least, that this account of the implications of geographical change for river boundaries is better understood as a presumption rather than a rule, and one that is only triggered in particular circumstances rather than in respect of river boundaries generally.

The ICJ has effectively avoided taking a view on the existence of a rule of accretion relating to international river boundaries. In some cases, this has been justified on the basis that no such change had taken place since the boundary was agreed upon (or its course acquiesced in).[24] In *El Salvador/Honduras* (1992), a Chamber of the Court also noted that 'the alleged rule originated in Roman law as a rule applicable to private property, not as a rule relating to rivers as boundaries of jurisdiction and administration'.[25] In other cases concerning river boundaries, the Court has clearly looked to the intentions of the parties (or arbitrator) establishing the boundary to determine its current location in circumstances of geographical

[22] This is well-illustrated by Attorney General Cushing's Opinion in respect of the Chamizal dispute: C Cushing, 'Arcifinious Boundaries' (1856) 8 *Opinions of the Attorney General of the United States* 175, 177. Most of the classic texts mention the accretion/avulsion distinction as a rule of international law, although nuances in accounts of its content deserve attention. There are also exceptions: Anzilotti and Bouchez agree that there is no general rule of international law governing the consequences of physical change in a river for a boundary delimited or defined by reference to it: see D Anzilotti, 'Intorno agli effete delle modificazioni del corso di un fiume sul confine fra due stati' in La Società Italiana per l'Organizzazione Internazionale (ed), *Opere di Dionisio Anzilotti: Scritti di Diritto Internazionale Publico*, vol 1 (Cedam, 1956) 701, 705; LJ Bouchez, 'The Fixing of Boundaries in International Boundary Rivers' (1963) 12 *ICLQ* 789, 807.

[23] ICJ Statute Art 38(1)(d).

[24] *El Salvador/Honduras* (1992), 546; *El Salvador v Honduras Application for Revision* (2003), 406–7; *Kasikili/Sedudu Island* (1999), 1065.

[25] *El Salvador/Honduras* (1992), 547.

change.[26] It has not endorsed a general rule of accretion or the accretion/avulsion distinction.

It is interesting to note in this regard the Court's finding in *Certain Activities* (2015) that the instruments establishing the boundary between Costa Rica and Nicaragua, which was defined as following the right bank of the San Juan River, clearly evidenced an intention to ensure Costa Rican rights of navigation in this watercourse.[27] It was on this basis that the Court concluded that the boundary must remain on the right side of the river to its mouth.[28] It is possible—in light of this interpretation—that not only accretion but avulsion affecting the course of the river might result in a corresponding change in the course of the boundary to ensure Costa Rica's right of navigation (though it was not found that substantial change had occurred in this case). This would be at odds with the accretion/avulsion distinction, which indicates that avulsive change should not affect the course of a boundary—the boundary remaining in the river's former bed. However, the instruments establishing the boundary between Costa Rica and Nicaragua along the San Juan suggest that it should be understood to shift with all types of subsequent geographical change, including avulsion.

In *Costa Rica v Nicaragua* (2018), the Court considered the implications of substantial geographical change on the location of the land boundary in the northern part of Isla Portillos on the Caribbean coast. It found that the submergence of a channel connecting the San Juan River with Harbor Head Lagoon precluded its use as the boundary.[29] According to the Court, '[s]ince there is no channel, there cannot be a boundary running along it'.[30] Somewhat opaquely, it concluded that 'in light of these findings . . . Costa Rica has sovereignty over the whole of Isla Portillos up to where the river reaches the Caribbean Sea'.[31]

It is important to recognize that the Court's reasoning here is not tantamount to an endorsement of the idea that a river boundary shifts with accretion and follows the former bed in cases of avulsion. No general rule regarding the implications of geographical change for river boundaries was identified or applied. Instead, the Court took the submergence of the feature formerly identified as the boundary to mean that it could no longer be used as a boundary. It held that the channel could no longer form part of the boundary because it no longer existed. Notably, this is not the only conclusion that may be drawn where geographical change or other developments result in the effective 'disappearance' of a feature used to define an international boundary. It may also be consistent with—and even required by—both the terms of a boundary treaty and general international law to treat the legal

[26] *Cameroon v Nigeria* (2002), 346; *Certain Activities* (2015), 703.
[27] *Certain Activities* (2015), 700, 703.
[28] Ibid.
[29] *Costa Rica v Nicaragua* (2018), 32.
[30] Ibid, 31.
[31] Ibid, 32.

boundary as persisting in the same course of the feature that no longer exists. What matters is the common intention of the parties as expressed in the instruments establishing the boundary. To understand the implications of such a change for the established boundary it is necessary to determine what the parties intended to achieve by defining the boundary as they did.

In *Costa Rica v Nicaragua* (2018), the Court did not clearly elaborate why the boundary could not continue to follow a channel that was now submerged by the sea. Its conclusion that the boundary followed the right bank of the San Juan to the point where this river meets the Caribbean Sea is nevertheless consistent with the terms of the 1858 Treaty and the Cleveland and Alexander Awards. It is clear that the parties intended to establish a boundary that followed the right bank of the San Juan until it ended in the sea. The boundary was defined in this way to ensure Costa Rica's access to this waterway, which the parties agreed was Nicaraguan.

Different boundary agreements may support different conclusions regarding the consequences of this type of geographical change. If, for example, there was evidence that the parties were not concerned with access to the river but with the preservation of territorial sovereignty over land located on either side, this would suggest that the boundary should not be affected by any subsequent change, whether accretion or avulsion. Of course, it may be difficult in these circumstances to identify the former location of a river or another geographical feature that has since changed. The appropriate response is to give the best possible effect to the common intentions of the parties in the now altered circumstances.

The First Alexander Award provides an excellent example of this response to the difficulty of ascertaining the facts at the time of delimitation. Alexander's decision 'to adopt what is practically the headland of to-day, or the northwestern extremity of what seems to be the solid land, on the east side of Harbor Head Lagoon' as the terminus of the land boundary between Costa Rica and Nicaragua was a response to the practical impossibility of identifying 'the extremity of Punta de Castillo, at the mouth of the San Juan River, as they both existed on the 15th of April 1858', which Cleveland had determined to be the terminus established by the 1858 Treaty.[32] This was a decision based on what was practically possible rather than what the law required, though the terms of the treaty informed this response to the practicalities. The Court's decision in *Costa Rica v Nicaragua* (2018) similarly gives effect to the parties' intention to establish a boundary that followed the right bank of the river to sea in changed geographical circumstances.

The accretion/avulsion distinction is a blunt instrument for determining the implications of geographical change for the course of a boundary and related questions of sovereignty. The effect of physical change in general and different types of physical change in particular will depend on the intention of the parties, whose views on this question are likely to depend upon the rationale for choosing a

[32] First Alexander Award, 220.

river boundary in the first place as well as its contemporary significance and use. Unless the intentions of the parties are made manifest in the boundary agreement or award, they must be deduced from the text, its context, and any relevant State practice. The same type of analysis is required where a State succeeds to an international boundary or an administrative division is transformed into an international boundary by operation of the principle *uti possidetis juris*.

The 1911 *Chamizal Case* is sometimes cited in support of an accretion/avulsion distinction in international law. Yet the implicit endorsement of this notion in the award at best qualifies as *obiter dictum*. The decision in the *Chamizal Case* is consistent with the approach taken to international boundary disputes before and since. Both in the majority decision and the dissenting and separate opinions of the US and Mexican commissioners, respectively, the treaties establishing and pertaining to the boundary are interpreted with a view to construing the intentions of the parties—the chief question being whether it was intended that the boundary should be fixed or ambulatory.

The 1911 decision sought to resolve a long-standing dispute between the United States and Mexico regarding title to the 'Chamizal tract'—some 600 acres of land that had originally formed part of the Mexican bank of the Rio Grande but ended up on the US side due to the southward migration of the river.[33] The 1848 Treaty establishing the boundary described it as passing up the middle of the Rio Grande and following 'the deepest channel, where it has more than one'.[34] The 1853 Gadsden Purchase Treaty affirmed that the boundary would be located in the middle of the river.[35] In 1884, the parties agreed that the boundary should shift with some types of change and not others.[36] In the Chamizal dispute, Mexico argued that the boundary was fixed up until 1884.[37] The United States claimed that it was ambulatory from the outset.[38]

There is some suggestion that the three commissioners responsible for the 1911 Award considered 'the ordinary rules of international law' to provide that a fluvial boundary would shift with accretion but not avulsion, though this view is implied rather than directly expressed. Significantly, these allegedly 'ordinary rules' were not applied in the given case, which, notably, was not distinguished as warranting an exception to the same.

In 1856, the Attorney General Caleb Cushing had provided the US–Mexico Boundary Commission with an Opinion regarding the implications of change in the course of the Rio Grande, advising that, according to 'the received rule of the law of nations... as laid down by all the writers of authority', a river boundary would

[33] *Chamizal* (1911), 317.
[34] Guadalupe Hidalgo Treaty (1848) Art V.
[35] Gadsden Purchase Treaty (1853) Art I.
[36] Convention Touching the Boundary Line (1884).
[37] *Chamizal* (1911), 317.
[38] Ibid.

shift with accretion but not avulsion.[39] This decision was subsequently quoted at length by the US Supreme Court in *Nebraska v Iowa* (1892)[40]—a judgment which continues to inform the Supreme Court's jurisprudence on river boundaries between the federation's constituent states.[41] Though Cushing cited a number of scholarly authorities in support of the alleged accretion/avulsion distinction, his analysis also appears to have been influenced by the earlier domestic jurisprudence of the US concerning river boundaries.

In *Chamizal*, the commissioners described the decision in *Nebraska v Iowa* (1892) as 'applying the ordinary rules of international law to a fluvial boundary between two States'.[42] They also described Cushing's 1856 Opinion as 'a valuable contribution to the subject by an authority on international law'.[43] Significantly, however, they did not take the rule of accretion described in that Opinion to determine the implications of geographical change for the boundary in the Rio Grande. Instead, it was noted that the Opinion and 'the occasional concurrence' with it expressed 'by some of the higher Mexican officials at the time it was given' cast doubt on whether 'the treaty of 1848, taken by itself, or the treaty of 1853, taken by itself indicated an intention to establish a fixed line boundary'.[44]

The commissioners concluded that these treaties could not be 'taken alone'.[45] They pointed to the fact the 1853 Treaty still described the boundary as the middle of the Rio Grande despite 'notable variations' in its course since 1848, which they took to suggest that the boundary moved with the river.[46] The commissioners also held that the 1884 Treaty specifying that the boundary would shift with erosion and accretion but not with 'any other change' (such as 'the cutting of a new bed' or 'deepening of another channel') was intended to apply to all changes affecting the course of the river (or its deepest channel) since the boundary was established in 1848 (that is, changes predating the 1884 Treaty as well as those following its conclusion). In *Chamizal*, then, the question of whether the boundary was ambulatory was determined by reference to the intentions of the parties to the relevant treaties as evidenced by the treaty text and subsequent practice. It did not depend upon any alleged rule of accretion or associated accretion/avulsion distinction.

Though Cushing's earlier Opinion was not applied in *Chamizal*, it is interesting to note how far it relies upon some problematic assumptions and generalizations about the reasons why States may choose a river boundary. Cushing did

39 Cushing, 'Arcifinious Boundaries', 175.
40 *Nebraska v Iowa* (1892), 363–5.
41 The 'tidelands' litigation concerning boundaries between state and federal jurisdiction over 'submerged lands' also appears to have been influenced by this case law. In turn, the tidelands cases have influenced the US understanding of the character of maritime limits under international law, the results of which are discussed in the Conclusion to this book.
42 *Chamizal* (1911), 331.
43 Ibid, 322.
44 Ibid.
45 Ibid, 321.
46 Ibid.

recognize that the implications of physical change affecting the course of the Rio Grande would '[depend], in part, on the terms of the treaty between the two republics prescribing the boundary line'.[47] He stressed, however, that the boundary described as proceeding 'up the middle' of the Rio Grande was 'not an astronomical or geographical line, but a natural object, defined by the treaty'.[48] Cushing went on to argue that 'the established principles of public law come in here to settle the question in all its relations'.[49] His account of those 'established principles', however, depends upon a particular—and questionable—understanding of the objectives underpinning the use of 'natural objects' such as mountains and rivers as a boundary.[50] The point, Cushing claimed, was that such features 'of themselves serve to *keep off* the public enemy'.[51]

The idea that rivers or mountain ranges constitute natural barriers has sometimes been used to justify their use as the boundary of a State—particularly in France, where the notion was also employed in the seventeenth century to justify territorial expansion.[52] As a generalization of the function of river boundaries, this idea has always been problematic: rivers often bring those on either side together rather than separating them. This account of the role of river boundaries also fails to reflect the particular concerns and objectives underpinning the decision of the United States and Mexico to describe part of their boundary as following the middle of the Rio Grande. Like many rivers, the Rio Grande has long been a shared resource, with both the United States and Mexico relying on its waters for irrigated agriculture as well as municipal and industrial uses.[53]

In his 1858 Opinion, Cushing argued that accretion must involve a change in the boundary because 'the territorial relations cannot be reversed by such imperceptible mutations in the course of the river'.[54] He also observed that 'the convenience of allowing the river to retain its previous function, notwithstanding such insensible changes in its course, or in either of its banks, outweighs the inconveniences'.[55] If, however, more substantial change should affect the course of the river, Cushing affirmed that the resulting 'injury by the loss of territory' is 'greater than the benefit of retaining the natural river boundary'.[56] It is on this basis that he considered avulsive change to leave the boundary 'in the middle of the deserted river bed'.[57]

47 Cushing, 'Arcifinious Boundaries', 175.
48 Ibid, 176.
49 Ibid, 177.
50 Ibid.
51 Ibid (emphasis in original).
52 P Sahlins, 'Natural Frontiers Revisited: France's Boundaries since the Seventeenth Century' (1990) 95 (5) *AHR* 1423–51.
53 JE Roth, 'The Rio Grande', MPEPIL Online, accessed 30 January 2018.
54 Cushing, 'Arcifinious Boundaries', 177.
55 Ibid.
56 Ibid.
57 Ibid.

The difficulty with this analysis is that it assumes that what is convenient and what is injurious remains the same for all States in all circumstances. In fact, there are cases where the value of a river as a shared resource may recommend its retention as the boundary even in cases of sudden and dramatic (avulsive) change. Gradual changes in the course of a river over time may still result in a loss of territory that the States establishing the boundary considered unacceptable. What matters is the common intention of the parties to the instrument establishing the boundary. Their response to subsequent geographical change may illuminate their original intentions or lead to subsequent agreement (including that established by conduct) modifying the existing boundary.

Cushing's analysis also fails to recognize that the 'convenience' of a river boundary may be primarily or exclusively due to the fact that this feature is mapped in a linear form. One reason why rivers have historically been used as boundaries has to do with their visibility; however, for a long time it has been their visibility on maps rather than on the ground that has been perceived as a key advantage. Where a mapped river is identified as the boundary, it is not necessarily the case that the parties intended the boundary to follow changes affecting the physical feature.[58]

The United States did not accept the 1911 Award[59] and the dispute over the Chamizal tract continued. It is worth noting that one reason given for the rejection of the Award was that the course of the river in 1864 could not be accurately determined in 1911.[60] In 1925, the International Boundary and Water Commission for the United States and Mexico (IBWC) began to discuss plans for the 'rectification' of the Rio Grande.[61] In 1930, it presented a detailed plan to the US and Mexican governments recommending the straightening and strengthening of the channel followed by an exchange of territory to leave to each State the land on their side of the reconfigured river.[62] In 1933, the United States and Mexico concluded a Treaty on the Rectification of the Rio Grande giving effect to this plan in a specified segment of the river.[63] Despite promising negotiations between the two States in 1932 and 1933,[64] the agreement did not deal with the Chamizal tract.

[58] The significance of maps and charts in connection with the legal implications of geographical change is treated in detail in Chapters 7 and 8.

[59] US Memorandum to Mexico (7 December 1911), 598–600.

[60] Ibid, 598; *Chamizal* (1911), 342 (Separate Opinion of the American Commissioner).

[61] See IBWC, Minute 61 (1925).

[62] IBWC, Minute 129 (1930).

[63] Convention for the Rectification of the Rio Grande, Art I.

[64] A solution mooted at this time was Mexico's transfer of the Chamizal tract to the United States in return for the United States cancelling obligations under the Pious Fund, which a 1902 Arbitration Award had held to require the annual payment of interest by Mexico to the United States (though Mexico had not paid this annuity since 1914): see KD Yielding, 'The Chamizal Dispute: An Exercise in Arbitration 1845–1945', Ph.D. thesis (Texas Tech University, 1973) 290–324; *The Pious Fund Case* (1902).

It was not until 1963 that the dispute over Chamizal was finally addressed. The Chamizal Convention provided for the relocation and concrete reinforcement of the Rio Grande in this section of the boundary, transferring the Chamizal tract to Mexico together with areas of land adjacent to and east of Cordova Island, which was itself divided equally between the two States through the physical relocation of the river.[65] In 1970, the two States concluded another treaty providing for the physical modification of the river to leave US land to its north and Mexican land to its south.[66] This Treaty also provided for a regular and regulated response to future changes affecting the course of the river, specifying that the boundary would shift with lateral movements due to erosion and accretion and authorizing the 'rectification' of the channel where tracts of land were left on the 'wrong' side. In the case of tracts of land under a specified size with a population below a specified maximum, failure to rectify the course of the river within a set timeframe would result in the relocation of the boundary to the new channel and the transfer of land to the State on whose side of the boundary it was located.[67] The State losing territory in this way would be compensated by a subsequent transfer of the same area of land in a future case of natural separation or rectification.[68] Finally, the Treaty provided for the execution of works to physically 'stabilise' the river against further change.[69]

While physically fixing the course of a river may in some circumstances be the only way to ensure both a stable boundary and mutual access to its resources, fixing a boundary in law and negotiating access and mutual management would generally appear more practical. The protracted dispute between the United States and Mexico regarding the boundary in the Rio Grande vividly illustrates the drawbacks of an ambulatory boundary. In this case, debates as to whether the nature of various changes affecting the river were of a type effecting change in the boundary were resolved by agreement and the physical concretization of the boundary in the relevant areas—the parties making further artificial adjustments to its course to facilitate land swaps.[70] This complicated solution is far from ideal. Yet the application of the alleged rule that a river boundary will shift in cases of accretion but not cases of avulsion, apart from being inconsistent with the intentions of the parties establishing the boundary, would not have had a better result. In this case, the parties were concerned to retain both territory on either side of the river and sovereignty over part of the river itself, which was a valued resource. Applying the accretion/avulsion distinction to the types of change affecting the Rio Grande would

[65] Chamizal Convention (1963); (1963) 48 *US DOS Bulletin* 199, 200.
[66] Boundary Differences Treaty (1970), Preamble, Arts I, II.
[67] Ibid, Art III (B).
[68] Ibid.
[69] Ibid, Art IV.
[70] Chamizal Convention (1963) Arts 1, 2. See also Convention for the Rectification of the Rio Grande (1933).

not have permitted this. As such, its application would not have been consistent with the intentions of the parties establishing this boundary. Nor would it have contributed to the boundary's stability.

The function of an international boundary is to divide territory in a stable manner, which is not to say that the boundary must be fixed. Locating an international boundary in a river may be 'convenient' for several reasons—for instance, to allow shared access to its resources. This does not mean that a boundary that moves with the river will always be desirable or that this type of fluidity was intended by the parties.

At most, the idea that a river boundary will move with accretion but not avulsion may operate as a presumption in connection with international river boundaries. It is, moreover, a rebuttable presumption that applies in a more restricted set of circumstances than typically suggested. Rather than automatically applying to every international boundary that follows the course of a river, the presumption will be triggered by certain considerations suggesting that an ambulatory boundary was intended. This is likely to be the case where the boundary was established in a river because of its significance to both States—for example, as a navigable waterway or source of freshwater or fish. The value of the river for both States may be reflected in the use of the thalweg or median line as the boundary rather than one or the other bank. Notably, however, where agreement on a river boundary is underpinned by a concern to ensure access to the body of water as a means of transport or for fishing or any number of social-cultural reasons or uses, it may also make sense to relocate the boundary in the event of *avulsion*. Whether this is the effect of a boundary agreement will depend upon a proper construal of the parties' intentions.

The principle of the stability of boundaries helps to explain why there is no presumption in favour of change in cases of avulsion. The issue is not just that the change in question is more sudden and substantial. It is that the relocation of a boundary to follow such change may require the transfer of substantial tracts of territory between neighbouring States. This is unlikely to be agreed to by a State whose overall territory is thereby reduced or where there is a special national interest in a particular tract of land (e.g. where it is populated by nationals). In these circumstances, stability may be best served by renegotiation of the boundary. At the same time, the loss or acquisition of territory as a result of boundary change in cases of avulsion will not always be considered problematic by the States concerned. What matters, fundamentally, is a proper construal of the relevant intentions. Where boundary change entails a loss or transfer of territory, a further presumption against the abandonment of territory unless clearly intended will also come into play.[71]

[71] On this further presumption, see Chapter 9.

IV. From the Rivers to the Sea

There is no evidence of or clear reason for a presumption that maritime boundaries comprised of a median line are ambulatory. Nor is there any reason to presume that maritime boundaries established on the basis of a more complex set of considerations and calculations will have a fluid character. The same concerns that may warrant the establishment of an ambulatory river boundary and, in certain circumstances, account for a distinction between the legal effects of accretive and avulsive change do not apply to international maritime boundaries.

There is no need for a maritime boundary to shift with coastal change to ensure that the States in question still have sovereign rights in the sea. The risk in the case of river boundaries is that geographical change may mean that a valued resource, the physical river, ends up entirely or more substantially in the territory of one or the other State if the boundary does not also move. This is not generally an issue in the case of maritime boundaries, where the change of potential relevance is that affecting the coast or other features where basepoints have been located for the purposes of constructing the boundary. Retaining a maritime boundary in the event of subsequent change affecting the coasts of either or both parties will not usually result in one or the other losing access to a valued resource. Indeed, shifting an established boundary in response to such change may be more likely to have this effect.

The particular method by which a boundary is delimited will not necessarily indicate whether it is fixed or ambulatory. The fact that the equidistance method is used to construct a boundary does not mean it will be ambulatory. The reasons which may recommend the equidistance method in certain circumstances—for example, the relative ease with which the method may be applied or the consistency of a median line with an 'equitable solution'[72]—do not imply that the parties also intend the boundary to shift in the event of subsequent geographical change affecting their coasts.

An equidistant or median line boundary is generally measured from a limited number of salient points on the coast or offshore features generating entitlement to maritime space. These salient points may be more prone to erosion and inundation than other parts of the coast. Far from suggesting that a boundary constructed by reference to these points will shift with or be invalidated by subsequent geographical change, this is consistent with and evidence of the legal irrelevance of such change.

In the *Black Sea Case* (2009), the ICJ held that '[e]quidistance and median lines are to be constructed from the most appropriate points on the coasts of the two States concerned, with particular attention being paid to those protuberant coastal points situated nearest to the area to the delimited'.[73] Noting that it was not bound

[72] Note that these advantages do not follow from use of the equidistance method in all circumstances, which is why the method is not obligatory: see Chapter 1.
[73] *Black Sea Case* (2009), 101.

to use the basepoints selected by the States in question for the purpose of unilaterally delimiting their maritime entitlements, the Court indicated that the 'appropriateness' of basepoints was to be assessed primarily by reference to coastal geography.

The choice of 'appropriate' points refers back to the notion that entitlement to maritime space projects from the coastal front. The selection of basepoints will also be informed by the functional objectives of maritime delimitation—namely, the construction of a boundary that can be known, respected, and enforced. The choice of salient points as basepoints further reflects the (legitimate) interest of the coastal State in maximizing the maritime area accorded to it in the delimitation process. Constructing an international boundary on the basis of the coastal configuration at the time of delimitation or on the basis of the coastal configuration represented in charts accepted by the parties is consistent with all of these considerations. While the same considerations do not prohibit the construction of a boundary that will shift with subsequent coastal change, they do suggest that an ambulatory maritime boundary should not be presumed. In cases where an ambulatory boundary is clearly established by agreement, these considerations further recommend the specification of when and how any subsequent coastal change will affect the location of the boundary. Such details may themselves serve as evidence of a common intention to establish an ambulatory boundary.

The legal relevance of 'coastal instability' has been considered in several delimitation cases. In *Nicaragua v Honduras* (2007), the ICJ chose to delimit the maritime boundary using an angle bisector rather than the equidistance method on the grounds inter alia that 'continued accretion at the Cape might render any equidistance line so constructed today arbitrary and unreasonable in the near future.'[74] Yet the point was not that coastal instability *as such* would have this effect. Coastal instability was understood to bear upon the 'feasibility' of selecting basepoints and constructing an equidistance line because the basepoints would have to be located on either side of an ambulatory land boundary in an area prone to substantial geographical change. The terminus of the land boundary was defined as the thalweg of the River Coco at its mouth. Because this part of the land boundary was ambulatory, the location of its terminus would follow changes in the location of the mouth of the River Coco. It was known that the location of the mouth of the river would change with future accretion and erosion of the delta.

While the Court referred to coastal change leaving basepoints 'uncertain', its concern was with basepoints located relative to the ambulatory land boundary rather than any or all basepoints on a changeable coast. The reason why it believed that 'any equidistance line ... constructed today' might be rendered 'arbitrary and

[74] *Nicaragua v Honduras* (2007), 742.

unreasonable' by future coastal change was due to the legal change supervening upon geographical change in this particular case—that is, the change in the location of the land boundary and its terminus.

Significantly, the Court did not suggest that a maritime boundary based on equidistance would change with the land boundary. Nor did it suggest that subsequent changes in the land boundary following changes in the river might mean that an established median line boundary would no longer be valid and binding. In *Nicaragua v Honduras*, the ambulatory character of the land boundary, evidenced by the terms of the 1906 Award according to an interpretation agreed on by the parties, was treated as part of the present reality bearing upon the maritime delimitation. The Court seems to have understood its own obligation to delimit a 'reasonable and equitable' maritime boundary to preclude the use of basepoints on either side of a land boundary that would subsequently change.

The decision in the *Black Sea Case* (2009) is somewhat more ambiguous regarding the legal relevance of coastal instability. The Court held that 'the geometrical nature of the first stage of the delimitation exercise leads it to use as base points those which the geography of the coast identifies as a physical reality at the time of the delimitation'.[75] In the course of justifying the selection of a basepoint at the end of the Sulina Dyke, it also observed that '[t]he land at this point is protected from shifts in the coastline due to marine processes'.[76] This does not seem to respond to any claim by the parties that the vulnerability of land might make it inappropriate as a locus for a basepoint. It may reflect a misunderstanding of the relevance of coastal instability in *Nicaragua v Honduras*.

The more recent award in *Bangladesh v India* (2014) is consistent with the decision in *Nicaragua v Honduras* (2007). It also picks up on the Court's emphasis on 'physical reality at the time of delimitation' in the *Black Sea Case* (2009). In *Bangladesh v India*, the Tribunal determined that future physical change affecting the configuration of the coast and leaving parts of it submerged was not legally relevant, even if it meant that basepoints used to construct an equidistance line would subsequently be left at sea.[77] Conversely, in *Nicaragua v Honduras*, physical change affecting the location of the mouth of the River Coco *was* legally relevant because an ambulatory land boundary had been lawfully established. In *Bangladesh v India*, the Tribunal held that the land boundary was not ambulatory and that its terminus in 'the midstream of the main channel of the Haribhanga River must be located as it was in 1947 at the time of the Radcliffe Award'.[78]

Bangladesh had recognized in its submissions in *Bangladesh/Myanmar* that the Court in *Nicaragua v Honduras* 'was concerned that today's equidistance line

[75] *Black Sea Case* (2009), 106.
[76] Ibid, 108.
[77] *Bangladesh v India* (2014), 62–3.
[78] Ibid, 48–9.

might look very different from tomorrow's equidistance line'.[79] Its further claim that the significance of coastal instability in the Bay of Bengal was analogous cannot be considered correct.[80] This claim ignores the fact that the Court in *Nicaragua v Honduras* was not concerned with coastal change as such but its consequences for the location of the land boundary. Unfortunately, the Tribunal in *Bangladesh v India* did not clearly distinguish *Nicaragua v Honduras* on this point, though it rejected Bangladesh's claim that a maritime boundary established today might become unreasonable or inequitable due to subsequent coastal change.[81] Instead, it merely observed that the *Nicaragua v Honduras* case 'considered the instability of a coast solely with respect to whether the establishment of base points was feasible'.[82] In *Bangladesh v India*, the Tribunal concluded that it was clearly 'feasible' to identify 'appropriate basepoints' for constructing an equidistance line as both Bangladesh and India had done so,[83] though it did not accept all of the basepoints proposed by the parties and independently identified additional points.[84]

In *Nicaragua v Honduras*, the Court had held that the basepoints proposed by the parties, including those used by Honduras to delimit its territorial sea, were not 'viable' for the purposes of constructing an equidistance line.[85] This was partly because the parties disagreed on the question of sovereignty over unstable islands that had emerged in the deltaic River Coco and upon which Honduras proposed to locate basepoints.[86] It also referred to the fact that even slight variations in the location of two proximate basepoints on such a sharply convex projection would produce significant differences in a line based on equidistance. The rejection of these basepoints and the equidistance method as a whole was also related to the Court's concern that 'continued accretion at the Cape might render any equidistance line so constructed today arbitrary and unreasonable in the near future', or as it was subsequently put, 'the configuration and unstable nature of the relevant coasts, including the disputed islands formed in the mouth of the River Coco, would make these base points ... uncertain within a short period of time'. [87] As already

[79] Bangladesh Reply (vol 1), 85, in *Bangladesh/Myanmar*. Cf *Nicaragua v Honduras* (2007), 742, where the Court observed that 'continued accretion at the Cape might render any equidistance line so constructed today arbitrary and unreasonable in the near future'.

[80] See Bangladesh Memorial (vol 1), 75–8, in *Bangladesh v India*.

[81] *Bangladesh v India* (2014), 62–3.

[82] Ibid, 116–17.

[83] Ibid, 63–4, 71, 99.

[84] Ibid, 73–5 (territorial sea); 102–5 (exclusive economic zone (EEZ) and continental shelf within 200 nautical miles (M)).

[85] The Court concluded more generally that the construction of an equidistance line was not feasible: *Nicaragua v Honduras* (2007), 745.

[86] Ibid, 704, 744. The Court explained that it made no finding as to sovereignty here 'because of the changing conditions'. This would appear to be an inadequate basis for deciding not to decide the issue. However, it may be justified insofar as the 'changing conditions' contributed to the parties' ongoing disagreement on the course of the land boundary in the river. The Court had not been asked to resolve this particular issue, which, given the character of the newly formed islands, seems to be what would have been required to determine sovereignty.

[87] *Nicaragua v Honduras* (2007), 742–3.

explained, the concern was that anticipated physical changes would affect the location of the ambulatory land boundary. The Court considered it inappropriate to construct a maritime boundary using basepoints on either side of a boundary that would soon shift.

Though the judgment in *Bangladesh v India* did not comment directly on the parties' disagreement on the meaning of 'feasible basepoints', the Tribunal's application of the concept indicates that it identified 'feasibility' with both 'technical possibility' *and* the broader question of whether basepoints were 'appropriate', which was understood to depend in part upon whether they '[reflected] the general direction of the coast'.[88] In *Bangladesh v India*, the Tribunal accepted that, as a matter of fact, the deltaic coast was unstable.[89] It emphasized, however, that the selection of basepoints was an exercise that referred to 'physical reality at the time of delimitation'.[90] Significantly, it took this to mean that 'it need not address the issue of the future instability of the coastline'.[91] It clearly considered the use of basepoints located on land at the time of delimitation to be appropriate even if coastal erosion meant they would be left at sea in the near future.[92]

In *Bangladesh v India*, the Tribunal decided not to use basepoints on low-tide elevations in view of their inconsistency with the criteria set out in the *Black Sea Case*, which indicated that 'protuberant coastal points' and points marking a significant change in the direction of the coast were 'most appropriate'.[93] As such, it did not have to address the question of whether the low-tide elevations on which India had located basepoints still existed. Nevertheless, the Tribunal clearly considered it inappropriate to rely on basepoints *already* left at sea by coastal erosion. It rejected or revised basepoints shown to be located seaward of the low-water line at the time of delimitation.[94]

The Tribunal held that its concern with 'physical reality at the time of delimitation' meant that (a) it 'need not consider whether instability could in some instances qualify as a special circumstance under [UNCLOS] article 15' for the purposes of delimiting the territorial sea,[95] and (b) that instability was not 'a relevant circumstance that would justify adjustment of the provisional equidistance line in the delimitation of the [EEZ] and continental shelf'.[96] As far as the delimitation of the

[88] *Bangladesh v India* (2014), 62–4.

[89] The Tribunal expressly stated that 'the relevant coast of Bangladesh is unstable' but appears to have accepted that this was also true of at least part of the Indian coast, referring to 'the instability of the coast of the Raimangal and Haribhanga estuary': *Bangladesh v India* (2014), 116.

[90] This expression is drawn from the *Black Sea Case* (2009), 41.

[91] *Bangladesh v India* (2014), 63.

[92] This is indicated by the Tribunal's selection of basepoints: ibid, 74–5.

[93] Ibid, 73–4.

[94] Ibid, 73–5, 103–5.

[95] Ibid, 71.

[96] Ibid, 116–17. Notably, Bangladesh had argued and India denied that relevant circumstances could justify an abandonment of equidistance in favour of another method and not just the adjustment of a provisional equidistance line: see Bangladesh Reply, 76–8, and India Counter-Memorial, 118, in *Bangladesh v India* (2014). Unfortunately, the Tribunal did not address this question. It referred

territorial sea was concerned, it appears to have considered the irrelevance of future change to the task of selecting basepoints to answer Bangladesh's arguments about instability as a 'special circumstance'.[97] In its rather brief consideration of coastal instability as a 'relevant circumstance' bearing upon the delimitation of the EEZ and continental shelf within 200M, the Tribunal recalled that it was exclusively concerned with 'present geophysical conditions'.[98] It also emphasized the uncertainty of predictions regarding future change, including 'the amount of coastal erosion or accretion'.[99] This seems to have been unnecessary given that maritime delimitation was held to be based on present facts—an approach that presumably means the accuracy or otherwise of predictions regarding future changes to those facts is irrelevant.

In *Bangladesh v India*, the Tribunal did not limit its consideration of geographical change to the question of the relevance of coastal instability to the task of constructing a maritime boundary (i.e. its relevance at the point of delimitation). It also commented on the stability of established boundaries in the event of geographical change. Bangladesh's account of the significance of coastal instability for an equidistance line during proceedings had been somewhat ambiguous—perhaps deliberately so. It argued that '[t]he highly unstable deltaic nature of the relevant coastlines makes it extremely difficult, if not impossible, to establish stable and reliable base points on which to construct a *meaningful* equidistance line.'[100] However, it also claimed that the 'unparalleled instability of the Bengal Delta makes any equidistance line inherently *unreliable*'.[101] Specifically, Bangladesh argued that '[t]he ever-changing character of the Delta's coast ... combined with the irregular, deeply indented nature of the coast, make any equidistance line *intrinsically unreliable and subject to change* as the coast itself changes in both the near term and the long term'.[102] It even asserted that 'in the foreseeable future the equidistance line will *migrate* west in the direction of India'.[103]

While this language suggests that Bangladesh's concern was that an equidistance line would be ambulatory in these circumstances, a review of these statements in context suggests that it sought to make a different point. Bangladesh pointed to

exclusively to the possibility of *adjusting* a provisional equidistance line, though not because it implicitly accepted India's position. Rather, it characterized Bangladesh's claim as relating exclusively to the adjustment of a provisional line—an argument that the State had in fact made in the alternative, proposing a very substantial adjustment with the same result as the application of the angle-bisector method: see *Bangladesh v India* (2014), 105; Bangladesh Reply (vol 1), 70, 122, in *Bangladesh v India* (where Bangladesh argues that this was the effect of the 'adjustment' in *Bangladesh/Myanmar*).

[97] *Bangladesh v India* (2014), 71.
[98] Ibid, 117.
[99] Ibid.
[100] Bangladesh Reply (vol 1), 48, in *Bangladesh v India* (emphasis added).
[101] Ibid, 77 (emphasis added).
[102] Bangladesh Reply (vol 1), 107, in *Bangladesh v India* (emphasis added).
[103] Bangladesh Memorial (vol 1), 109 (emphasis added).

forecasts indicating that 'more of India's deltaic coast will be submerged below future sea levels than [its own]'.[104] This meant that Bangladesh would be entitled to much more maritime space if an equidistance line was constructed after these changes—changes that it claimed would take place in the foreseeable future. It was on this basis that Bangladesh argued that

> To base a boundary that is intended to affect a permanent delimitation of the maritime areas appertaining to the Parties on basepoints located on a coast that is guaranteed to look very different in the future than it does today would be inconsistent with the dictates not only of equity but common sense.[105]

The Tribunal evidently disagreed. It held that the law provided for maritime boundaries that were both (a) based on physical geography at the time of delimitation (which may be subject to change) and (b) intended to be permanent (unless altered by agreement). It does not appear to have seen any inconsistency or inequity in this state of affairs.

Though Bangladesh may not have in fact suggested that an established boundary would either shift with subsequent coastal change or require renegotiation in this event, the Tribunal commented directly on these possibilities (appropriately, given the ambiguity of Bangladesh's claims). Emphasizing that 'maritime delimitations, like land boundaries, must be stable and definitive to ensure a peaceful relationship between the States concerned in the long term', it stated that

> In the view of the Tribunal, neither the prospect of climate change nor its possible effects can jeopardize the large number of settled maritime boundaries throughout the world. This applies equally to maritime boundaries agreed between States and to those established through international adjudication.[106]

The Tribunal also observed that '[t]he possibility of change in the maritime boundary established in the present case would defeat the very purpose of the delimitation.'[107] It emphasized '[t]he importance of stable and definitive maritime boundaries ... when the exploration and exploitation of the resources of the continental shelf are at stake', as well as '[t]he importance of such resources to a heavily populated State with limited natural resources', observing that the sovereign rights of coastal States, and therefore the maritime boundaries between them, must be determined with precision to allow for development and investment.'[108] '[S]table and definitive maritime boundaries' are also likely to be desirable where

[104] Ibid.
[105] Ibid, 109–10.
[106] *Bangladesh v India* (2014), 63.
[107] Ibid.
[108] Ibid.

neighbouring States are primarily interested in the exploitation of living resources in the territorial sea and EEZ. This illustrates the difference between the case of maritime boundaries and river boundaries. In the former case it will rarely be in the interests of the parties to establish an ambulatory boundary—though it should be reiterated that this is not prohibited. In the case of river boundaries, the value of the river itself as a shared resource may in some cases warrant the boundary shifting with the watercourse—though here too the decision to establish an ambulatory boundary depends upon the agreement of the States concerned.

It is interesting to compare the recent decision in *Costa Rica v Nicaragua* (2018) with *Bangladesh v India* (2014) and, indeed, *Nicaragua v Honduras* (2007). In *Costa Rica v Nicaragua* (2018), Nicaragua was found to have sovereignty over an enclave encompassing Harbor Head Lagoon and a sandbar separating it from the sea (a matter on which the parties agreed). The Court found that '[t]he instability of the sandbar separating Harbor Head Lagoon from the Caribbean Sea and its situation as a small enclave within Costa Rica's territory call for a special solution'.[109] It went on to suggest that 'should territorial waters be attributed to the enclave they would be of little use to Nicaragua, while breaking the continuity of Costa Rica's territorial sea'.[110] Somewhat surprisingly, it was on this basis that it determined that 'the delimitation of the territorial sea between the Parties will not take into account any entitlement which might result from the enclave'.[111]

The Court's reasoning here is problematic. The language suggests that Nicaragua might not be entitled to a territorial sea in respect of the sandbar. Given that the feature is above water at both high and low tide, there is no legal basis for this view. Entitlement to a territorial sea follows from nothing more than the possession of territorial sovereignty over coastal land, which was in this case clearly established. Indeed, as the sandbar is part of the mainland coast rather than an island, Nicaragua could also argue that it is entitled to an EEZ and CS in respect of this feature—the exceptional denial of entitlement to such zones in respect of islands classified as '[r]ocks which cannot sustain human habitation or economic life of their own' does not apply to a mainland coast. The Court observed that entitlement to a territorial sea in respect of this 'minor feature' would be of little use to Nicaragua and this may also be true of entitlement to an EEZ and continental shelf. Yet more needs to be said about why this might be a legal reason that counts against either or both Nicaragua's entitlement to maritime space here and its bearing upon the construction of a maritime boundary.

The Court refers to such entitlement as 'breaking the continuity of Costa Rica's territorial sea', but there is no legal right to a continuous territorial sea where the coastal territory generating such entitlement is broken by a segment of territory

[109] *Costa Rica v Nicaragua* (2018), 42.
[110] Ibid.
[111] Ibid.

belonging to another State. The Court's reasoning has a degree of consistency with the deeper rationale for coastal State jurisdiction in the waters off its shores—the idea that a coastal State has a kind of natural interest in the use of those waters for resource exploitation and security purposes. Nevertheless, the more general principles and specific rules which have been developed out of this underlying rationale do not allow a case-by-case assessment of the utility of a particular sea area to a particular State to affect the question of entitlement. As such, the Court's decision to ignore the sandbar in the delimitation of a maritime boundary between Costa Rica and Nicaragua appears to be at odds with the law. The delimitation of maritime space between two States can certainly be informed by practical considerations. Yet the Court's treatment of the Nicaraguan enclave is not justified on the basis of the reasons given.

It is notable that the Court also referred to the 'instability' of the Nicaraguan sandbar as a problem though it did not elaborate on this point.[112] It determined, moreover, to use basepoints 'located on salient points that are situated on solid land and thus have a relatively higher stability than points placed on sandy features' but the judgment fails to explain why this would be necessary.[113] There is an ostensible resonance between this insistence upon 'solid land' and the determination in the First Alexander Award that 'it best fulfills the demands of the treaty and of President Cleveland's award to adopt what is practically the headland of to-day, or the northwestern extremity of what seems to be the *solid land*, on the east side of Harbor Head Lagoon' as the site for the terminus of the land boundary, which was then more precisely defined.[114] Yet even if there were good reasons for taking the submergence of the former site of the land boundary terminus to prevent its continuing function as such (discussed above), there is no reason to think that the instability of the Nicaraguan sandbar enclaved within Costa Rican territory should preclude its appropriateness as a site for basepoints used to construct a maritime boundary.

The decision in *Costa Rica v Nicaragua* (2018) also considered the instability of a sandspit near the mouth of the San Juan River to militate against its use as a basepoint. In this regard, the Court concluded that '[t]he great instability of the coastline in the area of the mouth of the San Juan River, as indicated by the Court-appointed experts, prevents the identification on the sandspit of a fixed point that would be suitable as the starting-point of the maritime delimitation'.[115] On this basis it was considered 'preferable to select a fixed point at sea and connect it to the starting-point on the coast by a mobile line'.[116] Interestingly, the Court also referred to 'the fact that the prevailing phenomenon characterizing the coastline at the

[112] Ibid.
[113] Ibid, 40–1.
[114] First Alexander Award, 220 (emphasis added).
[115] *Costa Rica v Nicaragua* (2018), 38.
[116] Ibid.

mouth of the San Juan River is recession through erosion from the sea' as a reason for selecting a fixed point 2 nautical miles from the coast on the median line.[117]

Unlike the treatment of the Nicaraguan sandbar, this response to the instability of the coast at the terminus of the land boundary appears to be justified as a response to the prospect of future geographical change affecting the location of that terminal point, which might affect its 'appropriateness' as the starting point for the maritime boundary between the adjacent States.[118] In determining the course of the land boundary, the Court had emphasized a common intention (evidenced by the 1858 Treaty and subsequent Awards) that Costa Rica should retain sovereignty over the right bank of the San Juan until the river met the sea. It was because 'the prevailing phenomenon characterizing the coastline at the mouth of the San Juan River is recession through erosion from the sea' that 'the Court deem[ed] it appropriate to place a fixed point at sea . . . 2 nautical miles from the coast on the median line'.[119] Its concern was presumably that erosion would mean that the terminus of the land boundary would properly—that is, according to an interpretation of the instruments establishing the land boundary—be relocated further landwards. This follows from the Court's reasoning that submergence would mean that the present location of that terminus would no longer be consistent with the common intentions of the parties establishing the land boundary. The location of the starting point for the maritime boundary off the coast does not therefore reflect or respond to a belief that coastal change would otherwise result in the established maritime boundary changing its course.

The method by which a maritime boundary is constructed will not usually determine whether it is ambulatory or not. It is also necessary to consider the description of the established boundary in a treaty, award, or judicial decision. The fact that a boundary is described as a median line does not imply an ambulatory boundary in the absence of other evidence that this was intended. If—as is usual—the location of the basepoints used to construct this line and/or the terminal and turning points of the median line are specified by co-ordinates or depicted on charts, this may support the conclusion that the established boundary is—as is usual—fixed. Significantly, this does not mean that the specification of the boundary by co-ordinates or its depiction on a chart itself operates to fix what would otherwise be an ambulatory boundary. The point is that absent evidence to the contrary, such specification is consistent with an intention that the course of the established boundary shall remain fixed.

Baselines or boundaries in the form of straight lines connecting points defined by geographical coordinates are not always or necessarily permanently fixed. It remains entirely possible to define a boundary in this way at a particular point in

[117] Ibid.
[118] Ibid.
[119] Ibid.

time while also agreeing that its location will be subject to change in the future. The question is what, in this regard, has been agreed—either directly by the parties or through their agreement to be bound by a decision or award. As noted above, the subsequent practice of the parties may also be relevant here.

The character of a boundary as fixed or ambulatory depends upon what the parties have agreed, which is primarily a matter of what the treaty, judgment, or award provides. It is possible that reference to geographic co-ordinates may reflect an intention to fix the boundary against change affecting the basepoints by reference to which it is constructed. Such an intention will not be established if there is other clear evidence of agreement to an ambulatory boundary. In the *Chamizal* case, Mexico had argued inter alia that the treaties of 1848 and 1853 established a fixed rather than ambulatory boundary because they provided for the more precise definition of the course of the boundary by fixed measurements and stipulated that there should be no variation of that boundary other than by free, express, and mutual consent.[120] The Commission recognized that these treaties 'standing alone, might seem to be more consistent with the idea of a fixed boundary than one which would vary by reason of alluvial processes'. However, this could not override the countervailing support for an ambulatory boundary in the two States' subsequent practice.[121]

In the case of maritime boundaries—where there is no reason to assume that an ambulatory boundary would have any advantages associated with the function of an international boundary in the sea—very clear evidence that the parties have agreed to an ambulatory boundary will be required. In this context, the detailed definition of the location of maritime boundaries using charts and coordinates is consistent with the conclusion that the established boundary will not shift; yet its permanent character does not depend on such specification and the absence of these details will not independently prove an ambulatory boundary.

In the case of river boundaries, either a fixed or ambulatory boundary may be desirable depending on the objectives of the States concerned. A boundary that responds to these objectives through its fluidity or fixity is more likely to be consistent with the broader goal of stability in connection with international boundaries. In the case of maritime boundaries, stability is more likely to be served by fixed boundaries, though it remains lawful to establish an ambulatory maritime boundary and possible to do so in a manner that remains consistent with this overarching objective. To assume that a boundary is ambulatory in the absence of clear evidence that the parties have specifically agreed to this would, however, be at odds with the clear emphasis the law places on agreement as the basis for international boundaries. It would also be inconsistent with the principle of stability as it relates

120 *Chamizal* (1911), 320–1.
121 Ibid, 321, 325.

to international boundaries generally and as it has been elaborated in the 'legal order for the seas and oceans' that UNCLOS seeks to secure.[122]

V. The Principle of Stability in the Law of the Sea

A general principle of law supports the stability of boundaries of international significance. This principle applies not only to maritime boundaries between States but also to the limits established by the coastal State to mark both the different maritime zones within its jurisdiction and the point at which its jurisdiction gives way to the high seas and international seabed area.[123]

This appears to be one of the rare instances in which the general principle 'may be inferred from more specific rules of international law'.[124] Some of these 'specific rules' have already been discussed; the relevance of others to the question of the implications of geographical change for maritime jurisdiction will be elaborated upon in the following chapters. Associated doctrines include inter alia the principle of territorial integrity; the principle of the completeness of boundaries or the treaties establishing them, closely connected with the principle of effectiveness;[125] various aspects of the law governing the termination of treaties, including the express exclusion of reliance on fundamental change of circumstances as grounds for terminating an agreement establishing a boundary;[126] the survival of international boundaries beyond the treaty establishing them, whether conceptualized as a consequence of the principle of executed treaty provisions[127] or in terms of the notion of objective regimes; the principle of State succession to established boundaries and, in the case of newly independent States, the transformation of internal administrative borders into international boundaries under the principle *uti possidetis juris*; the injunction *quieta non movere* and its connection to the notion of historic rights;[128] and the doctrine of intertemporal law, encompassing both the basic principle of contemporaneity[129] and the carefully constrained notion of evolutive

[122] UNCLOS, Preamble.

[123] See generally KH Kaikobad, 'Some Observations on the Doctrine of the Continuity and Finality of Boundaries' (1983) 54 *BYIL* 119; G Marston, 'The Stability of Land and Sea Boundary Delimitations in International Law' in Blake (ed), *Maritime Boundaries* (Routledge, 1994) 144; M Shaw, 'Peoples, Territorialism and Boundaries' (1997) 8 *EJIL* 478.

[124] G Gaja, 'General Principles of International Law', MPEPIL Online, accessed 27 June 2017.

[125] *Interpretation of the Treaty of Lausanne* (1925), 20.

[126] It is also difficult to meet other conditions for termination in the case of boundary treaties. On geographical change and the termination of boundary treaties, see Purcell, 'Maritime Jurisdiction in a Changing Climate', 757–9 and Chapter 9 of this book.

[127] In the context of State succession, the fact that the treaty has been executed is not independently significant; the fact that it establishes an objective regime is.

[128] *Grisbådarna* (1909), 161.

[129] Casella suggests that the choice between (a) interpretation according to the principle of contemporaneity, and (b) reference to circumstances at the time of interpretation (as they have evolved) will depend upon the type of treaty under consideration, which may be categorized according to its effect. She identifies two possibilities: (i) treaties in which the parties have intended to create a *rule*, applicable

concepts.[130] The principle of stability that animates these rules can also be identified in the law of the sea as it relates to the establishment of both maritime boundaries and maritime limits.

As far as the interpretation of UNCLOS and the earlier law of the sea treaties is concerned, this general principle may be considered a 'relevant [rule] of international law applicable in the relations between the parties'.[131] Wolfrum argues more generally that 'principles may serve as a tool in the interpretation of positive legal norms' and that 'they are decisive elements in the establishment of the object and purpose of a given legal regime and the related interpretation of that norm'.[132]

The preamble to UNCLOS recognizes

> the desirability of establishing through this Convention, with due regard for the sovereignty of all States, a legal order for the seas and oceans which will facilitate international communication, and will promote the peaceful uses of the seas and oceans, the equitable and efficient utilization of their resources, the conservation of their living resources, and the study, protection and preservation of the marine environment.[133]

This broad statement of the 'object and purpose' of the treaty must be taken into account in an interpretation of its provisions; however, it is also those provisions that give the general aims of the treaty more concrete content. The more immediate aims of the provisions governing the establishment of both maritime limits and maritime boundaries are consistent with—and help to make apparent—the overall 'object and purpose' of the treaty.

At a general level, UNCLOS aims to secure stability and manage change in connection with the various interests in and uses of the sea by States and to some degree, through the medium of State rights and responsibilities, the interests of

to changing circumstances, and (ii) treaties creating a *situation*: S Cassella, 'Rééquilibrer les effets inéquitables d'une délimitation territoriale' (2009) *AFDI* 253, 264. Boundary treaties belong to the latter category.

[130] The way in which courts and tribunals have elaborated the notion of evolutive concepts means that an interpretation consistent with the law as it has developed is not strictly speaking a modification of the treaty. This is because such an interpretation is limited to cases where the expansion of the sense of a term over time should reasonably have been foreseen by the parties and is facilitated by the terms of the treaty—even while the particular way in which the concept would evolve was unknown. Thus in *Laguna del Desierto* it was concluded that the expression 'local water-parting' was not an evolutive concept (*Laguna del Desierto* (1994) 39), while in *Costa Rica v Nicaragua* (2009) it was concluded that the 'generic' term 'commerce' (in the phrase 'con objetos de comercio') would have been understood to have 'a meaning or content capable of evolving, not one fixed once and for all, so as to make allowance for, among other things, developments in international law': *Costa Rica v Nicaragua* (2009), 242–3. See also *Aegean Sea Continental Shelf Case* (1978), 21, on 'the territorial status of Greece'.

[131] VCLT Art 32(3)(c).

[132] R Wolfrum, 'General International Law (Principles, Rules, Standards)', MPEPIL Online, accessed 30 January 2018.

[133] UNCLOS, Preamble, para 4.

'mankind' and 'peoples'.[134] The legal order that the treaty upholds and develops is organized on the basis of a spatial division of maritime space associated with various configurations of State rights and responsibilities. The broad objectives of the Convention depend substantially upon the stability of the limits marking the different zones under national jurisdiction (in which the rights and obligations of the coastal State and foreign States vary), boundaries between national and international maritime areas, and maritime boundaries between States.

Stability does not necessarily mean fixity. Nor should it be presumed to stand in an oppositional relation to change. Attending to the relationship between geography and maritime jurisdiction clarifies the content of the principle of stability in this context, which bears upon the legal consequences of geographical change. As the following chapters further demonstrate, the role coastal geography is given in the construction and description of maritime limits and boundaries may help to ensure their stability and secure some of the related objectives identified in the Preamble to UNCLOS. It does not follow, however, that a general principle of stability or other aspects of the 'object and purpose' of UNCLOS would be served by maritime limits and boundaries that shift with subsequent geographical change.

Ambulatory boundaries are not necessarily at odds with the principle of stability. Where a particular agreement or rule provides that a boundary will shift in specified circumstances, the stability of that boundary and the legal order as a whole may be strengthened—especially where such change ensures that a boundary continues to serve its intended purpose (for example, where a river is a shared resource as well as a boundary). Yet boundaries may also be constructed or defined by reference to natural features in the absence of either agreement or a general rule regarding the implications of subsequent change affecting those features. In most of these cases, the reasons that account for the boundary being constructed or defined by reference to geography do not recommend that the course of the boundary is altered in the event of subsequent geographical change.

A boundary may be defined by reference to a geographical feature or a line on a chart that represents certain features of the natural environment[135] for reasons of convenience. The chief objective may be to designate a line that can be identified and observed by the States concerned. Thus the Court in the *Temple Case* (1962) concluded that

> the indication of the line of the watershed in Article I of the 1904 Treaty was itself no more than an obvious and convenient way of describing a frontier line objectively, though in general terms. There is … no reason to think that the Parties attached any special importance to the line of the watershed as such, as compared with the

[134] Ibid, esp paras 5–7; UNCLOS Part XI on 'the Area'.

[135] A watershed line, for example, is not a 'natural feature' as such. Nor is the low-water line along the coast. This distinction is elaborated in Chapter 7.

overriding importance in the interests of finality, of adhering to the map line as eventually delimited and as accepted by them.[136]

Maritime boundaries differ from boundaries directly defined by reference to a geographical feature such as a river or mountain range. A maritime boundary will not ordinarily trace the course of a natural feature. Indeed, the jurisprudence has made clear that the legal basis of entitlement to the continental shelf does not warrant the construction of a boundary that traces a trough, furrow, or rift in the seabed.[137] In the *Gulf of Maine Case*, the Chamber further indicated that it was 'not convinced of the possibility of discerning any genuine, sure and stable "natural boundaries" in so fluctuating an environment as the waters of the ocean, their flora and fauna', concluding that 'it would be vain to seek, in data derived from the biogeography of the waters covering certain areas of sea-bed, any element sufficient to confer the property of a stable natural boundary'.[138]

The construction of maritime boundaries responds to coastal geography in various ways and a fundamental objective is generally to ensure that the delimitation line responds to and respects the entitlement of each coastal State to a maritime area projecting from the coastal front into an area of overlap. This is a key feature of an 'equitable' delimitation. The role of geography in the law relating to the delimitation of maritime boundaries is connected with the legal basis of entitlement to maritime space—the idea that maritime jurisdiction follows from territorial sovereignty over coastal land. It is also tied up with a notion of 'equitableness' that gives expression to the basic equality of coastal States in terms of their interests and corresponding rights in the sea as well as the idea that maritime space should be proportionate to the coasts a State has. The particularity of a State's coasts is made comprehensible by the law's identification of a limited number of ideal-typical geographical 'facts' as relevant considerations in delimitation.

The connection between these 'facts' and a notion of what is 'equitable' refers back to the idea that the coastal State has a kind of natural interest in the use of the sea and its resources, including submarine resources, off its coasts. Coastal geography is given a role in delimitation that symbolically reflects, functionally secures, and also places limits on the relevant interests as an element of a broader 'legal order for the seas and oceans'.[139] The same conception of the coastal State's

[136] *Temple Case* (1962), 35. In the *Temple Interpretation Case*, the Court reiterated that it did not consider the location of the boundary in this area to depend upon the true location of the watershed line: *Temple Interpretation Case* (2013), 313, 315.

[137] See *Libya/Malta* (1985), 35–7. This case was concerned with the delimitation of the continental shelf within 200M, but seabed geology and geomorphology has not been considered significant beyond 200M either: see *Bangladesh/Myanmar* (2012); *Bangladesh v India* (2014); *Ghana/ Côte d'Ivoire* (2017).

[138] *Gulf of Maine* (1984), 277. But cf ibid, 317, where the Court observed that the notion of a natural distribution of fishery resources invoked by the United States in support of a boundary line prior to proceedings 'may have been justified for a delimitation concerning exclusive fishery zones alone, but less so for a "single" delimitation of both the EEZ and the continental shelf'.

[139] UNCLOS, Preamble.

interests and their place in a broader legal order makes sense of the role that non-geographical considerations (e.g. economic or security interests) may play in interstate maritime delimitation and explains why that role remains limited.

Geographical change subsequent to the establishment of a maritime boundary may directly affect coastal or offshore features that played a role in the construction of that boundary. Yet this will not necessarily mean that the established boundary no longer reflects the character of the States' entitlement to maritime space as a projection from their coastal fronts into an area of overlap. More importantly, the attentiveness of the delimitation process to this notion of projection from the coastal front does not mean that the law insists or allows a coastal State to insist that maritime boundaries should always reflect or respond to its coastal configuration and so change with changes to the coast. Instead, the idea of coastal projection and the associated role of geography in delimitation invest this process with a degree of objectivity, predictability, and fairness (equity).

These aspects of the delimitation process contribute to the timely and peaceful establishment of interstate maritime boundaries considered an essential element of a stable international order. This overarching objective helps to make sense of the role of geography in the construction and description of international maritime boundaries and, for that matter, unilaterally established maritime limits. Once these legal limits are lawfully established, the role of geography in the process has effectively done its work. There is no reason to think that subsequent geographical change should be legally relevant. Once established, international maritime boundaries—and maritime limits—are primarily valued as charted lines that can be respected and enforced over time.

This argument will be further elaborated in Chapter 9 of this book, which points to the difference between the significance of geographical circumstances (a) at the time and for the purposes of delimitation, and (b) after maritime limits or boundaries have been established. These differences have a logical parallel in a distinction between the creation and continuing existence of entitlement to maritime space, particularly where entitlement to particular maritime zones in respect of a particular feature (e.g. an island or archipelago) is subject to additional conditions.

For present purposes, it is worth reiterating that the principle of stability would not necessarily be compromised if there were a clear indication of when and how geographical change must be taken into account in the adjustment of legal limits and boundaries. In the case of unilaterally established maritime limits, however, there is no such indication in either conventional or customary international law. In these circumstances, it seems that stability would be undermined rather than enhanced by maritime limits that were continually contingent upon coastal geography—particularly given that coastal change is commonplace if not constant. Rather than assuming that this is a failing of the existing law, the incompatibility of such an arrangement with the clear value that the law places upon stability supports the conclusion that this interpretation of the relationship between maritime limits and coastal geography is mistaken.

In the case of international maritime boundaries, it is reasonable to expect States establishing an ambulatory boundary to provide some indication of when and how subsequent geographical change should be taken into account. This would also be good evidence that an ambulatory boundary was in fact intended. The principle of stability supports the conclusion that the ambulatory character of an international boundary should be clearly established by reference to the intentions evidenced by the particular boundary treaty, decision, or award. The mere fact that a boundary is described as the median line will not warrant a presumption that the boundary is ambulatory, even where there is no further specification of the exact location of this line.

VI. Conclusion

Recent jurisprudence has provided a very clear statement on the relevance—or, rather, irrelevance—of subsequent coastal change for established maritime boundaries. In *Bangladesh v India* (2014), the Tribunal emphasized that 'neither the prospect of climate change nor its possible effects can jeopardize the large number of settled maritime boundaries throughout the world'.[140] It noted that '[t]his applies equally to maritime boundaries agreed between States and to those established through international adjudication'.[141]

These observations stand out because they explicitly engage with the question of the implications of climate-related coastal change for established maritime boundaries. Yet the Tribunal's conclusions in *Bangladesh v India* were not novel but consistent with the treatment of dynamic geographical circumstances in connection with both land and maritime boundaries in previous cases. It is important to recognize that the Tribunal did not reject the possibility of coastal change ever influencing the delimitation *de novo* of a maritime boundary or the course of an established maritime boundary. The decision in *Bangladesh v India* is rather consistent with a broader jurisprudence that supports a distinction between (a) the possibility of establishing an ambulatory international boundary, and (b) the continuing validity of the agreement or decision establishing the boundary.

The principle of stability bears upon both questions, though it is the first that is the focus of the present chapter. There is no general legal rule prescribing that an international boundary between two or more States must shift with subsequent geographical change. This is true of both boundaries at sea and on land, including river boundaries. It remains possible for States to establish an ambulatory

[140] *Bangladesh v India* (2014), 63.
[141] Ibid.

international boundary by agreement, but this should be clearly proven not presumed. The question of whether a boundary is ambulatory is to be answered by a careful interpretation of the particular agreement, award, or decision establishing it, taking into account any relevant subsequent practice.

There is no presumption in favour of an ambulatory boundary, even in the case of international river boundaries. In the latter context, evidence that an ambulatory boundary was intended may trigger a secondary presumption that the effects of accretion will be distinguished from the effects of avulsion. This presumption is rebuttable. There may be cases where the movement of a boundary with avulsive change is clearly consistent with the parties' common intentions.

The function of international boundaries at sea and their significance in the spatial order of maritime jurisdiction makes it unlikely that a maritime boundary will be ambulatory, though it remains possible to establish a boundary with this character by agreement. If no agreement regarding the implications of subsequent geographical change for the boundary can be established, then it should be concluded that the boundary in question is not ambulatory. This is consistent with the priority of agreement in the law relating to international boundaries, recognized principles of legal interpretation, and a general principle of stability in connection with international boundaries.

The priority given to the stability of boundaries in international law is well established. As noted above, stability does not necessarily mean fixity. Boundary change that is regular and predictable—at least as far as the legal consequences of certain facts or circumstances are concerned[142]—remains consistent with and may even promote legal stability in the relevant sense. Establishing a boundary that is understood to alter with subsequent geographical change without specifying when and how such change is to occur is likely to undermine stability. These details cannot usually be inferred, even where the boundary in question is described as the median line. Such a line may be constructed by reference to specified basepoints, in which case alterations of the coast do not automatically indicate where new basepoints should be located. It cannot be assumed that unilateral changes to the territorial sea baseline by one of the States concerned will have a corresponding effect on the location of a median line boundary. Though this possibility is not excluded, it is a well-known rule of international law that unilateral changes to a boundary are not ordinarily permitted. In light of this rule, it is reasonable to conclude that unilateral changes to the territorial sea baselines will not have an effect on an established maritime boundary unless this is specifically agreed to by the States concerned.

The law relating to the unilateral delimitation of maritime space by the coastal State is more consistent with the law relating to the delimitation of maritime space between States than existing studies of the implications of climate-related change for maritime jurisdiction have recognized. This consistency has been obscured by

[142] It may be more difficult to anticipate if or when those facts or circumstances will arise.

the assumption that maritime baselines and most limits measured from them are ambulatory. Rothwell and Stephens accordingly suggest that the 'affirmation of stability in the context of maritime boundaries sits in stark contrast to the manner in which rising sea levels are addressed in the context of baselines ... with territorial sea baselines shifting landwards as the seas encroach'.[143] They consider the immobility of international maritime boundaries 'difficult to reconcile with the rapidly changing coastline conditions ... driven by sea level rise'.[144] This assessment fails to appreciate how and why the coast matters for both interstate and unilateral maritime delimitation. Specifically, it fails to recognize that the relationship does not logically or legally entail the continuing dependency of established maritime limits and boundaries on the coastal configuration. The law is not inconsistent in its approach to maritime limits and international maritime boundaries. What must be recognized is that maritime limits are *not ambulatory* for the same reasons that international maritime boundaries are not ordinarily ambulatory (i.e. in the absence of clear agreement to the contrary).

The law of the sea accords aspects of physical and human geography a legal significance that does not imply the ongoing contingency of maritime limits or boundaries on the persistence of the same geographical circumstances shown in contemporary charts or existing 'on the ground' at the point of their establishment. The role given to geography in this context is consistent with a broader concern to secure a stable 'legal order for the seas and oceans' through a spatial and functional division of State rights in the sea. This depends substantially upon maritime limits and boundaries being legally justified—a result of their construction in accordance with rules and methods that symbolically reflect the basic principle that entitlement to maritime space follows from the possession of territorial sovereignty over coastal land ('the land dominates the sea'). It also depends upon maritime limits and boundaries being functional—i.e. locatable and so observable and enforceable. The role of geography in the construction and description of maritime limits and boundaries serves these ends.

The law still allows neighbouring States to establish an ambulatory boundary by agreement. It also allows coastal States to revise unilaterally established maritime limits (other than the limits of the continental shelf) to inter alia take subsequent geographical change into account. Yet in neither case is this legally required. The law permits the establishment of an ambulatory maritime boundary by clear agreement and allows the coastal State to revise established maritime limits in response to geographical change as (a) an exercise justified by the geographical circumstances, that is (b) deliberately effected in a manner consistent with the concern to ensure that the relevant boundaries and limits are identifiable and observable, thereby allowing their effective operation in the division of State jurisdiction at sea.

143 D Rothwell, T Stephens, *The International Law of the Sea* (Bloomsbury, 2016) 413.
144 Ibid.

The exceptional prohibition of subsequent adjustments to the established limits of the continental shelf by the coastal State is consistent with the same vision of a stable legal order. As we have seen, this prohibition reflects a concern to preserve the international seabed area against the unilateral extension of national jurisdiction. It is not an exception to the alleged rule that maritime limits are generally ambulatory but an exception to the freedom of States to revise established maritime limits (the act of revision remaining subject to the rules and principles governing delimitation in the first instance).

The relocation of maritime limits and boundaries is in no way a requirement that follows from or is implied by the role of geography in the law relating to their construction. Given the natural variability of the coastal environment, such a requirement would be onerous and may lead to uncertainty regarding the location of limits and boundaries as well as their lawfulness and opposability. Perhaps more importantly, the role of geography in justifying the location and configuration of maritime limits and boundaries at the time of delimitation does not mean that geographical change leaves established limits and boundaries without justification. The symbolic role of geography in the rules and principles governing the construction of maritime limits and boundaries provides a principled basis for the delimitation process. This imbues the process itself with a certain rationality—providing reasons for allowing certain moves and denying others. It also contributes to the legitimacy of the resulting maritime limits and boundaries and thus acceptance of and respect for these legal limits by other States. Legitimacy and lawfulness in this regard refer back to the principled process of delimitation. As such, subsequent geographical change can have no bearing upon the lawfulness or legitimacy of established maritime limits and boundaries, which depends upon the adequacy of the delimitation process.

7

Projecting Change

The Map and the Territory

I. Introduction

The 'low-water line' may be more likely to evoke the image of a coast at low tide than the cartographical expression of a calculation of averages over time—at least for those who are not directly responsible for collecting or processing the relevant data or practically reliant on the resulting line. Yet it is the latter abstraction which Article 3 of the Convention on the Territorial Sea and Contiguous Zone (TSC) and Article 5 of the United Nations Convention on the Law of the Sea (UNCLOS) refer to as the 'normal baseline'. Because the low-water line may change over time, it is often assumed that the 'normal baseline' also changes over time, requiring a corresponding adjustment of zonal limits measured from it. More sophisticated versions of this thesis recognize that what matters is not merely a change in the configuration of the coast but the consequences of such change for a recalculation of the location of the low-water line.[1] Nevertheless, the intuitive plausibility of the notion that ambulatory maritime limits follow a 'naturally' ambulatory low-water line may have more to do with the image of a coast at low tide than an appreciation of either the factors involved in constructing the low-water line or the content of the baselines provisions.

Most versions of the ambulatory thesis rely implicitly upon an understanding that the definition of the normal baseline as the low-water line ties it to a changeable geographical feature. This has been taken to straightforwardly indicate that the baseline must change as that feature does. This line of reasoning has almost certainly done more work than Caron's argument from 'negative implication' in encouraging the ambulatory thesis. Indeed, its pervasiveness may explain why the deficiencies of Caron's more elaborate analysis have generally been overlooked.

The same logic is occasionally extended to so-called 'artificial' baselines—closing lines, straight baselines, and archipelagic baselines—which are understood to be subject to change due to the location of basepoints on the ambulatory low-water line or other changeable geographical features.[2] It remains interesting—and

[1] MW Reed, *Shore and Sea Boundaries*, vol 3 (US GPO, 2000), 185; Schofield, 'Rising Waters, Shrinking States', 209, 221–2; ILA-BC, Final Report, 3.

[2] Schofield, 'Rising Waters, Shrinking States', 211. However, Schofield also suggests that straight and archipelagic baselines might be legally fixed by the deposit of charts: ibid, 224 and cf discussion below.

Geographical Change and the Law of the Sea. Kate Purcell, Oxford University Press (2019). © Kate Purcell.
DOI: 10.1093/oso/9780198743644.001.0001

significant—that the notion of a 'naturally ambulatory baseline' is so rarely extended in this way. It is also notable that where it has been extended, it has also been suggested that 'artificial' baselines might in any case be legally 'fixed' by the deposit of the charts or lists of coordinates by which they are described.[3]

The process of reasoning leading to these conclusions is rarely made explicit. Both its form and substance, however, are connoted by a debate that *has* been carried on expressly. A number of scholars considering the implications of coastal change for maritime limits—the ILA's Committee on Baselines under the Law of the Sea (ILA-BC) in particular—have devoted considerable attention to the question of whether the normal baseline is the low-water line 'in fact' or as charted. The arguments advanced on this front have been presented as contributing to an enquiry into whether change in the low-water line legally requires the relocation of the normal baseline. In fact, the debate as a whole can be seen to presuppose the ambulatory thesis. Specifically, it appears to be premised on the understanding that the normal baseline *will* change when physical change means that a recalculated low-water line will differ from that currently shown on charts used to locate maritime limits. The issue has been framed as a question of *when* the legal change will take effect and whether it can be postponed (temporarily or indefinitely). As such, the ambulatory thesis is affirmed rather than interrogated. An examination of the terms of this debate nevertheless casts further light upon how and why that thesis is so often presupposed.

This chapter draws attention to and questions the transference of ideas regarding the natural variability of the coastal environment to maritime limits constructed or described by reference to geographic objects. This association or identification underlies both sides of the facts/charts debate. It is helpful to recall that the law relating to the unilateral and interstate delimitation of maritime space does not generally refer to geographical features as materially encountered but to their cartographic representation. The latter is never purely mimetic, even if it has a clear geographic referent and the reasons for its depiction relate to the materiality of the feature concerned (a low-tide elevation, for example, is charted because it is a navigational hazard and it is a navigational hazard because of its physical characteristics). It is not geography as such but its re-presentation on charts that facilitates the spatial organization of maritime jurisdiction.

The question of whether the baseline is a line on a chart or its geographic referent must be considered in the context of the relationship between cartography and jurisdiction in the law more broadly. It is important to recognize that the answer to this question is not necessarily an answer to the question of whether the low-water line or other types of baseline are ambulatory. In the existing literature, the question of whether the coastal State may rely upon the charted low-water line as the baseline *despite* subsequent coastal change typically supervenes on the view

[3] Schofield, 'Rising Waters, Shrinking States', 211.

that the normal baseline is ambulatory. At the same time, this formulation of the central question as one of 'facts or charts' helps us to understand why the ambulatory thesis has been presupposed. In short, a focus on geographical facts and charts is encouraged by and encourages a focus on accuracy and currency. Where these objectives govern, geographical change requires a response. What requires clarification in this context is whether these are objectives of the *law* and, if so, whether they translate into a legal requirement to adjust maritime limits to reflect coastal change.

The facts/charts debate focuses on the relationship between charts and the geographical features they represent. The problem is the straightforward identification of maritime limits—distinctly legal constructs—with one or the other. There is clearly a connection between the variable natural environment and the chart by virtue of the representational function of the latter, however mediated that may be by other interests and objectives. Charts are generally updated to reflect geographical change, particularly that relevant to their primary use for navigation. It may thus appear that the adjustment of the normal baseline in the event of coastal change is an inevitable consequence of the logic of charting. Legal limits, however, are neither natural facts nor the representation of such facts on charts. The chart is not the physical geography to which it refers and maritime limits are not the charted geographic features by reference to which they are constructed and described. The way in which maritime limits refer to charted geography is not identical with or even analogous to the way in which a chart refers to physical geography. Crucially, the law relating to maritime delimitation does not aspire to truth correspondence between coastal geography and jurisdictional limits.

II. The Facts/Charts Debate

The facts/charts debate is concerned with the question of whether the charted or 'actual' low-water line constitutes the normal baseline where there is a discrepancy between them. The initial formulation of this question in these terms appears to be attributable to Michael Reed, who identified it as an issue in the US 'tidelands cases' regarding rights to 'submerged lands'.[4] Though there may be other reasons for variance—for example, where charts or the surveys upon which they are based are inaccurate[5]—it is a question that has been directly associated with the prospect of intervening coastal change leaving an existing chart at odds with current geographical 'realities'.[6]

4 Reed, *Shore and Sea Boundaries*, vol 3, 178–85.
5 Ibid, 181-2.
6 Ibid, 177–83; ILA-BC, *Final Report*, 1–2, Annex 31–2; Schofield, 'Rising Waters, Shrinking States'.

The facts/charts debate has been taken up in the literature considering the implications of climate-related change for maritime limits, most notably by Clive Schofield and the ILA-BC (of which Reed was a member). In this context, the focus has been on the suggestion that a coastal State may rely on the low-water line shown in charts predating (or based on surveys predating) coastal change as the lawful baseline.[7] This proposal generally presupposes the ambulatory thesis; it is presented as a 'solution' or, at least, a stopgap with respect to the problem of ambulatory baselines.

Scholars such as Schofield who have elaborated on the legal basis for this solution have concentrated on the legal definition of the normal baseline, emphasizing the reference to the low-water line 'as marked on large-scale charts officially recognized by the coastal State'.[8] It is held to follow that 'it is the chart that is the legal document which can be relied upon'—an interpretation Schofield considers to be supported by the 'tendency [of legal authorities] to rely on the chart as the legal document on which to reply regarding the position of normal low water line baselines'.[9] The effect, he argues, is to '[allow] normal baselines to be invested with a degree of stability' in the sense that they will not change until—or unless—the chart is amended.[10]

Schofield associates the reference to the charted low-water line in UNCLOS Article 5 with two options that may be open to the coastal State concerned to preserve its maritime limits in the event of coastal change. First, the State may choose to officially recognize a particular chart representing coastal geography at a particular point in time for 'maritime jurisdictional purposes' as opposed to 'safety of navigation purposes where it would remain vital to show changes to coastlines over time'.[11] Alternatively, a State may adopt what Prescott and Bird have called 'a policy of masterly inactivity', electing not to update charts to reflect geographical change.[12] Notably, the latter strategy is only likely to be viable for as long as existing charts comply with requirements relating to safety of navigation. The coastal State's discretion will be limited by its responsibilities in this regard, including obligations under the International Convention for the Safety of Life at Sea (SOLAS) (1974).

Schofield expresses doubt about whether either 'policy' would be consistent with international law, though he suggests that this method of 'fixing' maritime limits 'would probably be effective as a matter of domestic law'.[13] Indeed, while

[7] ILA-BC, *Final Report*, 1–2, Annex 31–2; Schofield, 'Rising Waters, Shrinking States', 220–2.

[8] See esp Schofield, 'Rising Waters, Shrinking States', 220–4. See also Schofield and Freestone, 'Options to Protect Coastlines', 162. While Schofield reviews other options for 'fixing' maritime limits, including a 'liberal interpretation' of Article 7(2), the application of Article 76(9), and the possibility of reclassifying the relevant maritime areas as historic waters (a strategy he acknowledges is problematic), his work in this area has focused on the normal baseline in particular.

[9] Schofield, 'Rising Waters, Shrinking States', 220–1.

[10] Ibid.

[11] Ibid.

[12] Ibid, 221; Prescott and Bird, 'The Influence of Rising Sea Levels on Baselines', 297.

[13] Schofield, 'Rising Waters, Shrinking States', 225.

Schofield suggests that the charted line may be relied upon, he considers it 'likely that a tension would develop between the officially recognized chart for maritime jurisdictional purposes and (increasingly) reality as reflected in the charting used for navigation'.[14] He sees the recognition or non-recognition of claims based on geographical circumstances that have since changed as determinative of 'the utility of such policy'.[15]

It seems that Schofield, then, does not consider the charted low-water line to represent the legal limit notwithstanding changes in its 'actual position'. If the charted line were accepted as lawful notwithstanding subsequent geographical change, there would be no 'tension' between official charts showing maritime limits and navigational charts showing subsequent geographical change. This analysis betrays the belief that, unless the law changes, the ambulatory thesis and the consequences it identifies for maritime limits are inescapable. Schofield's view is that '[u]ltimately there may be a need for a new process or understanding regarding either the fixing of normal baselines and/or maritime limits'.[16] While he suggests that a new customary law to this effect may develop through State practice, he points to 'multilateral agreement on ... a revised legal regime applicable to normal baselines' as 'an alternative and arguably preferable approach'.[17] It is worth noting in this regard that the development of customary law would depend upon the States that engage in the relevant practice—i.e. retaining established baselines—also believing that this practice is lawful, which would not be the case if the ambulatory thesis were accepted.

Schofield's analysis does not challenge the view that the existing law provides for ambulatory maritime limits. Yet it suggests a rather particular understanding of *how* the law does so. While Schofield has also referred to Caron's arguments regarding UNCLOS Articles 7(2) and 76(9), his reasoning implies that Article 5 is in fact the primary source of the problem (ambulatory baselines) as well as a possible if temporary solution (reliance on charts predating coastal change).[18] Schofield and Arsana have recently set out this claim more explicitly, asserting that

> as the low-water line moves in response to sea level rise, so the 'normal' baselines and the maritime claims measured from them will shift. This is fundamentally because normal baselines are coincident with the 'low-water line along the coast as marked on large scale charts officially recognized by the coastal State (LOSC, Article 5)'.[19]

14 Ibid, 221.
15 Ibid.
16 Ibid, 229.
17 Ibid, 230.
18 Ibid, 210, 220.
19 Schofield and Arsana, 'Climate Change and the Limits of Maritime Jurisdiction', 134.

III. Article 5 and the 'Actual' Low-Water Line

To take Article 5 as both evidence of the ambulatory character of the normal baseline and a possible basis for preserving established baselines against change requires a somewhat problematic two-step interpretation of the provision. Without any textual justification, the article appears to be read as two separate clauses, providing first that 'the normal baseline ... is the low-water line along the coast' and second that the line is to be 'marked on large-scale charts officially recognized by the coastal State'. In this way a wedge is driven between the charted low-water line, which may be relied upon 'as a practical matter', and something thought of as the low-water line 'in fact', which either *is* the lawful baseline or is the line which charts showing the normal baseline must, as a matter of legal obligation, be adjusted to reflect.[20]

The ILA-BC's recent work on the normal baseline as defined in Article 5 also draws a distinction between the 'actual' low-water line and the charted low-water line.[21] The Committee's 'two-part mandate' was to 'identify the existing law on the normal baseline' and 'assess if there is a need for further clarification or development of that law'.[22] This was considered necessary in view of (a) the coastal impacts of climate change, (b) the artificial extension of existing coasts, (c) issues arising in *Nicaragua v Honduras* (2007) and *Guyana v Suriname* (2007) regarding the location of the normal baseline, and (d) the importance of the normal baseline for the construction of other types of baseline.[23] The ILA-BC's focus, however, was narrowed from the outset by the decision to structure its enquiry around the distinction between 'the charted low-water line and the actual low-water line', which was assumed but never demonstrated to be pivotal.[24] By taking the crucial question to be 'whether the Article 5 normal baseline is a line on a chart (the charted low-water line) or a line on the "ground" (the actual low-water line)',[25] the ILA-BC emphasized the difference between the 'actual' line and its depiction—terms already suggesting the priority of the former. While it noted a strong evidential presumption that the charted line was accurate, the ILA-BC concluded that where 'significant physical change [has] occurred so that the chart does not provide an accurate representation of the actual low-water line as the chosen vertical datum', the altered 'actual low-water line' and not the charted line is the 'legal normal baseline'.[26]

Both Schofield and the ILA-BC clearly consider changes to the normal baseline due to significant coastal change such as that associated with rising seas to

[20] See Caron, 'When Law Makes Climate Change Worse', 634, fn 76; Caron, 'Climate Change, Sea Level Rise and the Coming Uncertainty in Oceanic Boundaries', 9, fn 20.

[21] ILA-BC, *Final Report*, 3.

[22] Ibid, 1.

[23] Ibid, 1–2.

[24] ILA-BC, *Internal Discussion Document* (2010), 1–2; ILA-BC, *Final Report*, 2.

[25] ILA-BC, *Final Report*, 3.

[26] Ibid, 31.

be a serious problem. The ILA-BC has concluded that the low-water line shown on charts predating such change cannot be relied on as the legal baseline,[27] while Schofield has suggested it might be—if only temporarily and pending what is considered a necessary amendment of the law.[28] The difficulty with both views is that they depend upon a reading of Article 5 that is at odds with the ordinary meaning of its terms in their context and in light of the treaty's object and purpose.[29]

A. The Text

Article 5 of UNCLOS, like Article 3 of the TSC, refers in a single phrase to 'the low-water line along the coast as marked on large-scale charts'. There is a grammatical difference in the French text, which refers to 'la laisse de basse mer le long de la côte, telle qu'elle est indiquée sur les cartes marines à grande échelle reconnues officiellement par l'Etat côtier'. The comma placement does not alter the meaning of the phrase: the text that follows can only be understood to provide information about 'la laisse de basse mer', which is itself a cartographical construct—specifically, a category of tidal datum encompassing a range of definitions.

The 'low-water line' is not a term of art defined in either the TSC or UNCLOS. It is nevertheless clear that expression refers to the water line at low tide. It is also apparent that this cannot mean the line of low tide at a given locality on a given day. Beyond the fact that this variable line is not 'marked on large scale-charts', its use as a baseline would be impractical and inconsistent with the objective of ensuring the ready observance of maritime limits by sea users. A tidal datum, specifically a low-water datum, is the intended and appropriate point of reference.

B. The Low-water Line as a Cartographical Construct

The 'low-water line' is by definition a charted line and not a line on the ground that is subsequently represented on 'large-scale charts'. Of course, this cartographical construct does refer to and represent certain facts. However, it is important to understand the nature of the relevant facts and the manner of their representation.

The low-water line is a linear expression of averages based on measurements of variable heights of the tide at a limited number of particular points on the coast. Depending on the definition of low water used, the resulting line will rarely if ever correspond with the line of the tide at a particular place at any particular moment

[27] Ibid, 30.
[28] Schofield, 'Rising Waters, Shrinking States', 220–1.
[29] VCLT Art 31(1).

of time.[30] Whichever definition of low water is used, there will be substantial parts of the charted line that do not correspond with the 'actual low-water line' as it would be calculated at that particular point on the coast.

To understand these features of the low-water line, it is necessary to appreciate the physical and interpretive variability of the point at which land meets sea. The water line along coasts and offshore features is naturally fluctuating. It moves with tides which in most parts of the world have a 'semidiurnal' cycle of two low and two high tides each lunar day.[31] In the case of 'mixed' semidiurnal tides, the two low tides have different heights, as do each of the two high tides—a circumstance known as 'diurnal inequality'.[32] The two low tides are known as Lower Low Water and Higher Low Water, the two high tides as Lower High Water and Higher High Water.[33] While a diurnal component is responsible for mixed tides, there are relatively few areas where diurnal cycles with just one low and one high tide each day are dominant.[34]

Tidal range, the difference in height between consecutive low and high tides,[35] may vary over an approximately 27.5 day cycle, with fortnightly spring tides exaggerating both highs and lows, and neap tides in alternate weeks resulting in a reduced tidal range.[36] Tidal range is also influenced by local bathymetry, coastal configuration, and the width of the continental shelf.[37] The greatest tidal range in the world approaches 17 metres.[38] Yet even a relatively narrow tidal range can translate into significant horizontal distances between low and high tides where there is a low coastal gradient. The most extensive intertidal zones result from the combination of a high tidal range and a low gradient coast.[39]

The water line along a coast changes over the course of a day and across long period oscillations ranging from approximately 14 days to a month, and in the case of the nodal cycle, 18.6 years. So called 'tideless seas' such as the Baltic and Eastern

[30] The ILA-BC observes that '[t]he actual low-water line defined using the LAT datum will only be visible once every full metonic cycle of 18.6 years provided the meteorological conditions are normal. This means the low-water line will actually be underwater during all but the very lowest tides.': ILA-BC, *Final Report*, 32.

[31] US National Oceanic and Atmospheric Administration (NOAA) <http://oceanservice.noaa.gov/education/kits/tides/tides07_cycles.html> accessed 1 July 2012; Bird, *Coastal Geomorphology*, 25. A lunar or tidal day is approximately twenty-four hours and fifty minutes: IHO, *Hydrographic Dictionary* S-32 (5th edn, IHB, 1994), def. 1241.

[32] IHO, *Hydrographic Dictionary*, def. 1417.

[33] IHO, *Manual on Hydrography* (1st edn, IHB, 2005, as corrected), 264.

[34] Bird, *Coastal Geomorphology*, 25, 28.

[35] This will be 'the difference between mean high and mean low spring tides where the tides are semi-diurnal, or between mean higher high tide and mean lower low tide where the diurnal component introduces inequality in the levels of successive tides': ibid, 28.

[36] Each type of tide occurs twice over the lunar month, spring tides ordinarily coinciding with the first and third lunar phase, neap tides with the second and fourth (in the case of each tide, an interval of approximately 14.6 days): ibid, 26.

[37] S Haslett, *Coastal Systems* (Routledge, 2008), 78.

[38] This range has been recorded in Canada's Fundy and Unger Bays: <http://www.waterlevels.gc.ca> accessed 12 January 2012; Bird, *Encyclopedia of the World's Coastal Landforms*, 141–2.

[39] Haslett, *Coastal Systems*, 79.

Mediterranean are less influenced by astronomical tides but still experience 'meteorological tides'[40]—changes in the water line due to local meteorological conditions such as barometric pressure and wind, which may combine to produce storm surges[41] or negative surges.[42] These conditions can also interact with astronomical tides, affecting timing and height in the short term.[43] Longer term changes in the volume of water in the ocean associated with climate change (thermal expansion and greater input from other reservoirs, mostly land-based ice and water) have led to rises in mean sea level (MSL).[44] The pace and degree of global sea level rise is predicted to increase significantly (though not uniformly).[45] Mean sea level is affected regionally by changes in ocean circulation or atmospheric pressure and locally by vertical land movements, although the latter do not affect ocean volume.[46] As the MSL changes, so does the location of the low-water line.

A tidal datum is 'a standard elevation defined by a certain phase of the tide'.[47] It is generally an average based on measurements of the water level at a phase of the tidal cycle taken over a defined period, the 'tidal datum epoch'. Different countries use different tidal datum epochs, although the period is usually longer than 18.6 years to include a full lunar nodal cycle. While the relevant phase identified by UNCLOS Article 5 (and TSC Article 3) is low tide, this can be defined in a number of ways. Options include (a) the mean level—mean low water (MLW); (b) the mean level in conjunction with tidal range—mean low water springs (MLWS) or mean low water neap (MLWN); (c) 'the lowest tide level which can be predicted to occur under average meteorological conditions and under any combination of astronomical conditions'—lowest astronomical tide (LAT); and (d) lowest low water (LLW), which is 'an arbitrary level conforming to the lowest tide observed at a place, or somewhat lower'.[48]

Each of these definitions of the low-water line involves an abstraction from and generalization of measurements based on past records and, in some cases, probability-based predictions or approximations. Where averages or 'lowest lows' are based on tidal gauge measurements, a range of 'chart datum transfer techniques' may be used to 'provide the location of the low water line at sites along the coastline other than at tide gauge sites'.[49] As Maling notes '[t]he accuracy of the

[40] Meteorological tides are also known as 'radiational tides': DT Pugh, *Changing Sea Levels: Effects of Tides, Weather, and Climate* (CUP, 2004), 51, 129.

[41] Ibid, 129–31.

[42] Ibid.

[43] Land Information New Zealand <http://www.linz.govt.nz/hydro/tidal-info/tidal-intro/meteorological-effects> accessed 18 September 2013.

[44] IPCC, *Fifth Assessment Report*, Working Group II, 5.3.2.1.

[45] Ibid, 5.3.2.1–5.3.2.3.

[46] Ibid.

[47] US NOAA, 'Tides and Currents' <https://tidesandcurrents.noaa.gov/datum_options.html> accessed 6 February 2017.

[48] IHO, *Hydrographic Dictionary*, defs 3147, 3150, 3149, 2936, 2937.

[49] CLCS, *Scientific and Technical Guidelines*, 29.

delineation of the low-water line by interpolation depends to no small measure upon the density of the soundings which have been made in the area, the reliability of the tidal information used to reduce them to chart datum and the gradient of the beach'.[50]

The low-water line shown on a nautical chart '[depicts] the planimetric position of chart datum, for this is the level to which the soundings have been reduced and therefore represents zero depth at the appropriate state of the tide'.[51] It is important to recognize that '[t]he delineation of this line is therefore an "office compilation", being a boundary interpolated between the soundings and drawn at the time when these are reduced to chart datum and plotted'.[52]

Tide-coordinated aerial photography, and, more recently, satellite imagery and LIDAR (light detection and ranging) may be used to assist the charting of both the high- and low-water line. There are various challenges associated with the use of these technologies for charting a line reflecting the tidal datum;[53] however, the more important point for present purposes is that these technologies may only improve the accuracy of the cartographical representation of what is already a functional construct rather than a natural or morphological feature that can be directly identified on the ground. The character of the low-water line as a cartographical construct is unaltered by the fact that it may be possible to photograph the line of low-water in a particular place at a particular moment within a tidal datum epoch (a period of more than 18.6 years) when it corresponds with the selected tidal datum. The low-tide line 'on the ground' at that moment is not important either legally or cartographically; it is merely of use in the task of graphically representing the chart datum. Any concern with accuracy here relates to the accuracy of the charted line as a representation of the accepted definition of the tidal datum.

The chart datum functions cartographically as a 'permanently established surface from which soundings or tide heights are referenced'.[54] The chief objective from the perspective of the hydrographer and nautical cartographer is to ensure safety of navigation. Though the International Hydrographic Office has indicated a preference for LAT as the chart datum in areas with an appreciable tidal range, this is not obligatory and a range of definitions of the low-water line may serve as a navigationally safe chart datum.[55]

[50] DH Maling, *Measurements from Maps: Principles and Methods of Cartometry* (Pergamon, 1989), 242.
[51] Ibid, 241.
[52] Ibid.
[53] See CE Parish, 'Shoreline Mapping' in Yang and Li, *Advances in Mapping from Remote Sensor Imagery* (CRC Press, 2012) 145–68.
[54] IHO, *Hydrographic Dictionary*, def. 1222.
[55] IHO, *Regulations for International Charts and Chart Specifications* S-4 (4.7.0 edn, July 2017), B-405. See also IHO Resolution 3/1919, 'Chart Datum Definition', as amended 2008.

IV. The Legal Significance of the Low-Water Line

Both Schofield and the ILA-BC understand that 'the low-water line' is a tidal datum and not a physical tide line on the coast. Yet they have paid insufficient attention to the fact that the law refers exclusively to a line that is already charted by definition. Article 5 does not pick out 'the low-water line' as some non-cartographical matter of fact and require that it is 'marked on large-scale charts officially recognized by the coastal State'. It identifies the low-water line as the normal baseline in significant part because it is a linear representation of the 'coast' already marked on nautical charts.

To fully understand the legal significance of this charted line it is essential to note that it is not the only linear representation of the coast shown on nautical charts, which also depict some version of the high-water line. It is not necessarily the case that the low-water line (or some version of it) better represents the dividing line between land and sea, though it is important that the low-water line *does* represent this dividing line (albeit not exclusively). Instead, the low-water line appears to have been preferred to the high-water line because it allows the coastal State to maximize its maritime jurisdiction.

A. The Value of a Charted Line

The ILA-BC has concluded that the 'actual' low-water line is determined by applying the tidal datum used in charts officially recognized by the coastal State to the present coast—a recalculation of the chart datum taking into account 'evidence of the physical coastal realities or the actual coastal configuration'.[56] This assumes that it is the facts which the charted line seeks to represent which are legally significant rather than the charted line itself. These facts may indeed be significant to the hydrographer and cartographer as well as the navigator (the chief end user of nautical charts). Yet it is far from obvious that they are independently significant from the perspective of the law relating to maritime jurisdiction. The ILA-BC's account of the 'actual' low-water line also imports a concern with accuracy and currency in the representation of the relevant facts when there is no clear evidence that this is a concern of the law.

UNCLOS Article 5 has its origins in the work of the Second Sub-Committee of the Committee on Territorial Waters at the 1930 Hague Conference. The Second Sub-Committee's conclusions were not formally adopted but appended to the Committee's *Final Report* (lack of agreement on the breadth of the territorial sea

[56] ILA-BC, *Final Report*, 3.

precluding the adoption of a Convention on this topic in 1930).[57] They nevertheless proved influential in the subsequent development of the law on baselines.

In 1930, the Second Sub-Committee proposed that '[s]ubject to the provisions regarding bays and islands, the breadth of the territorial sea is measured from the line of the low-water mark along the entire coast'.[58] It also specified that 'the line of low-water mark is that indicated on the charts officially used by the coastal State, provided the latter does not appreciably depart from the line of mean low-water springs'.[59] In its 2012 report, the ILA-BC suggested that this draft provision 'did not refer to the line, per se, but to the chart datum that, when applied to that coast during the chart-making process, would result in that particular charted line'.[60] This is inconsistent with the record of negotiations, which indicate that it was the line shown on existing nautical charts that was considered to have advantages recommending its use as the baseline. An important virtue of the charted low-water line was and remains the fact that it could be immediately identified and observed.

The ILA-BC has argued that '[t]he insertion of the reference to charts' was a response to 'practical difficulties resulting from the absence of a universally agreed vertical datum for defining low water', stressing that this 'drafting innovation' was 'intended to address these difficulties, and was not intended to give primacy to the charted line'.[61] The drafting history does not support this analysis. The definition of low water as a vertical datum was not discussed in the abstract as distinct from and prior to the question of charting the same as a line. Instead, the fact that some version of the low-water line was (or was understood to be) shown on existing charts was one of the main reasons for its identification as an appropriate baseline.

The fact that different States used different definitions of the low-water line on existing nautical charts was expressly acknowledged at the Hague Conference but does not seem to have been considered a problem.[62] The general reference to 'the line of low-water mark'—already a reference to a *charted* line of low-water—was understood to cover the different definitions of low water in fact used in nautical charts around the world. But it was not *because* different definitions were used that the baseline was identified as the charted line. It was simply understood that the *charted* low-water line could be defined and established in a number of ways. The question of whether the charted line should have 'primacy' never arose because it was only ever the charted line which was identified as a candidate for the baseline (alongside closing lines for bays and rivers and what were later termed 'straight' baselines).

[57] Rosenne (1975/IV)) 1411, 1419–23.
[58] Ibid, 1419.
[59] Ibid.
[60] ILA-BC, *Final Report*, 11.
[61] Ibid, 11–12.
[62] Rosenne (1975/IV), 1419.

The Second Sub-Committee's proviso that 'the line of low-water mark ... indicated on the charts officially used by the coastal State' should not 'appreciably depart from the line of mean low-water springs' was consistent with the focus on the low-water line as a cartographical construct—a line shown on charts. It was also consistent with the definition of the baseline in terms covering the variety of tidal datums used on existing charts.

The suggestion that the 'low-water mark' should be the line of MLWS seems to have originated in the replies of South Africa, Australia, and Great Britain (India and New Zealand identifying with the British view) to a question from the Preparatory Committee for the Codification Conference. The Preparatory Committee had asked whether the baseline was the line 'of low-tide following the sinuosities of the coast; or a line drawn between the outermost points of the coast, islands, islets or rocks; or some other line'.[63] The aforementioned States referred to the MLWS as the baseline along the coast. Yet they did not suggest that this definition of the low-water line had any special virtues; rather, the MLWS seems to have been specified because the States in question used charts prepared by the British Admiralty which employed this particular tidal datum at the time.[64] Poland also mentioned the 'line of low-tide at spring tides' but in connection with a general system of straight baselines connecting the outermost points of the coast.[65]

Germany noted that it used MLWS for marine charts in the North Sea and MSL in the Baltic. Yet it also emphasized that (a) different methods were used to establish MLWS in the charts of different States, and (b) a number of States used other tidal datums 'to determine the base line'.[66] In view of these differences, Germany proposed that the definition of the baseline refer simply to the 'sea level adopted in the charts' of the coastal State.[67] Finland, on the other hand, considered that 'a definite decision should be reached as to which low-water mark should be adopted as the base line from which to count the breadth of territorial waters'.[68]

The Preparatory Committee noted 'the different meanings that can be given to the expression "low water"'.[69] It suggested that this was 'a question of a technical character' that governments 'may submit ... for examination by their experts so as to enable the latter to agree at the Conference upon the best expression to employ'.[70] While it left open the possibility that States might agree to specify a particular version of the 'low-water mark', it did not comment on whether this was necessary or desirable.

63 Rosenne (1975/II), 253–5.
64 IHO, *Manual on Hydrography*, 267.
65 Rosenne (1975/II), 255.
66 Ibid, 253.
67 Ibid.
68 Ibid, 254.
69 Ibid, 256.
70 Ibid.

There was no discussion of the expression 'low water' in the general meetings of the Committee on Territorial Waters at the Hague Conference, though an amendment proposed by the United States recommended that the limits of the territorial sea be measured from 'whatever line of sea level is adopted in the charts of the coastal State'—an even broader definition insofar as it did not specify a *low*-water line.[71] The matter was considered by the Second Sub-Committee, which had 'members ... drawn from the delegations of Chile, France, Germany, Great Britain, Greece, Italy, Japan, Norway, Poland, Portugal, Sweden, and the United States' and included M. François, Rapporteur for the Committee and later the International Law Commission's (ILC) Special Rapporteur on the territorial sea and high seas (including the continental shelf).[72] The only record of the Sub-Committee's work, however, is the proposed text and accompanying observations in its final report.[73]

In the Second Sub-Committee's view, 'divergences due to the adoption of different criteria on the different charts [were] very slight and [could] be disregarded'.[74] It explained that the proviso that the charted line should not 'depart appreciably from the line of mean low-water spring tide' was intended to 'guard against abuse' and 'would only be of importance in a case that was clearly fraudulent'.[75] Notably, it also characterized the MLWS as 'the more scientific criterion'.[76] Critically, the comparator here was the general definition of the baseline as 'the line of low-water mark' and not alternative definitions of the tidal datum (e.g. MLW, MLWN, LAT, or LLW). The MLWS was not considered more scientific than other tidal datums but more scientific than a general reference to 'the low-water line', which might admit abuse.

The Second Sub-Committee, contrary to the claims of the ILA-BC, did not consider 'the existence of multiple vertical datums to define the low-water line' a problem.[77] Instead, it expressly recognized that the low-water line shown on existing charts, whatever the vertical datum, could be used as the legal baseline. The proviso that this line should not 'depart appreciably' from the line of MLWS did not privilege this vertical datum over others—the Sub-Committee considered the difference between possible datums to be inconsequential, meaning that none of the alternatives would 'depart appreciably' from MLWS. Instead, the proviso was intended to prevent clearly 'fraudulent' claims. It anticipated the possibility that States might take advantage of the less 'scientific' expression, 'the line of low-water mark', to construct a line that did not correspond with *any* of the vertical datums in fact used on nautical charts.

[71] Rosenne (1975/IV), 1397, 1399.
[72] Ibid, 1278.
[73] Ibid, 1419.
[74] Ibid.
[75] Ibid.
[76] Ibid.
[77] ILA-BC, *Final Report*, 11.

The fate of the proviso during the preparatory work of the ILC for the 1958 Law of the Sea Conference (LOSC) confirms this account of its significance as well as the extent to which the identification of the low-water line as a baseline was a response to the fact that this line was shown on existing charts. The proviso was included in the Special Rapporteur's first report on the regime of the territorial sea in 1952.[78] In the course of the ILC's debates, Amado proposed its deletion on the grounds that 'if the low-water mark in official charts departed appreciably from the line of mean low-water spring tides, those charts would not be accurate and their validity would be questioned by any legal tribunal'.[79] He also expressed concern regarding the subjectivity of an assessment of whether a line departed 'appreciably' from MLWS, although Yepes thought that a dispute on this point could readily be referred to an international tribunal.[80]

Hudson objected more broadly to the definition of the low-water line as the 'normal' baseline, noting that 'it would be applicable only to a coast-line which confronted the sea' which 'was frequently not the case'—i.e. in the case of indented and island-fringed coasts.[81] In relation to the reference to MLWS, Hudson suggested that 'to accept a line indicated on official charts which, incidentally, frequently omitted to show the low-water mark properly, would be inconsistent with the judgment [in *Anglo-Norwegian Fisheries*]'.[82] Yet he was less concerned with 'accuracy' than the '[elevation of] the line of the low-water mark to a position of such importance' given the widespread use of 'an exterior or political coast-line' (i.e. straight baselines) to delimit the territorial sea and the recognition of the lawfulness of this practice in *Anglo-Norwegian Fisheries*.[83] In fact, the Court in *Anglo-Norwegian Fisheries* reinterpreted the so-called 'low-water mark rule' to encompass the use of straight baselines, which was presented as an application of the 'rule' rather than a departure from it. Both a baseline tracing the low-water line and straight baselines in appropriate circumstances were understood to '[show] the character of territorial waters as appurtenant to the land territory'.[84] Notably, the adjective 'normal', which had not been used by the Second Sub-Committee at the Hague Conference, was in fact deleted on this basis at the 1958 LOSC, though it was accidentally reintroduced in the course of drafting changes to remove then reinstate titles for the baselines provisions.[85]

[78] ILC Ybk 1952/II, 33.
[79] ILC Ybk 1952/I, 172.
[80] Ibid, 177–8.
[81] Ibid, 173.
[82] Ibid.
[83] Ibid.
[84] *Anglo-Norwegian Fisheries* (1951), 128–30.
[85] Because the word 'normal' had been deleted from the *text* of draft article 4 and no parallel amendment had been made to the *heading* of the ILC's draft article for the simple reason that article headings had at the time been entirely removed, the ILC's original heading was simply reinserted. In this way the 'normal baseline' was unintentionally revived as the title introducing text from which the adjective 'normal' had been deliberately removed: see UNCLOS I: III, 200; UNCLOS I: II, 61.

The reference to MLWS was provisionally retained in the Special Rapporteur's Second Report[86] and François was charged with investigating the Hague Baselines Committee's view of its purpose.[87] It was later deleted, though not on the grounds of the objections raised in 1952. The Committee of Experts consulted by the Special Rapporteur in 1953 interpreted the proviso in line with the views of the Hague Committee as '[covering] cases of possible bad faith on the part of States in determining the limits of their territorial waters'.[88] However, the experts concluded and the ILC agreed that its omission was 'hardly likely to induce Governments to shift the low-water lines on their charts unreasonably'.[89] In the commentary to its final draft articles, the ILC observed that

> The traditional expression 'low-water mark' may have different meanings; there is no uniform standard by which States in practice determine this line. The Commission considers that it is permissible to adopt as the base line the low-water mark as indicated on large-scale charts officially recognized by the coastal State.

This is also the approach taken in UNCLOS.

B. The Value of the Charted Low-water Line

At the 1930 Hague Conference, the 1958 LOSC, and UNCLOS III it seems to have been taken for granted that existing charts would show some version of the low-water line. McDougal and Burke claim that this assumption was unjustified, most charts showing only the high-water line, taken as the shoreline.[90] While it is true that charts of a certain scale will only show the low-water line where it is a discernible distance from the high-water line,[91] the 1958 and 1982 Conventions specify 'the low-water line along the coast as marked on *large-scale* charts'.[92] UNCLOS requires that closing lines, straight baselines, archipelagic baselines, and the lines delimiting roadsteads and the territorial sea, are shown on 'charts of a scale or scales adequate for ascertaining their position'.[93]

McDougal and Burke cite Boggs as authority for the claim that most 'ordinary sailing charts' will not indicate the low-water line.[94] However, 'sailing charts' are

86 ILC Ybk 1953/II, 65.
87 ILC Ybk 1952/I, 178.
88 ILC Ybk 1954/I, 64.
89 ILC Ybk 1953/II, 77; ILC Ybk 1956/II, 267.
90 M McDougal, W Burke, *The Public Order of the Oceans: A Contemporary International Law of the Sea* (YUP, 1962), 321.
91 UN Baselines Study, 3.
92 TSC Art 3; UNCLOS Art 5 (emphasis added).
93 UNCLOS Arts 16, 47(8) (archipelagic baselines).
94 McDougal and Burke, *The Public Order of the Oceans*, 321, fn 43.

the smallest scale nautical chart used for offshore navigation.[95] It is rather 'coast', 'coastal', or 'approach' charts used for inshore coastwise navigation which, as appropriate to their function, will be on a scale adequate to show the low-water line and other features relevant to the construction of straight baselines.[96] This is recognized by Boggs, who identifies a chart showing the approach to the Yangtze River at a scale of approximately 1:121,000 as 'the ideal type of chart from which to delimit the territorial sea—where precise delimitation is desired—because the low-tide line is clearly indicated.'[97] The 1989 UN Baselines Study recommends the use of charts at a scale of between 1:50,000 and 1:200,000.[98] The IOC, IHO, and IAG Advisory Board on the Law of the Sea (ABLOS) has suggested that '[t]he range of suitable scales will normally be from 1:100,000 to 1:1,000,000 for delimitation of the EEZ and continental shelf, while the scale for territorial boundary determinations should be of the order of 1:50,000 to 1:100,000'.[99] Ultimately, the language of the treaties makes it clear that the facility of showing the low-water mark and other baselines and zonal limits is determinative of whether a chart is of an adequate scale.

The designation of the low-water line rather than the high-water line as the baseline still deserves attention. While this was partly a response to the fact that the low-water line was shown on existing nautical charts, the high-water line was also charted—and on a larger number of available charts. Significantly, it appears that both lines were considered to (a) mark in an approximate way where land met sea, and (b) provide a more precise point for measuring the extent of the territorial sea and (later) other maritime zones. The difference between these two legal virtues is worth emphasizing. The concern to identify a more precise starting point for locating zonal limits should not be confused with a concern to more precisely represent the line of the coast in the baseline. The low-water line was valued for its precision in the first sense. It was not suggested that it was a more precise representation of the 'coast', though it was valued in part because it could be taken to represent (in a looser and symbolic sense, and as one among other possibilities) the dividing line between land and sea in many (though not all) geographical circumstances.

The high-water line also had these virtues; however, its use as the baseline does not seem to have been contemplated at the 1930 Hague Conference. This is explained by the influence of particular practices and documents on the Preparatory Committee's development of the 'Bases for Discussion'—in particular, the 1887

[95] IHO, *Hydrographic Dictionary*, def. 745; N Bowditch, *The American Practical Navigator* (US NIMA, 2002), 35.

[96] IHO, *Hydrographic Dictionary*, def. 712; Bowditch, *The American Practical Navigator*, 35.

[97] SW Boggs, 'Delimitation of Seaward Areas under National Jurisdiction' (1951) 45 *AJIL* 240, 252, fn 26.

[98] UN Baselines Study, 2.

[99] ABLOS, *Manual on Technical Aspects of UNCLOS*, 17.

North Sea Convention, which provided inter alia that '[t]he fishermen of [the States parties] shall enjoy the exclusive right of fishery within the distance of 3 miles from low-water mark along the whole extent of the coasts of their respective countries, as well as of the dependent islands and banks'.[100] The 1887 Convention was an important point of reference for bodies considering the regime of territorial waters prior to the Hague Conference, as well as the League of Nations Committee of Experts for the Progressive Codification of International Law (1925–28), which determined that the question of territorial waters was 'sufficiently ripe' for codification. The Institut de Droit International (IDI), International Law Association (ILA), and Harvard Research Group all specified the low-water line as the point of departure for measuring the limits of the territorial sea (subject to the use of closing lines across bays and, in some cases, special rules relating to islands),[101] as did the Committee of Experts in its Draft Convention.[102] This work was also drawn upon by the Preparatory Committee for the Hague Conference.[103]

In *Anglo-Norwegian Fisheries*, the Court had 'no difficulty in finding that, for the purpose of measuring the breadth of the territorial sea, it is the low-water mark as opposed to the high water mark, or the mean between the two tides,[104] which has generally been adopted [as the baseline] in the practice of States'.[105] The reason why States preferred the low-water line to the high-water line was presumably because this maximized their national maritime jurisdiction. It is interesting to note that the ILC's draft article relating to the normal baseline for a short time provided that the high-water line might be taken as the baseline if detailed charts indicating the low-water line were not available.[106] This amendment was proposed by Special Rapporteur François in 1953 at the recommendation of the Committee of Experts, which did not explain why it was considered necessary.[107] It was not discussed until 1954, when François explained that it was a practical solution allowing the mariner to determine the location of zonal limits where the low-water line was not charted.[108] The Commission adopted the amendment, but it was deleted the following year on the grounds that it may be taken to *require* use of the high-water line as the baseline by the coastal State in cases where detailed charts did not show the low-water line.[109]

100 North Sea Convention (1887) Art II.

101 See IDI, *Règles sur la définition et le régime de la mer territorial* (Paris,1894) Art II; IDI, *Projet de règlement relatif à la mer territoriale en temps de paix* (Stockholm, 1928) Art III; ILA Neutrality Committee, *Draft Convention on the Laws of Maritime Jurisdiction in Time of Peace* (Vienna, 1926) Art 5 (referring specifically to the 'low-water mark at ordinary spring tide'); Harvard Research, 'The Law of Territorial Waters' (1929) 23 (2) *AJIL Supplement* 241, 242) (referring to 'the mean low water mark').

102 Rosenne (1975/II), 98 (Art 2).

103 Rosenne (1975/I), xix.

104 Cf the accepted use of MSL on tideless seas.

105 *Anglo-Norwegian Fisheries* (1951), 128.

106 ILC Ybk 1953/II, 76.

107 ILC Ybk 1953/II, 77.

108 ILC Ybk 1954/I, 65.

109 ILC Ybk 1955/I, 196.

This episode illustrates the value of a charted line (whether the high- or low-water line and however defined) in allowing a determination of the location of maritime limits defined by distance with some precision. But it also points to the reasoning underlying the identification of the *low*-water line rather than the *high*-water line as the baseline. The proposed amendment was intended to facilitate respect of the coastal State's maritime limits in the absence of charts showing the low-water line. Its deletion was not based on the view that the high-water line could not be relied upon in these circumstances. It was prompted by a concern that '[t]he sentence in question could be construed as meaning that a State might be obliged to use the high-water line in cases where no charts were available'.[110] In other words, it was removed to clarify that the coastal State was entitled to use the low-water line as the baseline and could not be denied the right to do so purely on the grounds that the low-water line along its coast had not yet been determined (i.e. calculated on a chart).

Significantly, this does not mean that the low-water line was considered to exist as a matter of fact prior to its identification on a chart. Nor does it mean that sea users had to refer to such matters of fact in order to determine the location of the coastal State's maritime limits. If the high-water line was the only line shown on the available charts, it would be perfectly reasonable for States or sea users to refer to it in determining the extent of the coastal State's maritime jurisdiction, which they remain obliged to respect.[111] But the ILC was concerned to clarify that the coastal State remained entitled to use the low-water line as the baseline even if it could not determine the location of limits measured from the low-water line or enforce such limits until the low-water line was constructed on a chart. Use of the low-water line as the baseline was clearly understood to be an entitlement for the benefit of the coastal State. Its benefit over the high-water line is, of course, the extension of national maritime space.

C. The 'Fact' of Entitlement to Maritime Space and the 'Fact' of the Low-water Line

The ILC recognized that a mariner might rely on the charted high-water line to determine the location of maritime limits in the absence of charts showing the low-water line. It also recognized the continuing right of the coastal State to use the low-water line (which must still be charted) as the normal baseline. This points up a difference between (a) the fact that the coastal State is entitled to maritime space

[110] ILC Ybk 1955/I, 196.

[111] Legal obligations apply directly to sea users as a consequence of the jurisdiction of the coastal State in the relevant maritime zone. This is in no way inconsistent with the fact that UNCLOS is binding upon States rather than individuals.

regardless of whether there are charts showing the low-water line (or any coastal charts at all), and (b) the idea that there is an 'actual low-water line' that constitutes the legal baseline whether or not it has been depicted on a chart. While proposition (a) is perfectly correct, the same cannot be said about proposition (b). Yet some commentators have confused the two matters, pointing to the 'fact' of entitlement to maritime space as if it were also evidence that the 'actual low-water line' and not the charted low-water line is the legal baseline.

The ILA-BC has made this error more than once. For example, it has associated the statement in the 1989 UN Baselines Study that '[t]he low-water line along the coast is a fact irrespective of its representation on charts' and '[t]he territorial sea exists even if no particular low-water line has been selected or if no charts have been officially recognized' with the view that the 'actual' rather than charted low-water line is the legal baseline.[112] According to the ILA-BC, this conclusion is 'at odds with any contention that an international tribunal may not rely upon proffered evidence that a large scale chart is out of date or otherwise does not accurately depict the actual land/water interface at the designated datum'.[113] But the authors of the UN Baselines Study were not comparing the low-water line 'in fact' with the low-water line as charted, still less arguing that the former took priority over the latter as the legal baseline. The point was rather that entitlement to maritime space and the obligation to respect it do not depend upon the active establishment of maritime limits.

The next sentence of this passage (omitted by the ILA-BC) notes that '[f]or enforcement of regulations ... it is necessary to identify the location of the outer limit of the territorial sea, for which charts marking the low water line are required'.[114] The UN Baselines Study emphasized that the coastal State remains entitled to maritime space where it has not specified baselines and in the absence of charts showing the low-water line. It also recognized that the enforcement of regulations will prove difficult where the exact location of the limits of the territorial sea is unknown and would make a difference.

The assertion that the low-water line 'is a fact irrespective of its representation on charts' does not mean that it is a fact that can be relied upon to locate zonal limits in the absence of charts. Instead, the UN Baselines Study expressly notes that the identification of the limits of the territorial sea would require charts marking the low-water line. Far from suggesting that a charted low-water line could be compared with the 'fact' of the low-water line and that the latter was determinative of the location of the legal baseline, it is acknowledged that the limits of the territorial sea can only be located and enforced with exactitude where the low-water line is charted. This is because it is the charted low-water line that is the 'legal, normal

112 UN Baselines Study, 3; ILA-BC, *Final Report*, 23.
113 ILA-BC, *Internal Discussion Document*, 15.
114 UN Baselines Study, 3.

baseline'. Indeed, the charted low-water line was identified as the baseline partly *because* it allowed the limits of the territorial sea and other maritime zones to be more precisely defined and these more precise limits to be enforced.

The ILA-BC also refers to the judgment of the Australian High Court in *Li Chia Hsing* in support of the conclusion that 'the normal baseline exists even in the absence of officially recognized charts depicting it, that where the charted line does appear on officially recognized charts its accuracy may be challenged, and that, in some cases, the charted line may be found to be inaccurate on the basis of evidence to the contrary'.[115] In this regard, it points to Chief Justice Barwick's assessment that it is for the court to determine the location of the low-water line as a matter of fact, which he followed up with the observation that while 'a hydrographer's chart will provide cogent evidence of that fact, and a chart conforming to the specification in Art. 3 of the Treaty may be decisive internationally, particularly if a conventional baseline were adopted ... the fact of the low water mark cannot depend upon the existence of any such chart'.[116] The ILA-BC also quotes Justice Gibbs, who observed that

> it is impossible to suppose that it was intended by the Geneva Convention that the existence of a territorial sea should be dependent upon the existence of officially recognized large-scale charts showing the low-water line ... Article 3 ... must be regarded as doing no more than provide a means by which the low-water line may be evidenced. If there are charts of the kind mentioned they provide evidence (perhaps conclusive) of the position of the low water line.[117]

The difficulty is that neither the selected quotes nor any other part of the judgment suggests that the Court considered a divergence between the 'actual' and charted low-water line to cast doubt on the lawfulness of the charted low-water line as the normal baseline. Both Barwick and Gibbs were responding to the applicant's argument that, in the absence of charts indicating the low-water line, there can be no declared fishing zone at all and, according to the same logic, no other maritime zones including a territorial sea. Again, the point being made was that the coastal State remains entitled to the various maritime zones and may exercise its jurisdiction in those areas without more precisely defining their limits. Other States remain obliged to respect the rights of the coastal State and sea users will be subject to the regulations applying in the coastal State's maritime zones.

The ILA-BC's misreading of *Lia Hsing Chia* in this respect may have been encouraged by another aspect of the decision—the conclusion that the location of the low-water line and thus the limits of the fishing zone at the time of arrest was a matter of fact to be determined by the court. The Western Australian Supreme

[115] ILA-BC, *Final Report*, 19.
[116] *Li Chia Hsing* (1978), 192.
[117] Ibid, 195.

Court had come to the same conclusion in another case concerning the arrest of a foreign fishing vessel in Australian waters—*Chen Yin Ten v Little* (1976), to which the High Court positively refers. In *Chen Yin Ten*, the Supreme Court had also held that a determination of whether an island was capable of generating a fishing zone (the fishing zone in which the applicants were arrested) was a matter of fact for judicial determination. These aspects of both of *Lia Hsing Chia* and *Chen Yin Ten* follow from the fact that under Australian law the use of a foreign vessel for fishing or possession of a foreign vessel equipped for fishing in 'proclaimed waters' (now the 'Australian Fisheries Zone') was (and remains) a strict liability offence.[118] A defence of mistake to crimes of strict liability is now clearly provided in Australia's Criminal Code and was successfully relied upon by the applicants in *Mei Ying Su* (2008), who reasonably though incorrectly believed their foreign fishing vessel was outside Australia's fishing zone at the time of arrest.[119]

V. 'Artificial' Baselines and Geographical Change: Consistency in the Significance of Charts

Commentators who argue that the normal baseline is the 'actual' low-water line rather than the charted line sometimes identify this as an important point of difference from so-called 'artificial baselines'—straight baselines, archipelagic baselines, and closing lines.[120] Claims that the normal baseline is ambulatory are not always accompanied by claims that 'artificial' baselines are similarly subject to change where geographical change affects the features by reference to which they are constructed and described. This seems to be based on the belief that the mandatory charting of closing lines and straight and archipelagic baselines[121] 'fixes' them in a way that the low-water line is not fixed. It has also been suggested that the deposit of charts or coordinates showing 'artificial' baselines with the UN Secretary-General assures their continuing lawfulness or opposability notwithstanding coastal change affecting the relevant geographical features—at least for a time.[122] Some commentators have suggested that 'declaring' the position of the normal baseline might have an analogous effect.[123]

This analysis depends upon a distinction between the low-water line as a natural fact and 'artificial baselines' as charted lines that simply does not hold true. It also attributes undue significance to the due publicity and deposit obligations specified in the case of 'artificial' baselines and the absence of similar

[118] Australia Fisheries Act (1952) s 13; see also Fisheries Management Act (1991) ss 100, 101.
[119] *Mei Ying Su* (2008).
[120] See e.g. ILA-BC, *Final Report*, 8–9, 18.
[121] UNCLOS Arts 16, 47.
[122] Schofield, 'Rising Waters, Shrinking States', 224.
[123] Ibid.

specifications in the case of the normal baseline. The low-water line is also, by definition, a charted line. Yet the point is not that the low-water line, *like* so-called 'artificial' baselines, is fixed by charting. Such a claim would perpetuate a misunderstanding of the character of baselines of all types as well as the significance of charting in this connection.

The charted low-water line is also 'artificial'. It is the result of the selective representation of certain facts—or interpretations, estimations, and extrapolations of and from certain facts—by the hydrographer and cartographer, who undertake this exercise with particular and limited objectives in mind. Whereas the 'normal baseline' is already defined as the charted low-water line,[124] charting, due publicity, and deposit requirements apply to straight baselines and closing lines or the limits measured from them.[125] Archipelagic baselines must also be identified on charts or by coordinates to be duly publicized and deposited with the UN Secretary-General.[126] In the case of the normal baseline, however, no publicity or deposit obligations are expressly provided—a circumstance which the ILA-BC has taken to support the conclusion that the 'actual' low-water line as opposed to the charted low-water line is the legal baseline.[127]

The difference between the normal baseline and 'artificial' baselines in this regard has been overstated. Separate provisions in UNCLOS require that the outer limits of the EEZ and continental shelf are charted or defined by coordinates and that this information is given due publicity and deposited with the UN Secretary-General.[128] The Secretary-General is required to give due publicity to charts or coordinates identifying the limits of the continental shelf, which must also be deposited with the International Seabed Authority.[129] These charting, due publicity, and deposit obligations apply irrespective of which type of baseline is used—that is, they apply where the normal baseline is relied upon as well as where 'artificial baselines' are used.

It is true that there is no obligation to publicize or deposit charts or coordinates showing the normal baseline or the limits of the territorial sea or contiguous zone measured therefrom. Yet it is questionable how much can be made of this. Unlike straight baselines, archipelagic baselines, and closing lines, the location of the low-water line will in most cases *already* be duly publicized if it is 'marked

[124] UNCLOS Art 5. See also UNCLOS Arts 6 and 13, which apply the normal baseline to reefs and low-tide elevations in specified circumstances: UN Baselines Study, 1. Article 6 refers directly to the 'seaward low-water line of the reef, as shown by the appropriate symbol on charts officially recognized by the coastal State'. Although Article 13 does not mention charts directly, the 'low-water line' is already a cartographical construct. Low-tide elevations are usually charted as hazards to navigation: IHO, *Regulations for International Charts and Chart Specifications*, B-403.1(d).

[125] UNCLOS Art 16.

[126] UNCLOS Art 47(8), (9).

[127] See ILA-BC, *Final Report*, 8–9.

[128] UNCLOS Arts 75, 76(9), 84.

[129] UNCLOS Arts 76(9), 84.

on large-scale charts officially recognized by the coastal State'.[130] While 'artificial' baselines are constructed by reference to charted geographical features, they are not already shown on nautical charts.

The general availability of officially recognized charts showing the low-water line may also explain why there is no requirement to deposit this information with the UN Secretary-General. There is certainly no evidence that knowledge of and respect for the normal baseline and the limits measured from it was considered less important than knowledge of and respect for 'artificial' baselines and the limits measured from them. Nor is there any evidence that States considered it necessary to 'fix' so-called 'artificial baselines' against subsequent coastal change, still less that they sought to achieve such an objective through charting, due publicity, and deposit obligations.

If the absence of due publicity and deposit obligations relating to the normal baseline is properly understood to reflect the understanding that charts showing the low-water line were already widely available, it might be asked whether this also implies that States understood the normal baseline to consist of the low-water line on the most recent nautical charts used for coastwise navigation. It seems to have been considered unnecessary to give 'officially recognized' charts showing the low-water line due publicity or deposit them with the UN Secretary-General. The question is whether this means that it was also understood that the low-water line shown on the most accurate and up-to-date charts—those ordinarily or at least ideally used by mariners—would be the legal normal baseline.

This idea has not been developed in the literature, but it must be considered as another possible route to the claim that the normal baseline, at least, is ambulatory. The difficulty with this line of reasoning is that it implies that in the case of 'artificial baselines'—where due publicity and deposit obligation *do* apply—the production of new and updated charts for general use in navigation would *not* affect the lawfulness of established baselines. This would be a very significant distinction between the normal baseline on the one hand and 'artificial' baselines on the other. To derive this distinction from the mere fact that there is no direct requirement to publicize the normal baseline or deposit it with the UN Secretary-General would radically amplify a point of difference that is hardly emphasized by the treaty text. There is, moreover, nothing in the text or the drafting history of the law of the sea treaties that would make sense of such a distinction. There would seem to be no rationale for distinguishing between the normal baseline and 'artificial' baselines in terms of the consequences of the publication of new and updated charts.

Where the existing commentary considers the normal baseline alone to be ambulatory, it is sometimes suggested that charting itself or the definition of basepoints by sets of coordinates (rather than publicity or deposit with the Secretary-General) 'fixes' 'artificial' baselines against subsequent coastal change. The first point to be

[130] UNCLOS Art 5.

made in this regard is that if charting did have this effect, it would apply equally to the normal baseline which is also a charted line.[131] It is important to be clear that this is not the argument made in this chapter, which does not claim that charting 'fixes' the normal baseline in this manner. Rather, the problem lies with this account of the significance of charting—the idea that it might 'fix' legal limits that would otherwise change. The critical point is that charting requirements are not applied to definitions of the various types of baseline that otherwise suggest they would move in the event of coastal change. The law refers to charted features of the coast, but it is not the act of charting that serves to 'fix' baselines or zonal limits of any type.

VI. Conclusion

The drafting history shows that States moved to define baselines and zonal limits by reference to features shown on large-scale nautical charts because they wanted to define the limits of maritime jurisdiction more precisely and to facilitate the observation and enforcement of these more precise limits. These changes were a conscious departure from an earlier practice of more loosely defining the limits of the territorial sea by distance from the 'coast'. Charting maritime limits was not an innovation responding to and securing those limits against the well-known changeability of the coast. This does not mean that a State cannot rely on baselines defined by reference to the low-water line and other features on 'officially recognized' charts in circumstances of subsequent geographical change. But it supports the conclusion that the charting of baselines and zonal limits does not operate to fix baselines and zonal limits that would otherwise be ambulatory.

One of the chief objectives States sought to achieve by referring to common features on nautical charts to define and construct the different baseline types was to remove doubt regarding the location of maritime limits. Other considerations played a role—in particular, a concern to maximize the extent of the coastal State's maritime jurisdiction. The definition or construction of baselines by reference to the charted coast was also consistent with the legal basis for entitlement to maritime space—the possession of territorial sovereignty over coastal land.[132] It does not follow that baselines should change if physical changes later affect the charted geographical features by reference to which they were constructed or defined. Not only is there no express provision to this effect, an implicit rule with this result would be at odds with the clear intention of the drafters to ensure that the location

[131] While the location of the low-water line is not usually described by coordinates (which would be impractical), coordinates may be used to identify the salient points along it that are used to construct zonal limits.

[132] See Chapter 1.

of maritime limits could be identified and enforced with precision. It would also be at odds with the broader concern to ensure the stability of boundaries of international significance—particularly in the absence of specific provisions indicating when coastal change would invalidate established limits or trigger an obligation to revise them.

Reading in such a rule is also inconsistent with the drafting history, which clearly indicates that States were concerned to define baselines in terms allowing the use of existing charts for maritime delimitation. It was not intended that the determination of the location of the low-water line or the construction of other baselines should require time- and resource-intensive surveys of the coast and the preparation of new charts at the time of delimitation. As such, it should not be assumed that there is any obligation to engage in such activities for the purposes of ensuring the continuing lawfulness of established maritime limits.

Of course, new surveys may be undertaken and new charts prepared for other reasons—for instance, to ensure navigational safety. This brings us to a slightly different question regarding the significance of charts in connection with the law relating to maritime limits, which suggests another possible basis for the ambulatory thesis. This time, the reasoning can be understood to relate to baselines of all types. If States were aware that the nautical charts used for maritime delimitation would be updated to reflect changes affecting the features by reference to which baselines were constructed and described, it must be asked whether this implies an understanding that those baselines and the limits measured from them would be similarly subject to revision when charts were updated. This question is considered in Chapter 8.

8
Charting Change
Practices and Practicalities

I. Introduction

Scholars who have suggested that a particular low-water line might be preserved as the baseline if it is 'marked on large-scale charts officially recognized by the coastal State', as well as those who deny this possibility, tend to read Article 5 of the United Nations Convention on the Law of the Sea (UNCLOS) as if it identifies the normal baseline as the low-water line 'in fact', requiring that it be charted as a secondary matter. It is in light of this initial understanding that the words 'as marked on large-scale charts' appear as a legal loophole—a means of avoiding what the provision otherwise requires.

As explained in the previous chapter, this reading of Article 5 is not supported by the text or drafting history of the provision. The normal baseline is by definition a charted line. More precisely, it is 'the low-water line along the coast as marked on large-scale charts officially recognized by the coastal State'.[1] Acknowledging this much nevertheless points to a further possible argument in support of the ambulatory thesis—or at least, a variation that may be more legally persuasive than the idea that the law identifies the 'actual' rather than the charted low-water line as the normal baseline. It might be asked whether the definition of the normal baseline as a charted line and, more specifically, a line ordinarily shown on large-scale nautical charts can be taken to evidence a common intention that the baseline and zonal limits measured from it should change with the publication of new charts showing changes in the location of the low-water line.

This suggestion differs from the claim that the baseline is the 'actual' low-water line rather than the charted line. It is because the baseline *is* defined as the charted line that it could be inferred that States understood and intended it to be revised with relevant changes to the chart. This possibility has not been elaborated in the existing literature,[2] but, in the interests of assessing all possible grounds for

[1] UNCLOS Art 5.

[2] Schofield and Arsana's argument that Article 5 'does not specify either the age of the chart in question or whether it needs to be registered or recognized by an international body' offers one way of responding to this argument, though they do not discuss what defining the baseline as a charted line indicates about the expectations of the parties to the Convention on the Territorial Sea and Contiguous Zone (TSC) and UNCLOS: see Schofield and Arsana, 'Climate Change and the Limits of Maritime Jurisdiction', 142.

Geographical Change and the Law of the Sea. Kate Purcell, Oxford University Press (2019). © Kate Purcell.
DOI: 10.1093/oso/9780198743644.001.0001

the ambulatory thesis, it must be considered. Notably, if this were the basis for the ambulatory thesis, then the same reasoning would suggest that straight and archipelagic baselines and closing lines, which are also defined by reference to charted geographical features, must equally be amended if an updated chart shows relevant changes to the features concerned.

It is useful to distinguish this view from an assumption that the conditions relating to geographical circumstances in the baselines provisions apply on a continuing basis—a route to the ambulatory thesis discussed in Chapter 9. If baselines are ambulatory in the sense that they change with the charts by reference to which they are defined or described, they are so from the point of establishment. Their movement would be a consequence of (a) the definition of baselines by reference to features shown on nautical charts coupled with (b) an awareness of the fact that new charts may show changes to those features, where this is taken to imply (c) an understanding that baselines will automatically change or require revision with the publication of new charts. While the delimitation of maritime boundaries between States differs in important respects from the unilateral establishment of maritime limits by the coastal State, a comparison of the two cases helps to clarify the legal significance of the role of nautical charts in this context.

II. Accuracy and Currency in Nautical Charts

Nautical charts are ordinarily updated in order to improve their accuracy as a representation of current facts relevant to navigation—navigational safety in particular. This may involve revisions to reflect geographical change that has taken place since the chart was drawn. Updates may also improve the accuracy of the chart with respect to features that have not changed. Nautical charts may be based on source data of varying quality collected at various times. Notably, this means that baselines and zonal limits may have been established on the basis of 'facts' represented in charts which were out of date or incorrect at the time of delimitation.

It has been estimated that more than 50 per cent of soundings relied upon in modern charts were taken before 1939.[3] The most recent edition of the *Status of Hydrographic Surveying and Nautical Charting Worldwide* by the International Hydrographic Organization (IHO) identifies a number of areas which have never been surveyed or require resurveying at a larger scale or to modern standards.[4] The IHO has also found that '[a]lthough coverage of both paper and electronic charts has increased, in many cases there has not been a concomitant improvement in

[3] N Calder, *How to Read a Nautical Chart* (McGraw Hill Professional, 2002), 3.
[4] IHO, *Status of Hydrographic Surveying and Charting Worldwide* C-55 (IHB, 26 November 2018).

the source data from which they are derived'.[5] This is true of the two main types of electronic charts—raster charts and vector charts. The former are simply scans of paper charts, while the latter use 'intelligent data' about the features they represent, the accuracy of which still depends upon the accuracy of the surveys and other sources from which the data is drawn.[6]

The first formal discussion of the development of international surveying standards took place at the 1957 International Hydrographic Conference, the year before the first Law of the Sea Conference (LOSC).[7] The first recommended standards were published in 1968.[8] The latest edition of the IHO's Standards follows the growing practice in metrology of referring to degrees of uncertainty rather than 'accuracy' and 'error' in measurements.[9] This is because there is generally no 'true value' against which to compare measured depths.[10] The IHO Standards require a higher degree of certainty where measurements of depth are particularly important for navigational safety (a matter of under-keel clearance).[11] The IHO currently recommends that States replace or supplement source information on existing paper charts with an indication of 'Zones of Confidence' in Electronic Chart Display and Information Systems, which categorize surveyed areas based on the accuracy and currency of source data to indicate the reliability of different parts of a chart for the purposes of safe navigation.[12] It appears that the new Electronic Navigational Chart Product Specification currently being developed by the IHO will use other methods to indicate data quality on electronic charts.[13]

Because the law (non-coincidentally) refers to geographical features typically marked on large-scale charts, new surveys and other information about those features, including changes affecting them, are likely to be forthcoming at some point. Where the information matters for navigational safety this will usually or ideally be sooner rather than later. 'Notices to mariners' regularly circulate information relating to the location and character of hazards to navigation, which may be manually transferred to charts by users and, in some cases, either or both published on new 'print on demand' paper charts and made available in a format suitable for download and integration with raster charts and Electronic Navigational Charts.[14]

[5] Executive Summary in IHO, *Status of Hydrographic Surveying* C-55 (IHB, 2011). The data collated in the current edition of C-55 (2018) confirms that this is still the case (later editions do not provide summaries).

[6] ABLOS, *Manual on Technical Aspects of UNCLOS*, Chs 3, 4.

[7] IHO, *Standards for Hydrographic Surveys* S-44 (5th edn, IHB, 2008), 1.

[8] Ibid.

[9] Ibid.

[10] Ibid.

[11] Ibid, 1, 5–6.

[12] IHO, *Transfer Standard for Digital Hydrographic Data* S-57 (3.1 edn, IHB, 2010), Appendix B1.

[13] IHO Data Quality Working Group, 'Safe Navigation with Uncertain Hydrographic Data: The Representation of Data Quality in the IHO S-101 Data Model:' (6 June 2012) *Hydro International* at <https://www.hydro-international.com/content/article/safe-navigation-with-uncertain-hydrographic-data> accessed 13 February 2017.

[14] See e.g. US NOAA, 'Chart Updates' at <https://nauticalcharts.noaa.gov/charts/chart-updates.html> accessed 12 October 2019.

When and how new information is gathered and communicated to mariners depends upon State capacity. The IHO notes that maritime safety information is deficient in many regions, especially Africa and the Caribbean.[15] Many developing countries do not have the capacity 'to collect, collate and promulgate urgent navigational safety information in a timely manner'.[16] As such, there may be a considerable lapse of time between the event of geographical change and any record of it. There may be further delays before the information is disseminated, even where it is relevant to navigational safety.

As far as maritime delimitation is concerned, new information may include two potentially relevant types of fact, which must be carefully distinguished as raising distinct legal questions. First, new information may reveal that certain facts were inaccurately represented in the charts relied upon for delimitation without suggesting that those facts have changed. This raises the question of (a) whether it is sufficient to refer to existing charts for delimitation or if facts on the ground must be taken into account, and (b) whether, in either case, new information about those facts means that maritime limits or boundaries based on them are no longer lawful and/or must be redrawn. Alternatively, new information may reveal that geographical circumstances taken into account in the delimitation process have since changed. The question in these circumstances is whether subsequent change can bring into question maritime limits or boundaries lawfully established on the basis of charts or geographical facts as they were at the time of delimitation.

III. The Legal Relevance of the Accuracy and Currency of Charts

The question of whether and when a maritime boundary might be ambulatory was discussed in Chapter 6, where it was shown that the construction of a boundary by reference to geographical circumstances (whether indicated by charts or other evidence) does not of itself imply an ambulatory character. It remains instructive to consider how the accuracy and currency of charts has been dealt with in the jurisprudence relating to maritime delimitation between States, particularly given the inferences the International Law Association's Baselines Committee (ILA-BC) has drawn from this case law in connection with its conclusions regarding the ambulatory character of maritime limits.

In its 2012 report, the ILA-BC reviewed a selection of domestic and international cases with a particular question in mind. The Committee asked whether the courts had been prepared to accept evidence of the 'actual' location of the low-water line where this departed from the charted low-water line, and whether they

[15] Executive Summary, 'Status of MSI' in IHO, *Status of Hydrographic Surveying* (2011).
[16] Ibid.

considered the former to prevail over the latter. The nature of this enquiry led to some distortion of the jurisprudence.

The ILA-BC seems to have assumed that references to information about the current location of the low-water line rather than (only or primarily) charts showing the low-water line signified that the 'actual' low-water line and not the charted line was the legal baseline. As already discussed, the Committee on more than one occasion mistakes (a) the point that entitlement to maritime space exists regardless of whether maritime limits have been specified for (b) the identification of the 'actual' low-water line as the lawful baseline. It also fails to recognize that admitting more current or accurate evidence of the location of the low-water line does not imply that the charted low-water line relied upon as the normal baseline must be up to date and factually accurate *at all times* and may be challenged on this basis.

Evidence of the location of the low-water line that looks beyond existing charts has been admitted in several delimitation cases. However, this is because one or both of the parties involved has asserted its right to benefit from the most current and accurate information regarding geographical circumstances *at the time of delimitation*. This assertion must be clearly distinguished from the understanding that an established boundary must be adjusted in response to subsequent geographical change. Crucially, it must also be recognized that this practice does not lend support to the conclusion that the normal baseline used for unilateral delimitation is ambulatory.

Unless 'historic title' or 'special circumstances' justify another approach, the delimitation of the territorial sea by a court or tribunal will usually begin with the construction of a provisional equidistance line measured from the baselines in fact employed by the coastal State to locate its maritime limits. This is not the low-water line according to any and all evidence at the time of delimitation. It is the low-water line shown on charts officially recognized by the State for the purposes of unilateral delimitation and any established straight or archipelagic baselines. Where States have not established baselines for unilateral delimitation, the selection of basepoints for delimiting the territorial sea, like the selection of basepoints for delimiting the exclusive economic zone (EEZ) and continental shelf, will refer to the 'physical reality at the time of delimitation'.[17]

Critically, the emphasis in the jurisprudence on 'physical reality at the time of delimitation' does not refer to facts on the ground as compared with the representation of coastal geography in charts. The law has been developed on the understanding that both unilateral and interstate delimitation will be based on geographical circumstances as represented in existing charts. More current or accurate evidence of geographical circumstances may be taken into account at the time of delimitation, but this is by no means legally required. Taking this evidence

[17] *Black Sea Case* (2009), 106.

into account in the delimitation process, moreover, does not imply that new information showing inaccuracies or subsequent geographical change will necessitate the revision of established maritime limits and boundaries. The coastal State remains free to revise its maritime limits (with the exception of the limits of the continental shelf) to take such new information into account, though this is a matter of discretion. Neighbouring States equally remain free to renegotiate an established boundary on this basis, though this will depend upon their agreement.

A. Accuracy and Currency at the Point of Delimitation

The ILA-BC has pointed to several maritime delimitation cases in support of the conclusion that the normal baseline is the low-water line 'in fact' rather than 'as charted', extrapolating from this that changes in the 'actual' low-water line also alter the normal baseline. Several problems with this analysis have already been discussed. There are further difficulties with this reading of the jurisprudence as it relates to the relationship between charts and other evidence of 'facts on the ground'.

The jurisprudence does not support the conclusion that the law *requires* interstate delimitation to be based on the most accurate picture of geographical facts at the time of delimitation. There are cases in which States have looked beyond existing charts to other evidence of the geographical circumstances obtaining at the time of delimitation. There have also been objections to charts on the basis that they fail to accurately represent the relevant geographical circumstances. But this does not mean that delimitation based on charts that are inaccurate or out of date is *unlawful*. Nor does it mean that subsequent evidence that a chart was inaccurate or out of date will indicate the *invalidity* of the boundary, still less allow or require a change in its course.

(i) Accuracy, currency, and the priority of agreement

Legal principle and State practice support the conclusion that interstate delimitation need not be based on the most accurate and current geographical information possible. The priority of agreement in interstate delimitation is relevant here. The right to establish an international boundary by agreement includes the right to agree to use particular charts for this purpose. As Schofield and Arsana point out, 'it is not unusual for two States to agree on the use of a particular chart for maritime delimitation, even though the chart may no longer depict the current coastline/baselines'.[18] This is reasonably common practice in delimitation by direct agreement between States.

Where a third party is tasked with delimitation, agreement between the parties on the charts to be used is also unlikely to be questioned. Courts and tribunals have

[18] Schofield and Arsana, 'Climate Change and the Limits of Maritime Jurisdiction', 142.

not independently assessed the accuracy or currency of charts in such cases. This may be understood as a matter of deference to the parties' agreement. Yet it is also consistent with a legal regime that not only permits delimitation based on existing charts but has many features that reflect an understanding that delimitation will ordinarily be based on a cartographic view of the coast.

There is no reason to think that the accuracy and currency of charts is assumed in the absence of arguments to the contrary. The experts involved in maritime delimitation would be aware that many charts in use are based on older surveys including information that may be inaccurate or out of date. The jurisprudence clearly indicates that it is sufficient to rely upon recent charts of an adequate scale for delimitation. In some cases, emphasis has also been placed on the fact that the charts in question have been mutually recognized by the parties, even if they dispute their use for delimitation.[19] There are several cases that have stressed the importance of the 'physical reality at the time of delimitation'; however, the 'physical reality' in this regard has not been identified with 'facts on the ground' as opposed to those represented in charts.

(ii) Physical reality at the time of delimitation

In *Tunisia/Libya* (1982), the International Court of Justice (ICJ) held that 'what must be taken into account in the delimitation of shelf areas are the physical circumstances as they are today; that just as it is the geographical configuration of the present-day coasts, so also it is the present-day sea-bed, which must be considered'.[20] The point being made, however, was that '[i]t is the outcome, not the evolution in the long-distant past, which is of importance'.[21] The Court rejected the parties' arguments that the geological history (Libya) or geological composition (Tunisia) of the seabed could determine its character and extent as the 'natural prolongation' of their land territory.[22] The 'physical circumstances as they are today' were not contrasted with charted geographical circumstances. Indeed, the delimitation was based on the charted coast.[23]

In the *Black Sea Case* (2009), the Court stated that it 'must, when delimiting the continental shelf and exclusive economic zones, select base points by reference to the physical geography of the relevant coasts'.[24] Yet it did not contrast this exercise with the selection of basepoints by reference to charts but with the use of basepoints already defined by the coastal State for the purpose of establishing its maritime limits.[25] When the Court in the same case insisted that 'the geometrical

[19] See e.g. *Ghana/Côte d'Ivoire* (2017), 97. The treatment of charts in this case is discussed further below.

[20] *Tunisia/Libya* (1982), 54.

[21] Ibid.

[22] Ibid, 52–4.

[23] See ibid, 61–4, 87–91.

[24] *Black Sea Case* (2009), 108.

[25] Ibid.

nature of the first stage of the delimitation exercise leads it to use as base points those which the geography of the coast identifies as a physical reality at the time of the delimitation', it went on to clarify that this 'geographical reality covers not only the physical elements produced by geodynamics and the movements of the sea, but also any other material factors that are present'.[26] Rather than contrasting 'physical reality at the time of the delimitation' with charted geography, the Court's point was that the selection of basepoints could refer not only to natural features of the coast but also to man-made structures—in this case, the Sulina dyke.[27] Both the natural and man-made features considered by the Court were those shown on existing charts provided by the parties.[28]

In *Bangladesh v India* (2014), the Tribunal also emphasized its '[concern] with the "physical reality at the time of the delimitation"' and, specifically, the question of 'whether the choice of base points located on the coastline and reflecting the general direction of the coast is feasible in the present case and at the present time'.[29] Again, this was not a differentiation between facts on the ground and those shown on charts. The Tribunal's point was that the boundary would respond to geographical circumstances 'at the time of the delimitation' and need not take into account any future coastal change.[30] The Tribunal also noted the difference between its earlier identification of the terminus of the existing land boundary and the maritime delimitation. The former task had required the identification of 'the geographical features and the coast line as they were in 1947'.[31] Conversely, the Tribunal was required 'to delimit *de novo* the territorial sea, exclusive economic zone, and continental shelf' and 'must therefore choose base points that are appropriate in reference to the time of the delimitation, i.e. the date of its Award'.[32] The contrast here was between (a) 'the geographical features and the coast line' in 1947 and (b) 'the geographical features and the coast line' at the time of delimitation. It was not a distinction between geography as charted and on the ground.

The difference between existing charts and contemporary facts on the ground was nevertheless an issue in *Bangladesh v India*. The parties disagreed 'on the accuracy of the maps and charts produced, due in particular to the rapid erosion of the coastline'.[33] More specifically, Bangladesh argued that five of India's proposed basepoints should be rejected as they were located on low-tide elevations (LTEs) that no longer existed—i.e. features no longer above water at low-tide.[34]

26 Ibid, 106.
27 Ibid.
28 See written proceedings in the *Black Sea Case* at <https://www.icj-cij.org/en/case/132/written-proceedings>.
29 *Bangladesh v India* (2014), 62–3.
30 Ibid.
31 Ibid, 62.
32 Ibid.
33 Ibid, 64.
34 Ibid, 58–9.

Two of these basepoints were located on South Talpatty/New Moore Island, which Bangladesh claimed to have 'disappeared permanently below the surface in the late 1980s or early 1990s'.[35] Bangladesh objected to a further two basepoints on Mandarbaria/Clump Island, arguing that coastal erosion had left them under water.[36] India argued that the LTEs still existed and that the basepoints on Mandarbaria/Clump Island were located on land.[37] It also argued that 'it is universal practice to select base points in accordance with maritime charts, and all modern charts depict South Talpatty/New Moore as a low-tide elevation'.[38]

The Tribunal's initial response to these arguments was to appoint an expert hydrographer to assist it in interpreting the relevant information.[39] It also conducted a site visit prior to the oral hearings with its expert in attendance.[40] It is only on rare occasions that members of the ICJ or an arbitral tribunal have participated directly in site visits.[41] Site visits by court-appointed experts are more common, as are visits by experts appointed by the parties. The site visit by the tribunal in *Bangladesh v India* appears to be the only time such an exercise has featured in a maritime delimitation case. The case indicates, moreover, that there are good reasons why courts and tribunals do not generally conduct site visits in this context.

The LTEs in question were not sighted during the visit. Only breakers and water discolouration were seen in the vicinity of South Talpatty/New Moore Island. Bangladesh argued and India denied that this proved the features were permanently submerged. India recalled its earlier reservations as to the utility of an aerial survey to identify basepoints, arguing that (a) neap tides would affect visibility as the lowest tide would be above the lowest astronomical tide, (b) the visit did not coincide with the time of lowest tide, and (c) 'poor meteorological conditions' further hindered visibility.[42]

Following the site visit, the Tribunal requested that the parties provide further information on

> (a) the appropriateness of ... proposed base points situated on the current land coastline ... given their appreciation of the stability of those coastlines: and
> (b) the appropriateness of ... proposed base points situated on low-tide elevations ... given their appreciation of the visibility and stability of those features.[43]

[35] Ibid, 58.
[36] Ibid, 59–60.
[37] Ibid, 60–1.
[38] Ibid, 60.
[39] Ibid, 3.
[40] Ibid. See also Procedural Order No 1, available at <https://pca-cpa.org/en/cases/18/> accessed 4 January 2019.
[41] MA Becker, C Rose, 'Investigating the Value of Site Visits in Inter-State Arbitration and Adjudication' (2017) 8 *JIDS* 219, 219–20.
[42] *Bangladesh v India* (2014), 60; *Bangladesh v India* (2014), Hearing Transcript, Day 3, 297–300.
[43] *Bangladesh v India* (2014), Hearing Transcript, Day 4, 363.

According to counsel for India, the Tribunal also 'invited the Parties "to indicate any alternative base points to those already submitted", on the assumption (without deciding, as [the Tribunal] put it) that stability and visibility may be relevant factors in the selection of base points for the purpose of maritime delimitation'.[44]

As discussed in Chapter 6, the Tribunal rejected the argument that instability could make a site inappropriate as a location for basepoints. It considered it legally irrelevant that 'within a few years … the low tide elevations chosen by India will likely have changed or disappeared'.[45] The Tribunal also noted that '[w]hereas it was important in the past to rely on permanent coastal features for the identification of boundaries at sea, satellite navigation systems now allow users of the oceans to easily locate any geodetic point without resorting to the actual physical features used at the date of delimitation'.[46]

Article 6(3) of the Convention on the Continental Shelf (CSC) may be briefly revisited in connection with this point—in particular, the specification that lines 'should be defined with reference to charts and geographical features as they exist at a particular date, and reference should be made to fixed permanent identifiable points on the land'. This does not suggest that 'fixed points on land' should serve as basepoints to determine the median line. Rather, such points are proposed as anchors making it possible to identify the location of the boundary notwithstanding any subsequent coastal change. The intention was that '[t]he *turning points of boundary lines* should be related to fixed points on land, such as a church, a beacon, or a lighthouse'.[47] This reflects an understanding that a median line boundary is ordinarily fixed rather than ambulatory—the point being to facilitate the identification of its course as fixed at the point of establishment. Article 6(3) also supports the conclusion that a boundary based on a particular chart remains effective notwithstanding later evidence of inaccuracies or subsequent geographical change. It provides for the definition of a boundary by reference to particular charts at a particular time—that is, without taking into account subsequent amendments to either improve the chart's accuracy or reflect subsequent geographical change.

The Tribunal's conclusions in *Bangladesh v India* regarding the irrelevance of instability did not answer the question of whether the permanent submergence of features shown as LTEs on current charts would preclude their use as basepoints. In fact, the Tribunal did not answer this question directly at all, though aspects of its approach remain informative.

The Tribunal noted that the site visit had 'confirmed the location, visibility and protuberance of the base points' on the mainland coast but 'did not confirm the visibility of the base points located on low tide elevations, with the possible

[44] Ibid.
[45] *Bangladesh v India* (2014), 62.
[46] Ibid, 63.
[47] UNCLOS I: VI, 93 (emphasis added).

exception of the base point situated on South Talpatty/New Moore Island'.[48] It held that '[b]reakers observed in that area did signal the existence of a feature, although it was not apparent whether the feature was permanently submerged or constituted a low-tide elevation'.[49] The Tribunal concluded that '[i]n any event, whatever feature existed could in no way be considered as situated on the coastline, much less as a "protuberant coastal point"'.[50] On this basis it determined that 'South Talpatty/New Moore Island is not a suitable geographical feature for the location of a base point'.[51] It more generally rejected the use of basepoints on LTEs as inconsistent with 'the criteria elaborated . . . in the *Black Sea* case and confirmed in more recent cases', concluding that such features could not be considered 'protuberant coastal points'.[52]

This conclusion is rather suspect given that LTEs are elsewhere considered part of the 'legal coast'. While the Tribunal referred to UNCLOS Article 5 in this connection,[53] the baselines provisions recognize a variety of baseline types that depart from the low-water line along the coast of a mainland or island, including Article 13 on LTEs. Article 12 of the TSC and Article 15 of UNCLOS refer generally to 'the baselines from which the breadth of the territorial seas of each of the two States is measured', which may include baselines of various types in various combinations. In any event, the Tribunal's conclusion that basepoints could not be situated on LTEs as a matter of alleged legal principle meant it was unnecessary to determine (a) whether the LTEs were in fact above water at low-tide or permanently submerged, and (b) whether permanent submergence prevented their use as basepoints. It also appears to have been unnecessary to conduct a site visit.[54]

Notably, the Tribunal also rejected several other proposed basepoints on the basis that the coordinates 'plotted to seawards' of the low-water line.[55] It appears to have considered it necessary for basepoints to be located on the low-water line rather than at sea. Significantly, however, it was by reference to *charts* provided by the parties that the Tribunal both determined that the proposed basepoints lay beyond the low-water line and identified alternatives.[56] The Tribunal indicated that its selection of basepoints would be determined 'by reference to the physical geography at the time of the delimitation and to the low-water line of the relevant coasts'.[57]

48 *Bangladesh v India* (2014), 74.
49 Ibid.
50 Ibid.
51 Ibid.
52 Ibid, 73.
53 The Tribunal cites *Eritrea/Yemen*, but in that case Article 5 was invoked in support of the decision to rely on the low-water line rather than the high-water line for interstate delimitation—a decision consistent with the right of States to benefit from the more seaward line: *Eritrea/Yemen (Phase II)* (1999), 44. It was also recognized that basepoints could be located on LTEs though none were—an alleged LTE was found (by reference to existing charts) to be permanently submerged: ibid.
54 This point is emphasized in Becker and Rose, 'Investigating the Value of Site Visits', 238–9.
55 *Bangladesh v India* (2014), 74–5, 103–4.
56 See Technical Report by the Tribunal's Hydrographer: *Bangladesh v India* (2014) A-1, A-3.
57 *Bangladesh v India* (2014), 64.

To this end, it resolved to 'avail itself of the most reliable evidence, resulting from the latest surveys and incorporated in the most recent large scale charts officially recognized by the Parties in accordance with article 5 of the Convention'.[58]

While this formulation suggests that accuracy and currency matter, the decision to refer only to information 'incorporated in the most recent large scale charts officially recognized by the Parties' indicates that such charts are sufficient for delimitation—even if other evidence suggests a discrepancy with facts on the ground. The Tribunal allowed that basepoints could be located on Mandarbaria/Clump Island and Moore Island but rejected the proposed coordinates as plotting seaward of the charted low-water line. The Tribunal did not consider whether any of the proposed coordinates were more consistent with facts on the ground, as Bangladesh alleged. It simply gave priority to the low-water line depicted on 'the nautical charts provided by the parties'.[59]

It is interesting to compare this aspect of the Tribunal's reasoning with *Ghana/Côte d'Ivoire* (2017), where a Special Chamber of the International Tribunal for the Law of the Sea (ITLOS) constructed an equidistance line based on BA Chart 1383, which relied on data from the 1840s, though a more current chart was available.[60] This decision was based on the fact that the new chart used 'different methods ... for the survey of the Ivorian and Ghanaian coasts' and that the parties' common use of the older chart up until 2014 was a good indication of their 'common confidence in [its] reliability'.[61] The Special Chamber nevertheless noted its agreement with Côte d'Ivoire that 'a more recently prepared chart is preferable in principle'.[62] The Chamber also accepted Ghana's argument that the consistency of the older chart with the data underlying the newer chart was evidence that the coast was not, as Côte d'Ivoire had alleged, unstable[63]—though the new chart was sufficiently different to the old (due to the method of charting) to mean that its use for delimitation would make a difference.[64]

While the Special Chamber indicated that more recent charts were preferred as a matter of principle, it clearly did not consider the principle in question to mandate the use of the most up-to-date information regarding coastal geography for delimitation purposes. Instead of insisting that the inadequacies of Côte d'Ivoire's new chart with respect to Ghana's coast be remedied, the Chamber accepted the older chart based on much less recent data. This is consistent with the development of the law relating to maritime delimitation, which has not required States to go

[58] Ibid.
[59] Technical Report, *Bangladesh v India* (2014) A-1, A-3.
[60] *Ghana/Côte d'Ivoire* (2017), 97.
[61] Ibid.
[62] Ibid.
[63] Ibid, 92.
[64] Ibid, 96.

beyond existing charts to establish their maritime boundaries, even if this has been permitted.

The role of charts in delimitation suggests that site visits will rarely if ever be appropriate in a maritime delimitation case. As discussed in Chapter 7, the low-water line is a cartographical construct and may not correspond with a visible line between land and sea at any stage of the tide or only rarely. India was right to argue that the failure to sight an alleged LTE could not prove that it did not exist or could not be relied on for maritime delimitation.

It is interesting to compare this set of circumstances to those in *Nicaragua v Colombia* (2012), where the Court held that more recent evidence relating to small features on the submerged bank of Quitasueño—photographs and measured heights in a report by Colombia's expert—showed them to be 'above water at some part of the tidal cycle and thus to constitute low-tide elevations'.[65] The photograph evidence was probative though not independently determinative—the Court applying a different tidal model to that used in the expert report to assess measured heights and identifying one feature as an island.[66] This does not mean the failure to sight proposed basepoints in *Bangladesh v India* (2014) could have determined whether they qualified as LTEs. Photographic evidence showing a feature above water at some stage of the tide may be probative in a way that a lack of visibility at any stage of the tide is not. A lack of visibility alone is unlikely to prove that a feature is not above any and all possible definitions of low or high-water. Visibility makes it clear that the same feature would at least be above low water according to a range of definitions of the same.

The Court's decision in *Nicaragua v Colombia* (2012) was based on geographical information that went beyond existing charts. Indeed, the Court privileged the expert report 'based upon actual observations of conditions at Quitasueño and scientific evaluation of those conditions' and objected to charts provided by Nicaragua on the grounds that they 'were prepared ... to show dangers to shipping at Quitasueño, not to distinguish between those features which were just above, and those which were just below, water at high tide'.[67] It also dismissed 'surveys conducted many years (in some cases many decades) before the present proceedings' as irrelevant, insisting that the legal character of the features in question would depend upon 'the contemporary evidence'.[68]

These comments on the map evidence must be treated carefully. The Court's objection to charts 'prepared in order to show dangers to shipping' must be put in context, as charts showing dangers for navigation (that is, large-scale nautical charts showing the coast) are, of course, the charts chiefly relied upon for both unilateral and interstate delimitation. It is important to recognize that the Court

65 *Nicaragua v Colombia* (2012), 645.
66 Ibid.
67 Ibid, 644.
68 Ibid.

was responding to Colombia's claim that the charts did not accurately reflect geographical circumstances at the time of delimitation—circumstances it was entitled to benefit from in the construction of a maritime boundary.

(iii) Distinguishing rights from requirements

In its pleadings, Colombia had argued that

> [w]hether a feature qualifies as an island or a low-tide elevation is a question of present-day fact. That some other government may not have recognized that feature as an island at some earlier point of time is not decisive, or even particularly relevant. Nor is it decisive that the feature in question 'has never been reflected on nautical charts as an island but always as a low-tide elevation'.[69]

It cited *Qatar v Bahrain* (2001) in support of the last contention—specifically the Court's finding that Qit'at Jaradah was an island despite being charted as an LTE.[70]

The Court in *Qatar v Bahrain* explained that it had 'carefully analysed the evidence submitted by the Parties' and 'weighed the conclusions' of their experts before coming to this conclusion.[71] It paid particular attention to the fact that Qatar's experts 'did not themselves maintain that it was scientifically proven that Qit'at Jaradah is a low-tide elevation'.[72] Instead, they had concluded that Bahrain's surveys 'did not provide a basis for a definitive determination whether it is an islet or a low-tide elevation'.[73] The Court, however, considered the evidence sufficient to establish that Qit'at Jaradah was 'a naturally formed area of land, surrounded by water, which is above water at high tide'.[74] It did not comment specifically on the charts representing Qit'at Jaradah as an LTE but seems to have accepted that other scientific evidence of the position of this feature above water at high tide would prevail.

The treatment of Qit'at Jaradah in *Qatar v Bahrain* (2001) is analogous to the approach taken to Quitasueño in *Nicaragua v Colombia* (2012). In both cases, the Court gave weight to contemporary evidence at odds with existing charts in response to a State's assertion of its right to benefit from facts as they stood at the time of delimitation. Crucially, this does not mean that States are *required* to base their claims on geographic information that goes beyond that shown on recent large-scale charts. Nor is a court or tribunal tasked with delimitation ordinarily required to look beyond existing charts to ensure that delimitation is based on the most current and accurate geographical facts. If, however, a party presents probative evidence relating to relevant geographical circumstances that differs from the

[69] Colombia Rejoinder, 93, in *Nicaragua v Colombia* (2012).
[70] *Qatar v Bahrain* (2001), 99.
[71] Ibid.
[72] Ibid.
[73] Ibid.
[74] Ibid.

charted information, a court or tribunal will be required to take such evidence into account. Legally, this does not signify the general priority of such information over the charts. Instead, it responds to the right of the coastal State to claim as much as the contemporary geographical circumstances permit. This covers a range of claims that point to evidence of geographical facts at variance with existing charts, including evidence that charted geographical circumstances relied upon by another party no longer obtain.

In *Guyana v Suriname* (2007), Guyana challenged a basepoint proposed by Suriname on the grounds that the low-water line on which it was located was not accurately charted.[75] Suriname maintained that the chart was accurate and reflected the recent accretion of a mud shoal in the area that had extended its coast. The ILA-BC has emphasized that 'neither party contended that the chart was dispositive, even though it was a large-scale chart officially recognized by the coastal State'.[76] Both States submitted further evidence of the configuration of the coast at the time of delimitation, which the tribunal relied upon for its decision to accept the basepoint.[77]

The ILA-BC understands this decision to support the conclusion that 'the charted low-water line may be challenged before an international tribunal on the basis that it does not reflect accurately the actual low-water line'.[78] This is correct; however, it does not imply that the 'actual' low-water line will always take priority over the charted low-water line at the time of delimitation, still less that it will continue to constitute the legal baseline post-delimitation. Suriname successfully argued that it should be able to take advantage of the accretion of its coast at the time the boundary was delimited.[79] It argued that 'small changes in the shape or presence of low-tide features along a coast, whether due to accretion or erosion or other natural processes that change the configuration of the low-water line, can lead to very substantial changes in the provisional equidistance line, particularly in adjacent state situations'.[80] This point concerns the impact of erosion and accretion on the construction of an equidistance line *at the time of delimitation*. It should not be mistaken for a belief that such change would affect an established equidistance line. *Guyana v Suriname* supports the proposition that the construction of a maritime boundary may *not only* be based on existing charts but *may also* refer to other information regarding current geographical facts. This does not mean that such information will necessitate changes in the location of a maritime boundary once it is established.

75 *Guyana v Suriname* (2007), 128.
76 ILA-BC, *Final Report*, 13.
77 *Guyana v Suriname* (2007), 128.
78 ILA-BC, *Final Report*, 13.
79 Suriname Rejoinder in *Guyana v Suriname* (2007), 108.
80 Ibid.

The law still accepts and, indeed, anticipates interstate delimitation based on recent large-scale charts officially recognized by the parties. The jurisprudence relating to the delimitation of maritime boundaries between States also recognizes that the low-water line constituting the normal baseline for the purposes of unilateral delimitation (which may play a role in the delimitation of the territorial sea according to the 'equidistance-special circumstances rule') is a charted low-water line. It remains appropriate to defer to probative evidence that the location of the low-water line is other than that shown in charts at the time an international boundary is delimited if (a) a State insists on the right to locate basepoints on the low-water line as calculated at that time, and (b) there is no obligation to locate basepoints on the established territorial sea baselines (e.g. in delimiting the EEZ/continental shelf or where 'historic title' or 'special circumstances' justify alternative basepoints for delimiting the territorial sea). Notably, a difference between the location of the low-water line at the time of delimitation and the charted line taken as the territorial sea baseline will not itself constitute a 'special circumstance'. This is because the law clearly permits the coastal State to rely on the charted line and other cartographic representations of the coast for unilateral maritime delimitation.

In relation to unilateral delimitation, the TSC and UNCLOS suggest that reference to current charts is appropriate and sufficient for constructing baselines. The law was deliberately crafted to allow States to establish baselines by reference to the charts they already had with a view to facilitating the timely establishment of readily identifiable and observable maritime limits.[81] It did not require an investigation into the accuracy and currency of these charts or the information on which they were based.

More recently, it appears that some States in practice refer to geographical information from a variety of other sources, including aerial photographs and satellite imagery.[82] Schofield suggests that States seek out 'whatever information ... is the best quality and most up to date' for the purposes of constructing maritime limits or at least identifying the normal baseline (the low-water line).[83] It is not clear that this practice is widespread. Nor is there clear evidence that it reflects an understanding that the law *requires* delimitation on the basis of the most current and accurate information regarding relevant geographical circumstances. As such, the practice cannot be taken to signify either agreement on an interpretation of the law of the sea treaties or the emergence of a customary rule to this effect.

It is worth considering whether the law would countenance the use of charts known to be inaccurate or out of date to construct maritime limits. The technical experts consulted by States participating in the Hague Conference and the three law of the sea conferences were no doubt aware that existing charts were based on

[81] See Chapter 7.
[82] Schofield, 'Rising Waters, Shrinking States', 221.
[83] Ibid.

surveys that were not necessarily accurate or up to date. There remains a difference between allowing the use of existing charts notwithstanding this fact and allowing the use of charts known to be out of date or inaccurate where more current and accurate charts are available.

The reference to charts 'officially recognized by the coastal State' clearly indicates that it is for the coastal State to determine which chart it will use to establish the normal baseline. The point, however, was to clarify that the State could rely on current charts showing any one of the possible low-water lines and that another State or sea user could not insist that maritime limits must be measured from a different low-water line.[84] 'Officially recognizing' a chart known to be obsolete or inaccurate for unilateral delimitation purposes where more current and accurate charts are available may be inconsistent with the obligation to interpret and perform the law of the sea treaties in 'good faith'.[85]

Notably, this does not mean that there is an obligation to seek out more current or accurate information than that shown on existing charts. Nor does it mean that continuing to rely on maritime limits established on the basis of a chart that becomes out of date or inaccurate due to subsequent geographical change departs from a 'good faith' interpretation or application of the treaty law. The definition of the 'normal baseline' refers to 'charts officially recognised by the coastal State' in an account of what is required and permitted in the *establishment* of maritime limits. It permits the coastal State to make use of existing charts indicating the location of the low-water line according to any one of the standard definitions at the point of delimitation. A finding of 'bad faith' at this stage may be warranted where a more accurate and current chart could easily be relied upon. If there is evidence that existing charts are out-of-date or inaccurate but alternatives are not available, there will be no 'bad faith' on the part of a State proceeding to establish maritime limits based on those charts. The law clearly admits and anticipates the use of existing charts for unilateral delimitation; it does not require that States prepare new ones.

In both unilateral and interstate delimitation, it remains open to the States concerned to make use of more recent or accurate geographical information, though this is not obligatory. A point of difference flows from the role of agreement in interstate delimitation. It is appropriate for a court or tribunal to accept a chart where the parties have agreed to its use for the purposes of interstate delimitation—even if more current and accurate alternatives are available. However, if a party objects to a chart on the grounds that it is inaccurate or out of date or introduces other evidence of the existence, location, or character of relevant geographical circumstances (i.e. there is no agreement), it is appropriate for the court or tribunal to take

[84] See Chapter 7.

[85] VCLT Arts 26, 31; UNCLOS Art 300. Gardiner notes that 'the combination of good faith and taking account of object and purpose results in an outcome that is more likely to reflect effectively the true intentions recorded in the text than would a purely literal approach': R Gardiner, *Treaty Interpretation* (2nd edn, OUP, 2015), 172.

this evidence, if probative, into account. This follows from the right (not obligation) of States to insist on a boundary that responds to geographical circumstances obtaining at the time of delimitation, which may be expressed as a concern with the currency and accuracy of charts. Crucially, such a concern does not imply that the boundary will move with the subsequent revision of charts to improve their accuracy or record changed geographical circumstances.

There is no legal requirement that charts relied upon for interstate delimitation must be accurate and current. Arguments regarding the currency and accuracy of charts are rather legally relevant where a coastal State insists upon the right to benefit from more current or accurate information about geographical circumstances obtaining at the time of delimitation. These arguments reflect an understanding that the definition of a boundary is temporally specific—referring to geographical circumstances shown in particular charts or otherwise demonstrated to exist at the time of delimitation. Far from implying that the boundary will move with the subsequent revision of charts, they signal an effort by the State concerned to secure the greatest advantages possible in the construction of a boundary that will not subsequently change.[86] In some cases, for some States, it may be advantageous to rely on existing charts that do not accurately represent current geographical circumstances. This is entirely lawful. However, a State that can obtain an advantage from showing that contemporary geographical circumstances differ from those shown in the existing charts will have the benefit of being able to insist on its right to have the delimitation reflect geographical circumstances obtaining at the time.

It is worth noting that States delimiting an international maritime boundary may be more concerned with accuracy and currency regarding geographical circumstances than States unilaterally establishing maritime limits, except in the case of the limits of the continental shelf. This follows from the fact that subsequent unilateral adjustments of an international boundary are not permitted by law unless specifically provided for in a boundary agreement.[87] Conversely, the coastal State remains entitled to revise established maritime limits with the exception of those in the continental shelf.[88] In the case of international maritime boundaries, subsequent changes will depend on agreement between the parties. It is also extremely difficult to unilaterally terminate or withdraw from a boundary treaty.[89] The coastal State is likely to seek to maximize its maritime jurisdiction on the basis of contemporary geographical circumstances in both unilateral and interstate delimitation. Yet there is greater impetus to do so where subsequent revision is not

[86] As noted in Chapter 6, States may still establish an ambulatory maritime boundary by agreement; however, the intention to do so would have to be clearly established and is not evidenced by arguments regarding accuracy or currency at the time of delimitation.
[87] See Chapter 6.
[88] See Chapters 3 and 4.
[89] See Chapter 9.

permitted (in the case of the limits of the shelf) or likely to depend upon a new interstate agreement[90] (in the case of an international maritime boundary).

B. New Information about Past Facts

The law does not require that unilateral or interstate delimitation is based on the most accurate and current geographical information possible. It nevertheless recognizes the relevance of probative evidence that contemporary geographical circumstances differ from geographical circumstances represented on existing charts (which remain the usual basis for delimitation). Such evidence may be relied on by the State unilaterally establishing its maritime limits. It must be taken into account where a State insists upon its right to benefit from contemporary circumstances in interstate delimitation. States will usually only go beyond the charts where this allows them to maximize their claims to maritime space—either directly or (in interstate delimitation) by objecting to the claims of another State.[91]

The legal significance of geographical information at odds with existing charts bears upon the question of whether new information about geographical circumstances taken into account in the delimitation process permits or requires the adjustment of established maritime limits or boundaries. The possibility under consideration here is the discovery of new information regarding geographical circumstances as they were at the time of delimitation—not information about subsequent geographical change. It appears that the legal relevance of such new information is limited.

It has been shown that the normal baseline was deliberately defined in a manner allowing use of the low-water line shown on existing charts to establish maritime limits. The law does not require that charts are updated to ensure their currency or accuracy at the time of delimitation. Other baseline types are also defined by reference to standard features on nautical charts. The law is concerned with the timely establishment of precisely defined lines, the construction of which reflects the idea that 'the land dominates the sea', and the location of which can be readily ascertained. This does not depend upon a high degree of accuracy in the representation of geographical facts. It also suggests that new information revealing inaccuracies in geographical information relied on for delimitation—including the publication of revised charts—will not warrant the revision of established maritime limits.

The considerations of principle underpinning the law relating to maritime limits in this regard are somewhat analogous to those underpinning the law relating to

[90] The limited circumstances that might justify the revision of a judicial or arbitral decision establishing a boundary are discussed in the following section.

[91] It is important to be clear that such an objection may be recognized as an expression of the right to benefit from existing geographical circumstances—it does not mean that there is a requirement to look beyond existing charts.

international maritime boundaries. Maritime boundaries may be established by treaty or the decision of an international court or tribunal. International law protects such boundaries against unilateral change (unless specifically provided for in the boundary treaty or another agreement between the States concerned). It strictly limits the circumstances in which termination or withdrawal from a boundary treaty or the revision of a boundary award or decision will be permitted.[92] As discussed in Chapter 6, the principle of stability is expressed in a number of doctrines that serve to protect established boundaries.

A State seeking to challenge an established boundary on the grounds that delimitation was based on maps or charts subsequently shown to be out of date or inaccurate will have limited options. It might argue that an error of fact invalidated its consent to a boundary treaty or that a boundary decision or award must be revised due to the discovery of facts unknown to the parties or the court or tribunal at the time the decision or award was made. It will be necessary to prove inter alia that the error or ignorance pertained to a matter of fact that was essential to the party's consent to the boundary treaty or would have been a 'decisive factor' in the judgment or award. This is not obviously the case where a map or chart is shown to have been out of date or inaccurate. The significance of the discovery of new information about past facts will depend upon the intentions of the parties or the decision-maker and how these intentions relate to the use of maps or charts in the construction and definition of the boundary.

(i) Error, ignorance, and international boundaries

Article 48(1) of the Vienna Convention on the Law of Treaties (VCLT) provides that '[a] State may invoke an error in a treaty as invalidating its consent to be bound by the treaty if the error relates to a fact or situation which was assumed by that State to exist at the time when the treaty was concluded and formed an essential basis of its consent to be bound by the treaty'. Article 48(2) indicates that this will not be possible 'if the State in question contributed by its own conduct to the error or if the circumstances were such as to put that State on notice of a possible error'. Article 48(3) clarifies that '[a]n error relating only to the wording of the text of a treaty does not affect its validity' (such an error may instead be corrected[93]).

Newly discovered facts may also warrant the revision of a judicial decision or arbitral award, including a decision or award establishing a boundary.[94] The ICJ is

[92] See Chapter 9.

[93] VCLT Art 79. An obligation to correct the error only applies if the parties agree that there is an error.

[94] Conversely, the fact that there is an essential error cannot mandate the revision of a treaty by the parties (as opposed to indicating its invalidity or nullity). Revision of a bilateral treaty (the usual form of a boundary treaty) depends on the consent of all parties. As Klabbers notes, a multilateral treaty may be effectively revised without unanimous consent: J Klabbers, 'Treaties, Amendment and Revision' in MPEPIL Online, accessed 5 December 2018. Here too, however, revision is not independently justified by 'essential error'.

specifically authorized by its Statute to revise earlier decisions if certain conditions are met.[95] While the Statute for ITLOS does not provide for the revision of decisions, this is addressed in the Tribunal's Rules.[96] Other cases of arbitration may be covered by the rules set out in the 1899 and 1907 Hague Conventions for the Pacific Settlement of International Disputes, which indicate that '[t]he parties can reserve in the 'Compromis' the right to demand the revision of the Award'.[97] It has been suggested that the authority to revise an award might otherwise be an implied or inherent power of an arbitral tribunal.[98] This seems at odds with idea that States may expressly 'reserve ... the right' to 'demand' revision, which implies that the right is otherwise forfeited in the interests of the finality of the award. The same concern with finality accounts for the strict conditions applying to the revision of a judgment or award where this possibility is admitted, including time limits on requests.

The rule of revision as formulated in these instruments does not refer specifically to 'error' but may cover cases mapping onto this category in the law of treaties. Requests for revision will be considered where they are 'based upon the discovery of some fact of such a nature as to be a decisive factor, which fact was, when the judgment was given, unknown to the [Court or Tribunal] and ... the party requesting revision, always provided that such ignorance was not due to negligence'.[99]

The treatment of error in the 1969 VCLT was heavily informed by the decision in the 1962 *Temple Case*—a boundary dispute in which the significance of a discrepancy between a mapped line purporting to represent the watershed line and the 'true' watershed line was at issue. In that case, the ICJ found that the non-correspondence of the mapped line taken as the boundary with the 'true' watershed line, although an error, did not invalidate Thailand's consent to the boundary as shown on the map. As well as finding that Thailand's authorities had the opportunity to identify and rectify the alleged error (which they did not do),[100] the Court paid careful attention to the common intentions of the parties in defining the boundary as they did. It concluded that '[t]here is ... no reason to think that the Parties attached any special importance to the line of the watershed as such, as compared with the overriding importance in the interests of finality, of adhering to the map line as eventually delimited and as accepted by them'.[101]

[95] ICJ Statute Art 61; see also Permanent Court of International Justice (PCIJ) Statute Art 61.
[96] ITLOS Rules Arts 127–9.
[97] Hague Convention (1899) Art 55; Hague Convention (1907) Art 85.
[98] This argument is noted by Rosenne, though he does not make the same claim: S Rosenne, *Interpretation, Revision, and Other Recourse from International Judgments and Awards* (Martinus Nijhoff, 2007), 5.
[99] PCIJ Statute Art 61; ICJ Statute Art 61; ITLOS Rules Art 127. The Hague Conventions refer to 'the discovery of some new fact calculated to exercise a decisive influence upon the Award': Hague Convention (1899) Art 55; Hague Convention (1907) Art 85.
[100] *Temple Case* (1962), 26.
[101] Ibid, 35.

Notwithstanding Thailand's continuing objections to the 1962 judgment, the Court's reasoning regarding the Annex I Map line was and remains consistent with the law relating to international boundaries generally.[102] Notably, the Court insisted that its understanding of the significance of the Annex I Map was justified as a matter of treaty interpretation and not only on the basis of the parties' subsequent acceptance of the mapped line. After concluding that 'the acceptance of the Annex I map by the Parties caused the map to enter the treaty settlement and to become an integral part of it',[103] the Court specified that this did not involve a departure from the terms of the existing treaty. It explained that a proper interpretation of the treaty as a whole would take into account the fact that

> In general, when two countries establish a frontier between them, one of the primary objects is to achieve stability and finality. This is impossible if the line so established can, at any moment, and on the basis of a continuously available process, be called in question, and its rectification claimed, whenever any inaccuracy by reference to a clause in the parent treaty is discovered. Such a process could continue indefinitely, and finality would never be reached so long as possible errors still remained to be discovered. Such a frontier, so far from being stable, would be completely precarious.[104]

Significantly, this does not mean that a mapped boundary will always prevail notwithstanding errors in its representation of facts on the ground. This depends upon the intentions of the parties or third party delimiting the boundary, as evidenced by the text of the treaty or decision and any relevant subsequent practice.[105]

In some cases, it may clearly be intended that the boundary should accurately follow the course of a particular feature (e.g. a river or watershed) either at a particular time or on a continuing basis (the latter case amounting to the establishment of an ambulatory boundary). It will still need to be established that the assumed accuracy of the mapped line in tracking the feature in question was an essential basis for the party's consent to the boundary treaty. It will also need to be shown that the State alleging error did not contribute to it by its own conduct and that 'the circumstances were [not] such as to put that State on notice of a possible

[102] Thailand again argued that the mapped line could not be the boundary as it 'departs in significant respects from the watershed line stipulated in the 1904 Treaty' in the *Temple Interpretation Case* (2013), 305. The parties disagreed on whether the 1962 judgment had 'decided with binding force that the Annex I map line represents the frontier'. The Court declined to answer this question as it went beyond an interpretation of the operative part of the judgment: ibid, 301, 317. It nevertheless observed that the judgment that the Temple was in Cambodian territory followed from a finding that the map line was the boundary: ibid, 306–17.

[103] *Temple Case* (1962), 33.

[104] Ibid, 34.

[105] See Chapter 6.

error'. In this context, an awareness of the limitations of the surveys or maps relied on will be relevant.

In the case of a request for the revision of a judicial or arbitral decision, the newly identified fact must be 'of such a nature as to be a decisive factor' and unknown to the court and parties at the time the decision was made (such ignorance not being due to negligence). It is possible to imagine cases where a newly identified fact would have had a decisive influence on a delimitation decision—for example, where charts omitted an island belonging to one of the parties and generating entitlement to maritime space. Ignorance of this kind of fact remains unlikely and may be considered negligent. An awareness that the charts relied upon were not entirely accurate or up to date—and, as such, may have contained errors relating to relevant geographical circumstances—will also bear upon an assessment of whether a newly discovered fact can properly be considered a 'decisive factor'.

The notion of 'a decisive factor' does similar work to an 'essential basis of consent' in relation to errors of fact in the case of treaties. It must be shown that the parties and, in third-party delimitation, the court or tribunal, assumed the accuracy and currency of the cartographic representation of geographical circumstances and that their consent or decision was premised on such accuracy and currency. This will be difficult to establish where a boundary was based on charts known to rely on older surveys and so potentially contain inaccuracies.

Where error is alleged to invalidate a party's consent to a treaty, then a general awareness of the potential inaccuracy of maps or charts may mean that 'the circumstances were such as to put that State on notice of a possible error'.[106] Even if the party was not 'on notice' in this sense, it would need to be shown that the error related to 'a fact or situation . . . assumed by that State to exist at the time . . . the treaty was concluded' and '[forming] an essential basis of its consent to be bound'.[107] This criterion may be satisfied by evidence that the State (a) reasonably assumed that the charted geographical circumstances used to delimit the boundary accurately tracked facts on the ground and (b) would not have agreed to the boundary if it knew this was not the case. This will not be established where it appears that a State was content to take a mapped line as the boundary in the context of a general awareness that the map may be out of date or inaccurate.

Where a State seeks the revision of a boundary decision, a general awareness of the potential inaccuracy of charts will not necessarily prevent it from successfully arguing that it was ignorant of a specific new fact. Yet such a fact may not qualify as a 'decisive factor' if it was accepted that the decision could properly be based on existing charts notwithstanding inaccuracies—including the omission or misrepresentation of what would otherwise be relevant geographical facts.

[106] VCLT Art 48(2).
[107] VCLT Art 48(1).

(ii) The importance of intention

The definition of a boundary by reference to maps or charts known to be inaccurate (or possibly so) does not invariably mean that the parties or court or tribunal were content to make use of cartographic lines and points regardless of whether they in fact corresponded with features on the ground. The particular terms in which the boundary is defined, its relationship with the maps or charts used to construct the boundary or indicate its course, and the approach taken to demarcation must all be taken into account. In the case of a boundary treaty, the subsequent practice of the parties may also be relevant.[108]

The complexities here are usefully elaborated by reference to the decisions in *Encuentro/Palena* (1966), *Laguna del Desierto* (1994), *Laguna del Desierto Revision/Interpretation* (1995), and *Cameroon v Nigeria* (2002). None of these disputes involved a claim that consent to a boundary treaty had been invalidated by error and only the 1995 *Laguna Del Desierto Case* involved a request for revision of a previous decision. Yet all four cases cast light on the relationship between error and the intentions of the parties to a boundary agreement or a court or tribunal tasked with delimitation.

Alvarez-Jimenez has argued that the ICJ has effectively 'corrected mistakes' in boundary treaties through interpretation in accordance with Articles 31 and 32 of the VCLT.[109] It is more accurate to say that a number of decisions by the Court and other tribunals have demonstrated that existing boundary agreements and awards may remain effective notwithstanding a range of errors. Rather than the errors being 'corrected', it has been possible to give effect to the original intentions of the parties or arbitrators despite them.

Both *Encuentro/Palena* and *Laguna del Desierto* concerned disputes between Chile and Argentina regarding the interpretation and application of a 1902 Award clarifying the course of a boundary defined by an 1881 Treaty and 1893 Protocol.[110] For present purposes, the most interesting aspect of *Encuentro/Palena* is the way in which the Court of Arbitration dealt with a lack of correspondence between (a) the boundary described in the 1902 Award, the associated Report, and the 'Award Map' and (b) certain facts on the ground.

The Award had provided that from a 'fixed point on the River Palena, the boundary shall follow the River Encuentro to the peak called Virgen'.[111] The Report elaborated that 'crossing the Palena at this [fixed] point, opposite the junction of the River Encuentro, [the boundary] shall then follow the Encuentro along the course of its western branch to its source on the western slopes of Cerro Virgen'.[112]

[108] VCLT Art 31(3)(b). On this point see also Chapter 6.

[109] A Alvarez-Jimenez, 'The International Court of Justice's Use of the Vienna Convention in the Interpretation of Boundary Agreements: 2000–10' (2012) 3 (2) *JIDS* 409, 417–28. He also suggests that the Court has extended the principles in these provisions in an unorthodox fashion.

[110] *Encuentro/Palena* (1966), 112.

[111] Ibid, 142.

[112] Ibid.

The Award Map indicated a line fitting this description.[113] This line, however, followed the tributary known as the River Salto to its source on Cerro Virgen. More precisely, it followed the course of the River Salto mapped by Argentina but misnamed the Encuentro, part of which was only an approximation (a pecked line showing that the river was known to exist but had not been accurately located).[114] This river was also misidentified in the text of the Award and the Award Map as the Encuentro. During demarcation, a boundary post was erected at the confluence of the Palena and the real Encuentro, upstream of the Salto.[115] It subsequently became clear that this river did not fit the description in the Arbitrator's Report or the depiction in the Award Map.[116]

The parties agreed that 'a geographical error of some kind was made in 1902–03' but disagreed on 'what the error was'.[117] Argentina argued that the Salto had been misnamed the Encuentro in the Award and Map, which led to the erroneous placement of Boundary Post 16.[118] Chile argued that the Boundary Post 'was correctly placed and that the error consisted mainly of the wrong depiction of the topography on the Award Map with the result that, contrary to the Arbitrator's real intention in 1902, the Award makes the boundary pass through Cerro de la Virgen instead of through the mountain which Chile later came to call "Pico Virgen" or "Pico de la Virgen" '.[119] The error on this account lay in the misidentification of the course and source of the Encuentro.[120]

There are some peculiarities in the *Encuentro/Palena* decision that follow from the parties' agreement that Boundary Post 16 could not now be moved.[121] The question for the Court was whether the boundary between Posts 16 and 17 remained 'unsettled' and, if so, how the 1902 Award could be 'interpreted and fulfilled' in this sector.[122] The Court found that the boundary was settled between Post 16 and the confluence of the two channels of the real Encuentro—neither of which had its source on Cerro Virgen—because there was no difficulty in 'applying the Award to the ground'.[123] Specifically, the description of the boundary as '[following] the River Encuentro' was taken to be readily '[applied] to the ground' insofar as there was 'no difficulty about identifying and following that river as far as the Confluence'.[124] This looks like an *ex post facto* rationalization of the fact that

[113] Ibid, 152.
[114] Ibid, 150–2.
[115] Ibid, 153, 155.
[116] Ibid, 155.
[117] Ibid, 167.
[118] Ibid, 131, 167.
[119] Ibid, 167.
[120] Ibid, 127.
[121] Ibid, 153.
[122] Ibid, 112, 163–4.
[123] Ibid, 169.
[124] Ibid, 154, 169.

the Court could not revisit the placement of Post 16. Other than carrying the name Encuentro, this was not the river described in the 1902 Award, Report, and Map.

In determining the course of the boundary beyond the confluence to Cerro Virgen—a section considered unsettled due to the difficulty of 'applying the Award to the ground'—the Court sought to give effect to the intentions of the arbitrator as indicated by the Award, Report, and Map, which had been 'frustrated by an incorrect appreciation of the geography'.[125] It determined that the chief intention was that the boundary should follow a river to the peak of Cerro Virgen, the latter being singled out as a 'strong, well-marked, and unmistakable topographical feature'.[126] As neither channel of the actual Encuentro had its source here, the Court determined that it would give best effect to the arbitrator's intentions to follow the 'major channel' of that river 'until it begins to deviate in a marked degree from the direction of Cerro de la Virgen, at which point the line must leave the Encuentro altogether and make for Cerro de la Virgen in a manner as far as possible consistent with the general practice of the Award'.[127] This line did not follow a river to its source in Cerro Virgen but made its way from the Encuentro to this peak along the local water-parting, which had been used to define the boundary elsewhere.[128]

It is interesting to compare the Court's solution to that proposed by a Mixed Commission in 1955, which had been based on the assumption 'that the boundary must pass through the source of the Encuentro'.[129] The Court did not consider the Arbitrator's chief intention to have been that the boundary should follow a river to its source. Instead, the terms of the 1902 Award and Report indicated that the boundary should pass through the peak of Cerro Virgen—an intention related to the concern to ensure that the boundary, once fixed, would be readily identifiable.[130]

Encuentro/Palena differs from the *Temple Case* in that the Court did not insist on the mapped line. Too much should not be made of this—identifying the mapped line as the boundary was not an option given the terms of the *compromis* and the circumstances relating to Boundary Post 16. The Court in any case indicated that the line shown on the Award Map was consistent with the intentions of the arbitrator notwithstanding the misidentification of the River Salto as the Encuentro.[131] Unable to depart from a starting point that already diverged from the mapped line (Boundary Post 16), it emphasized the arbitrator's intention that the boundary should pass through the peak of Cerro Virgen as a clearly identifiable landmark. In this regard, it was intended that the boundary should correspond

125 Ibid, 174–7.
126 Ibid, 170, 177.
127 Ibid, 177.
128 Ibid, 180.
129 Ibid, 171.
130 Ibid, 170, 177.
131 Ibid, 152, 176.

with a natural feature. Conversely, the definition of the boundary as following a river wrongly identified as the Encuentro was largely a matter of convenience based on the understanding that this river had its source in the Cerro Virgen. It was intended that the boundary should rise to this peak—not that it should follow the actual Encuentro to its source wherever it lay.

Like the *Temple Case, Encuentro/Palena* shows that the use of geographical features to describe a boundary may be no more than a means to an end. It does not necessarily reflect an intention that the boundary should follow the actual configuration of that feature on the ground. As such, errors regarding the location of the feature on the ground may not prevent the intentions of the parties or decision-maker establishing the boundary from being fulfilled. *Encuentro/Palena* illustrates the importance of the intentions of the arbitrator and (indirectly in this case) the parties to a boundary treaty in determining the course of a boundary that appears uncertain due to error. The Court did not correct the error—its interpretation ensured that the error would not prevent those intentions from being fulfilled.

Laguna del Desierto (1994) concerned the 'interpretation and fulfilment' of the 1902 Award with respect to another section of the Chile–Argentina boundary—that between Boundary Post 62 and Mount Fitzroy. The Award had defined the boundary in this part as:

> lines ... fixed across Lake Buenos Aires, Lake Pueyrredôn (or Cochrane) and Lake San Martin, the effect of which is to assign the western portions of the basins of these lakes to Chile and the eastern portions to Argentina, the dividing ranges carrying the lofty peaks known as Mounts San Lorenzo and Fitzroy.[132]

The Arbitrator's Report described the boundary as '[following] the median line of the Lake [San Martin] southwards as far as a point opposite the spur which terminates on the southern shore of the Lake in longitude 72°47'W, whence the boundary shall be drawn to the foot of this spur and ascend the local water-parting to Mount Fitzroy'.[133] Boundary Post 62 was placed on the southern shore of Lake Saint Martin in 1903.[134] There was no further demarcation of the boundary between this point and Mount Fitzroy.

In this case, the parties disagreed on the meaning of 'the local water parting' in the Report. Argentina argued that the expression was not defined by the Award but should be taken to refer to a specific section of a water-parting generally understood to mean an 'unbroken line ... between two predetermined points' that 'at each of its points, separates river Basins' and 'cannot cross rivers or lakes'.[135] This meant that a local water-parting could coincide with the continental water parting that separated

[132] *Laguna del Desierto* (1994), 20.
[133] Ibid.
[134] Ibid.
[135] Ibid, 38.

waters draining to the Pacific from those draining to the Atlantic.[136] Chile argued that the 'local water-parting' separated 'waters which flow into a single ocean' and could not coincide with the continental water-parting.[137] It initially claimed that 'there is no continuous "local water-parting" which carries the line from boundary post 62 to Mount Fitzroy', i.e. that 'the description of the boundary in the 1902 report does not conform with the geographical reality'.[138] Chile later claimed that its proposed boundary followed the 'local water-parting', though it crossed some surface water and partly coincided with the continental water-divide.[139]

The Court found that the term 'water-parting' meant 'the line which divides . . . two separate directions of surface flow of the waters or, in other words, the line at which two slopes of the land surface intersect vertically'—this being both (a) the definition used by the parties in their submissions for the 1898–1902 arbitration, and (b) the ordinary meaning of 'water-parting' at the time.[140] The Court also found that 'the 1902 Award considers a local water-parting to be one which runs between two points, at least one of which is not located on the continental divide'.[141] Noting that the Award Map represented the boundary in the disputed sector by a pecked line, the Court concluded that '[b]y defining the frontier as a "local water-parting", the Arbitrator opted for a natural feature whose exact location was not known'.[142]

To 'fulfil' this part of the Award it was necessary to identify the 'actual configuration' of the local water-parting as defined.[143] The Court commissioned a 'geographical expert' for this task[144] with a majority concluding that the line identified by the expert was the boundary.[145] Chile had argued that this 'application of the 1902 Award in the light of geographical knowledge acquired subsequently would be tantamount to its revision by means of the retroactive assessment of new facts'.[146] Rejecting this argument, the Court noted that '[t]he land remains unchanged. Thus, the local water-parting between boundary post 62 and Mount Fitzroy existing in 1902 is the same as the one which can be traced at the time of the present arbitration'.[147]

In a subsequent request for interpretation and revision of the 1994 Award, Chile argued inter alia that the Court had erred in concluding that the line identified by the expert was identical to the 'actual configuration' of the water-parting in 1902. Chile submitted that glacial movement between 1902 and 1994 meant that it was

136 Ibid.
137 Ibid.
138 Ibid, 39.
139 Ibid.
140 Ibid, 39–43.
141 Ibid, 44.
142 Ibid.
143 Ibid, 50.
144 Ibid, 48.
145 Ibid, 53.
146 Ibid, 50.
147 Ibid.

not.[148] It also objected to the location of the boundary on the surface of glaciers 'subject to constant movement and change', arguing that this rendered them 'unsuitable as sites for the delineation of frontiers by means of water-partings'.[149]

This last claim alleged an error of law rather than fact and could not be a basis for revision (which is not tantamount to appeal).[150] The Court nevertheless commented on its substance, emphasizing that 'as a legal concept the stability of frontiers does not depend on possible changes which may occur in the ground across which the frontiers run, changes which constitute a strictly physical phenomenon'.[151] It noted that the 'option was open' for States establishing a boundary 'on a moving glacier or along a river whose *thalweg* shifts its course ... to agree that the frontier shall follow the shifts of the glacier or *thalweg* or to "fix" the frontier at the moment when it is delineated'.[152] The mere fact that the physical geography was mobile did not prevent the establishment of an immobile boundary.

With respect to Chile's contention that 'the local water-parting established as the frontier by the 1994 Award is not the same as the one which existed in 1902', the Court found that there was no clear evidence of any intervening change.[153] More importantly, it clarified that it was in any case 'legally immaterial' whether the water-parting identified in 1994 was 'the same as the one which physically existed in 1902'.[154] The Court had not considered the identification of the water-parting in 1994 as the boundary to be justified because the 'land had not changed' since 1902. Instead, it found that the 1902 Award made clear that the boundary was to follow the water-parting on the ground but its specific location had not been determined at the time or since. To give effect to the 1902 Award in 1994, the Court had to determine the line of the water-parting at the time of its decision. This did not offend the 'principle of contemporaneity' requiring the interpretation of a boundary agreement or award in light of the law and facts at the time it was made. The Court had interpreted the 1902 Award in precisely this context and found that the boundary was intended to follow the actual course of the local water-parting when determined on the ground. Its course on the ground was not determined before it was identified by the Court's expert in 1994.

Chile had also criticized the 1994 decision for its treatment of the Award Map, arguing that the line identified by the Court failed to respect the general direction of the mapped line and points that it passed through.[155] In response, the Court explained that '[t]he 1994 Award stated that the established frontier is in accordance with the

[148] *Laguna del Desierto Revision/Interpretation* (1995), 163, 167–8.
[149] Ibid, 164.
[150] Ibid, 158, 166.
[151] Ibid, 164.
[152] Ibid, 166.
[153] Ibid, 165.
[154] Ibid, 170.
[155] This argument featured in the dissenting opinions of Pohl and Benadava in *Laguna Del Desierto* (1994), 53–149.

1902 Award map, as the Court interpreted this latter instrument with respect to the significance of its pecked line'.[156] The pecked line had been taken to confirm that the boundary was to follow the course of the actual water-parting, which had not been identified at the time the Award and accompanying Map were made. There was no obligation to follow the course of this pecked line, which indicated only the two points between which the location of the actual water-parting had to be determined

It is interesting to compare *Encuentro/Palena* and the *Laguna del Desierto* cases with *Cameroon v Nigeria* (2002), where the Court, confronted with the definition of the boundary as passing through 'the source' of the Tsikakiri river and the fact that the Tsikakiri river did not have one source but many, determined that its task was 'not to identify the "geographical" source of the Tsikakiri, but to identify the source through which the drafters of the Thomson-Marchand Declaration intended that the boundary should pass'.[157] In this regard, the Court emphasized that the drafters 'intended to designate a point which could be readily identified both on maps and on the ground'.[158] It concluded that the source of the river most clearly meeting this criterion should be taken as the relevant point in the boundary.[159]

Where a boundary is defined by reference to one or more geographical features, the chief intention may be to ensure that it can be identified, respected, and enforced. A mapped line that fails to respect the true course of a natural feature may be consistent with this intention. In other cases, it may be intended that the boundary should follow a feature on the ground because this inter alia (a) allows the boundary to be respected in the absence of demarcation by boundary posts, (b) ensures States on either side have access to the feature (e.g. a river), or (c) respects each State's established title to territory on either side of the feature as located on the ground. In some cases, it may be clear that the boundary was intended to follow the feature on the ground[160] though the rationale is not apparent.

Even where it is clearly intended that a boundary should correspond with a feature on the ground, further evidence may be required to establish an intention that the boundary should accurately correspond with current facts. Such an intention cannot be assumed but must be clearly evidenced where it is claimed that a lack of accuracy or currency in the geographical information relied upon for delimitation invalidates a boundary treaty or warrants the revision of a boundary decision. In many cases, boundaries are established on the basis of geographical information known to be in fact or potentially out of date or inaccurate. In many cases, a failure to accurately track geographical circumstances on the ground

[156] *Laguna del Desierto Revision/Interpretation* (1995), 180.

[157] *Cameroon v Nigeria* (2002), 374.

[158] Ibid, 375.

[159] Ibid.

[160] This would seem to be the case, for example, where it is provided that demarcation should more accurately specify the boundary by reference to geographical circumstances on the ground.

will not prevent the intentions of the parties or court or tribunal establishing the boundary from being fulfilled.

(iii) Instability and ambulatory boundaries

It is important to be clear that the circumstances under discussion involve new information about past facts. Facts coming into existence after the conclusion of a treaty will not usually indicate that consent to it was based on an error of fact. Nor will such subsequent developments ordinarily justify the revision of a judicial or arbitral decision, which is intended to remedy the failure to consider a fact obtaining at the time of decision which would have been 'a decisive factor'. Subsequent geographical change, as such, will not generally invalidate a party's consent to a boundary treaty or justify the revision of a boundary decision.

It remains possible that subsequent geographical change could evidence the fact that geographical circumstances were unstable at the time of delimitation. Error or a case for revision could be made out if such instability was unknown when the boundary was delimited and, crucially, *if* it could be established that the stability of the feature in question was assumed and a basis for consent to a boundary treaty or 'a decisive factor' in a boundary decision. In this regard, however, it is useful to recall the Court's observation in *Laguna del Desierto* (1995) that 'the stability of frontiers does not depend on possible changes which may occur in the ground across which the frontiers run'.[161] The relevance of the physical stability of a feature will depend on whether the established boundary is ambulatory or, as is more usual, fixed, which depends upon a construal of the intentions of the parties or court or tribunal establishing the boundary.

New evidence of geographical instability is likely to be irrelevant if the boundary is fixed. If the boundary is ambulatory, at least some types of subsequent change were anticipated and could not be considered unknown. If it is provided that the boundary will only shift with certain types of geographical change, other change is irrelevant. A case of error or grounds for revision might still be made out if new information shows that a feature is more unstable than previously thought. Significantly, it must also be shown that the feature was unstable or prone to the relevant change at the time of delimitation, though this fact was unknown. Where later developments produce instability or vulnerability to change, the relevant fact cannot be said to have existed at the time of delimitation so cannot qualify as a fact that would have been determinative if known. The implications of such subsequent developments for the established boundary must take into account the temporal dimensions of the law, which—as Chapter 9 elaborates—distinguishes between the rules and principles governing the creation of a boundary and those governing its continuing existence.

[161] *Laguna del Desierto Revision/Interpretation* (1995), 164.

IV. Foreseeable Practicalities? The Implications of Charting Practices

There is no legal requirement that maritime limits or boundaries must be established on the basis of the most current and accurate geographical information available at the time of delimitation. States delimiting a maritime boundary may agree to rely on particular charts for this purpose regardless of their currency or accuracy. More accurate evidence of contemporary geographical facts will take priority in third-party delimitation where a State argues that it is entitled to claim more (or the other State less) on this basis. Yet the law permits and, indeed, anticipates delimitation by reference to existing nautical charts. Accordingly, there is no reason to assume that more current and accurate geographical information becoming available after the establishment of maritime limits or boundaries will invalidate or warrant revision of the same. Nevertheless, it was presumably known that existing nautical charts would be updated at some point in response to new information revealing inaccuracies in their representation of geographical circumstances or subsequent geographical change. A key question is whether this implies an understanding that maritime limits and boundaries would be revised as charts were updated.

In the case of maritime boundaries, it is relatively easy to establish that this will not ordinarily be the case. The law clearly indicates that boundaries are to be based on charts relied on by the parties at the time of delimitation and possibly other evidence of the contemporary circumstances. An array of rules consistent with the principle of the stability of boundaries supports the conclusion that the use of existing charts to delimit a maritime boundary—which is standard practice—neither implies that boundary is ambulatory nor indicates that it will only be justified in its current configuration until the next update of the relevant charts. International boundaries, including maritime boundaries, are intended to have a long life and the law serves to ensure this.

Practical considerations might appear to support the conclusion that maritime limits must be revised as charts are updated. States negotiating the law of the sea treaties were no doubt aware that the same nautical charts used to determine and display maritime limits would be updated to show changes to coastal geography and the low-water line. It is important that mariners using those charts for navigation are aware of jurisdictional limits. If coastal geography changes and limits do not, mariners may need to refer to separate (historical) charts showing existing limits or collate this information.

There was no discussion at the law of the sea conferences of the logistical challenges that might arise from either the use of separate charts for maritime limits and navigation or the transposition of information indicating the fixed location of maritime limits. This does not necessarily suggest that States envisioned that limits would be redrawn as charts were updated. There was equally no discussion of procedures for updating charted limits or the central question of whether geographical change triggers such an obligation. Other aspects of the law weigh against the conclusion that the role of charts in delimitation means that maritime limits must be revised as charts are updated.

UNCLOS requires baselines or zonal limits to be defined by geographical coordinates or charted with sufficient accuracy and at a scale facilitating translation into coordinates.[162] As the Tribunal observed in *Bangladesh v India* (2014), 'satellite navigation systems now allow users of the oceans to easily locate any geodetic point without resorting to the actual physical features used at the date of delimitation'.[163] Prior to the development of satellite navigation systems, baselines and zonal limits were defined in a manner deliberately designed to facilitate the accurate identification of their position by sea users.

Under UNCLOS, deposit and due publicity requirements apply to straight baselines and closing lines or 'the limits derived therefrom', archipelagic baselines, and the limits of the EEZ and continental shelf.[164] The absence of a parallel requirement for the 'normal baseline' is not significant given that the low-water line is 'marked on large-scale charts officially recognized by the coastal State'.[165] Deposit and due publicity requirements ensure that established maritime limits can be located and respected by members of the international community and sea users over time. They also reflect an understanding that charts showing maritime limits have special status and authority as expressions of the will of the coastal State in the exercise of its rights and fulfilment of its responsibilities under conventional and customary law. The requirement that charts be deposited with the UN Secretary-General must be situated in the practice of the UN Secretary-General as the named depositary for UNCLOS and other legal instruments. The Secretary-General is considered the appropriate custodian for multilateral treaties of 'worldwide interest'.[166] Charts showing maritime limits have a legal and not merely practical significance.[167] They are legally binding instruments with consequences for parties to UNCLOS and States generally.

The role of these charts as expressions of the will of the coastal State means they are no longer just one iteration of a series of nautical charts subject to revision in accordance with new geographical information bearing upon requirements for navigational safety. The law makes use of existing nautical charts to facilitate the coastal State's timely delimitation of its entitlement to maritime space. But the officially recognized, deposited, and duly publicized chart showing maritime limits is a legal instrument expressing the will of the coastal State in the exercise of its rights and fulfilment of its responsibilities regarding the delimitation of national maritime space in the law of the sea.

Though it was presumably understood that nautical charts would ordinarily be updated to reflect new information clarifying existing geographical information or evidencing later geographical change, the law is clearly concerned to ensure that the location of maritime limits established by the coastal State at a particular point in time

[162] UNCLOS Arts 5, 6, 16, 47(8), 75, 76(9), 84.
[163] *Bangladesh v India* (2014), 63.
[164] UNCLOS Arts 16, 47(9), 75(2), 76(9), 84.
[165] UNCLOS Art 5.
[166] UNOLA, *Summary of Practice of the Secretary-General as Depositary of Multilateral Treaties* (UN Publications, 1999), 7.
[167] Cf Caron, 'When Law Makes Climate Change Worse', 634.

and by reference to particular charts can be ascertained and so respected by other States and sea users. If it had been assumed that the State would have to revise maritime limits with the publication of new charts, it would be reasonable—given this clear concern—to expect some provision relating to the deposit and due publicity of 'officially recognized' amendments. As it stands, the law is concerned to both facilitate and regulate the act of delimitation by the coastal State but does not impose further requirements to adjust established limits in response to subsequent geographical change.

It is important to be clear that the 'officially recognized' charts showing maritime limits do not independently secure maritime limits against change or constitute the source of their lawfulness despite such change. The point is not that States may rely on charted limits as a kind of legal loophole in the face of subsequent geographical change.[168] Rather, the approach taken to charts in the law is consistent with a system which provides for delimitation at a particular point in time by reference to existing nautical charts. Requiring the coastal State to prepare, deposit, and duly publicize specific charts or lists of coordinates identifying the location of its maritime limits ensures that those limits, defined at a particular point in time, can be continue to be located and so respected and enforced. The use of existing nautical charts facilitates the timely and relatively regular establishment of maritime limits. This does not imply any obligation to adjust lawfully established maritime limits in response to later updates to nautical charts, including those recording subsequent geographical change.

V. Conclusion

The rules relating to baselines and zonal limits are clearly directed towards their construction at a particular point in time—the moment of delimitation. The role of charts in this context does not imply an understanding that maritime limits will necessarily be revised as charts are updated, although the coastal State retains the option of redrawing established maritime limits (except the limits of the shelf) to take advantage of updates that allow it to further maximize its entitlement to maritime space.

The temporal dimensions of the law relating to maritime limits are in this regard aligned with the temporal dimensions of the law relating to international maritime boundaries. The following chapter will examine the question of temporality in greater detail. For present purposes, it is clear that the role of nautical charts in the delimitation process does not imply a legal obligation to revise maritime limits or maritime boundaries as charts are updated for navigational purposes.

The requirements for accuracy and currency in nautical charts attendant on their primary use for navigation do not have a direct parallel in the law relating to maritime delimitation. A State may, at the time of delimitation, take advantage of geographical information that is more current and accurate than that shown in

168 Cf Schofield, 'Rising Waters, Shrinking States', 220–1, as discussed in Chapter 7.

existing charts to maximize its entitlement to maritime space or counter the claims of a neighbouring State. Yet the law considers existing charts an adequate basis for delimitation notwithstanding the fact that they may be to varying degrees out of date or inaccurate. States negotiating the law of the sea treaties and the technical experts they consulted would have been well aware that charts are not regularly updated and may be somewhat inaccurate as a representation of current facts. This was not considered an obstacle to their use as the basis for determining entitlement to maritime space and its spatial specification.

It is worth emphasizing that even if the law did require delimitation to be based on the most accurate and current geographical information available at that time, this would not imply a legal requirement to amend established maritime limits where subsequent geographical change means the information relied on for their construction is no longer accurate or current. A finding that the law requires accurate and current information regarding the location of the low-water line or other coastal features at the time of delimitation does not amount to a finding that the law requires maritime limits or boundaries to reflect the most accurate and current information about these 'facts' on a continuing basis. The legal principle underpinning the first requirement does not recommend the second. The error involved in taking the rules and principles that govern the construction of maritime limits and boundaries to condition their continuing existence is discussed in Chapter 9.

As the Conclusion to this book will further elaborate, State practice shows that many States do not revise their maritime limits when nautical charts are updated or when they otherwise become aware of subsequent geographical change. Where States have revised their limits in response to such developments, this does not clearly evidence a belief that such revision is legally required. The law recognizes the right of the coastal State to establish maritime limits in accordance with the rules and principles governing their construction. This implies the right to redraw those limits in accordance with the same rules and principles—including in circumstances where geographical circumstances have changed. This, crucially, is a matter of permission rather than obligation. The right to revise maritime limits—as an option—is confirmed by the exceptional restriction of the same right in the case of the limits of the continental shelf, which must be 'permanently described'. As we shall see, at least two States do appear to believe that maritime limits *must* be revised as charts are updated. Yet this does not counter the weight of State practice and other evidence of the content of the law in this regard. The role of charts in delimitation is consistent with the conclusion that maritime limits are not ambulatory and that revision in response to the updating of charts is not legally required.

9

Conditions over Time

Lessons from the *Island of Palmas*

I. Introduction

The relevance of the temporal dimensions of the law relating to maritime limits and boundaries for the question of geographical change has already become apparent through the analyses developed in the previous chapters. The significance of the law's temporality becomes even clearer when we turn to consider what may be the most influential assumption underpinning the ambulatory thesis—the assumption that the conditions set out in the baselines provisions require satisfaction on a continuing basis.

Again, this has not been expressly advanced as an argument in support of the theory of ambulatory maritime limits. Yet this line of reasoning is evident where scholars considering the implications of coastal change (and climate-related change in particular) (a) refer to real or hypothetical examples of established baselines, and (b) assess their lawfulness or the extent to which they allegedly 'must' or 'will' change by reapplying the baselines provisions to real or hypothetical circumstances of geographical change. This exercise assumes that the baselines provisions do not merely govern the construction of maritime limits but apply as conditions which must continue to be met. If established baselines are constantly reassessed against the baselines provisions, then the lawfulness of maritime limits is effectively conditional upon the coastal geography informing their location remaining unchanged—or unchanged in material aspects picked out by the baselines provisions.

It is worth reiterating that this route to the ambulatory thesis can be distinguished from the idea that baselines share the variability of the natural features to which they refer. If the latter assumption were correct (and it has been argued that it is not), baselines would be ambulatory from the point of establishment. Their movement would be a consequence of the decision to use variable 'natural' features as the baseline or the locus of basepoints (discussed in Chapter 7) or the decision to define baselines by reference to features shown on nautical charts that are ordinarily revised in light of new and current information (discussed in Chapter 8). This can be distinguished from the continual assessment of baselines against the terms of the baselines provisions and their adjustment in accordance with the same. The fact that commentators often rely on a combination of these assumptions in their

Geographical Change and the Law of the Sea. Kate Purcell, Oxford University Press (2019). © Kate Purcell.
DOI: 10.1093/oso/9780198743644.001.0001

arguments is indicative of a general failure to properly articulate the grounds for the ambulatory thesis.

The assumption that established baselines must continue to meet the conditions set out in the baselines provisions has a clear parallel in arguments that geographical change may result in the loss of entitlement to maritime space. In this context, change affecting the conditions precedent for entitlement has been considered to affect the continuation of the right. It has been suggested, for example, that a loss of entitlement to maritime space may result where geographical change means that a feature no longer meets the definition of an island as 'a naturally formed area of land, surrounded by water, which is above water at high tide' or falls into the category of '[r]ocks which cannot sustain human habitation or economic life of their own'.[1] These conclusions appear to be based on the understanding that the continuing possession of these partly geographical attributes is a condition for continuing entitlement to maritime space. It has been suggested that continuing entitlement to archipelagic waters is similarly conditional on continuing qualification as an archipelagic State as well as continuing satisfaction of the rules governing the construction of archipelagic baselines.[2] More generally, loss of territorial sovereignty over coastal land is understood to result in a loss of the entitlement to maritime space generated by that coast. This last case, as we shall see, should in fact be distinguished from the case of entitlement to maritime space in respect of an island or archipelago.

There are a number of difficulties with the foregoing interpretation of the law. Primarily, it is not obvious that the conditions governing the establishment of entitlement to maritime space or the construction of maritime limits are also conditions that govern the continuing existence of such entitlement or the continuing lawfulness of established maritime limits. Yet the possibility that the conditions for the establishment of legal rights, status, or limits may not be identical to the conditions for their persistence does not seem to have been contemplated in the commentary considering the legal implications of geographical change for maritime jurisdiction in the law of the sea. Perhaps as a corollary, insufficient attention has been paid to the particular character and content of the conditions for the establishment of (a) entitlement to maritime space generally, (b) entitlement to the

[1] See e.g. Soons, 'The Effects of a Rising Sea Level', 217–19, though Soons argues that entitlement to a continental shelf may be retained as a result of its limits being permanently fixed. As will be discussed in this chapter, this appears to confuse the question of entitlement to maritime space with its delimitation. Grote Stoutenburg argues that an island may not be downgraded to a 'rock' but on the basis that such a feature could still meet the requirements of UNCLOS Article 121(3): Grote Stoutenburg, *Disappearing Island States*, 152–4. This argument is based on the same assumption that the conditions for entitlement to maritime space in respect of an island apply on a continuing basis. Charney uses the same reasoning to conclude that an island may be downgraded to a rock, emphasizing, significantly, the parallel with 'ambulatory baselines' in this regard: Charney, 'Rocks that Cannot Sustain Human Habitation', 867–8, fns 23, 25. See also Freestone and Pethick, 'Sea Level Rise and Maritime Boundaries', 76; Schofield and Freestone, 'Options to Protect Coastlines', 146–7.

[2] See e.g. ILA Sea Level Rise Committee, Conference Report (2018), 10.

various maritime zones in the case of islands, (c) entitlement to archipelagic waters, (d) maritime limits, and (e) international maritime boundaries. In particular, insufficient attention has been paid to the temporal dimension of these conditions.

In the case of international maritime boundaries, it is not usually argued that the continuing lawfulness or effectiveness of the established boundary depends on the persistence of factors taken into account in their construction. Yet the irrelevance of subsequent geographical change in this context is often attributed to a supervening principle of the stability of international boundaries. There has been a failure to recognize that the irrelevance of subsequent geographical change also follows from or is consistent with the role of geographical circumstances as elements bearing upon the construction of the boundary rather than conditions for its continuing existence. As such, there has been a failure to recognize the consistency between the law relating to interstate maritime delimitation and the law relating to both entitlement to maritime space and unilateral maritime delimitation in this regard.

The temporality of the law relating to entitlement to maritime space, maritime limits, and international maritime boundaries is usefully clarified by an application of Max Huber's valuable distinction between the creation of rights and their 'continued manifestation', as developed in the 1928 *Island of Palmas Case*. The question of the implications of geographical change for maritime jurisdiction does not concern a change in the law; it is concerned with change affecting certain facts taken into account in the establishment of entitlement to maritime space or its delimitation. The distinction between the creation and continuing existence of rights which underpins Huber's account of the two branches of intertemporal law nevertheless casts light on the legal significance of such change. Indeed, applying this distinction to the law of maritime jurisdiction may both clarify and illustrate the value of Huber's account of the second branch of the doctrine of intertemporal law, which has attracted criticism largely in proportion to the extent that it has been misunderstood.

II. Intertemporal Law: Huber's Insight

In the 1928 *Island of Palmas Case*, Judge Huber observed that

> [t]he same principle which subjects the act creative of a right to the law in force at the time the right arises, demands that the existence of the right, in other words its continued manifestation, shall follow the conditions required by the evolution of law.[3]

Critics of this claim have mostly followed Jessup, who sought to demonstrate its apparent absurdity in his comment on the arbitration in the same

[3] *Island of Palmas* (1928), 845.

year.[4] Jessup called upon his readers to consider a situation in which State A acquires Island X from State B in a particular year (T1) through a peace treaty following a war in which State A is the victor. State A undertakes no further sovereign acts in respect of Island X. Two hundred years later (T2), the acquisition of territory by a victor from the vanquished at the conclusion of a war is no longer considered lawful. According to Jessup, the application of the second branch of Huber's doctrine of intertemporal law in these circumstances would mean that at T2 'A would no longer have good title to island X but must secure a new title on some other basis or in accordance with the new rule'.[5] The 'retroactive effect' of the law would demand 'reacquisition' in a manner consistent with new developments.[6]

Jessup's hypothetical was intended to demonstrate that it would be unreasonable, impractical, and at odds with existing practice to '[demand] that the existence of the right ... shall follow the conditions required by the evolution of law'.[7] In fact, his example illustrates how far Huber has been misunderstood. Huber has been charged with a failure to understand the logical consequences of his own argument. He is seen to be endorsing a contradiction—the second element of his principle of intertemporal law effectively nullifying the first. Yet Huber quite correctly emphasized that it is 'the *same principle*' which demands that the creation of rights and their continued existence are judged by the law contemporary to them.[8]

Huber's point may be clarified once it is recognized that the conditions relating to the acquisition of territory (or the creation of rights) are not necessarily the same as those relating to its continued possession (or the continuing existence of rights). Of course, the law that applies at T2, 200 years after the acquisition of territory, may provide that the persistence of State A's territorial sovereignty depends entirely upon the lawfulness of its acquisition at T1, that is, 200 years earlier. It cannot, however, be assumed that the law contemporary to that acquisition and by reference to which its lawfulness is properly determined can fully account for, or will necessarily have anything at all to say about, the conditions subsequently applying to State A's *continued* territorial sovereignty over the area concerned—a question of how territory may be lost rather than how it may be acquired. As Huber pointed

[4] P Jessup, 'The Palmas Island Arbitration' (1928) 22 *AJIL* 735. Similar criticisms have been made by W Versfelt *The Miangas Arbitration* (Kemink, 1933), 14–16, 149; P Malanczuk, *Akehurst's Modern Introduction to International Law* (7th edn, Routledge, 1996), 156; A D'Amato, 'International Law, Intertemporal Problems' in R Bernhardt (ed), *Encyclopedia of Public International Law* (2nd edn, North-Holland, 1992) 1234, 1235; J Dugard, *International Law: The South African Perspective* (3rd edn, Juta, 2005), 128–30. Elias accepts Jessup's account of the consequences of Huber's view, even if he notes that 'in practice other principles of interpretation and application of intertemporal law such as acquiescence, prescription, desuetude, and the rule against nonretroactivity of treaty provisions would operate to make it impossible for the second element of the doctrine to work injustices': T Elias, 'The Doctrine of Intertemporal Law' (1980) 74 *AJIL* 285, 286–7; see also I Brownlie, *Principles of Public International Law* (7th edn, OUP, 2008), 125.

[5] Jessup, 'The Palmas Island Arbitration', 740.

[6] Ibid.

[7] *Island of Palmas* (1928), 845.

[8] Ibid (emphasis added).

out, the establishment of a right can be distinguished from its continued existence. The lawfulness of its establishment cannot be brought into question by subsequent changes to the law which would not now permit such a right to be established (at all or in the same manner or circumstances). Yet questions as to whether the right then lawfully established continues to exist may arise as a result of, and be properly answered by, the contemporary law.

III. Intertemporal Law: Huber's Error

While Huber is not guilty of the mistake with which he is commonly charged, a different error in his application of the dual principle of intertemporal law in the *Island of Palmas* may have encouraged the misinterpretation of his argument. In that case, the United States had claimed inter alia that Spain had title over Palmas (or Miangas) on the basis of discovery, that this title was recognized by subsequent treaties, and that it was ceded by Spain to the United States under the 1898 Treaty of Paris.[9] The Netherlands argued that there was no proof of Spanish title by discovery or any other mode of acquisition. Alternatively, it argued that if Spain did have title at any point, it had been lost prior to 1898 and could not therefore have been ceded to the United States. The Netherlands claimed that 'the belonging of Miangas to native states under Netherland sway, the successive acts of paramountcy, conventions with native principalities, acts of administration etc. of the Netherlands begun in a period when neither Spain nor any other power exercised sovereignty over that region, and continuing afterwards and until 1898 without any protest by any foreign government, converged in validly establishing Netherland sovereignty'.[10]

In his 1928 Award, Huber explored both (a) the consequences if, according to the law at the time, Spain's discovery of the island established a 'definitive title of sovereignty' without requiring 'any act, even symbolical, of taking possession', and (b) the consequences if that discovery, according to the law contemporary with it, established only an 'inchoate title' requiring completion.[11] It was in the course of considering the first possibility (as a hypothetical, reserving judgment on whether 'mere' discovery was a 'complete' root of title at the time) that Huber made his now famous claim that '[t]he same principle which subjects the act creative of a right to the law in force at the time the right arises, demands that the existence of the right, in other words its continued manifestation, shall follow the conditions required by the evolution of the law'.[12] It was in his application of this principle that Huber made a serious error.

[9] Ibid, 837.
[10] Netherlands Memorandum (National Printing Office, The Hague, 1925), 21.
[11] *Island of Palmas* (1928), 846.
[12] Ibid, 844.

The arbitrator pointed to 'the principle that occupation, to constitute a claim to territorial sovereignty, must be effective', which he considered to have been 'laid down' in the nineteenth century based upon 'a tendency already existing and especially developed since the middle of the 18th century'.[13] While this is clearly a rule relating to the acquisition of territorial sovereignty (the creation of title), Huber suggested that it would be 'incompatible with this rule of positive law' if a region not under the 'effective sovereignty of a State' were to 'be reserved for [its] exclusive influence ... in virtue solely of a title of acquisition which is no longer recognized by existing law, even if such a title ever conferred territorial sovereignty'.[14]

The problem here is not that Huber failed to apply the first branch of the doctrine of intertemporal law as he defined it. He did not assess the Spanish acquisition of territorial sovereignty over the Island of Palmas by reference to the nineteenth-century requirement of effective occupation. Rather, his argument was that the evolution of the law in this regard also changed what was required for the *maintenance* of title.[15] Assuming for the sake of argument that Spain had a complete title based on discovery, Huber's question was 'whether sovereignty yet existed at the critical date, i.e. the moment of conclusion and coming into force of the Treaty of Paris', which was alleged to have transferred Spanish sovereignty over the island to the United States.[16] His conclusion was that that even if 'mere' discovery did create a complete title and did not require subsequent sovereign acts according to the law in the first part of the sixteenth century, the law by the nineteenth century required an exercise of 'effective sovereignty' for that title to be maintained.[17]

This account of what nineteenth-century international law required for *continuing* territorial sovereignty (the maintenance of the right) was entirely extrapolated from what nineteenth-century international law required for the *acquisition* of territorial sovereignty (the creation of the right). Specifically, Huber inferred from the fact that nineteenth-century international law required occupation to be effective 'to constitute a claim to territorial sovereignty' that nineteenth century international law also required an effective exercise of territorial sovereignty for title to be maintained.[18] In Huber's view, then, territorial sovereignty could be *lost* through a lack of effectiveness. Significantly, Huber also expressed the view that, in this context, 'the question of an abandonment properly speaking of sovereignty by one State in order that the sovereignty of another may take its place does not arise'.[19]

[13] Ibid, 845–6.
[14] Ibid, 846.
[15] Ibid, 839, 846.
[16] Ibid, 845.
[17] Ibid, 845–6.
[18] Ibid, 846.
[19] Ibid.

Kohen has concluded that Huber's view was that 'Spain had never acquired sovereignty over Palmas' and that 'consequently he considered it unnecessary to examine whether Spain had abandoned its purported right'.[20] In fact, Huber suggested that the question of abandonment did not arise in the course of considering the hypothetical possibility that 'mere' discovery *had* established a definitive Spanish title.[21] He considered it unnecessary to consider the question of abandonment because he concluded that 'at the present time'—i.e. when considering the continuing existence of a title based on discovery—'there is no sovereignty'.[22] He did not conclude that there was 'no sovereignty' because Spain never acquired it. Instead, he determined that there was no sovereignty because Spanish title based on discovery (taken hypothetically to have established a complete title) could not have *persisted* in the absence of effective acts of sovereignty. Huber's suggestion was that territorial sovereignty acquired through discovery would in any case have been lost through a subsequent failure to 'manifest' or display effective sovereignty.

This account of the circumstances in which a definitive title to territory may be lost cannot be considered correct. Yet while this error may have encouraged some scholars to misconstrue and accordingly reject Huber's account of the second branch of intertemporal law, it by no means undermines the value of that account and the distinction between the creation and continuing existence of rights upon which it turns. Indeed, it is by reference to this same distinction that it is possible to see where Huber went wrong.

If it is concluded that a right (in this case, title to territory) was established at a particular point in time according to the law contemporary to it (in this case, hypothetically, that Spain's discovery of the island constituted a complete and definitive root of title according to the contemporary law), then the proper question is whether Spain's territorial sovereignty was lost after this point and prior to the cession of Spanish territory to the United States in 1898. Huber's mistake was to claim that Spanish title was lost before 1898 as a result of the failure to exercise effective sovereignty. In fact, both the law prior to 1898 and the law since would not admit the loss of established title to territory simply by virtue of the failure to exercise effective sovereignty.

By the nineteenth century, international law had come to require that if occupation was to establish a title to territory, it must be effective.[23] There was also increasing support for the view that effective acts of sovereignty were required to 'complete' title based on discovery. Notwithstanding some disagreement between scholars on this point, it seems that nineteenth-century international law also recognized a transfer of territory from one State to another where the original title-holder acquiesces in 'the continuous and peaceful display of actual power' by

[20] M Kohen, 'Territory, Abandonment', *MPEPIL Online*, accessed 22 February 2016.
[21] *Island of Palmas* (1928), 846.
[22] Ibid.
[23] Ibid, 839.

another State (i.e. 'effectivités'), a situation sometimes referred to as acquisition of territory by 'prescription'.[24] Yet there is no evidence that the increasingly important role of effective occupation or 'the peaceful and continuous display of State authority'[25] in the *acquisition* of territory had a parallel in the law relating to the *loss* of territory—at least not as Huber construed it. In fact, there seems to have been a strong presumption against the loss of territorial sovereignty. This is given expression in the law's insistence upon abandonment—or acquiescence tantamount to abandonment—by State A as a condition for the acquisition of the same territory on the part of State B by 'the peaceful and continuous display of State authority' (i.e. acquisition of territory by occupation or prescription).[26]

While Huber suggested that even a 'complete' title could be lost by a mere failure to exercise 'effective sovereignty', the law has long required more than this. In the period under consideration by Huber (1609 to 1868), the failure to exercise effective sovereignty could not independently result in either (a) a loss of territorial sovereignty by State A leaving room for its acquisition by State B by occupation or (b) State B's displacement of State A's title by prescription. In neither case could the acts of State B independently result in a loss of territorial sovereignty by State A. State A must have either clearly abandoned its territory or acquiesced in State B's claim to sovereignty.

24 Ibid, 857; L Oppenheim, *International Law: A Treatise*, vol 1 (1st edn, Longmans, Green & Co, 1905), 293–6.

25 *Island of Palmas* (1928), 867.

26 This aspect of prescription in the law of nations was emphasized by a number of early modern and eighteenth-century scholars with substantial influence on the subsequent development of practice and doctrine: see H Grotius, *The Rights of War and Peace* [1646] (Liberty Fund, 2005) vol 2, Book II, Ch IV; S Pufendorf, *Of the Law of Nature and Nations* [1729] (Clarendon, 1934), Book IV, Ch XII; C Wolff, *The Law of Nations Treated According to a Scientific Method* [1743] (Clarendon, 1934), Ch III; E Vattel, *Law of Nations* [1758] (Liberty Fund, 2008), Book II, Ch XI. It has been suggested that 'Grotius rejected the usucaption of the Roman law, yet adopted from the same law *immemorial* prescription for the law of nations': Oppenheim, *International Law*, vol 1 (1905), 293 (the same view is retained in R Jennings, A Watts (eds), *Oppenheim's International Law* (9th edn, OUP, 2008), 705). This is not quite right as Grotius treats the lapse of time as potentially probative evidence that territory has been abandoned, suggesting that such abandonment rather than the mere passage of time is a condition for acquisition of title by prescription. Possession since 'time immemorial' is simply strong evidence that any former right has been relinquished: see Grotius, *The Rights of War and Peace*, vol 2, Book II, Ch IV. A number of nineteenth-century jurists also referred expressly to presumed abandonment as an element of prescription—'presumed' here meaning tacit rather than express abandonment: see e.g. T Twiss, *Law of Nations Considered as Independent Political Communities – On the Rights and Duties of Nations in Time of Peace* (2nd edn, Clarendon Press, 1884), 212–13; H Wheaton, *Elements of International Law* (2nd edn, Little, Brown & Company, 1863), 803–4. Other scholars of this period refer to tacit consent as having a similar effect: see e.g. the views of late-nineteenth-century authors summarized by E Nys, *Le Droit International Les Principes, Les Theories, Les Faits*, vol 2 (Castaigne, 1905), 37–9; also Oppenheim, *International* Law, vol 1 (1905), 294–6. Cf Phillimore, who explicitly denies that abandonment by the previous owner is a necessary element of prescription: R Phillimore, *Commentaries upon International Law*, vol 1 (T & JW Johnson, 1854), 221. Though it is not possible to develop this argument further here, Phillimore's insistence on 'firm discrimination' between prescription and abandonment followed by occupation ignores the consistency between the requirements for tacit consent in cases of prescription and abandonment of territory generally—particularly, the burden of establishing a State's intention to relinquish its territorial sovereignty.

Linderfalk, agreeing that territory could only be lost by abandonment, has suggested that 'the law of the 18th century considered such a failure [to exercise sovereignty over the island] tantamount to abandonment exactly'—Huber therefore being right in his account of the reason why territorial sovereignty was lost but wrong not to recognize this as abandonment.[27] This leaves Huber's basic error untouched. It is also inaccurate as an account of abandonment. In the eighteenth century and since a strong presumption against abandonment has meant that its establishment requires more than a mere failure to engage in sovereign acts in respect of a territory. Specifically, the law demands evidence of an *intention* to abandon—the *animus derelinquendi*—that is determined by reference to objective facts.[28] Thus in the *Clipperton Award* (1931) the arbitrator concluded that '[t]here is no reason to suppose that France has subsequently lost her right by *derelictio*, since she never had the *animus* of abandoning the island, and the fact that she has not exercised her authority there in a positive manner does not imply the forfeiture or an acquisition already definitively perfected'.[29] Notably, while the fact that Clipperton Island was uninhabited was the reason for concluding that sovereign acts were not required to 'perfect' the French title,[30] the award does not suggest that the absence of a population also altered the conditions for continuing sovereignty—i.e. justifying continuing sovereignty notwithstanding the State's failure to exercise it. The absence of an intention to abandon the territory was fully determinative.[31]

Huber thought that '[i]t seems ... natural that an element which is essential for the constitution of sovereignty should not be lacking in its continuation'.[32] Specifically, he considered it 'natural' that if 'an act of effective apprehension' were now required for the creation of title (and, in his view, this was an essential element of conquest and accretion as well as discovery and prescription in nineteenth-century international law) it would also be required for territorial sovereignty to persist.[33] If title had been acquired at an earlier time when the law did not require such 'effective apprehension', then that acquisition of territory would not be invalidated by subsequent changes in the law. Yet continuing rights of territorial

[27] U Linderfalk, 'The Application of International Legal Norms over Time: The Second Branch of Intertemporal Law' (2011) 58 *NILR* 147, 158.

[28] See note 26 above; *Delagoa Bay Award* (1875), 157–61; *Clipperton Award* (1931), 394; *Lighthouses Case* (1937), 36–46; *Belgium/Netherlands* (1959), 227–30; *Pedra Branca* (2008), 50–1, 96; Kohen, 'Territory, Abandonment'; G Marston, 'The British Acquisition of the Nicobar Islands, 1869: A Possible Example of Abandonment of Territorial Sovereignty' (1999) 69 (1) *BYIL* 245, 262–3.

[29] *Clipperton Award* (1931), 394 (emphasis added).

[30] See also *Eastern Greenland Case* (1933), 45–6; *Indonesia/Malaysia* (2002), 682; *Pedra Branca* (2008), 36. In connection with the acquisition of territory, effectiveness in respect of an uninhabitable territory may require relatively little in the way of sovereign acts.

[31] See also the Court's emphasis on Malaysia's lack of protest against Singapore's acts *à titre de souverain* in respect of Pedra Branca/Pulau Batu Puteh in its finding that the sovereignty had passed from Malaysia to Singapore by 1980: *Pedra Branca* (2008), 50–1, 95–6.

[32] *Island of Palmas*, 839.

[33] Ibid.

sovereignty following from this initial acquisition would be subject to the evolution of the law, which Huber took to require 'effective sovereignty'.[34] It is in this account of the content of the law as it relates to continuing territorial sovereignty that Huber's chief error lies.

The increasing importance of effectiveness as a condition for acquiring territorial sovereignty has *not* in fact been accompanied by the development of the law to make continuing territorial sovereignty dependent upon continuing effectiveness. To put the point more sharply, the law has not come to recognize that loss of territory may follow from ineffectiveness alone in circumstances where the title-holder does not intend or consent to the abandonment of territory. Nor would such a rule be a 'natural' corollary of effectiveness as a condition for the acquisition of territory.

By the nineteenth century, the law relating to the acquisition of territory appears to have changed in such a way as to give effective occupation a far greater role than it previously had (certainly when compared to the fifteenth and early sixteenth centuries). Yet it did not 'naturally' follow—logically or legally—that the loss of effective sovereignty would bring about a loss of title to territory. In fact, the converse is true. The law came to impose more stringent requirements for the acquisition of territory in the context of inter-imperial competition over remote lands. Competing powers insisted upon effective occupation to counter Spanish and Portuguese claims to title based on 'mere' discovery or papal grant. Yet the concern that more stringent conditions should apply to the acquisition of territory was consistent with a concern that stringent conditions should apply to the *loss* of territory—i.e. that lawfully acquired title in remote areas should not easily be lost to competitors. Specifically, it seems to have been an established principle of international law, certainly by the nineteenth century and arguably well beforehand, that territorial sovereignty could only be lost by abandonment.[35] In circumstances where another State had engaged in 'the peaceful and continuous display of State authority', the territorial sovereignty of the original title holder could not be lost without express or implicit acquiescence tantamount precisely to abandonment and subject to the same stringent conditions. Requiring more to establish title to territory (i.e. effective occupation) was consistent with requiring more to establish the loss of territory lawfully acquired (i.e. an *animus derelinquendi* subject to a high standard of proof).

[34] Ibid, 839, 846.

[35] See e.g. Grotius, *The Rights of War and Peace*, vol 2, Book II, Ch IV; Vattel, *Law of Nations*, Book II, Ch XI, esp § 145.and other sources referred to in note 26 above.

IV. Reassessing the *Island of Palmas Case*: The Acquisition and Loss of Territory

Huber did not conclude that Spain had in fact established a definitive title by discovery but went on to consider the possibility that its title was rather 'inchoate'. The arbitrator again referred to nineteenth-century law in his account of what was required for 'completion'—namely, effective occupation.[36] He seems to have used nineteenth-century standards to assess acts predating the nineteenth century—a move difficult to reconcile with the first branch of the principle of intertemporal law.[37] This could be rationalized as an application of the second branch of the principle of intertemporal law—the relevant question being whether the 'inchoate' title persisted. However, Huber did not clearly establish that an 'inchoate' title based on discovery would be lost if a State failed to effectively occupy the territory within a reasonable period. It is not enough in this regard to point to the new requirement for effective occupation as a condition for the creation of title. While it is not obvious that nineteenth-century international law protected 'inchoate' title to the same extent or in the same manner as it protected a fully established title, an investigation into the conditions governing the maintenance or loss of 'inchoate' title is precisely what the principle of intertemporal law requires.

Huber did not undertake such an investigation but he did proceed to consider the possibility that the United States retained an 'inchoate' title to the Island of Palmas based on Spanish discovery. The arbitrator concluded that such 'an inchoate title ... cannot prevail over a definite title founded on continuous and peaceful display of sovereignty'.[38] Indeed, he even suggested that an 'inchoate title ... based on display of State authority' would prevail over an inchoate title based on discovery.[39] This suggests that what was being assessed was relative title.[40] Yet Huber was comparing what he considered to be an 'inchoate' title based on 'mere' discovery with 'prescription' on the part of the Netherlands.[41] Prescription requires abandonment

[36] *Island of Palmas* (1928), 846.

[37] Ibid.

[38] Ibid, 869.

[39] Ibid, 870. This implies that an 'inchoate' title based on discovery will not preclude another State from claiming territorial sovereignty over the same piece of land based on effective occupation. If this is true, it is difficult to see what work 'inchoate' title based on discovery does.

[40] Ibid, 846.

[41] Prescription is a term used by some scholars though rarely in international jurisprudence. Huber himself uses the expression tentatively. Nevertheless, the situation he describes satisfies all the conditions for prescription in international law, where that concept is understood to require not only the open, peaceful, and effective display of sovereignty by State A, but acquiescence tantamount to abandonment by State B: see *Island of Palmas* (1928), 868; WE Beckett, 'Les questions d'intérêt général au point de vue juridique dans la jurisprudence de la Cour permanente de Justice internationale' (1934) 50 *Recueil des Cours* 189, 220; R Jennings, *The Acquisition of Territory in International Law* (MUP, 1963), 22. Cf Brownlie, who argued that the Netherlands' title was rather relative, there being no usurpation of one sovereign by another as in the classic case of prescription: Brownlie, *Principles of Public International Law*, 147–8, 155–6; Crawford, *Brownlie's Principles*, 230–1. Insisting upon 'usurpation'—implying seizure without consent—may be faithful to the private law concept from which the analogy is drawn; yet it is at odds with the international doctrine. As O'Keefe has observed, the development of the

on the part of the title-holder, which may take the form of acquiescence in another State's public exercise of sovereignty over the territory in question. If such acquiescence is established and title is properly said to be acquired by prescription, then there is no residual 'inchoate' title to be compared with that acquired by the 'usurping' State. If the Netherlands acquired title to the Island of Palmas by prescription, then the United States had no continuing title based on discovery—inchoate or otherwise—with which the Netherlands' title could be compared and its relative strength assessed.

In *Island of Palmas*, Huber assumed that the conditions for maintaining a complete title and completing an 'inchoate title' based on discovery were the same as the conditions for the acquisition of territory by occupation according to nineteenth century law. Specifically, he assumed that in all cases what was required was effective occupation, which he identified with a peaceful and continuous display of sovereignty.

This account of the requirements for the maintenance of title to territory cannot be considered correct. It is also doubtful whether the 'completion' of title based on discovery required as much.[42] Yet the arbitrator did not commit the error with which he is commonly charged. He did not suggest that developments in the law relating to the acquisition of territory by discovery apply retrospectively to either invalidate title established on the basis of the previous law or show it to be incomplete subject to the satisfaction of new conditions. Although he insisted that bare discovery is a form of acquisition 'no longer recognized by existing law, even if ... [it] ever conferred territorial sovereignty',[43] this is not the basis upon which he suggested that the discoverer (Spain) or its successor (the United States) did not presently possess sovereignty over the island. Rather, Huber argued that if discovery *did* establish either a definitive or inchoate title, territorial sovereignty was subsequently lost due to a failure to meet the conditions for its persistence according to the law at the time the question of its continuing existence was raised. He erred in his account of the substance of the law in this regard.

Huber suggested that the question of continuing sovereignty arises where competing claims to title are accompanied by subsequent sovereign acts:

> [I]f the contestation is based on the fact that the other Party has actually displayed sovereignty, it cannot be sufficient to establish the title by which territorial

analogy by international adjudicators has resulted in a concept 'more attuned to the horizontality and voluntarism of the international legal order', in which 'acquiescence on the part of the title-holder' reformulated as 'tacit recognition' is essential: R O'Keefe, 'Legal Title versus *Effectivités*: Prescription and the Promise and Problems of Private Law Analogies' (2011) 13 *ICLR* 147, 187–8.

---

[42] Some scholars have argued that symbolic acts, such as the erection of crosses and marks, were considered sufficient to transform discovery into full title up until the beginning of the nineteenth century: A Keller et al, *Creation of Rights of Sovereignty through Symbolic Acts, 1400–1800* (Columbia University Press, 1938), 148–9.

[43] *Island of Palmas* (1928), 846.

> sovereignty was validly acquired at a certain moment; it must also be shown that the territorial sovereignty has continued to exist and did exist at the moment which for the decision of the dispute must be considered as critical.[44]

Significantly, this is what State B claiming an existing and prior title against State A must demonstrate where State A argues that State B no longer possesses territorial sovereignty, even if it possessed title at an earlier time. Evidence of 'the actual display of State activities, such as belongs only to the territorial sovereign'[45] may be presented by State B in these circumstances, but the absence of such a display of sovereignty cannot independently establish a loss of title. What must be demonstrated is an intention to abandon territory or acquiescence in the exercise of sovereignty by another State.

The fact that State B has not displayed sovereignty may still be relevant in cases where State A has undertaken effective sovereign acts to the extent that it supports a finding of acquiescence in the competing claim. Absent the relevant *animus derelinquendi*, however, it cannot be determinative. Thus in the *Delagoa Bay Award*, it was concluded that a temporary weakening or even loss of Portuguese authority did not amount to a loss of sovereignty leaving it open to the British to conclude treaties of cession with indigenous leaders.[46] It was because the British had concluded these treaties that the question of whether Portugal had continuing sovereignty—or conversely, had lost its title—was raised. However, the 1875 Award confirms the importance of the intention of the original title-holder in this context; 'l'affaiblissement *accidentel* de l'autorité Portugaise' could not terminate Portuguese sovereignty.[47]

V. The Creation and Continuing Existence of Status, Rights, and Legal Limits

The significance of Huber's distinction between the creation and continued existence of rights extends beyond questions relating to the acquisition and loss of territory. It is of particular value as a framework for understanding and critiquing the assumption that the same conditions govern both the *establishment* of entitlement to maritime space, maritime limits, and maritime boundaries

[44] Ibid, 839.

[45] Ibid.

[46] *Delagoa Bay Award* (1875), 161. Notably, the Award takes Portugal to have acquired the territory in question by discovery in the sixteenth century followed by occupation in the seventeenth and eighteenth centuries. It does not explain how this was compatible with the presence of the indigenous Tsonga population organized into the chieftaincies of Tembe and Mapoota or elaborate on what the law at the time of the acquisition of territory had to say on this point.

[47] Ibid (emphasis added).

and the *subsistence* of entitlement to maritime space, maritime limits, and maritime boundaries.

Though the focus of this book is the law of the sea, it is worth noting the relevance of the same distinction to the legal questions arising as climate-related change threatens to leave territory uninhabitable or even submerged below rising seas. Whether either or both loss of territory and loss of statehood ensue—interrelated possibilities—is likely to depend substantially upon the intentions of the affected States regarding their territory and status, together with recognition of continuing territorial sovereignty or statehood by other States. These factors are likely to play a different and much more significant role in relation to the continuing existence of both territorial sovereignty and statehood than they do in the acquisition of territory or the creation of States.

As far as continuing territorial sovereignty is concerned, it is relevant that land lost to the weather and waves will not be subject to a competing claim to title by another State. The fact that loss of territory may entail or contribute to the extinction of the State may also have implications for an assessment of whether territory is lost by virtue of these developments. Crawford points to the 'priority' of 'the category of statehood ... over the category of acquisition of territory' at the birth of a new State, which means that its 'definitive establishment. ... on certain territory defeats claims by other States that relate to the whole of that territory'.[48] The same 'priority' of 'the category of statehood' may mean that continuing statehood implies continuing territorial sovereignty where the territory at risk of being lost is also the territorial basis for the State.

The priority of statehood is further confirmed by the fact that, while territorial sovereignty is difficult to *lose*, it may be *abandoned* directly or indirectly by acquiescence in claims to sovereignty over the same area by another State. In both circumstances, an *animus derelinquendi* or intention to abandon is essential. Abandonment is a unilateral act which depends upon and affirms the agency of the State—as does the presumption against unintended loss of territory. If a State's abandonment of its whole territory were to bring about its extinction as a State, it might be considered suicide: a final act of agency entailing the extinction of the agent. Yet even here the presumption in favour of continuing statehood may do considerable life preserving work. A State which actively abandons its territory may still insist upon its statehood, in which case recognition by other States may play an important role. Recognition in these circumstances should be distinguished from recognition of a new State at the point of its creation. Insofar as effectiveness has not been proven to be a requirement of *continuing* statehood, withdrawing recognition on the basis of a loss of effectiveness would appear to be unjustified.

[48] J Crawford, *The Creation of States in International Law* (2nd edn, OUP, 2007), 48.

A. Entitlement to Maritime Space

The distinction between the creation of rights and their continued existence is also applicable to entitlement to maritime space, with important consequences in terms of the implications of geographical change. While Huber was concerned with the question of which law should apply *ratione temporis*, his distinction allows for the possibility that the creation of a right and its continuing existence may be subject to different legal conditions. The law applying to the creation of a right may indicate that certain facts—for example, certain geographical circumstances—must be present or taken into account in certain ways. The first branch of the principle of intertemporal law indicates that if the law governing the creation of the right subsequently changes, this will not usually affect a right already established on the basis of the previous law. If the law does not change but the geographical circumstances to which it refers do, the lawfulness of the establishment of the right (prior to that change) will not be in question. Whether such change affects the maintenance of the right—its continued existence—is a separate legal question.

Although it is not impossible that the same or similar conditions should govern the creation of a right and its continued existence, there must be a sound basis for such an interpretation where the applicability of the same conditions to both cases is not expressly provided. While Huber expressed the view that '[i]t seems ... natural that an element which is essential for the constitution of sovereignty should not be lacking in its continuation',[49] there is no basis for a presumption to this effect and what 'seems natural' will depend on the circumstances. In many cases, it will not be considered desirable that the right (or legal limit) should always meet the conditions it was required to meet for its establishment. It will not obviously or often be desirable for a right (or legal limit) to change with changes affecting the facts taken into account in its establishment. While Huber suggested that effectiveness was not only required for the acquisition of territory but 'equally for the maintenance of the right',[50] it has been argued above that the conditions for the creation of a right and its continued existence differ in this context. Although effectiveness plays a central role in both the acquisition of territory and the creation of States,[51] it appears that the radical diminution and even loss of effectiveness will not automatically bring about a loss of territory or statehood. In both cases, there is a difference in substance between the law applying to the creation of rights or status and the law relating to the continuing existence of the same rights or status.

It is worth clarifying that Huber directly considered the possibility of such a difference in substance between the law governing (a) the acquisition of territory and (b) continuing sovereignty in his conjectural examination of the consequences if

[49] *Island of Palmas* (1928), 839.
[50] Ibid.
[51] Crawford, *The Creation of States*, esp Ch 2.

discovery without effective occupation were sufficient to establish a definitive title. On this version of events, effectiveness was understood to be essential for the continuation of sovereignty but not its initial establishment. It is the possibility of such a difference that most clearly brings out the significance of Huber's argument that developments in the law may bear upon the question of continuing sovereignty but cannot undermine the past establishment of legal title. The developing law could (and in Huber's view did) require effectiveness for continuing sovereignty and this could affect the State's continuing rights. If, however, the developing law had altered the conditions for the acquisition of territory by discovery to require further acts of effective occupation, the new law could not be invoked to challenge the original acquisition at a time when no such requirement applied.

The distinction between the creation and continuing existence of rights remains legally significant even if the law governing the creation of the right and the law relating to its continuing existence are identical. If—for the sake of argument and contrary to the existing law—effective occupation *was* a condition for the acquisition of territorial sovereignty *and* a condition for continuing sovereignty, a State that had acquired territory by way of effective occupation but subsequently failed to maintain effective authority could lose its territorial sovereignty. Yet this would not impugn the original acquisition—a fact which may have consequences for an assessment of whether sovereign acts might be invalid or null and in what sense (e.g. *ex tunc, ex nunc*, voidable but not yet void).

In international legal and political discourse regarding the impacts of climate change, it is often suggested that the inundation of an island due to rising sea levels will result not only in the displacement of any local population but also (and relatedly) the loss of entitlement to maritime space. As a matter of doctrine, this is understood to follow from the legal definition of an island in both the Convention on the Territorial Sea and Contiguous Zone (TSC) and the United Nations Convention on the Law of the Sea (UNCLOS) as 'a naturally formed area of land, surrounded by water, which is above water at high tide'.[52] This definition precedes and conditions the proposition that islands will generate entitlement to the full complement of maritime zones[53]—under UNCLOS, a territorial sea, contiguous zone, exclusive economic zone (EEZ), and continental shelf. Article 121(3) of UNCLOS further provides that entitlement to an EEZ and continental shelf will be exceptionally denied in the case of a subcategory of islands characterized as 'rocks which cannot sustain human habitation or economic life of their own'.

The same reasoning that suggests inundation of an island by rising seas may result in the loss of entitlement to maritime space has been extended to low-tide elevations (LTEs), legally defined as 'a naturally formed area of land which is

[52] TSC (1958) Art 10; UNCLOS Art 121(1).

[53] TSC (1958) Art 10; Convention on the Continental Shelf (CSC) (1958) Art 1(b); UNCLOS Art 121(1), (2).

surrounded by and above water at low tide but submerged at high tide'.[54] It has also been suggested that the right to 'draw straight archipelagic baselines' enclosing 'archipelagic waters', which depends upon qualification as an 'archipelagic State', might be jeopardized by geographical change.[55]

As argued in Chapter 1, the law's provision for the extension of the limits of the territorial sea from LTEs is better understood as a rule relating to delimitation rather than entitlement to maritime space. Nevertheless, the provisions on LTEs and archipelagic States, which are formulated as rules governing the construction of baselines, point up the interplay between the legal rules and principles governing entitlement to maritime space and those governing its delimitation. If maritime features no longer qualify as islands, LTEs, or archipelagos, this may have implications for their use in the construction of both maritime limits and international maritime boundaries.

Under the law of the sea, a 12-nautical-mile (M) territorial sea may be measured from an LTE lying wholly or partly within the territorial sea of the mainland or an island.[56] It is often assumed that the right to measure the limits of the territorial sea from an LTE will be lost if erosion, subsidence, or rising sea levels (independently or in combination) mean that the feature is no longer 'above water at low tide'. A shift in the location of the baseline used for measuring the territorial sea may also leave an LTE beyond its outer limits. Evidently a loss of entitlement to the territorial sea generated by a mainland coast or island would also preclude its measurement from LTEs formerly located within this maritime zone.

The definition of an archipelago under Article 46 of the 1982 Convention refers to 'islands, interconnecting waters and other natural features', though the key requirement is that these 'natural features' are 'so closely interrelated' that they 'form an intrinsic geographical, economic and political entity, or … historically have been regarded as such'. Evidently, the phrase 'historically … regarded as such' may become critical if physical change compromises the geographical, economic, and political interrelationship of the 'natural features' comprising an archipelago. Yet, as we shall see, other legal reasons count against the conclusion that geographical change will have consequences for established archipelagic baselines.

The prospect that loss of entitlement to certain maritime zones may follow from geographical change affecting the feature 'generating' such entitlement must be examined in connection with the related idea that the submergence of land or loss of habitability and associated population displacement might result in the loss of territory and even statehood in international law. The possibility of loss of entitlement to maritime space *as a whole* due to the loss of territorial sovereignty over coastal land or the loss of statehood can in fact be distinguished from the possibility

[54] TSC Art 11; UNCLOS Art 13.
[55] UNCLOS Arts 46, 47.
[56] TSC Art 11; UNCLOS Art 13.

of loss of entitlement to particular maritime zones. If territorial sovereignty over coastal land is indeed lost, then it follows from the principle of appurtenance that entitlement to maritime space generated by that coastal land will also be lost. In this case, the basic condition for entitlement to maritime space may reasonably be held to apply to both the creation of the right and its continuing existence. This is not obviously true of the conditions governing entitlement to a territorial sea, EEZ, and continental shelf in respect of an island or entitlement to archipelagic waters.

(i) Loss of entitlement to maritime space as a whole

Under the existing law, entitlement to maritime space follows from the possession of territorial sovereignty over coastal land. In view of the character of entitlement to maritime space as an 'appurtenance' to land territory, it appears that an intention to retain such entitlement cannot do as much work as the intention to retain land territory—at least, not in the event of a loss of territorial sovereignty over coastal land. This does not mean that a State is not permitted to abandon its entitlement to maritime space. The point is that abandonment is not the only means by which entitlement to maritime space may be lost and an intention to retain such entitlement may be insufficient to secure continuing rights.

In his dissenting opinion in *Anglo-Norwegian Fisheries*, Judge McNair asserted that entitlement to a territorial sea, which was granted '[t]o every State whose land territory is at any place washed by the sea', could not be refused: '[t]he possession of this territory is not optional, not dependent upon the will of the State, but compulsory.'[57] No evidence was offered in support of this claim, which is at odds with the general approach to sovereignty and jurisdiction in international law. While entitlement to a territorial sea does not depend upon an active claim by the coastal State, there does not appear to be any legal reason why a State could not actively relinquish its entitlement to maritime space in part or whole. Land territory can be abandoned where clearly intended[58] and there is no reason to think that this is not or should not be possible in the case of entitlement to maritime space. Here too there is likely to be a presumption against abandonment with a correspondingly high standard of proof to ensure that a State is not deprived of its fundamental rights against its will.

Notably, locating maritime limits at less than the maximum distance from the baseline permitted by law will not usually entail abandonment of the remainder. This point does not appear to have been fully appreciated by Thirlway, who distinguishes between 'potential' and 'actualised' rights to maritime space to argue that the former give way to the latter upon delimitation. Specifically, Thirlway suggests that 'pre-determined boundaries' (an unsatisfactory characterization of zonal limits at the maximum distance from the baseline insofar as it underplays

[57] *Anglo-Norwegian Fisheries* (1951), 160.

[58] See Kohen, 'Territory, Abandonment'.

the coastal State's responsibility for and discretion in defining those limits more precisely) 'presumably yield to those actually claimed, if the State concerned claims less than its "entitlement" '.[59] Thirlway identifies the continental shelf as the sole exception to this rule on the basis that entitlement exists *ipso facto* and *ab initio*[60] as opposed to 'rights [existing] when *and to the extent that* they have been expressly claimed by the coastal State'.[61]

Thirlway's argument here is problematic and should not be confused with the relatively straightforward point that some maritime zones must be proclaimed for the coastal State's jurisdiction therein to be enforceable. Proclamation is required for a coastal State to enforce its rights and lawfully exercise its responsibilities in a contiguous zone, an EEZ or exclusive fishery zone (EFZ), and, following *Qatar v Bahrain*, archipelagic waters.[62] This requirement does not alter the fact that all coastal States are in principle entitled to an EEZ and contiguous zone based on no more than their possession of territorial sovereignty over coastal land (together with the additional conditions for entitlement to an EEZ in respect of an island). Similarly, certain States qualify for entitlement to archipelagic waters based on their fulfilment of the criteria identified by the law. If they meet the definition of an 'archipelagic State' then they are entitled to make use of archipelagic baselines.[63]

The coastal State has a vested right to maritime space. Thirlway suggests that this right is 'inchoate' until such time as it is spatially specified.[64] The difficulty with this characterization is that it suggests that entitlement to maritime space is in some sense incomplete until maritime limits are established. In fact, the coastal State's entitlement to maritime space must be respected regardless of whether it has established maritime limits, although rights to maritime space that require proclamation need not be observed until they are in fact proclaimed. This does not mean that entitlement to maritime space requiring proclamation is any more 'inchoate' than entitlement to maritime zones that need not be proclaimed. Proclamation neither establishes nor completes a title, as Lauterpacht notes, but is 'a means by which a title, claimed or acquired, is announced'.[65] However,

> [t]hat does not mean that [proclamation] is meaningless or unnecessary ... [It is a] proposition of order and orderliness which requires that a person—or a state—asserting a claim, however inherently valid, must make his claim known by a formal pronouncement or notification. This is so especially if the subject of the

[59] Thirlway, 'The Law and Procedure of the ICJ 1960–1989: Supplement, 2007', 114.
[60] *North Sea Cases* (1969), 22.
[61] Thirlway, 'The Law and Procedure of the ICJ 1960–1989: Supplement, 2007', 113 (emphasis added).
[62] *Qatar v Bahrain* (2001), 103.
[63] UNCLOS Arts 46, 47.
[64] Thirlway, 'The Law and Procedure of the ICJ 1960–1989: Supplement, 2007', 114–16.
[65] H Lauterpacht, 'Sovereignty over Submarine Areas' (1950) 27 *BYIL* 376, 418.

> claim in question is novel in character, undefined in extent, and likely to require determination in relation to similar claims by other persons or states.[66]

Until a coastal State defines its maritime limits more precisely, its jurisdiction in maritime zones not requiring proclamation must be respected and may be enforced in an area approximated by reference to the low-water line (and closing lines across rivers[67]). The coastal State's jurisdiction in maritime zones requiring proclamation need not be observed and cannot be enforced—but this does not mean that the coastal State's *entitlement* to these zones is 'inchoate' or incomplete.

Thirlway also suggests that the extent of a coastal State's maritime entitlement in principle is reduced to whatever the State in fact claims.[68] He identifies the limits of the continental shelf as an exception, speculating that

> If … there is any distinction between the areas which a State is entitled to claim by way of EEZ, and the *ipso facto* and *ab initio* entitlement to continental shelf, it would presumably have to be that a claim to a lesser area of continental shelf than that entitlement leaves the full entitlement still existing in some legal limbo.[69]

Thirlway goes on to argue that this idea of a residual entitlement existing 'in limbo' is 'unrealistic' as far as the delimitation of the shelf between opposite or adjacent States is concerned. He observes, correctly, that 'a delimitation, agreed or judicial, between two areas of shelf must be final and determinative; one party could not claim to re-open the matter on the basis that it had, in ignorance, failed to insist on everything the law gives it'.[70] Yet this is an *ignoratio elenchi* as far as the question of residual entitlement is concerned. It is perfectly possible to insist upon the final and binding character of international maritime boundaries while accepting that one or both of the States concerned may claim a more extensive area of entitlement should the agreement be renegotiated.

Thirlway is more prepared to accept that the 'full entitlement' of the coastal State to the continental shelf may continue to exist 'in some legal limbo' where a coastal State unilaterally establishes its limits at less than the maximum distance from the baseline or isobath. If anything, however, the reverse is true. Rather than the continental shelf being the only zone in which residual entitlement may survive the establishment of an outer limit at a distance less than the full entitlement, it is

[66] Ibid, 418–19.

[67] Evidently, use of the low-water line as the baseline will not be possible at the mouth of a river, though arcs of circles may be constructed from points on its banks.

[68] Thirlway, 'The Law and Procedure of the ICJ 1960–1989: Supplement, 2007', 114. It might be added that its extent in principle is also its extent in practice where precise limits have not been established. This is also the case where those limits have been established at the maximum distance from the baseline or by reference to the outer edge of the continental margin.

[69] Ibid.

[70] Ibid.

the only zone in which the coastal State is precluded from subsequently adjusting the limits it has unilaterally established. As such, it is the only zone in which there can be no residual entitlement beyond limits established at less than the full extent of the available entitlement, whereas this is a possibility in the case of all other maritime zones.

In general, zonal limits established at less than the maximum permissible distance from the baseline may be binding without entailing the relinquishment of a more extensive entitlement provided by law. It seems reasonable to impute a high standard of proof of intention to relinquish maritime entitlement given the important sovereign rights at issue. As has already been observed, the relevant analogy is abandonment of territory. Thirlway's suggestion that maritime entitlement that is not actively claimed is left hovering 'in some legal limbo' implies the fantastic where the facts are unremarkable. With the exception of the outer limits of the continental shelf, zonal limits may be established at different distances up to the maximum extent provided by law at different points in time. The extent to which the establishment of an international maritime boundary limits the national maritime jurisdiction of a State may change if the boundary is renegotiated. This applies equally to a maritime boundary dividing the continental shelf between States.

The possibility of renegotiating a maritime boundary delimiting the continental shelf between States is fully consistent with the rule that where the limits of the shelf are unilaterally established (in cases where there is no overlap with the entitlement of another State) those limits cannot subsequently be changed. The exceptional requirement that the limits of the shelf must be established once and for all has nothing to do with the fact that rights to the shelf exist *ipso facto* and *ab initio*. Instead, it follows from the fact that this zone is coterminous with the international seabed area. Because the outer limits of the continental shelf only double as the limits of the Area where there is no overlap with another State's national maritime space, permanence is only required in these circumstances—that is, in the case of the unilaterally established limits of the continental shelf.

Though the law requires a clear intention to abandon entitlement to maritime space this does not mean that abandonment is the only means by which entitlement to maritime space may be lost. Unlike the law of territory and the law relating to statehood, the law of the sea as it relates to entitlement to maritime space as a whole does identify conditions for the creation of this right that are also properly understood to condition its continuing existence. While the law relating to maritime jurisdiction is similarly concerned with stability, this concern does not warrant the retention of entitlement to maritime space where territorial sovereignty over the coastal land generating such entitlement has been lost. According to the principle of appurtenance, entitlement to maritime space automatically accompanies territorial sovereignty over coastal land. While it is not always the case that the conditions for the creation of the right and its continuing existence are the same, the close tie between territorial sovereignty and entitlement to maritime space—figured as 'natural' in the law[71]—does appear to function as a condition for national maritime jurisdiction on a continuing basis.

The continuing character of maritime space as an appurtenance of coastal territory means inter alia that the transfer of the latter ordinarily involves the automatic transfer of the former. Thus in the 1909 *Grisbådarna Case* it was concluded that 'maritime territory' is 'automatically' transferred with the cession of the coastal territory to which it appertains.[72] The fact that the transfer of territorial sovereignty to State B carries with it entitlement to maritime space without any particular action or attitude on the part of State A with respect to that maritime entitlement indicates that it is the transfer of territorial sovereignty that matters—the intentions of State A with respect to the sea being irrelevant. It is consistent with the law in this regard for a State's loss of territorial sovereignty over coastal land in circumstances where that territory is not transferred to another State to be automatically accompanied by a loss of entitlement to maritime space.

Where territorial sovereignty passes from one State to another, it is theoretically possible though practically unlikely that some or all of the maritime rights appertaining to the transferred territory could be left with the transferring State by express agreement.[73] While the principle of appurtenance may not prohibit such an unusual arrangement, it does not follow that the desire of a single State to retain its entitlement to maritime space notwithstanding the loss of territorial sovereignty would be independently sufficient to secure this end.

In the first scenario there are just two (directly) interested States. Entitlement to maritime space retained by State A would otherwise have passed to State B (which agreed to State A retaining these rights). The legal basis for this arrangement is agreement between the States concerned. In the second scenario, a single State is concerned to retain entitlement to sea areas when it no longer possesses territorial sovereignty over adjacent coastal land. Those sea areas would otherwise revert to high seas or sea areas properly appertaining to another coastal State by virtue of its territorial sovereignty over coastal land. In this context, the coastal State's interest alone does not appear to be a sufficient legal basis for continuing entitlement to maritime space. Interstate agreement in the first case might prevail over the

71 See Chapter 1.

72 *Grisbådarna* (1909), 159. The Court's assumption in *Grisbådarna* that the cession of territory and appurtenant maritime entitlements automatically entails the delimitation of maritime boundaries is, however, at odds with international law at the time of the decision and since: ibid, 159–60. Entitlement to maritime space is transferred with coastal territory and an established maritime boundary may also be inherited (Article 11 of the Vienna Convention on Succession of States in respect of Treaties (VCSS-T) (1978) will apply to existing maritime boundary agreements). Where no boundary has been established, however, cession itself will not automatically establish one—though in certain cases involving cession of the coastal territory of neighbouring States, the particular circumstances may demonstrate that there was agreement on a maritime boundary at the same time.

73 In these circumstances, the agreement would be the legal basis for the transferring State's rights to maritime space. This means that any failure of the agreement—i.e. its invalidity or termination—may leave the relevant entitlement with the State now in possession of the coastal territory (at least if it is void *ex tunc*).

ordinary principle according to which entitlement to maritime space is automatically transferred with coastal territory. However, the existing law does not support the conclusion that a coastal State's desire to retain entitlement to maritime space taken alone is an interest or intention that may prevail over the same principle, which suggests that the loss of maritime space will also automatically accompany the loss of territorial sovereignty over coastal land.

(ii) Loss of entitlement to particular maritime zones

The continuing dependency of entitlement to maritime space as a whole on continuing territorial sovereignty might be assumed to have a parallel where entitlement to certain maritime zones is subject to additional conditions. This is not the case. The principle linking the possession of territorial sovereignty over coastal land with a general entitlement to maritime space also indicates that loss of the former would be accompanied by loss of the latter. However, the rules further specifying the circumstances in which entitlement to particular maritime zones may be claimed in respect of an island or archipelago do not indicate that loss of entitlement will follow if subsequent change means these circumstances no longer obtain.

The definition of an island as a naturally formed area of land above water at high tide can be considered a condition for entitlement to maritime space with respect to such a feature.[74] This specification was a response to concerns that States were claiming or might claim entitlement to the full complement of maritime zones from artificial islands or LTEs.[75] The same concern accounts for the definition of an LTE as 'a naturally formed area of land which is surrounded by and above water at low tide but submerged at high tide' and the specification that '[w]here a low-tide elevation is wholly situated at a distance exceeding the breadth of the territorial sea from the mainland or an island, it has no territorial sea of its own'. This clear differentiation between islands and LTEs was intended to restrict claims to maritime space in respect of the latter. Yet provision for the measurement of the territorial sea from LTEs within the territorial sea generated by the mainland or an island also recognized the interest of the coastal State in extending this maritime zone. The law facilitates such an extension in a regular and constrained manner.[76]

The definition of these features by reference to high and low tide raises the question of whether erosion and inundation may result in an island either being legally 'downgraded' to an LTE or, in the case of total submergence, losing all entitlement to maritime space. If an LTE is no longer above water at low tide, the question arises whether it may continue to be used as a basepoint for measuring the breadth of the territorial sea generated by the mainland coast or an island. While

[74] TSC Art 10; CSC Art 1; UNCLOS Art 121(1), (3).
[75] See Chapter 1.
[76] Ibid.

some commentators seem to have considered a loss of maritime space in these circumstances to be a logical corollary of the legal definition of an island and LTE, insufficient attention has been paid to the temporality of the law and its object and purpose.

The provisions on islands and LTEs in the TSC and UNCLOS begin by identifying what an island or LTE is.[77] They do so, however, in order to clarify how the coastal State may use these features in determining (a) in the case of an island, entitlement to the territorial sea, contiguous zone, EEZ, and continental shelf, and (b) in the case of an LTE, the outer limits of the territorial sea.[78] In the case of LTEs, it is made clear that the coastal State cannot claim a territorial sea from an LTE situated beyond the territorial sea of the mainland or an island.[79] The object of distinguishing between islands and LTEs was to prevent extensive claims to maritime space based on the latter.

This restriction was intended to constrain the coastal State in its claims. It is not clear that it has any further application once these claims have been made manifest (most likely through delimitation[80]), unless of course the claims fail to respect the restriction in question. Crucially, placing restrictions on the use of minor maritime features to extend the maritime jurisdiction of the coastal State does not mean that a claim justified and made manifest at a particular point in time (T1) would no longer be justified due to geographical change at a later date (T2). While the States negotiating the TSC and UNCLOS were concerned to limit claims to maritime space based on relatively minor geographical features, there is no indication at all that they were concerned with the question of the *continuing existence* of entitlement to maritime space or proposed to condition this in any way. The legal definition of islands vis-à-vis LTEs was understood to limit and regulate the coastal State's claims to maritime space. There is no evidence that States considered it appropriate or inevitable that claims properly justified in this regard could subsequently be undermined by the vagaries of nature.

A similar analysis can be applied to UNCLOS Article 121(3), which provides that '[r]ocks which cannot sustain human habitation or economic life of their own shall have no exclusive economic zone or continental shelf'. As discussed in Chapter 1, the purpose of this provision was again to place limitations on the coastal State's claims to maritime space, this time in response to the development of the concept of the EEZ and a new concern to protect the international seabed area as the common heritage of mankind. The decision to restrict entitlement to maritime space in the case of 'rocks' was again a response to and constraint on claims

[77] TSC Arts 10(1), 11(1); UNCLOS Arts 13(1), 121(1).

[78] TSC Arts 10(2), 11(1)(2); UNCLOS Arts 13(1)(2), 121(2)(3). See also CSC Art 1.

[79] TSC Art 11(2); UNCLOS Art 13(2).

[80] Delimitation will usually indicate whether a State claims a territorial sea alone or together with an EEZ and continental shelf in respect of an island (or an alleged island). This does not alter the fact that entitlement exists prior to and in the absence of the specification of maritime limits.

that had been or might be made by States seeking to extend their jurisdiction. The exceptional denial of entitlement to an EEZ and continental shelf on the basis that an island lacked capacity to 'sustain human habitation or economic life' was a rule relating to the *creation of rights*. There is no evidence that States considered the same conditions to apply to the *continuing existence* of entitlement to an EEZ and continental shelf in respect of an island. Article 121(3) does not clearly establish that the *loss* of capacity to 'sustain human habitation or economic life' would result in the loss of entitlement to these maritime zones.

As already noted, the delimitation of entitlement to maritime space is the most common manifestation of a coastal State's claim to such entitlement. There remains an important distinction between entitlement to maritime space and its delimitation, which some commentators have failed to properly appreciate. Soons, for example, has argued that the permanence of the outer limits of the continental shelf means that entitlement to this zone will continue even 'while the object which generated these sovereign rights no longer exists'.[81] This conclusion is entirely unwarranted by the law. The rules and principles governing the establishment of maritime limits only apply where entitlement to maritime space exists. The rationale for the provision for permanent limits of the continental shelf, moreover, by no means recommends their retention where other circumstances indicate that the State is no longer entitled to this maritime zone. As discussed in Chapter 4, the law provides for the permanent description of the limits of the continental shelf in order to protect and preserve the international seabed area beyond national jurisdiction. If a coastal State's entitlement to a continental shelf was indeed lost, this would not raise the risk of further incursions into the international seabed area but result in its enlargement.

The key question here is whether entitlement to the continental shelf *has* been lost. The fact that the limits of the continental shelf cannot be retained where entitlement to this maritime zone *is* lost does not mean that entitlement to this maritime zone *will* be lost due to geographical change affecting an island's capacity to sustain human habitation or economic life of its own. The fact remains that the rule denying entitlement to an EEZ and continental shelf in the case of '[r]ocks which cannot sustain human habitation or economic life of their own' is concerned with the creation of rights rather than their continuing existence. States were not concerned to specify the consequences if an island properly qualifying for these maritime zones subsequently lost the capacity to sustain human habitation or economic life of its own.

Huber's distinction between the creation and continuing existence of rights reminds us that the content of the law in each case—the conditions it specifies—is not necessarily identical. It is not qualitatively the same thing for (a) a State to be denied entitlement to an EEZ and continental shelf by the terms of a treaty to which

[81] Soons, 'The Effects of a Rising Sea Level', 218–19.

it has committed itself (a condition understood to apply to its claims, including past claims, as a result of this commitment) as it is for (b) a State to lose entitlement to an EEZ and continental shelf which it has already claimed in accordance with the (new) law due to an island's subsequent loss of capacity to sustain human habitation or economic life of its own. The legal consequences of UNCLOS Article 121(3) coming into force for a particular State are those described in situation (a). Conversely, there is no evidence whatsoever that this provision was intended to have the consequences described in situation (b). The provision was not developed as a condition for continuing entitlement to an EEZ and continental shelf in respect of an island. The fact that States saw fit to preclude claims to an EEZ and continental shelf in the case of 'rocks' does not mean that they also considered it appropriate to deprive a State of its established entitlement to these maritime zones because subsequent developments, which might include geographical change, had the unfortunate consequence of a loss of capacity to sustain human habitation or economic life. The rule was designed to prevent what was considered opportunism not to punish either misfortune or, indeed, a loss of capacity brought about by the actions of the State itself. To conclude otherwise is to ignore the treaty text, which shows its temporal specificity as a condition for claims to maritime space in the first instance. The object and purpose of these conditions is to restrict and regulate such claims. This interpretation is confirmed by the drafting history.[82]

The conditionality of entitlement to 'archipelagic waters' upon qualification as an 'archipelagic State' raises a similar question of whether subsequent geographical change or other developments might result in a loss of this status and so the loss of archipelagic waters. The implications of geographical change for the location of established archipelagic baselines are covered by the discussion of maritime limits below. The question here is whether a State may lose the right to use these baselines to enclose archipelagic waters, which has been identified as a question of entitlement to maritime space and not merely its delimitation.

According to UNCLOS Article 46, an ' "archipelagic State" means a State constituted wholly by one or more archipelagos and may include other islands'. An 'archipelago' is defined as 'a group of islands, including parts of islands, interconnecting waters and other natural features which are so closely interrelated that such islands, waters and other natural features form an intrinsic geographical, economic and political entity, or which historically have been regarded as such'. Without assuming that this is a condition for continuing entitlement to archipelagic waters, it may be noted that subsequent environmental change would have to be

[82] See the work of Sub-Committee II, Seabed Committee: Seabed Committee Report (1973/I), 56–7; debates in the Second Committee on the regime of islands: UNCLOS III: II, 278–89; proposals by Romania, Turkey and (collectively) Algeria, Dahomey, Guinea, Ivory Coast, Liberia, Madagascar, Mali, Mauritania, Morocco, Sierra Leone, Sudan, Tunisia, Upper Volta and Zambia: UNCLOS III: III, 228–33; Romania's comment in the plenary: UNCLOS III: I, 128; Main Trends Paper: UNCLOS III: III, 140–1; Informal Single Negotiating Text (ISNT) Art 132: UNCLOS III: IV, 170–1.

substantial for an archipelago to no longer constitute a 'closely interrelated' 'group of islands' and other natural features in a geographical sense. The definition also refers to 'an intrinsic geographical, economic and political entity', which indicates that geography is a factor rather than fully determinative. Finally, the law considers the fact that a group of islands, interconnected waters, and other natural features have 'historically been regarded as' an 'intrinsic geographical, economic and political entity' to be sufficient to establish its character as an archipelago. This means that a State which in practice treats the islands, interconnecting waters, and other natural features of the archipelagos composing it as a unified geographical, economic, or political entity and is recognized as so doing is properly considered an archipelagic State. Of course, the definition of an 'archipelago' is not independently determinative but significant as an element of the definition of an archipelagic State as 'a State constituted wholly by one or more archipelagos', which 'may include other islands'. As argued in Chapter 1, what is stressed in this definition is the *constitution* of a State by one or more archipelagos, which are its defining feature.

The fact that an archipelago need only have been 'historically . . . regarded' as 'an intrinsic geographical, economic and political entity' may be thought to facilitate its continuing qualification as such notwithstanding subsequent change, whether geographical, economic, or political. Yet it is by no means necessary to rely on this clause as a legal loophole to prevent loss of status as an archipelagic State and, accordingly, the loss of entitlement to archipelagic waters.

In Part IV of UNCLOS, satisfaction of the legal definition of an 'archipelagic State' and an 'archipelago' is framed as a precondition for the right to draw archipelagic baselines. Article 46 defines the terms used in Article 47, which provides that '[a]n archipelagic State may draw straight archipelagic baselines joining the outermost points of the outermost islands and drying reefs of the archipelago' and sets out specific rules for their construction. It is thus made clear that the definition of an archipelagic State and the archipelagos constituting it must be satisfied for a State to claim archipelagic waters. These definitions serve as conditions for the creation of the right. There is no evidence that States were concerned with the continuing existence of entitlement to archipelagic waters following the lawful establishment of archipelagic baselines.

The weight given to historical attitudes—specifically, the fact that a group of islands, interconnecting waters, and other natural features have been 'historically regarded' as 'an intrinsic geographical, economic and political entity'—does not reflect a concern that an archipelago might lose its character as such due to subsequent change, geographical or otherwise. Instead the law recognizes the significance of the particular way in which archipelagic States have understood and responded to their own special character as a justification for entitlement to archipelagic waters in the first instance.

Archipelagic States sought to secure the same kind of interests that entitlement to the territorial sea had already recognized and secured for States generally, arguing that these interests were not adequately secured by the application of the ordinary rules to a State composed wholly or mainly by archipelagos.[83] At UNCLOS III, it was emphasized that the general rules governing entitlement to national maritime space would not allow the archipelagic State to 'safeguard the integrity of its territory, the political, social and cultural unity of its people, the cohesion of its economy, and the needs of its national security'—the 'general rules' being understood to secure the coastal State's interests in this regard in other circumstances.[84]

Kopela emphasizes that 'the archipelagic regime was conceived and promoted during UNCLOS III as a means of protecting the interests and needs of the people living in the archipelago'.[85] Yet the States advocating this regime sought to secure recognized *State* interests rather than the interests of the inhabitants of archipelagos directly or generally. Contrary to Kopela's contention, neither their arguments nor the resulting text suggests that 'the interests and needs of archipelagos are identical regardless of their political status' or that there is, as such, no justification for the application of the regime set out in UNCLOS Part IV to archipelagic *States* rather than archipelagos generally.[86] It should be noted in this regard that while the rules governing the construction of straight baselines were drawn on in the formulation of the rules governing the construction of archipelagic baselines, they were not justified on the same basis. Indeed, the reasons supporting the use of straight baselines could not have justified entitlement to sovereignty over the extensive sea areas enclosed by archipelagic baselines.

The regime of archipelagic waters responds to the call for an internationally recognized form of jurisdiction adequate in content and configuration to the special unity of land and sea over considerable distances where States are composed wholly or mainly of archipelagos. The law does not insist on proof of this unity as a matter of objective fact but recognizes and respects as a sufficient condition for entitlement to archipelagic waters the historically evidenced understanding of the State that these 'group[s] of islands, including parts of islands, interconnecting waters and other natural features' constitute 'an intrinsic geographic, economic and political entity'.

This is clearly a condition for entitlement to archipelagic waters in the first instance. It does not follow that subsequent geographical, economic, or political change (short of a total loss of territorial sovereignty over coastal land) can result in the loss of status as an archipelagic State. Rather than directly facilitating the maintenance of archipelagic status—which is unnecessary—the role of a historical

[83] Evensen Report: UNCLOS I: I, 299; Indonesia, 'Communique to Japan concerning Territorial Waters' (13 December 1957); UNCLOS II: II, 72, 74–7, 286.
[84] UNCLOS III: II, 260 (Indonesia and Burma).
[85] Kopela, *Dependent Archipelagos*, 232.
[86] Cf ibid, 232–3.

understanding of the unity of an archipelago as part of the basis for entitlement to archipelagic waters signals that States were concerned to give effect to the special self-understanding of archipelagic States as a unity encompassing land and sea. This does not suggest an ongoing conditionality upon geographical circumstances remaining unchanged. Nor does it suggest that 'regarding' an archipelago as a unity is a condition for its continuing existence.

It remains possible for a State to abandon its claim to archipelagic waters. However, the possibility of abandonment (an option rather than an obligation) does not mean that the actual or perceived unity of groups of islands, interconnecting waters, and other natural features—even in the event of substantial geographical change—is necessary to retain entitlement to archipelagic waters. Not only is there no express requirement to this effect—the definitions set out in UNCLOS clearly functioning as conditions precedent for claims to archipelagic waters in the first instance—there is no basis for inferring that the conditions for the creation of the right are in this case the same as the conditions for its continuing existence. Chiefly, it is neither logical nor necessary to infer the punitive from the permissive. To assume that the conditions enlivening the option to claim archipelagic waters are also conditions for continuing entitlement to the same would be to ignore the key difference between (a) allowing a State composed of archipelagos to benefit from an enclosure of waters that responds to the geographical, economic, and political unity of the land and water within and (b) depriving the same State of this benefit because it suffers subsequent geographical change with serious economic and political consequences threatening or undermining the unity of its archipelagos.

It is again one thing to grant a right to claim archipelagic waters and quite another to insist that subsequent geographical change will necessarily deprive a State of such entitlement where it is already established and relied upon to 'safeguard the integrity of its territory, the political, social and cultural unity of its people, the cohesion of its economy, and the needs of its national security'.[87] Though entitlement to archipelagic waters responds to natural and human facts, it does not follow that subsequent change affecting those facts and already damaging to the archipelagic State's interests must result in a loss of entitlement to this maritime zone. The conditions for the creation of the right reflect a concern to further the interests of the archipelagic State. To take the same conditions as requirements for continuing entitlement to maritime space is to convert a right into an obligation and render the interests that the regime of archipelagic waters seeks to protect vulnerable to the vicissitudes of nature. Far from being either expressly provided for or implied by the law, this result would distort and undermine it.

[87] UNCLOS III: II, 260 (Indonesia and Burma).

(iii) The artificial preservation or reinforcement of natural features

The definition of both LTEs and islands as 'a naturally formed area of land' as well as the reference to 'natural features' in the definition of an archipelago raises the further question of whether the reinforcement or reconstruction of such features by 'artificial' means (e.g. the addition of concrete or erection of other structures on a natural feature that would otherwise be submerged) may have consequences for their continuing capacity to generate entitlement to maritime space. Evidently, this idea depends upon the same assumption that 'naturalness' is not only a condition for the creation of entitlement but a condition for its continuing existence. This involves a failure to understand the objectives of the law as well as its temporal dimension.

In the *South China Sea Arbitration*, the Tribunal found that 'external additions or modifications intended to increase [the] capacity [of an island] to sustain human habitation or economic life of its own' were not consistent with the notion of 'human habitation' or 'economic life' referred to in Article 121(3).[88] Capacity depending on such 'artificial' intervention was not considered to satisfy the conditions for entitlement to an EEZ and continental shelf under that provision.[89] Notably, this does not mean that interventions intended to preserve an existing capacity to sustain 'human habitation' or 'economic life' will disqualify an island from entitlement to these maritime zones—though such measures are unnecessary if their sole purpose is to justify continuing entitlement to the same.

In its 2016 Award, the Tribunal expressly concluded that a 'rock cannot be transformed into a fully entitled island through land reclamation'.[90] It reasoned (correctly) that '[i]f States were allowed to convert any rock incapable of sustaining human habitation or an economic life into a fully entitled island simply by the introduction of technology and extraneous materials, then the purpose of Article 121(3) as a provision of limitation would be frustrated'.[91] This reasoning implies, however, a difference between cases where such measures are used to 'convert' a rock into a fully entitled island in this way and cases where an island that is or was already capable of sustaining human habitation or economic life of its own is subject to various interventions involving 'the introduction of technology and extraneous materials'. While the former measures are at odds with the object and purpose of Article 121, the latter measures, which may help to preserve a local population or local economic activities, are not.

In the *South China Sea Arbitration*, the Tribunal pointed to a close relationship between 'natural' physical geography and 'natural' human interests and practices as both justifying and restricting rights to an EEZ and continental shelf in respect of

88 *South China Sea Arbitration* (2016), 227.
89 Ibid.
90 Ibid, 214.
91 Ibid.

an island. It took Article 121(3) to refer to the 'natural capacity' of a feature to support 'human habitation'—which was taken to refer to 'the natural population of the feature'—or 'economic life of [its] own'—which was taken to refer to 'the life and livelihoods of the human population inhabiting and making its home on a maritime feature or group of features' (at least 'ordinarily').[92] In determining whether an island had the capacity to support either human habitation or economic life understood in this way, the Tribunal referred to both 'physical conditions' and 'the historical use to which [the feature] has been put', though it was careful to note that the absence of evidence of historical use was not determinative (e.g. it might still be argued that a feature has capacity though it has not historically been utilized).[93]

The emphasis on 'natural' capacity and the 'natural' physical conditions in the Award was linked to the object and purpose of Article 121(2), which is to limit entitlement to an EEZ and continental shelf to cases where a local population has an interest in and will benefit from activities in these maritime zones. Yet it does not follow from this rationale that an island that comes to require measures using technology or 'extraneous materials' to prevent or mitigate changes to natural conditions that support its 'capacity to sustain human habitation or economic life of [its own]' will be disqualified from entitlement to an EEZ and continental shelf. The appropriate analogy here is coastal protection or land reclamation activities along a mainland coast, which do not disqualify a coastal State from entitlement to the full complement of maritime zones in respect of that area. The objective of preventing the extension of national maritime jurisdiction through claims to entitlement based on artificial islands does not mean that States should be penalized for undertaking activities to protect existing islands.

Under UNCLOS Article 13, LTEs do not independently generate entitlement to maritime space but may be used to measure the outer limits of the territorial sea where they are located within its original circumference as measured from the mainland or an island.[94] Here, too, it may appear that measures to protect a feature from erosion or submergence such as the addition of concrete could mean that it no longer qualifies as 'a naturally formed area of land which is surrounded by and above water at low tide but submerged at high tide' and, as such, cannot be used to extend the limits of the territorial sea.

In this case, the fact that the rule clearly refers to the construction of baselines as an exercise at a particular point in time is significant, as the following section elaborates. It is also relevant that the rule does not respond to any independent value of LTEs located within the territorial sea of a mainland or island States but to the interests of coastal States generally in extending the territorial sea. The artificial preservation or reinforcement of features that were otherwise 'naturally formed'

[92] Ibid, 227–8.
[93] Ibid, 230–1.
[94] See Chapter 1.

areas of land 'surrounded by and above water at low tide but submerged at high tide' does not undermine the object and purpose of the law, which is to facilitate an extension of the territorial sea in a regular way and subject to clear limits. This does not mean, however, that artificial preservation or reinforcement is *required* to justify the continued use of LTEs as basepoints in the measurement of the outer limits of the territorial sea.

Artificial reinforcements may allow an LTE to support a lighthouse or another installation. In the absence of such an installation, it is difficult to see any reason for reinforcing an LTE in the territorial sea of a mainland or island. Such a practice would appear to be predicated on the belief that the permanent submergence of an LTE would preclude its continuing use as a basepoint—or at least a concern that this might be the legal effect of such change.

As Chapters 6 and 8 have explained, probative evidence that a feature is permanently submerged may indeed preclude its use in the construction of a new maritime boundary, though States may agree to rely on charts predating such change for the purposes of interstate delimitation. In the unilateral construction of maritime limits, it seems that a State may make use of an LTE shown on existing charts regardless of whether it in fact remains above water at low-tide at the time of delimitation. In both cases, the law indicates the circumstances to be taken into account in the *delimitation process*. This does not imply that the permanent submergence of an LTE after the establishment of maritime limits or boundaries or the registration of this change on a chart will bring the established legal limits into question.

The coastal State may take advantage of (and is constrained by) the rule allowing the measurement of the territorial sea from LTEs at the time of delimitation. This rule governs the construction of maritime limits, not their continuing existence. It does not imply that established maritime limits would no longer be lawful or must be revised if an LTE were subsequently permanently submerged. The law applying to the continuing existence of maritime limits indicates only that the coastal State is entitled but not obliged to revise those limits with the exception of the limits of the continental shelf.

As a general rule, measures to preserve or reinforce natural features against erosion or inundation will not independently disqualify a State from continuing entitlement to maritime space in respect of that feature. Nor will they bring established maritime limits or boundaries into question. It is important to recognize, however, that the same activities are not *necessary* to preserve entitlement to maritime space or established limits and boundaries. The point is not that a State may preserve its entitlement to maritime space by artificial preservation of the features generating it. The distinction between the creation and continuing existence of rights means that such entitlement will persist notwithstanding subsequent geographical change. Efforts to transform a rock into an island capable of sustaining human habitation or economic life of its own, an LTE into an island, or a submerged feature into an LTE purely for the purposes of generating entitlement to maritime space or extending established maritime limits would be at odds with the conditions for the creation of the right. The artificial reinforcement of an existing island or LTE, however, will not cause the loss of an established entitlement to maritime space or prevent the continuing use of an LTE as a basepoint.

B. Maritime Limits

The assumption that maritime limits must be continually reassessed and revised by reference to the treaty provisions governing their establishment may be the most influential of the unstated grounds for the ambulatory thesis. Yet it is an assumption entirely unsupported by 'the ordinary meaning to be given to the terms of the treaty in their context and in the light of its object and purpose'.[95] The treaty provisions in question have a specific temporal scope: they are expressly concerned with the act of delimitation by the coastal State, which takes place at a particular point in time.

Articles 7, 10, 47, and 50 of UNCLOS refer to the *drawing* or *demarcation* of baselines. Articles 14 and 16 refer generally to the *determination* of baselines using methods set out in the baselines provisions. Similar if not identical terminology is employed in the TSC. In both the 1958 and 1982 Conventions, zonal limits are to be actively *delimited*. Article 8 of the TSC and Article 11 of UNCLOS highlight the fact that the drawing of baselines and the location of zonal limits are two aspects of a single task, specifying how ports are to be treated 'for the purpose of delimiting the territorial sea'. UNCLOS Article 3 refers to the right of the coastal State 'to *establish* the breadth of its territorial sea up to a limit not exceeding 12 nautical miles, *measured* from baselines *determined* in accordance with this Convention'.[96]

Articles 5, 6, and 13 of UNCLOS provide that the 'baseline *is* the low-water line' (Articles 5 and 6 further specifying the low-water line 'as charted'), while Article 9 specifies that 'the baseline *shall be* a straight line across the mouth of [a] river' flowing directly into the sea.[97] These provisions might be considered more temporally ambiguous based on the text alone; however, their location within the baselines provisions as a whole (an essential context for determining their ordinary meaning) indicates that they are also intended to govern the establishment of maritime limits. While they describe the normal baseline and closing line, this functions as an instruction to the coastal State in the exercise of delimitation. There is no reason to think that these articles, unlike the other baselines provisions, import an additional duty to ensure that, once established, the normal baseline or closing line will continue to correspond with the low-water line or a line across

[95] Vienna Convention on the Law of Treaties (VCLT) Art 31.
[96] Emphasis added.
[97] Emphasis added.

the mouth of the river, respectively. In practice, States do not differentiate between these formulations but apply them all (as appropriate) in the delimitation process.

It is clear from the treaty text that these provisions are intended to govern the construction of baselines by the coastal State. As such, other States can objectto the baselines established by reference to these provisions (and have done so). There is no textual basis, however, for treating the baselines provisions as conditions that apply over time. Nor is such an understanding consistent with the broader objectives of the law relating to maritime limits and maritime jurisdiction more generally.

As Chapter 1 explains, the baselines provisions refer to a limited number of ideal-typical geographical circumstances. Specifically, the law makes use of the abstract forms and standardized symbols representing geography in the static, spatial grid of a nautical chart. Rules for the construction of baselines that refer to geography as both represented and abstracted in nautical charts have a practical and symbolic function. They allow coastal States to unilaterally delimit their national maritime jurisdiction in an efficient and systematic way amenable to scrutiny by other States or a legal authority tasked with resolving a dispute. They also give expression to the general principle that 'the land dominates the sea'—that is, the principle that national maritime jurisdiction follows from territorial sovereignty over coastal land. In both cases, the overarching objective is to ensure or secure a stable legal order for the oceans.

The crucial point is that the work done by geography in this regard is done at the time of delimitation. The practical benefits of referring to coastal geography as shown on a particular nautical chart would be largely confounded if coastal States were required to reassess and revise their baselines against the baselines provisions on a continuing basis. The fact that the geographical features picked out by the baselines provisions—the low-water line and low-lying features—are ordinarily subject to change would mean that baselines and the zonal limits measured from them would change frequently if those provisions were continually reapplied. The potential for disputes between States regarding the lawfulness of established baselines would increase with the expectation of their revision to take into account changed geographical circumstances. An obligation to reapply the baselines provisions would be onerous both upon the coastal State and parties relying on its maritime limits in practice, which may change frequently even if it were argued that only changes shown in charts must be taken into account. Indeed, the very fact that the relevant geographical features (or cartographic constructs) *are* ordinarily subject to change supports the conclusion, based on the ordinary meaning of the treaty text, that such reapplication and revision is not required.

There is no reason to think that the establishment of baselines at a particular point in time, in the absence of a *duty* to continue to reassess and revise them but subject to a *right* in most cases (with the exception of the limits of the shelf) to do so, is at odds with the principle that the 'land dominates the sea' in general or as expressed in the baselines provisions. This principle by no means implies that maritime limits should shift with changes to physical geography. This much is demonstrated by the fact that the same principle plays a similar role in the delimitation of maritime boundaries between States—boundaries which will not ordinarily be subject to change once established. Geographical change subsequent to the establishment of an international maritime boundary is not thought to cast doubt on its consistency with the principle that 'the land dominates the sea', which is given effect in the delimitation process. There is nothing to suggest that the significance of this principle in the unilateral establishment of maritime limits is any different. Unilaterally established maritime limits constructed in accordance with the relevant treaty provisions will also give effect to the principle that 'the land dominates the sea', which does not further demand their adjustment in response to subsequent coastal change.

C. International Maritime Boundaries

The delimitation of a maritime boundary will be substantially based on the geographical circumstances obtaining at the time and, in most cases, geographical circumstances reflected in contemporary charts.[98] There is, however, an important distinction between the process of delimitation and the boundary it produces. Simply because certain factors are taken into account in the delimitation process does not mean that the resulting boundary depends upon their persistence.

(i) From delimitation to established boundaries

The law relating to maritime boundaries supports a distinction between the conditions governing the construction of a boundary and the conditions governing its continuing existence. Maritime boundaries—particularly those delimited by a court or tribunal—will usually be based on geographical circumstances at the time of delimitation, in particular, the configuration of the coasts and the presence of such features as islands. At the time of delimitation, States will generally seek to locate the boundary relative to the most protuberant points on the coast. This is consistent with the idea that maritime jurisdiction is naturally appurtenant to and a projection from the 'legal coast' or 'coastal front'. It is not assumed, however, that these geographical circumstances must remain unaltered for the established boundary to remain lawful and effective.

Protuberant points on the coast are by definition particularly vulnerable to the action of the weather and the sea—processes that may result in geographical change. While there have been a few occasions in interstate delimitation disputes where a State has argued that the physical stability of an area of land is a

[98] See Chapter 8.

precondition for its use as an appropriate site for basepoints used in the construction of a maritime boundary,[99] the jurisprudence does not support the conclusion that maritime boundaries are premised upon—and may stand and fall with—the persistence of the geographical circumstances taken into account in their construction. As discussed in Chapter 6, coastal instability may be relevant to delimitation where it has consequences for the location of an established land boundary—i.e. where the established boundary is ambulatory. Taken alone, however, instability and the prospect—even the certainty—of future geographical change will not mean that an area of coastal land is an inappropriate site for basepoints.[100]

In *Bangladesh v India*, the Tribunal made clear that the prospect of future change was irrelevant because the construction of a maritime boundary was based on the 'physical reality at the time of the delimitation' and would be unaffected by geographical change subsequent to its establishment.[101] The Tribunal correctly drew a line between present geographical circumstances and future coastal change. It is worth noting that there was another way in which coastal instability could have been taken into account at the point of delimitation. The dynamism of the deltaic coastline could reasonably be considered a present reality, even if its particular and continuing consequences for the configuration of the coast (specific changes that would only be seen in the future) were not. Bangladesh seems to have treated coastal instability as a present reality in the construction of its baselines in 1974. In its view, the fluctuations of its deltaic coast meant that the low-water line did not represent a clear dividing line between land and sea and that the shallow waters adjacent to its coast '[pertained] to the character of inland waters'.[102] This was taken to justify the location of basepoints offshore on the basis of depth.

By taking coastal instability into account at the time of (unilateral) delimitation in this way, Bangladesh was not trying to prevent future coastal change from affecting the baseline on the understanding that baselines were ambulatory. Nor was it attempting to anticipate future change and take it into account at the time of delimitation based on the belief that, once established, baselines were permanently fixed. Coastal instability was simply treated as part of the geographical reality at the time of delimitation. As discussed in Chapter 3, Bangladesh did not consider the dynamism of the deltaic coast to prevent the establishment of basepoints on it—it did not assume that the baseline would shift with the coast. Instead it pointed to the dynamism of the coast as evidence of the close relationship between land and sea in the waters off its coast, on the basis of which it sought to justify a practice of locating basepoints offshore.

There are elements of the same reasoning in Bangladesh's case for delimitation by an angle bisector in its dispute with India, though the argument is not clearly

99 See Chapter 6.
100 *Bangladesh v India* (2014), 63, 74–5. See Chapter 6.
101 *Bangladesh v India* (2014), 62–3.
102 Platzöder (1983/IV), 14 (15 October 1974).

developed. It is possible that Bangladesh's objection to 'equidistance's excessive focus on micro-geographic features' and preference for a method that refers to 'macro-geography' (in its view, an angle bisector)[103] could have been strengthened by reference to the extent to which the fluctuating coastline blurred the dividing line between land and sea. While it is not clear that the Tribunal would have accepted this reasoning, it would at least have been compatible with the principle that delimitation should refer to present geographical realities.

The relevance of geographical circumstances obtaining at the time of delimitation to the construction of the boundary follows from the notion that the maritime entitlements to be delimited are a projection from the coastal front.[104] Justifying the construction of a boundary on this basis responds to the demand that delimitation (especially by a court or tribunal) should be principled and not arbitrary. The same considerations of principle do not mean that a boundary should respond to subsequent changes in the coastal configuration or, indeed, changes to other circumstances informing the location of that boundary.

It is one thing to demand that delimitation should be effected in a principled manner, another to demand that maritime boundaries should continue to respond to changes affecting coastal geography after their establishment. If the latter were in fact a demand made by States or, indeed, by the law, one would expect all maritime boundaries to be ambulatory. As it stands, maritime boundaries are ordinarily fixed. Though the law does not prohibit an ambulatory boundary, it does not presume that a boundary will have this character.[105] Geography—specifically, the naturally changeable geography of the coasts—plays a role in the delimitation process. It does not condition international maritime boundaries on a continuing basis. Reference to a simplified, cartographical representation of coastal geography facilitates the construction and definition of a boundary that can be clearly identified on a chart and is, as such, readily observed and enforced over time.

The continuing effectiveness of international maritime boundaries notwithstanding subsequent geographical change is reinforced by restrictions upon the circumstances in which boundary agreements can be terminated or withdrawn from and boundary awards challenged. Once established, international boundaries are not easily changed. Even the termination of a boundary agreement will not necessarily affect the boundary that agreement has established. The restrictions on termination of or withdrawal from a boundary agreement are consistent with the idea that factors taken into account in the construction of such a boundary need not persist for the boundary to remain lawful and effective.

[103] Bangladesh Memorial, vol 1, 111, in *Bangladesh v India*.
[104] See Chapter 1.
[105] See Chapter 6.

(ii) Fundamental change of circumstances

Article 62(2)(a) of the VCLT recognizes that '[a] fundamental change of circumstances may not be invoked as a ground for terminating or withdrawing from a treaty... if the treaty establishes a boundary'. The application of this rule to maritime boundaries was affirmed in the *Aegean Sea Continental Shelf Case*[106] and its rationale is as applicable here as in the case of land boundaries. While international boundaries will usually be constructed by reference to circumstances obtaining at the time of their establishment, the chief objective is the stable division of areas subject to sovereignty or sovereign rights between two or more States.[107] While stability in this sense may be achieved by an ambulatory boundary,[108] it would be seriously jeopardized by allowing a State to unilaterally terminate or withdraw from a boundary on the basis that circumstances obtaining at the time of delimitation have since changed.

In general, unilateral acts will not affect the location of an international boundary unless the boundary agreement or award expressly provides otherwise. This applies to the unilateral adjustment of maritime baselines and zonal limits by the coastal State.[109] State practice shows that where maritime baselines have been redrawn, international boundaries established by reference to them have not been reopened for negotiation or challenged on this basis.[110]

It is worth noting that there is in any case a high threshold for the termination of or withdrawal from a treaty on the basis of a fundamental change of circumstances. The general rule is that '[a] fundamental change of circumstances which has occurred with regard to those existing at the time of the conclusion of a treaty, and which was not foreseen by the parties, *may not* be invoked as a ground for terminating or withdrawing from the treaty'.[111] An exception to this general rule is admitted where '(*a*) the existence of those circumstances constituted an essential basis of the consent of the parties to be bound by the treaty; and (*b*) the effect of the change is radically to transform the extent of obligations still to be performed under the treaty'.

Even if it were not expressly provided that this exception does not apply to boundary treaties, it is unlikely that the cumulative conditions would be met in cases of geographical change subsequent to the establishment of a maritime boundary. In some cases, the relevant change may have been unforeseen, though there is no reason to think that States would not be aware of the ordinary

[106] *Aegean Sea Continental Shelf Case* (1978), 35–6.

[107] Ibid. Cf Árnadóttir, who suggests that the same concern with stability does not apply to maritime boundaries because the latter 'generally fluctuate with changes to the coastal front'—an assumption that has been contested at length in this book: S Árnadóttir, 'Termination of Maritime Boundaries Due to a Fundamental Change of Circumstances' (2016) 32 (83) *UJIEL* 94, 95.

[108] See Chapter 6.

[109] Ibid.

[110] Tanaka, *Predictability and Flexibility*, 231.

[111] VCLT Art 62(1) (emphasis added).

vulnerability of protuberant points on the coast to subsequent change. It would also need to be shown that the assumed persistence of the affected geographical circumstances was an 'essential basis' for the parties consent to the boundary agreement.[112]

The role of geography in the delimitation of maritime boundaries indicates that States will usually (though not necessarily, where the boundary is freely agreed) consider the boundary to be equitable in part because of the manner in which it responds to geographical circumstances obtaining at the time. The role of geography in this context can be understood to respond to the notion that entitlement to maritime space projects from the coastal front. As such, the manner in which the delimitation of a boundary responds to coastal geography may be considered an 'essential basis' for the parties' consent to the resulting boundary. This does not mean, however, that the assumed persistence of the same geographical circumstances was an 'essential basis' for their consent. Even if it could be established that the States in question believed that these circumstances would not subsequently change, it would also have to be shown that they considered it necessary for the boundary to be based on geographical circumstances that would not change.

The notion of an 'essential basis of consent' must also be read in conjunction with the requirement that 'the effect of the change is radically to transform the extent of obligations still to be performed under the treaty'. Insofar as the chief obligation is to respect the established boundary, subsequent geographical change will not '[increase] the burden of the obligations to be executed to the extent of rendering the performance something essentially different from that originally undertaken'.[113] It is worth noting that there might be a better chance of establishing a fundamental change of circumstances meeting this condition in the case of an ambulatory boundary. If, for example, it could be shown that (a) States believed that the change to which the ambulatory boundary was agreed to respond would be gradual or infrequent, (b) this understanding was an 'essential basis of consent' to the boundary treaty, and (c) subsequent developments meant that more radical or frequent change necessitated the more radical and frequent adjustment of the boundary according to the terms of the agreement, then this could be considered to increase the burden of the obligations to be performed to a substantial degree.

Of course, termination or withdrawal on the basis of a fundamental change of circumstances is in any case excluded in the case of boundary agreements. The appropriateness of this exclusion is not altered by the fact that certain types of geographical change subsequent to the establishment of an ambulatory boundary could increase the burden on the parties to continually adjust that boundary in response. Instead, such difficulties point to the importance of clearly specifying what

[112] This is analogous to the requirements for establishing error invalidating consent, discussed in Chapter 8.
[113] *Fisheries Jurisdiction Case* (1973), 65.

type of change an ambulatory boundary will respond to and when. It also suggests why choosing to establish an ambulatory maritime boundary may be unwise.

States establishing an international boundary, including a maritime boundary, are generally concerned to construct a boundary that is capable of being respected and observed over time. Boundaries are negotiated or delimited by a court or tribunal with an eye to the longevity of the resulting line (and, indeed, with an awareness of the fact that boundaries cannot be terminated on the grounds of a fundamental change of circumstances, at least since the conclusion of the VCLT). This does not suggest a belief that the geographical circumstances by reference to which a maritime boundary is delimited will remain unchanged. It reflects an understanding that the role of geography in maritime delimitation does its work at the time the boundary is established.

Even if boundary agreements were not protected by the rule in VCLT Article 62(2)(a), admitting unilateral termination of or withdrawal from such agreements on the basis of geographical change would be at odds with the structure of the law. The foregoing reflections on (a) whether the persistence of geographical circumstances taken into account in the delimitation process may be an 'essential basis for consent' and (b) whether subsequent geographical change might 'radically ... transform the extent of obligations still to be performed under the treaty' highlight the difference between the conditions for the construction of a boundary and the conditions for its continuing existence. The law gives geography a role in the delimitation process but does not provide for boundaries that are continually contingent upon the naturally variable coast. While a boundary that is contingent upon coastal geography in this way can be established by agreement (an ambulatory boundary), the law governing the delimitation of maritime boundaries does not propose to set out conditions that will govern the continuing existence of the boundary after its establishment. The rules and principles that do apply to the latter question favour the persistence of the boundary notwithstanding a fundamental change of circumstances.

(iii) Impossibility of performance

According to Article 61(1) of the VCLT, '[a] party may invoke the impossibility of performing a treaty as a ground for terminating or withdrawing from it if the impossibility results from the permanent disappearance or destruction of an object indispensable for the execution of the treaty'. In its commentary on the draft version of this article, the International Law Commission (ILC) noted that 'the type of cases envisaged by the article [are] the submergence of an island, the drying up of a river or the destruction of a dam or hydro-electric installation indispensable for the execution of a treaty'.[114]

[114] ILC Ybk 1966/II, 256.

It is reasonable to consider the submergence of an island to amount to its 'permanent disappearance or destruction' and coastal erosion could also be considered to have this result for those parts of the coast that are washed away or submerged. Yet these geographical circumstances may be taken into account in the construction of a maritime boundary without remaining objects that are 'indispensable for the execution of the treaty'. As Soons notes, 'it remains very well possible... to continue to respect the boundary line of the delimitation agreement' notwithstanding the submergence of an island taken into account in its construction.[115] This is as true of an ambulatory boundary as it is of a fixed boundary—the only difference being that this type of change may necessitate a change in the course of an ambulatory boundary.

The application of the rule regarding impossibility of performance to the case of geographical change subsequent to the establishment of a maritime boundary again points up the difference between the question of the construction of such a boundary and its continuing existence. Geographical circumstances play a role in the delimitation process but their persistence is not a necessary condition for the continuing effectiveness of the boundary.

VI. Conclusion

The law relating to entitlement to maritime space, maritime limits, and international maritime boundaries has an important temporal dimension. The legal implications of geographical change in this context must be assessed in light of the important distinction between the creation and continuing existence of rights elaborated by Max Huber in the 1928 *Island of Palmas Case*. Huber's understanding of this distinction requires clarification and a serious error in his account of its implications in terms of the law of territory must be corrected. Yet a re-examination of the arbitrator's analysis of the two branches of intertemporal law confirms its acuity and shows how the second branch in particular has at times been misunderstood. An appreciation of the way in which the law governing the creation of a right may differ from the law governing its continuing existence is not only of value where the implications of a change in the law are to be assessed. The distinction also helps to make sense of the difference between (a) the role of geography in the 'generation' of entitlement to maritime space and the establishment of maritime limits and boundaries, and (b) the implications of subsequent geographical change for continuing entitlement to maritime space and established maritime limits and boundaries.

Huber's distinction between the creation and continuing existence of rights helps to illuminate the basic error involved in the assumption that the conditions

115 Soons, 'The Effects of a Rising Sea Level', 228.

governing the establishment of entitlement to maritime space, maritime limits, and maritime boundaries necessarily govern the persistence of entitlement to maritime space, maritime limits, and maritime boundaries as well. By carefully distinguishing the legal question of what is required for the creation of a right from the legal question of what is required for its subsistence or loss it is possible to see that the conditions are not necessarily identical and to appreciate why this is the case.

It has been argued above that the conditions for the acquisition of territory or the creation of the State differ from the conditions for continuing territorial sovereignty or statehood, and that this is largely because of a concern with stability in an international legal order which still takes the territorial State as its primary unit. For better or worse, this notion of stability has encouraged the development of laws that make territory and statehood difficult to acquire and even more difficult to lose. It is consistent with this vision of international legal order to limit the possibility of territory or statehood being lost unintentionally—i.e. through a loss of effectiveness.

In the case of entitlement to maritime space, the picture is slightly different. According to the principle that 'the land dominates the sea', it is necessary and sufficient for a State to possess territorial sovereignty over coastal land to justify its entitlement to an 'appurtenant' area of national maritime space. The priority of territorial sovereignty in this relationship of appurtenance means that territorial sovereignty over coastal land is also a condition for the persistence of entitlement to maritime space. The intentions of the coastal State matter here in relation to the loss of territory but cannot prevent the loss of entitlement to maritime space automatically accompanying the loss of territorial sovereignty over coastal land. To retain its entitlement to maritime space, the coastal State must fight for its continuing territorial sovereignty over the land to which that entitlement appertains. Insofar as such a fight reflects an intention to retain territorial sovereignty, it may be sufficient to achieve this end—and necessary where there are claims to the contrary.

This coincidence between the conditions for entitlement to maritime space in general and the conditions for its continuing existence is unusual. In many circumstances, a qualitative difference between the creation of a right and the loss of an existing right will be reflected in the conditions that the law specifies as necessary or sufficient to bring about these very different results. This is true of the conditions for entitlement to particular maritime zones in respect of islands or archipelagos and the rules and principles governing the construction of maritime limits and boundaries, which differ from the conditions for continuing entitlement to these maritime zones and the persistence of maritime limits and boundaries.

The treaty provisions invoked in support of the idea that certain types of geographical change will precipitate a loss of entitlement to maritime space in respect of an island or archipelago or necessitate the revision of maritime limits are in fact chiefly concerned with the creation of rights, not their continuing existence. They set out the conditions in which a State may claim maritime space in respect of an island or enclose the waters of its archipelagos within archipelagic baselines. They specify rules for the construction of baselines and zonal limits. These provisions are largely unconcerned with the question of continuing entitlement to maritime space or the persistence of maritime limits. When the law does engage with this question, moreover, it does not suggest that the conditions bearing on claims to maritime space in respect of an island or archipelago or the construction of maritime limits must continue to be satisfied if entitlement to maritime space and established limits are to be retained.

Provision for the permanent establishment of the limits of the continental shelf evidently relates to the persistence of these limits.[116] What this indicates, however, is that the limits of the continental shelf, once established, cannot be revised by the coastal State. This is presented as an exception implying the general rule that the coastal State is entitled—though not obliged—to revise established limits in the case of other maritime zones.

UNCLOS Article 7(2), which specifies that straight baselines on deltaic coasts 'shall remain effective until changed by the coastal State in accordance with this Convention', similarly points to a right (not an obligation) to revise established baselines. It also indicates that any subsequent redrawing of baselines and zonal limits will be governed by the treaty rules relating to the construction of these legal limits. As the Conclusion to this book will further elaborate, this application of the law governing the 'creation of the right' is entirely appropriate as in these circumstances maritime limits are established anew. If the State does not opt to revise established limits, however, the same law has no application. It certainly does not mandate the revision of maritime limits or signal a loss of their lawfulness or effectiveness in the event of geographical change.

As well as being inconsistent with the temporal specificity of the treaty text, such an effect is by no means implied by the role of geography in the law. As we have seen, using the cartographical representation of the coast to spatially specify the rights of the coastal State in the sea and to both advance and constrain its interests in this regard serves a number of purposes. It ensures a principled consistency with the key principle that 'the land dominates the sea', which captures the legal basis for entitlement to national maritime space as a whole. A schematic treatment of geography brings a measure of order to unilateral maritime delimitation and the delimitation of maritime space by a court or tribunal. It usefully informs interstate delimitation by negotiation, supporting the peaceful and timely establishment of international maritime boundaries.

The additional conditions for entitlement to maritime space in respect of an island, the conditions for entitlement to archipelagic waters, the provisions

116 The prohibition on subsequent revision is also relevant to the construction of the limit in the first instance, raising the stakes both for the coastal State concerned to maximize its entitlement and other interested parties concerned to ensure that its limits are consistent with rules directed towards the preservation of an international seabed area.

governing the construction of maritime limits, and the methodologies specified in the treaty law and developed in the case law for the construction of maritime boundaries are concerned inter alia with ensuring that claims to maritime space and their delimitation in the same general circumstances by coastal States around the world are subject to the same broad standards. Associating certain rights and obligations or, more accurately, permissions and limitations with ideal types of coastal geography contributes to the generality of the law as well as its adaptability to local circumstances. By providing for a relatively regular response to common geographical circumstances, the law realizes a kind of proportional equality between coastal States in terms of their interests and corresponding rights in adjacent seas.[117] This notion of proportional equality is key to the (in some respects idiosyncratic) concept of equity in the law of the sea.[118]

The role of geography in the law of the sea contributes substantially to ensuring that claims to national maritime space and its delimitation are orderly and principled. Using the spatial schema of the cartographic representation of the coast to specify the jurisdiction of the coastal State also facilitates the observance and enforcement of these legal limits. Significantly, all of these benefits are realized at the point of delimitation and will not be lost in the event of subsequent geographical change. The role geography plays in ensuring that claims to national maritime space and its delimitation are orderly, principled, and practical in terms of both establishment and observance contributes to the end goal of a division of maritime space and associated rights and obligations that is intended to persist over time. The work geography does in this regard is done at the time claims to maritime space, maritime limits, and international maritime boundaries are lawfully established. While the effects are enduring, they do not depend upon geography remaining unchanged.

[117] See Chapter 1.
[118] Ibid.

Conclusion

The Limits of Geographical Change

I. Introduction

This book has sought to both elaborate and critique the arguments and assumptions underlying the ambulatory thesis. It has found that there is no basis in the existing law for the view that States are required to adjust established maritime limits in response to geographical change, or, as a variant, the view that those limits shift automatically to reflect such change. The law relating to maritime limits is in this sense consistent with the law relating to international maritime boundaries, which also grants geography a significant role in the delimitation process without implying that established boundaries are (for this reason) vulnerable to subsequent geographical change. The legal framework which allows the establishment of ambulatory international boundaries by clear agreement but does not admit any presumption of this character responds to the significance of sovereignty and sovereign rights at sea. It reflects the understanding that legal limits which mark the spatial extent of a coastal State's sovereignty and sovereign rights should not be vulnerable to change in unintended ways.

The principle of stability does not exceptionally secure international maritime boundaries against subsequent change. Rather, the role of geography in the law relating to both maritime limits and maritime boundaries is already consistent with the concern to secure 'a stable legal order for the seas and oceans'. It facilitates delimitation across a range of settings in a principled and relatively regular manner and results in legal limits that can be readily observed and enforced. The valuable work that reference to geography does in this regard by no means implies an ongoing vulnerability to subsequent geographical change, which would undermine the stability that the role of geography in the law helps to secure.

The role of geography in connection with entitlement to maritime space (as distinct from its delimitation) also reflects a concern with order and stability. The loss of territorial sovereignty over coastal land will result in the loss of entitlement to maritime space appurtenant to that territory; however, while geographical change may play a role in this process, it will not independently bring it about. Geographical change will not jeopardize a State's established entitlement to maritime space in respect of an island or its entitlement to archipelagic waters where territorial sovereignty is retained. The law that both authorizes and restricts these

Geographical Change and the Law of the Sea. Kate Purcell, Oxford University Press (2019). © Kate Purcell.
DOI: 10.1093/oso/9780198743644.001.0001

claims to maritime space in the first instance does not imply the vulnerability of established rights to subsequent geographical change. The law relating to islands and archipelagic States is clearly concerned to regulate claims to maritime space, not to condition entitlement once established. There is no basis for assuming that the same conditions govern the initial claim and the continuing existence of entitlement. Such an assumption fails to appreciate the qualitative difference between the creation of a new right and the loss of an established right, which are (appropriately) governed by different conditions.

The foregoing chapters have sought to elaborate and interrogate both the explicit and implicit reasoning underpinning the view that maritime limits are ambulatory and the related idea that entitlement to maritime space is vulnerable to subsequent geographical change. The claim that some types of international maritime boundary will necessarily shift with coastal change has also been considered. It has been argued that neither the underlying reasoning nor the alleged results are supported by the existing law. The law does not require the adjustment of maritime limits in response to geographical change. Nor does it follow from the existing law that such change will automatically result in a loss of entitlement to maritime space. The question of whether an international maritime boundary is ambulatory depends upon the terms of the agreement and will not be readily presumed. It remains important to be clear about what the law of the sea does require of a State in the event of change affecting its coasts and to distinguish these obligations from what the law permits.

II. Rights and Obligations in Circumstances of Geographical Change

The action of the weather and waves may effect a variety of changes in coastal geography. Hydrographic offices with an interest in the accurate representation of current geographical facts (according to their own standards) and a responsibility for navigational safety may be bound to record and report such changes. The relationship between the State and its hydrographic authority is not one of agency; the hydrographic authority is usually an organ of the State. As Anzilotti explained in 1912, '[t]here is no distinction between organ and State: there are not two different subjects, one of which acts for the other; there is one single subject, the State, which declares its intent and acts through its own organs'.[1] This does not alter the fact that the State, acting directly or through this organ, is the authoritative agent of change as far as the location of maritime limits is concerned. Where it has established lawful and effective maritime limits, the coastal State is not legally required to redraw them in response to subsequent geographical change or the revision of

[1] D Anzilotti, *Corso di diritto internazionale*, vol 1 (Athenaeum, 1912), 206, translation in AP Sereni, 'Agency in International Law' (1940) 34 *AJIL* 638, 639.

existing charts to record such change.[2] It may nevertheless *elect* to redraw its maritime limits (with the exception of the limits of the continental shelf) on the basis of a range of considerations, which are not restricted by law (though the construction of any new baselines and limits remains governed by law). These considerations may legitimately include an interest in reconfiguring baselines and zonal limits to encompass additional resources or extend the total maritime area under national jurisdiction.

The coastal State may take advantage of geographical change admitting the seaward extension of jurisdiction (e.g. the accretion or reclamation of land) to bring resources beyond former limits—for example, mineral deposits or fisheries—under national jurisdiction. In most cases, the advantage will follow the relocation of the limits of the exclusive economic zone (EEZ) rather than the territorial sea. The sovereign rights in which coastal States are most interested run across both zones and relocating the limits of the territorial sea further seaward will not facilitate access to new resources where these are already the subject of sovereign rights in the EEZ. As the coastal State is not entitled to redraw the limits of the continental shelf once established, it will exceptionally be prevented from taking advantage of change affecting either the coast or submarine features by reference to which the continental shelf is unilaterally delimited. It may be recalled, however, that the coastal State's jurisdiction in the EEZ includes sovereign rights to explore and exploit resources of the seabed and its subsoil, as well as superjacent waters.[3]

The overall extent of the coastal State's jurisdiction may be increased by the expansion of internal waters. In the event of coastal accretion or the emergence of a geographical feature suitable for use as a basepoint, limits must still be located at or within the distance from this point specified by law. However, the application of the arcs of circles method (which requires that limits are to be measured from the nearest point rather than all points on the baseline) may result in more sea space being included within the jurisdiction of the coastal State. If a low-tide elevation (LTE) emerges in the territorial sea as measured from the mainland or an island, the coastal State may use that feature as a basepoint to measure the limits of the existing territorial sea, which will extend its total area.[4]

A new geographical feature generating entitlement to some or all of the recognized maritime zones may extend the total sea area under national jurisdiction.

[2] This remains true where maritime limits are either or both established and periodically revised by a hydrographic body as an organ of the State. A State may choose to define its maritime limits by reference to the most current official charts produced by such a body, though it is not legally required to do so. The State may also define its maritime limits in this way where the hydrographic body is not its organ or agent—the official status of limits established by that body following from the State's decision to treat them as such.

[3] United Nations Convention on the Law of the Sea (UNCLOS) Art 56(1)(a).

[4] UNCLOS Art 13. Unless the new LTE is located at the outer edge of the territorial sea of the mainland or an island, this will not usually push the existing limits of that zone seaward by a full 12 nautical miles (M).

The coastal State will be entitled to the full complement of maritime zones in respect of a newly emerged island meeting the conditions in Article 121 of the United Nations Convention on the Law of the Sea (UNCLOS). Notably, the prohibition on revision of the limits of the shelf once established should not prevent a State from claiming a *new* entitlement to a continental shelf in respect of a new island or where an existing island becomes newly 'capable of sustaining human habitation or economic life of its own'. As no right to a continental shelf in respect of such a feature previously existed, no limits will yet have been permanently established.[5]

It is clear that a coastal State may derive certain advantages from the revision of maritime limits in response to certain types of geographical change. It is important to recognize that the law, which does not *require* that a coastal State redraw its maritime limits in response to coastal change, equally does not restrict its right to do so—there is no legal basis for objecting to a State taking advantage of geographical change in this way.

New claims to entitlement and the revision of maritime limits remain subject to the conditions specified by the law. As argued in Chapter 9, this does not mean that the relevant rules and principles condition entitlement to maritime space or the lawfulness of maritime limits on a continuing basis. There is no legal basis for objecting to maritime limits on the grounds that the geographical circumstances by reference to which they were constructed have since changed. Delimitation will ordinarily be based on geographical circumstances in existing charts or otherwise shown to obtain at the time. As Chapter 8 explains, this does not mean that established limits will be open to challenge on the grounds that relevant facts obtaining at the time of their construction were unknown or inaccurate. Nor does it mean that a State wishing to take advantage of geographical change in a particular area by redrawing some baselines and zonal limits is legally obliged to adjust all established baselines and limits to accord with the geographical circumstances obtaining at that time. The requirements relating to the construction of maritime limits apply if, when, and where the State elects to revise established limits. There is nothing in the existing law to suggest that a State could not choose to redraw baselines and zonal limits along some parts of its coast but not others.

The proposition that States may both (a) benefit from geographical change by making new claims to maritime space and revising established limits where the change is advantageous (e.g. accretion) and (b) avoid the loss of maritime space or retreat of maritime limits where the change is disadvantageous (e.g. erosion and inundation) directly challenges one of the most basic assumptions at work in the ambulatory thesis. It is often taken as given that the ability of the coastal State to benefit from the revision of its maritime limits where natural and in some cases artificial or

[5] It is not obvious that the time limit on submissions to the Commission on the Limits of the Continental Shelf (CLCS) should preclude the establishment of the limits of the shelf beyond 200M in the case of a newly emerged island.

man-made change results in the seaward extension of its coast means that it should also bear any losses consequent upon geographical change. Thus the International Law Association's Baselines Committee (ILA-BC) has taken the view that 'it follows that if the legal baseline changes with human-induced expansions of the actual low-water line to seaward, then it must also change with contractions of the actual low-water line to landward'.[6] This entails a serious misunderstanding of the law as it applies to all types of geographical change (including both accretion and erosion) and some types of man-made coastal change.

The ILA-BC has discussed the right of the coastal State to extend its maritime jurisdiction in the event of a 'territorial gain' in connection with man-made changes to the coast in particular.[7] While the law of the sea expressly provides that artificial islands and other offshore installations and structures will not generate entitlement to maritime space,[8] it provides that permanent harbour works shall be treated as part of the coast.[9] There is also some evidence of State practice supporting the location of baselines at the outer edge of reclaimed land extending the natural coast.[10]

Significantly, this does not mean that, as the ILA-BC put it, 'the legal baseline changes with human-induced expansions of the actual low-water line to seaward'.[11] Article 11 provides only that 'permanent harbour works which form an integral part of the harbour system' will be treated as part of the coast 'for the purpose of delimiting the territorial sea'. This means that the coastal State may elect to redraw its baseline to include new harbour works, or, in other words, that 'harbour works are regarded as forming part of the coast' at the time the State establishes or chooses to revise its maritime limits. Similarly, State practice suggests that a coastal State *may* establish baselines at the outer edge of reclaimed land. It does not indicate that baselines either shift automatically or *must* be revised to take reclaimed land into account.

As has been argued at length in this book, there is no foundation in treaty law or custom for a legal obligation to adjust established maritime limits in response to geographical change. This is also true where the change in question is man-made. The coastal State is rather entitled to make such adjustments unless this is specifically prohibited. It is specifically prohibited in the case of the limits of the shelf and the construction of artificial islands and other man-made features offshore. The State may otherwise take advantage of geographical change where this serves

[6] ILA-BC, *Final Report*, 28.

[7] Ibid, 25–8.

[8] UNCLOS Art 60(5), (8). Safety zones may be established.

[9] UNCLOS Art 11.

[10] ILA-BC, *Final Report*, 28; C Carleton, 'Problems Relating to Non-natural and Man-made Basepoints under UNCLOS' in Symmons (ed), *Selected Contemporary Issues in the Law of the Sea* (Martinus Nijhoff, 2011) 31, 52–5.

[11] ILA-BC, *Final Report*, 28.

its interests. It remains at liberty to retain its established maritime limits notwithstanding such change.

There is nothing illogical or contrary to common sense in this state of affairs. As argued in Chapter 9, there is no generally applicable reason why the conditions governing the creation of a right or regime should also govern its continuing existence. Whether or not these conditions vary depends upon the law in the particular case. Thus the fact that territory may be acquired by natural accretion does not mean that the erosion or submergence of land results in a loss of territory. As discussed, there are good reasons—or at least reasons consistent with international law more broadly—why the legal conditions in which territory may be lost require more than the attrition or reversal of the conditions in which territory may be gained. A concern to ensure the stability of territorial situations in the interests of international order and peace is foremost among them. The related concern to ensure the stability of boundaries of international significance helps to explain why the law of the sea does not provide for maritime limits that are continually contingent upon the notoriously variable geography of the coast and other maritime features.

III. Opting for Ambulatory Limits

The decision to redraw maritime limits may be taken on a case-by-case basis or the coastal State may adopt a general policy of revising its limits based on the most recent charts.[12] A State may even adopt a policy of revising limits based upon the most recent geographical information available or particular sources of it, such as Notices to Mariners. The adoption of policies of this type may in certain circumstances amount to the unilateral assumption of an obligation to revise maritime limits in the specified circumstances that is enforceable by other States.[13] Depending on the character of the obligation assumed, it may even result in new charts or other evidence of changed geographical circumstances being directly opposable to the coastal State. It is important to be clear, however, that the source of these legal effects is the unilateral act of the coastal State, which binds that State alone. The possibility that specific obligations may follow from unilateral acts in this context does not alter the fact that there is no general obligation to revise established maritime limits as charts are updated or evidence of subsequent geographical change becomes available.

The bulk of State practice is consistent with the conclusion that maritime limits are not ambulatory. This finding does not depend upon evidence that a certain

[12] See note 2.

[13] ILC, 'Guiding Principles Applicable to Unilateral Declarations of States' (2006), UN Doc A/61/10, 370–6; *Nuclear Tests (Australia v France)* (1974), 267; *Nuclear Tests (NZ v France)* (1974), 473.

number of States do not update their limits in the event of geographical change, as compared with the number that do. Practice in this regard is mixed, and this is consistent with the conclusion that the decision to redraw maritime limits in response to subsequent geographical change is discretionary. What matters is the absence of an official view on the part of States that retaining existing limits notwithstanding geographical change is illegitimate or requires special justification,[14] or that revision in response to geographical change is required under international law.

There are two States whose practice represents an exception to this general state of affairs. The United States treats its baselines and the zonal limits measured from them as 'ambulatory and subject to revision based on accretion or erosion of the charted low water line'.[15] The Netherlands also considers its normal baseline, defined as the '0-metre depth [line] ... published in the official nautical charts of the Hydrographic Service', to 'change when a new 0-metre depth line appears in the nautical charts'.[16] It adjusts the zonal limits measured from this line accordingly.[17] Notably, both States take the *normal* baseline in particular to be ambulatory, rather than baselines generally. While the United States does not use straight baselines as a matter of principle (or policy),[18] the Netherlands does not consider straight baselines to be ambulatory.[19] It does not rely on UNCLOS Article 7(2) in this regard but appears to take straight baselines generally to be fixed upon establishment.

While both States understand the location of their maritime limits to change as the coast changes, neither considers this an automatic process. In the United States, an interagency baseline committee is responsible for reviewing and approving the limits indicated on official charts. New editions of those charts are considered to supersede the previous 'official limits'.[20] The Dutch Hydrographic Service updates maritime limits several times a year on the basis of its own new and updated charts, with amendments publicized in Notices to Mariners, on its website, and through a mailing list.[21]

[14] If a State relies expressly on UNCLOS Article 7(2) in this regard, it may be relying on the express indication in that provision that baselines need not be adjusted even if geographical change is significant. Further evidence would be required to establish that the State considers the provision an exception to a general rule requiring the adjustment of baselines to reflect geographical change.

[15] US Office of Coast Survey, 'U.S. Maritime Limits and Boundaries', <http://www.nauticalcharts.noaa.gov/csdl/mbound.htm> accessed 11 September 2013.

[16] Royal Netherlands Navy, Hydrographic Service, 'Maritime Zones and Boundaries', <https://english.defensie.nl/topics/hydrography/maritime-zones-and-boundaries> accessed 10 January 2015.

[17] Ibid.

[18] Nor are the US states permitted to use straight baselines for the purposes of delimiting their maritime entitlements under domestic law—the choice 'rests with the Federal Government' given that its exercise may entail the extension of national jurisdiction: *US v California* (1965), 168.

[19] Royal Netherlands Navy, Hydrographic Service, 'Maritime Zones and Boundaries', <https://english.defensie.nl/topics/hydrography/maritime-zones-and-boundaries> accessed 10 January 2015.

[20] See US Office of Coast Survey, 'U.S. Maritime Limits and Boundaries'; NOAA, *US Coast Pilot*, vol 3 (45th edn, US GPO, 2012), 32.

[21] See Royal Netherlands Navy, Hydrographic Service, 'Maritime Zones and Boundaries', <https://english.defensie.nl/topics/hydrography/maritime-zones-and-boundaries> accessed 10 January 2015.

The practice of the United States and the Netherlands in this regard is consistent with the right of all coastal States to revise established maritime limits (with the exception of the limits of the shelf). Yet it is evident that neither State considers such revision to be optional. Rather, both States understand accretion and erosion to *legally require* the adjustment of established maritime limits. Moreover, they appear to understand the source of this legal obligation to be the generally applicable law relating to maritime limits. This distinguishes their practice from a case of unilateral action giving rise to specific obligations. Here, the conduct of each State expresses an understanding that they are bound by the law relating to maritime limits generally rather than manifesting a will to be bound by a unilateral act.[22]

There is no evidence that the understanding of the law that underpins the practice of the United States and the Netherlands is shared by States generally. For the practice of these two States to have a broader significance, it must be shown that other States parties to the law of the sea treaties agree with the interpretation of the law upon which this practice is based.[23]

While the Netherlands is party to both the 1958 Geneva Conventions on the Law of the Sea and UNCLOS, the United States is not a party to the latter instrument. It remains bound by the 1958 Conventions and the customary law of the sea, including those parts of UNCLOS with customary status.[24] As a matter of practice, the United States appears to consider itself bound by the rules and principles identified in UNCLOS as governing unilateral delimitation.[25] To the extent that these

[22] On unilateral acts see ILC, 'Conclusions Relating to Unilateral Acts of States', UN Doc A/CN.4/L.703, 20 July 2006.

[23] VCLT Art 31(3) (a), (b).

[24] UNCLOS has both codified and contributed to the development of customary international law. See T Treves, 'The Development of the Law of the Sea since the Adoption of UNCLOS', paper given at the FNI Conference, 'The World Ocean in Globalization: Challenges for Marine Regions', Oslo, 21–23 August 2008, 13.

[25] The US Office of Coast Survey considers the baselines provisions in UNCLOS to be 'substantively the same as those under the 1958 Convention' (<https://web.archive.org/web/20131012232558/http://www.nauticalcharts.noaa.gov/staff/law_of_sea.html> accessed 12 September 2013), although technically the 1958 TSC will apply to the extent of any inconsistency unless the relevant part of UNCLOS can be considered custom. The outer limits of US maritime zones are located consistently with UNCLOS on the basis of measurements of distance from the low-water line and closing lines across bays and rivers: see US Office of Coast Survey, 'U.S. Maritime Limits and Boundaries'. Since 2001, a government task force has been collecting and analysing data in support of the US claim to an extended continental shelf area: US State Department, 'Defining the Limits of the U.S. Continental Shelf' <https://2001-2009.state.gov/g/oes/continentalshelf//index.htm> accessed 14 August 2011. It is not entirely clear whether this information must or indeed can be submitted to the CLCS pursuant to UNCLOS Art 76(8) unless the United States accedes to the Convention: cf the reading of Annex II, Art 4 by Oude Elferink (A Oude Elferink, 'The Commission on the Limits of the Continental Shelf', MPEPIL Online, accessed 28 February 2018) with arguments advanced by McDorman (T McDorman, 'The Entry into Force of the 1982 Convention and the Article 76 Outer Continental Shelf Regime' (1995) 10 *IJMCL* 165, 179–85; McDorman, 'The Role of the Commission on the Limits of the Continental Shelf', 303–4, fn 11) and, more recently, Baumert (Baumert, 'The Outer Limits of the Continental Shelf', 861–9). While States parties may have a general interest in encouraging US respect of the treaty regime despite its non-accession, it may be felt that a non-party should not benefit from the legitimizing effect of a CLCS recommendation. At the same time, it may be in the best interests of all States that the limits of non-parties are subject to this process, which operates to both constrain and bestow certainty on the limits of the shelf as the limits of the Area.

depart from the provisions of the 1958 Conventions, this suggests that the United States considers them custom.

The practice of the United States cannot be taken as evidence of 'the agreement of the parties regarding [the] interpretation' of UNCLOS, though it may be taken into account in an assessment of whether any such agreement regarding the interpretation of the 1958 Conventions has been established between the States parties.[26] The practice of the Netherlands with respect to its maritime limits may be considered an application of UNCLOS as interpreted by that State. The practice of both States may also contribute to the development of customary international law, though in this regard it is necessary to differentiate between acts understood by the State concerned to implement a treaty obligation and acts understood to (also or otherwise) be required by custom.[27] In general, practice bearing on the identification or development of customary law will be difficult to identify given the wide participation of States in UNCLOS and the absence of clear statements that a particular rule is considered to have both conventional and customary status. The Netherlands refers directly to UNCLOS as the governing instrument in connection with the establishment and revision of maritime limits.[28] There is no evidence that it considers these rules (as it understands them) to have customary status. As noted above, the United States does seem to consider these rules to have customary status.

The practice of the United States and the Netherlands has not been supported by parallel practice or responses on the part of other States sufficient to establish that the parties to the law of the sea treaties agree to an interpretation supporting the theory of ambulatory maritime limits.[29] Nor is there a general practice accepted as law that might evidence a customary rule to this effect. Indeed, there is even a disjunction between the practice of the United States and that of the Netherlands. While both States understand international law to require the adjustment of baselines in response to coastal change, the United States treats this as a rule of customary law while the Netherlands considers it an obligation under treaty law. The legal significance of their practice thus varies. This disjunction is unaltered by the fact that the United States understands the treaty law to reflect custom. It would have to be shown that the Netherlands also took this view for the practice of the two States to converge (i.e. as evidence of a customary rule requiring the revision of baselines in response to coastal change).

As far as the practice of other States is concerned, it would have to be demonstrated that (a) States parties to the law of the sea treaties or coastal States

[26] VCLT Art 31(3)(b).

[27] See ILC, 'Draft Conclusions on Identification of Customary International Law, with Commentaries' (2018), UN Doc A/73/10, 139.

[28] See Royal Netherlands Navy, Hydrographic Service, 'Maritime Zones and Boundaries', <https://english.defensie.nl/topics/hydrography/maritime-zones-and-boundaries> accessed 10 January 2015.

[29] VCLT Art 31(3)(a)(b).

generally revise their maritime limits in the event of geographical change, or that (b) States with interests materially affected by the practice of the United States and the Netherlands in revising baselines in this manner acquiesce in that practice.[30] Crucially, it would also have to be demonstrated that States which (a) revise their maritime limits in the event of geographical change or (b) acquiesce in the American and Dutch practice in this regard *act on the basis of a belief that such revision is legally required.* There is no evidence that this is the case. Revising limits or respecting limits that are revised in response to geographical change is also consistent with the understanding that such revision is permitted not required.

It is worth noting that a policy of periodically reviewing maritime limits at specified intervals is one way of implementing the coastal State's right to revise maritime limits other than those delimiting the shelf. Without further evidence, it cannot be taken to imply a belief that revision is required because the coast may have changed in the interim. Finland (party to both the Convention on the Territorial Sea and Contiguous Zone (TSC) and UNCLOS) provides an interesting example in this regard. Its 1956 Act on the Delimitation of Territorial Waters indicated that the specified basepoints would be 'corrected at intervals of thirty years'.[31] The article in which this clause appears suggests that 'correction' was understood to entail a reapplication of the criteria by reference to which those basepoints had been 'chosen':

> (1) that they are above sea-level more than one half day per year, on the average, at low-water levels during the ten-year period preceding the year when this law takes effect; (2) that their distance from one another is at most twice the width of the marginal sea; and (3) that the inner territorial waters will be as extensive as possible.[32]

In 1995, Finland not only revised its baselines but amended the criteria for their construction described in the 1956 Act, providing that 'the base points ... shall be selected from among points located above the mean water level at a certain epoch, designated on the basis of long-term water level measurements' and that '[e]ven points below the said level may be used ... provided that they are at least periodically within sight and a lighthouse or other installation permanently above the sea level has been built on them'.[33] The text was also adjusted to indicate that '[t]he base points and the location of the landward limits of the internal waters ... shall be *reviewed* every thirty years'.[34]

[30] Not all adjustments of maritime limits will materially affect the interests of other States to a degree requiring a response.
[31] See Finland, Territorial Waters Delimitation Act (1956) Art 4(3).
[32] Ibid.
[33] Finland, Territorial Waters Delimitation Act (1956) as amended.
[34] Ibid.

It is possible that the original legislation anticipated the specification of 'the width of the marginal sea' in the treaty law (that is, a legal development that might warrant the 'correction' of basepoints more than twice the specified distance apart or allow their situation at a greater distance from one another if the breadth of the territorial sea were extended).[35] Yet what makes the Finnish example particularly interesting is that both the original and amended legislation seem to anticipate that the thirty-year review will entail the adjustment of baselines to take geographical change into account. At the same time, the very fact that a thirty-year interval is specified suggests that the State does not consider geographical change in the interim to bring established maritime limits into question. There is nothing to suggest that the review at thirty years was thought to be required by international law (though the legislation may create such a requirement as a matter of domestic law). Rather, it appears that the Act provides for the periodic revision of basepoints to ensure the regular realization of the advantages (in terms of the seaward extension of maritime space) following from the land uplift that continually forms new skerries on the Finnish coast (extending Finnish land by about 10km^2 per year).[36] Far from reflecting a belief that international law requires the revision of baselines in the event of geographical change, the Act can be understood as an assertion of the right of the coastal State to retain established baselines (e.g. for thirty years) and decide if and when it will revise them.

Other States may revise their baselines more regularly, and in some cases, there are indications that this is thought to be required by law in order to take coastal change into account. The website of Geoscience Australia, for instance, refers to the fact that Australia's territorial sea baseline (TSB) which was 'originally determined in the early 1970s based on small scale mapping supported by some aerial photography' is now based on data that has been 'completely revised using the most appropriate and current source information available, such as State mapping data, hydrographic charts and satellite imagery'.[37] It also notes that while this baseline is 'generally consistent with hydrographic charts', '[p]hysical changes to the coast and improved methods of locating the LAT line [taken as the normal baseline] in the future may lead to differences between the TSB and the information depicted

[35] Finland at the time claimed a 4M territorial sea and would have been aware that the breadth of the territorial sea would be debated at the 1958 Law of the Sea Conference (LOSC), with some States supporting a narrower 3M territorial sea and others its extension up to 12M: see ILC Ybk 1956/II, 265–6. To the extent that this is 'anticipated' by the Finnish Act, the intention may have been to prevent agreement upon a 3M limit affecting the established basepoints for another thirty years—though in fact domestic legislation could not have prevented a new international rule to this effect applying to Finland as a party to the TSC. It is notable that the 1956 Act is not worded in a way to prevent the earlier adjustment of baselines if this were considered advantageous (for instance, if a 12M territorial sea were approved and a benefit could be obtained by locating basepoints more than 8M apart).

[36] M Koskenniemi, M Lehto, 'Finland and the Law of the Sea' in Treves and Pineschi (eds), *The Law of the Sea: The European Union and its Member States* (Martinus Nijhoff, 1997) 127, 129.

[37] Geoscience Australia, 'Computing Australia's Maritime Boundaries', <http://www.ga.gov.au/scientific-topics/marine/jurisdiction/maritime-boundaries> accessed 28 March 2016.

on charts in certain areas'.[38] Geoscience Australia maintains a database indicating Australia's maritime limits, the abstract for which states that

> Geoscience Australia is committed to the maintenance of the maritime boundaries data to ensure it reflects the changing nature of Australia's coastline and hence the various maritime zone limits. The data reflects the location of the coastline within the constraints of available source material at the time of production.[39]

The digital representation of Australia's maritime limits is understood to be consistent with both UNCLOS and the domestic Seas and Submerged Lands Act (SSLA) (1973), and it is expressly noted that 'in the event of an inconsistency between maritime boundaries data and the baselines and limits under the legislation, the latter prevails'.[40] Yet while neither UNCLOS nor the domestic legislation (including Proclamations under the Act[41]) specify that the normal baseline is ambulatory, Geoscience Australia adjusts its location (and the limits measured from it) as new data becomes available regarding the current position of the LAT line. This suggests a belief that such adjustment is required by law, though in the circumstances this remains deniable by the State concerned.

The Australian example differs from that of the United States and the Netherlands in that the relevant belief regarding what the law requires is not expressly stated. This does not mean that inferences cannot be drawn. Yet the fact that the State could plausibly claim that it adjusts its baselines because it is entitled, not required, to do so underscores the ambiguity of the evidence on which any inference regarding its beliefs is based. This ambiguity must be taken into account in an assessment of whether the relevant practice can bear upon the interpretation of the treaty law. Under VCLT Article 31(3), subsequent agreements and subsequent practice matter to the extent that they are 'objective evidence of the understanding of the parties as to the meaning of the treaty'.[42] The ILC has also emphasized that '[t]he weight of a subsequent agreement or subsequent practice as a means of interpretation under article 31, paragraph 3, depends, *inter alia*, on its clarity and specificity'.[43]

Significantly, even if it is reasonable to conclude that Australia's revision of its baselines in response to geographical change is understood by that State to be required by UNCLOS (by way of the domestic SSLA), it cannot be concluded this is

38 Ibid.

39 Geoscience Australia, 'Seas and Submerged Lands Act 1973 – Australian Maritime Boundaries 2014a – Geodatabase', <http://dx.doi.org/10.4225/25/5539DFE87D895> accessed 12 October 2016.

40 Geoscience Australia, 'Australian Ocean Governance and Relevant Legislation', <http://www.ga.gov.au/scientific-topics/marine/jurisdiction/amsis/australian-ocean-governance-and-relevant-legislation> accessed 12 October 2016.

41 SSL (TSB) Proclamation (2016, previous 2006).

42 ILC, 'Draft Conclusions on Subsequent Agreements and Subsequent Practice' (2018), Conclusion 3.

43 Ibid, Conclusion 9.

an interpretation on which States parties to UNCLOS agree. There are simply too few instances of States applying the treaty law in a manner that clearly reflects an understanding that the adjustment of maritime limits is required in the event of coastal change. This is also true where State practice might evidence a rule of customary law or contribute to its development (i.e. where it is the practice of a non-party or where the State party clearly indicates that it considers the rule to have customary as well as conventional status). It is doubtful whether the Australian charting practices can be considered to contribute to the development of a customary law at all, as they are clearly understood by the relevant authorities to give effect to domestic legislation and treaty law.[44]

A review of State practice suggests that only the United States and the Netherlands can be reliably understood to revise their maritime limits in response to coastal change because they believe the law requires this. Their implementation of this belief in practice has not given rise to circumstances in which protest would be expected (and thus acquiescence implied). Notably, neither the United States nor the Netherlands has objected to other States maintaining baselines despite geographical change affecting features of the coastline bearing upon their establishment—action that might have provoked a response. This does not mean that either State understands its own practice of revising limits in response to coastal change to be discretionary or based upon a unilaterally assumed obligation. It does, however, indicate some inconsistency in that practice further attenuating its capacity to contribute to custom[45] (particularly given the energetic US policy of protesting baselines claims it considers unlawful or 'excessive' on other grounds[46]).

There are historical and local circumstances which may explain why the Netherlands and the United States have come to understand the law relating to maritime limits differently to other States. While a full contextualization of their divergent practice is beyond the scope of the present study, several factors appear relevant. In the case of the Netherlands, the State's interest in land reclamation is significant and a concern to extend maritime jurisdiction with the land may well have been coupled with the mistaken belief that this would depend on a general rule that changes in the baseline followed changes in the coast. It is notable that the National Hydrographic Service's statement on 'changes in maritime zones' expressly illustrates the alleged rule that 'the baseline, and thus the zones, change when a new 0-metre depth line appears in the nautical charts' with the example of 'the construction of Maasvlakte 2 [which] pushed the Dutch coastline westward',

44 See ILC, 'Draft Conclusions on Identification of Customary International Law'.

45 On the requirement that the relevant practice must be both general and consistent, see ibid, Conclusion 8 and commentary, 135–8.

46 US DOS, 'United States Responses to Excessive Maritime Claims'; US DoD, *Maritime Claims Reference Manual* (2014), <https://www.jag.navy.mil/organization/code_10_mcrm.htm>; JA Roach, RW Smith, *United States Responses to Excessive Maritime Claims* (2nd edn., Martinus Nijhoff, 1996); Roach and Smith, *Excessive Maritime Claims*.

allowing the Netherlands to '[gain] 55 square kilometres of territorial sea'.[47] As argued above, the law in fact supports the right of coastal States to revise baselines to take land reclamation into account without requiring such adjustment in the event of any and all changes to the coast, whether natural or man-made.

The United States' understanding of the ambulatory character of maritime limits has been influenced by the 'tidelands' litigation concerning boundaries between state and federal jurisdiction over 'submerged lands'. Notably, the US Supreme Court's treatment of river boundaries between constituent states also seems to have influenced its treatment of the question of state-federal boundaries in the sea.

In litigation following the conclusion of the Submerged Lands Act (SLA) in 1953, the US Supreme Court held that the 'coast line' taken as the starting point for measuring the '3 geographical miles' (or in certain circumstances, up to 3 marine leagues[48]) of submerged lands granted to the states was ambulatory.[49] This was considered to follow from the finding in *US v California* (1965) that the baselines provisions of the TSC should control the meaning of 'coastline' defined in the SLA as 'the line of ordinary low water along that portion of the coast which is in direct contact with the open sea and the line marking the seaward limit of inland waters'.[50] In the *Texas Boundary Case* (1969) (and subsequently the *Louisiana Boundary Case* (1969)), the Supreme Court asserted that the TSC provides for an ambulatory normal baseline—'coastline' under the SLA therefore meaning 'the modern, ambulatory coastline'.[51] There is no support for this interpretation of the TSC in *US v California* (1965). Two aspects of this decision may nevertheless have encouraged the subsequent attribution of an ambulatory character—in the sense of conditionality upon geographical change—to the baseline.

In *US v California*, California had expressly argued that baselines are 'ambulatory' but used this term to refer to the possibility of change in the legal definition of the baseline over time rather than the movement of the baseline with the coast. California suggested that any such changes permitting the seawards expansion of 'inland waters' would also extend the state's entitlement to submerged lands—the latter being measured from the outer limit of inland waters.[52] The Supreme Court rejected this 'open ended view of the Act' on the grounds that inter alia '[a]llowing

[47] See Royal Netherlands Navy, Hydrographic Service, 'Maritime Zones and Boundaries', <https://english.defensie.nl/topics/hydrography/maritime-zones-and-boundaries> accessed 10 January 2015.

[48] Rights to the seabed extend 'to the boundary line of each such State where in any case such boundary as it existed at the time such State became a member of the Union, or as heretofore approved by Congress, extends seaward (or into the Gulf of Mexico) beyond three geographical miles': (2002) 43 USC §1301. In the case of states claiming rights to submerged lands either up to 3M or a historic boundary within this distance (an alternative to the 3 geographical miles guaranteed to all states regardless of their historical maritime claims), the 3M will be measured from the 'boundaries of the State' (including its coastline) as it existed at the time of entry into the Union: *US v Louisiana* (1967), 159–60.

[49] *Texas Boundary Case* (1969), 4–5; *Louisiana Boundary Case* (1969), 32–4.

[50] *US v California* (1965), 164–5.

[51] *Texas Boundary Case* (1969), 4–5; *Louisiana Boundary Case* (1969), 32–4.

[52] *US v California* (1965), 166.

future shifts of international understanding respecting inland waters to alter the extent of the [SLA] grant would substantially undercut the definiteness of expectation which should attend it.'[53]

Though the Court rejected California's claim that the SLA provided for baselines that were 'ambulatory' in this particular sense, the same term was picked up in the *Texas Boundary Case* (1969) where it was associated with geographical rather than legal change.[54] The 1969 decision also identified the concept with an obligation rather than a right to adjust established baselines. This may have been encouraged by the observation in *US v California* (1965) that 'artificial accretions' (i.e. reclaimed land), like natural accretions, become part of a State's territory.[55] Yet it does not follow that baselines must be ambulatory. Indeed, the Court did not draw this conclusion in 1965. In its judgment, a connection was drawn between the fact that territory may be acquired by natural accretion or land reclamation and the right to measure maritime limits from the outer edge of harbour works recognized in TSC Article 8. The supplemental decree following the 1965 decision provided that

> the coastline is to be taken as heretofore or hereafter modified by natural or artificial means, and includes the outermost permanent harbor works that form an integral part of the harbor system within the meaning of Article 8 of the TSC.[56]

This definition of the coastline 'as ... modified by natural or artificial means' was emphasized in the *Texas Boundary Case*, where it was taken to confirm the ambulatory character of baselines under the TSC and thus the SLA.[57] Yet the 1965 decision and 1966 decree were concerned with the right to extend entitlement to submerged lands where the coast is extended by natural or artificial means. The point was that (a) artificial and natural additions to a coast constitute part of the territory, and (b) maritime limits and so too limits under the SLA may be measured from the 'coastline' of newly accreted or reclaimed land and 'the outermost permanent harbor works that form an integral part of the harbor system'.[58]

The right to measure maritime limits from new land or harbour works is clearly not the same thing as an obligation to adjust the baseline in response to natural or artificial coastal change. There appears to be no legal basis for the Supreme Court's assumption of the latter by reference to the former in the *Texas Boundary Case*.

53 Ibid.

54 The different usage in *US v California* (1965) was not discussed.

55 See *US v California* (1965), 166–7.

56 *US v California* (1966), 449.

57 *Texas Boundary Case* (1969), 5.

58 The Supreme Court has subsequently interpreted this rather narrowly to mean 'structures erected ... for protective purposes, or for enclosing sea areas adjacent to the coast to provide anchorage and shelter': *Louisiana Boundary Case* (1969), 37, fn 42; see also *US v California* (1980), 7. In response to the Federal Government's concern that the states may use artificial extensions of the coast to push their entitlement seaward, the Supreme Court has pointed out that constructions in or over navigable waters must be approved by the Federal Government, which may condition its approval on the baseline for measuring submerged lands remaining fixed: *US v California* (1965), 176; *US v Alaska* (1992), 585.

The co-option of the notion of 'ambulatory baselines' to describe conditionality upon coastal change may have been encouraged by the common characterization of rivers such as the Mississippi as ambulatory and the Supreme Court's familiarity with the accretion/avulsion distinction, which it had held to apply to river boundaries between the federation's constituent states.[59] The positive law offers little support for the conclusion that baselines must be ambulatory. Indeed, the terms of the 1953 SLA suggested that the baseline for measuring State jurisdiction over submerged lands was fixed. The definition of 'lands beneath navigable waters' specified that this includes lands below non-tidal waters 'up to the ordinary high water mark as heretofore or hereafter modified by accretion, erosion, and reliction'.[60] The reference to the low-water line and the outer limit of inland waters was not similarly qualified.[61] It was the Supreme Court that effectively read the same terms in.

In 1986, an amendment to the SLA specified that 'any boundary between a State and the United States under this Act ... which has been or is hereafter fixed by coordinates under a final decree of the United States Supreme Court shall remain immobilized at the coordinates provided under such decree and shall not be ambulatory'.[62] Such boundaries are excepted from the rule that state jurisdiction over the seabed should not extend beyond either 3 geographical miles or 3M (as applicable), covering the possibility that coastal erosion may leave a fixed boundary beyond this distance. This amendment was prompted by the 'inconvenience of an ambulatory coastline' acknowledged in the *Louisiana Boundary Case* (1969). In that case, the Court had suggested the 'resolution of the problems through appropriate legislation or agreement between the parties', which 'might, for example, freeze the coastline as of an agreed-upon date.'[63] It is the formulation of the problem that accounts for this solution.

Louisiana had argued that the SLA would admit different definitions of the 'inland water line' for different states, proposing that the line fixed by the Coast Guard from time to time for the purposes of regulating navigation should be used in Louisiana given the particular vulnerability of its coast to change due to the shifting Mississippi and extreme storms in the Gulf.[64] The Court preferred the federal government's argument that the definitions in the TSC applied for the purposes of

[59] *Texas Boundary Case* (1969), 4–5; *Louisiana Boundary Case* (1969), 32–4. There is an interesting relationship between US Supreme Court's approach to interstate river boundaries and the history of the Chamizal dispute. For present purposes, it is sufficient to note that the domestic decisions lend support to the conclusion that the United States considers the accretion/avulsion distinction a rule of international law. This position, which has not called for or resulted in any reactive practice by States outside the US–Mexico boundary dispute, does not alter the conclusions drawn in Chapter 6.

[60] SLA (1953); (2002) 43 USC §1301(a).

[61] (2002) 43 USC §1301(c).

[62] Outer Continental Shelf Lands Act Amendments (1986), Tit. VIII, § 8005; see SLA (1953); (2002) 43 USC §1301(b)(2).

[63] *Louisiana Boundary Case* (1969), 18–19, 34.

[64] Ibid, 32–3.

the SLA in all states.[65] It considered 'the desirability of "a single coastline for both the administration of the [SLA] and the conduct of our future international relations"' to be a 'countervailing policy consideration' that might outweigh 'the policy in favor of a certain and stable coastline, strong as it is'.[66]

This apparent policy conflict points to the error in the Supreme Court's understanding of what the international law of the sea requires. The TSC already provided for baselines that were 'certain and stable' insofar as they need not (as a matter of obligation) though could (as an option) be adjusted in response to coastal change. It would be consistent with this international regime to treat baselines under the SLA as fixed or, indeed, to allow the use of a fixed line in Louisiana and a regularly adjusted line in other states. A misunderstanding of the position in international law led first to a judicial interpretation of domestic law producing the 'problem' of ambulatory baselines followed by a revision of that domestic legislation to resolve the problem by fixing state–federal boundaries by decree.

The US jurisprudence distorts rather than illuminates international law as it relates to maritime limits. It is also questionable whether the approach taken in the US tidelands cases can contribute to international law in this area. In view of the consistency of these domestic judicial decisions with the practice of other branches of government in the United States, it is reasonable to treat them as evidence of the practice of that State capable of contributing to custom.[67] Still, at least one member of the ILA-BC, Sienho Yee, had doubts about the relevance of this case law to a study of baselines under international law.[68] As he observed, '[t]he complicated dynamics of the relationship between the United States and its component states cast doubt on the value of the U.S. practice in dealing with federal-state relations as practice within the meaning of Article 38(1)(b) of the ICJ Statute.'[69] Even if there is at times considerable scope for analogical reasoning between international law as it relates to States and the domestic law of federal States as it relates to their constituent units, the division of title to submerged lands between the states and the federal government in the United States has a complicated history that must be taken into account.

Though the US Supreme Court has drawn on international law in connection with questions concerning maritime limits and boundaries, its analysis has been shaped by the history of state–federal relations in the United States as well as the particular arguments of the parties in contentious cases and the facts bearing upon their rights according to the particular statutory regime. Insofar as this has encouraged the conclusion that international law provides for ambulatory maritime

[65] Ibid, 33–4.
[66] Ibid, 34.
[67] See A Roberts, 'Comparative International Law? The Role of National Courts in Creating and Enforcing International Law' (2011) 60 *ICLQ* 57, 62.
[68] ILA-BC, *Final Report*, 20, fn 128.
[69] Ibid.

limits, the domestic lens seems to have produced a misinterpretation of the law of the sea. This misinterpretation has been reinforced by its reiteration in domestic jurisprudence, legislation, and policy. It now informs the US approach to the unilateral delimitation of its national waters.

In view of the foregoing, it is unsurprising that both state and federal governments in the United States have considered ambulatory limits a problem. It is equally unsurprising that the SLA has been amended to resolve this problem by allowing the limits between state and federal maritime jurisdiction to be fixed by decree.[70] As far as international law is concerned, however, there is no need to 'fix' maritime limits against change. These limits are not ambulatory—international law does not require their adjustment in response to geographical change. As discussed in Chapter 6, there are in some circumstances good reasons to agree to an ambulatory interstate boundary—for instance, where the boundary follows a river valued as a shared resource. These reasons do not apply in the case of maritime limits, which best serve their purpose when they are not contingent upon the changeable coast. This is also generally true of maritime boundaries between States, though the parties remain free to agree on an ambulatory boundary if they wish.

It is notable that no other State appears to consider its own maritime limits or those of other States to require adjustment in the event of changes to the low-water line or other geographic features by reference to which they were constructed. Some States revise their maritime limits regularly, while others rely on limits constructed many years ago. There is no evidence that these varying practices are based upon an understanding that the law requires limits to be adjusted in response to geographical change and only allows their retention where geographical circumstances remain unchanged.

In order to pre-empt their invocation as counter-examples, it is worth setting out explicitly how this conclusion holds up against two well-known but not always well-analysed instances of State practice, both featuring the UK. The first is the British abandonment of its claim to an EEZ in respect of Rockall. The second is the UK's abandonment of a proposed basepoint for the delimitation of the continental shelf with Belgium on the basis of a survey indicating that the feature concerned (Shipwash Sands) was no longer above water at low tide.[71]

The UK abandoned its claim to a 200M fishery zone in respect of Rockall, a barren island some 480 kilometres off the west coast of mainland Scotland, upon accession to UNCLOS.[72] Crucially, this was a response to what the UK considered to be a *change in the law* applying to it—the application of Article 121(3), which provides that '[r]ocks which cannot sustain human habitation or economic life of

[70] SLA (1953); (2002) 43 USC §1301(b).

[71] DH Anderson, 'Belgium-United Kingdom: Report Number 9-17' in Charney and Alexander (eds), *International Maritime Boundaries*, vol 2 (ASIL/Martinus Nijhoff, 2004) 1901, 1903–4, 1906.

[72] Hansard, HC (series 6) vol 298, col 397W (21 July 1997); Hansard, HC (series 6) vol 299, col 481W (31 July 1997).

their own shall have no [EEZ] or continental shelf.' The claim was not abandoned in response to geographical or other change altering or destroying the capacity of the island to sustain human habitation or economic life of its own. It offers no support for the conclusion that a previously established entitlement to an EEZ and continental shelf would be lost in these circumstances. What it does suggest is that the UK did not consider customary international law to preclude entitlement to the full complement of maritime zones around an island in the circumstances detailed in Article 121(3), at least not prior to 1997. Notably, the UK continues to measure its 200M EEZ from the St Kilda archipelago off the west coast of the Scottish mainland, despite the last permanent inhabitants of Hirta Island being voluntarily evacuated in 1930.[73] It has also lodged a submission claiming an extended continental shelf in the Hatton Rockall area, though its claim to entitlement to this maritime zone is not based on Rockall but the Scottish mainland and islands including the St Kilda archipelago.[74]

The second case to be considered is the UK's abandonment of a proposed basepoint on Shipwash Sands during the negotiation of a maritime boundary with Belgium. The UK is reported to have 'formally abandoned' this basepoint in response to information that it had 'been eroded by natural processes to such an extent that it no longer dried at low-water'.[75] This is in fact entirely consistent with the right of States to insist upon delimitation according to the geographical circumstances obtaining at the time and to look beyond the existing charts in this regard—the UK's move recognized Belgium's right to object to the use of Shipwash as a basepoint in these circumstances. As argued in Chapter 8, this does not mean that it is legally obligatory to look beyond the charts or ascertain the most accurate picture of the relevant geographical circumstances possible for the purposes of delimitation. Even more crucially, the case does not lend support to the idea that basepoints that have *already* been used to construct established maritime limits and boundaries may no longer be relied on due to subsequent geographical change.

The erosion of Shipwash Sands did not prompt the UK to make any changes to its established maritime limits. Britain had extended its territorial sea to 12M in 1987, but the baseline in the area was defined only in general terms as the low-water line on the mainland, islands, and LTEs within the territorial sea—the UK had not specified which features it considered LTEs.[76] The UK's response to the fact that Shipwash Sands was no longer above water at low tide in the course of negotiating an international maritime boundary was in keeping with the role that

73 National Trust for Scotland, 'St Kilda', <http://www.kilda.org.uk> accessed 7 July 2013.

74 UK Submission to CLCS (2009). Ireland and Denmark have made submissions with respect to the same area, while Iceland has indicated that it will do the same: see Ireland Submission to CLCS (2009); Denmark Partial Submission to CLCS (2009); Iceland Partial Submission to CLCS (2008).

75 See Anderson, 'Belgium-United Kingdom: Report Number 9-17', 1904.

76 Territorial Sea Act (UK) (1987) (extending the territorial sea); Territorial Waters Order in Council (UK) (1964) defining baselines (straight baselines were established in some areas, but not in the vicinity of Shipwash).

the law gives geography in the delimitation process. It does not suggest that the State would consider the erosion of a basepoint already used to establish maritime limits to legally require their revision.

Shipwash Sands has since re-emerged and, in view of its location within the territorial sea generated by the mainland, the UK is entitled to use this feature as a basepoint to measure the outer limits of this maritime zone. The boundary with Belgium in the continental shelf has been unaffected by this development—unsurprisingly given the presumption against unilateral changes to an established boundary. While the terms of an agreement or other clear evidence of the parties' intentions may serve to rebut this presumption,[77] a different amendment by Exchange of Notes between the UK and Belgium confirms its application in this case.[78]

The Shipwash example may be briefly compared to the US case concerning Dinkum Sands, which the ILA-BC cites as supporting the view that facts on the ground rather than charts are determinative of the location of maritime limits.[79] In *US v Alaska* (1997), the Supreme Court upheld the determination of the Special Master that Dinkum Sands was not an island—a characterization contested by Alaska, which sought to measure the outer limit of its submerged lands from the feature.[80]

Dinkum Sands was not within the 3-mile belt of submerged lands measured from the mainland or an island. As such, it was held (by analogy to the rule regarding LTEs in international law) that it would only generate further entitlement to submerged lands if it could be classified as an island.[81] The Special Master concluded that Dinkum Sands did not meet the TSC's definition of an island because surveys conducted between 1981 and 1983 indicated that it was 'frequently below mean high water'.[82]

Dinkum Sands had been treated as an island by the United States for the purposes of measuring the breadth of its territorial sea (pursuant to the TSC) up until 1984. This practice ceased in the same year that the Special Master heard evidence from the United States and Alaska regarding its physical attributes.[83] The issue was not that the feature had changed since it was first treated as an island (though it was subject to seasonal change due to its composition of ice and gravel). Rather, it was understood to have been *mischaracterized* as an island—its regular loss of elevation leaving

[77] A high standard of proof is likely to apply in view of the principle of the stability of boundaries. If it was not expressly provided when and how the boundary may be unilaterally adjusted, it will be difficult to rebut the presumption that it cannot be: see further Chapter 6.

[78] Exchange of Notes amending the 1991 Agreement (UK, Belgium: 2005).

[79] ILA-BC, *Final Report*, 20–1.

[80] *US v Alaska* (1997), 22–32.

[81] Ibid, 22.

[82] See *US v Alaska* (1997), 23, 29–30.

[83] According to the ILA-BC, an amendment to this effect was made at the US Baseline Committee Meeting of July 17, 1984: ILA-BC, *Final Report*, 20, fn 134.

it below high tide so often that it was not considered to meet the legal definition of an island. Whether or not this is a reasonable construal of the criterion 'above water at high tide' (which is arguably satisfied if the feature is above high tide at all), it is a conclusion concerning the lawfulness of the claim to a territorial sea in the first instance rather than its continuing lawfulness in the event of geographical change.

The Special Master found that Dinkum Sands did not in fact qualify as an island, not that it had lost its status as such due to subsequent geographical change. The decision to stop measuring the breadth of the territorial sea from it may thus be considered to have corrected an error made at the point of delimitation (and repeated in subsequent revisions of the limits of the territorial sea). The United States abandoned its claim to a territorial sea in respect of Dinkum Sands because it was understood that this feature did not in fact qualify as an island generating entitlement to this maritime zone. It did not abandon this claim in response to geographical change meaning that the feature was no longer above water at high tide.

State practice in respect of Rockall, Shipwash Sands, and Dinkum Sands does not support the conclusion that entitlement to maritime space will be lost or that established maritime limits must be adjusted in response to later geographical change. Of course, the broader practice of the United States suggests that it does consider maritime limits to be ambulatory in this sense and the Netherlands also considers the normal baseline to move with the coast. Yet this limited State practice does not establish either an authoritative interpretation of the law of the sea treaties or a customary rule to this effect. In fact, neither the treaty law nor custom *requires* the revision of maritime limits in response to geographical change. Nor does the law imply that entitlement to maritime space, once lawfully established, will be lost if geographical circumstances change. Equally, however, a coastal State that *elects* to adjust its maritime limits in the event of geographical change will not have breached international law. This is clearly permitted by the law, even in cases where it is based on a misunderstanding of what the law requires.

IV. Conclusion: Beyond the Ambulatory Thesis

The idea that maritime limits and some maritime boundaries might be 'ambulatory' has been considered at length in this study, which has also examined the related idea that entitlement to maritime space may be lost as a consequence of geographical change. The chief aim has been to elaborate and critique the arguments driving the ambulatory thesis, which also underpin predictions regarding the loss of entitlement to maritime space in the context of climate change. An effort has been made to expose and unsettle the assumptions on which this reasoning is based.

Projections regarding the coastal impacts of climate-related change have focused attention on the implications of erosion, inundation, and loss of habitability for maritime jurisdiction. Scholars of the law of the sea have overwhelmingly characterized this as a 'novel problem', and it is from this standpoint that the existing law has been judged unequal to the task of responding to the resulting harms. Indeed, the law is understood to compound the losses that will be suffered by providing that maritime rights are eroded with the coast. As such, the 'solution' is thought to ultimately require new law—even if tactical stop-gaps can be identified along the way.

This book challenges the prevailing characterization of the problem and concludes that the proposed solutions are unnecessary. It locates the impacts of climate change within a broader category of geographical change of potential significance for maritime jurisdiction. The existing scholarship has paid insufficient attention to the fact that the law was developed with full knowledge of the ordinary variability of the coastal environment and the features picked out in the baselines provisions in particular. The fact that change as rapid, substantial, and widespread as that accompanying climate change was not foreseen does not mean that the law does not already address the phenomenon of geographical change in a manner consistent with the broad goal of securing a stable legal order for the seas. Indeed, a detailed study of the positive law shows that geography plays a key role in securing the stability of this legal order without implying that its key components—entitlement to maritime space, maritime limits, and international maritime boundaries—remain at the mercy of the vagaries of nature.

It is important to recognize that neither geography nor geographical change map onto one side of the real or apparent binary oppositions often understood to constitute a source of tension in the law of the sea—e.g. general law and particular facts, objective and subjective considerations, stability and change. Scholars engaging with the question of the implications of climate-related change for maritime jurisdiction are clearly concerned that the stability of the international legal order is threatened by the prospect of increasingly rapid and extreme coastal change. Yet where the ambulatory thesis is advanced or affirmed, the nuances of 'stability' as an objective of the law of the sea and international law more generally are often lost. Above all, there is a tendency to identify stability with fixity and instability with change.

The detailed analysis of the law relating to maritime jurisdiction in this book helps to clarify the content of stability as a goal in this context. The law governing the construction of maritime limits is concerned with the establishment of ascertainable and so observable limits that are drawn consistently with generally applicable rules. Similar considerations account for the law relating to the construction of maritime boundaries, though States negotiating a boundary may agree to take other considerations into account (a court or tribunal is more constrained). Maritime limits and boundaries that cannot be identified and therefore respected are a source of instability. So too are limits and boundaries that are unduly vulnerable to legal challenge, whether through the courts or (as is more usual in the case of maritime limits) diplomatic protests.

The law relating to maritime jurisdiction furthers stability by insisting upon maritime limits and boundaries that are clearly defined. It is also in the interests of stability that it refrains from imposing excessively strict and exacting requirements on the coastal State. Instead, the law makes use of broad and somewhat flexible standards with a principled basis in the notion that 'the land dominates the sea'. It does not impose strict rules of construction, which may hamper the delimitation process and encourage objections to the resulting limits. Stability is served by maritime limits and boundaries that are readily established, identifiable, observable, and generally accepted by States.

The role of geography in the rules governing the construction of maritime limits and boundaries contributes substantially to this end. The law makes use of the spatial schema of nautical charts, where the complexity of coastal geography is already reduced to points and lines facilitating the construction of zones and limits which can be readily identified and observed. Referring to a limited number of ideal-typical geographical circumstances allows the application and, to some degree, adaptation of general rules to the diverse circumstances of coastal States globally. The principle that 'the land dominates the sea' is symbolically expressed in the identification of certain features of the coastal front as points of reference for locating the limits of different maritime zones and constructing interstate boundaries. All of these factors contribute to what appears to be a principled, regulated, and equitable system of delimitation, and thus to acceptance of that system and the limits and boundaries produced. The relationship between geography and entitlement to maritime space, maritime limits, and maritime boundaries is mediated by and directed towards particular legal objectives. Correspondingly, though not solely as a consequence, there is no synchronism or relationship of legal obligation between the fact of geographical change and either the loss of entitlement to maritime space or the redrawing of established maritime limits and boundaries.

In connection with international maritime boundaries (and international boundaries generally), the principle of stability means inter alia that the movement of an established boundary with subsequent geographical change will not be readily presumed. The intention to establish an ambulatory boundary should be clearly evidenced, though it need not be explicit (unless the circumstances indicate that an ambulatory boundary could only be established by express specification). As the Tribunal emphasized in the *Laguna del Desierto Revision and Interpretation Case* (1995),

> A boundary is an eminently legal concept. An international boundary consists of the contact line of the spatial spheres of validity of two State legal orders. In contrast... Chile postulates a physical concept of boundary and thus concludes that a frontier on a glacier is subject to the same shifts as the glacier. But this occurs only if a legal rule so prescribes and it does not depend on the natural conditions.[84]

[84] *Laguna del Desierto Revision/Interpretation* (1995), 166.

There is no legal rule that requires the relocation of a maritime boundary in response to coastal change.

The law relating to maritime jurisdiction reflects the more general truth that change is not by definition inconsistent with stability, although stability may demand reason and regularity in such change there is. The rules and principles relating to entitlement to maritime space and its delimitation make strategic and symbolic use of 'land' in a particular sense—as geography and, particularly, the cartographic representation of geography—to construct maritime jurisdiction as a spatial order. There is, however, no direct relationship or correspondence between stability and change in land and stability and change in law. The law of the sea has, indeed, been largely unconcerned with the dynamic materiality of geography. Instead, it makes use of the cartographical representation of coastal geography symbolically and for practical reasons—the symbolism itself having a practical role in ensuring that entitlement to maritime space and its delimitation is organized (and both facilitated and constrained) on a principled basis.

This clarification of what the existing law does with geography and, relatedly, what this can and cannot be understood to imply about the significance of geographical change, does not exclude the possibility that a change in the law to take more account of geographical materiality, including its dynamism, may be appropriate—particularly in the Anthropocene.[85] It is reasonable to conclude, however, that any such 'taking account' in the form of a simple equation of physical change with legal change would be likely to cause more harm than good. There are good reasons why the existing law does not make such an equation, though this is not to say that the manner in which it does conceptualize geography is beyond critique.

Scholars who advance or accept the ambulatory thesis overwhelmingly view its consequences as a problem to be overcome. They have canvassed a variety of ways to 'fix' baselines and thus the zonal limits measured from them against rising seas. These include measures to physically protect the coast against change and legal responses such as the increased use of straight baselines (where the law is considered

[85] See e.g. S Elden, 'Legal Terrain—The Political Materiality of Territory' (2017) 5 (2) *LRIL* 199, 222–4; P Steinberg, 'Free Sea' in Legg (ed), *Spatiality, Sovereignty and Carl Schmitt: Geographies of the Nomos* (Routledge, 2011) 270, 272–3; P Steinberg, K Coddington, 'From Ice Law to ICE LAW: Constructing an Interdisciplinary Research Project on the Political-Legal Challenges of Polar Environments' (2015) *Arctic Yearbook* 1–8. Here, too, there is value in a clearer understanding of the role of both geography and geographical change in the existing law. Steinberg's argument that 'UNCLOS reifies a distinction between land and water' that is incapable of dealing adequately with the phenomenon of ice, for example, is problematic insofar as it ignores aspects of the law of the sea that conceive of an interrelationship and interplay between land and sea in a manner that relates ideas relating to physical properties with ideas about human interests and use in a more nuanced way. The ambulatory thesis has played a role in making ice look more problematic than it is under the existing law. In this regard, it is useful to recall inter alia the broader and somewhat flexible concept of the legal 'coast' in the modern law of the sea, discussed in Chapter 1

to unusually permit the retention of this type of baseline, at least temporarily, in the event of coastal change). More ambitiously, several scholars have proposed the amendment of UNCLOS, the negotiation of a new treaty, or the development of a new customary rule through State practice.[86]

There are acknowledged problems with and obstacles to all of these proposed 'solutions'. Hard or soft engineering responses directed towards protecting features used in the construction of maritime limits may be at odds with and deflect resources away from measures required to protect the coastal environment, population, and infrastructure from rising seas and storm surges. States are likely to be unwilling to reopen a treaty which took almost a decade to negotiate (UNCLOS) and the negotiation of separate or supplementary agreements may reopen the seemingly intractable disputes suppressed if not accommodated by the 'package deal' approach at UNCLOS III. The development of custom would depend upon the belief of States retaining established limits in the event of coastal change that this practice is permitted by law. This is denied by the ambulatory thesis thought to necessitate a new customary rule to this effect.

Fortunately, these are difficulties that may be avoided altogether. This study has argued that there is no need for measures to physically or legally 'fix' maritime limits against coastal change or to secure continuing entitlement to maritime space in circumstances where geography has changed but territorial sovereignty is not in question. The existing law does not provide for ambulatory maritime limits or condition continuing entitlement to maritime space on geographical circumstances remaining unchanged. As such, the law need not be amended, supplemented, or replaced in order to overcome the undesirable consequences that would follow if entitlement to maritime space and maritime limits were contingent upon geography in this way. As it stands, States wishing to retain established entitlement to maritime space and unilaterally established maritime limits in the event of coastal change are permitted to so, unless they no longer possess territorial sovereignty over coastal land (which also depends, it has been argued, on whether they intend to give it up). States have always been free to agree on fixed maritime boundaries and, unless there is clear evidence that an ambulatory boundary was intended, there will be a presumption that established boundaries will not shift with subsequent changes to the coast or the baselines used for the unilateral delimitation of maritime space.

[86] See Prescott and Bird. 'The Influence of Rising Sea Levels on Baselines', 292–8; Caron, 'When Law Makes Climate Change Worse', 639–52; Caron, 'Climate Change, Sea Level Rise and the Coming Uncertainty in Oceanic Boundaries', 12–17; Freestone and Pethick, 'Sea Level Rise and Maritime Boundaries', 78–9, 83–7; Schofield, 'Sea Level Rise and Options to Secure Maritime Jurisdictional Claims', 411–14; Schofield, 'Rising Waters, Shrinking States', 214–30; Hayashi. 'Sea Level Rise and the Law of the Sea', 79–90; Schofield and Arsana, 'Climate Change and the Limits of Maritime Jurisdiction', 141–4; Schofield and Freestone, 'Options to Protect Coastlines', 150–63; Rayfuse, 'Sea Level Rise and Maritime Zones', 181–90.

Electing to retain established maritime limits or favouring fixed over ambulatory maritime boundaries will not halt the damaging effects of erosion and inundation on coastal environments, populations, and infrastructure. It will not ensure that fish stocks are still available or that the exploitation of mineral resources will continue to be either acceptable or profitable. Whether the current system of rights and duties under the law of the sea remains appropriate in the context of climate change is debateable.[87] Yet the automatic loss of entitlement to maritime space and retreat of maritime limits with increasing coastal erosion and inundation is not part of the problem.

The modern law of the sea is directed towards and generally achieves a stable division of maritime space, which brings a degree of order to the multiple uses of the sea by multiple actors. This is not a static arrangement, although change is regulated in the interests of stability. Maritime limits are established by deliberate action on the part of the coastal State through a process governed by law and may be revised the same way. Maritime boundaries established by agreement or the decision of a court or tribunal may be revised by subsequent agreement, which will be informed by the same general principles governing interstate delimitation. States negotiating or renegotiating a boundary will be bound by the applicable treaty law, though they may agree to depart from some of the principles developed in the case law by agreement and take other considerations into account. Entitlement to maritime space does not ordinarily depend on any particular act by the coastal State but follows automatically from the possession of coastal land (though in some cases entitlement must be proclaimed to be enforceable[88]). Additional conditions must be satisfied to establish claims to maritime space in respect of an island and claims to archipelagic waters. The State remains free to relinquish any or all of its established entitlement to maritime space.

The law gives geography a key role in the additional conditions for claims to maritime space and the construction of maritime limits and boundaries. It follows that geography will play the same role in any revision of maritime limits or renegotiation of maritime boundaries. It does not follow that subsequent geographical change will necessarily precipitate the loss or alteration of established

[87] It is worth noting that the extent of national maritime jurisdiction is not necessarily a problem in this context. As Jennings observed in 1972, 'a more constructive approach to … [t]he extension of national jurisdiction', which is 'something that has already happened on quite a large scale', may be to 'harness it to the purposes of international law and regulation for the general benefit' rather than simply object to it: R Jennings, 'A Changing International Law of the Sea' (1972) 31 (1) *CLJ* 32, 48. Though Jennings did not have the particular problems associated with climate change in mind, certain qualifications of the rights of States at sea, already associated with duties regarding inter alia the preservation of the marine environment, might support mitigation of and adaptation to climate change. More radical changes to the content of State rights and obligations at sea may be required in response to climate change. These changes, too, could be made without altering the spatial extent of coastal State jurisdiction in the sea. Of course, it might still be desirable to limit or reduce the area of sea space in which States possess jurisdiction: the point is that changes to the content of national maritime jurisdiction and not just its spatial extent should be considered in the context of climate change.

[88] See Chapter 9.

rights and legal limits. The law neither expressly provides nor implies that such a serious displacement of sovereignty and sovereign rights—prejudicial not only to the interests of the coastal State but to the stability of the legal order as a whole—should accompany 'the meaningless plungings of water and the wind'[89] against the changeable coast.

[89] Wallace Stevens, 'The Idea of Order at Key West' [1934] in *The Collected Poems of Wallace Stevens* (Vintage Books, 1990) 128, 129.

Bibliography

ABLOS, *Manual on Technical Aspects of UNCLOS* C-51 (4th edn, IHB, 2006).
Alexander, LM, 'Baseline Delimitations and Maritime Boundaries' (1982–83) 23 *VJIL* 503.
Alvarez-Jimenez, A, 'The International Court of Justice's Use of the Vienna Convention in the Interpretation of Boundary Agreements: 2000–10' 3 (2) (2012) *JIDS* 409.
Anderson, D, 'Belgium-United Kingdom: Report Number 9-17' in Charney and Alexander (eds), *International Maritime Boundaries*, vol 2 (ASIL/Martinus Nijhoff, 2004) 1901.
Anderson, D, 'Negotiating Maritime Boundary Agreements: A Personal View' in Lagoni and Vignes (eds), *Maritime Delimitation* (Martinus Nijhoff, 2006) 121–41.
Anderson, D, 'The Principle of Reasonableness in the Law of the Sea' in Hestermeyer et al (eds), *Co-Existence, Cooperation and Solidarity: Liber Amicorum Rüdiger Wolfrum*, vol 1 (Martinus Nijhoff, 2012) 657.
Anderson, D, 'Some Aspects of the Regime of Islands in the Law of the Sea' (2017) 32 *IJMCL* 316.
Anzilotti, D, 'Intorno agli effete delle modificazioni del corso di un fiume sul confine fra due stati' in La Società Italiana per l'Organizzazione Internazionale (ed), *Opere di Dionisio Anzilotti: Scritti di Diritto Internazionale Publico*, vol 1 (Cedam, 1956) 701.
Anzilotti, D, *Corso di diritto internazionale*, vol 1 (Athenaeum, 1912), 206, translation in Sereni, AP, 'Agency in International Law' (1940) 34 *AJIL* 638.
Aquarone, M, 'The 1985 Guinea/Guinea-Bissau Maritime Boundary Case and its Implications' (1995) 26(4) *ODIL* 413.
Are, F, Reimnitz, E, 'An Overview of the Lena River Delta Setting: Geology, Tectonics, Geomorphology and Hydrology' (2000) 16 (4) *JCR* 1083.
Árnadóttir, S, 'Termination of Maritime Boundaries Due to a Fundamental Change of Circumstances' (2016) 32 (83) *UJIEL* 94.
Bateman, S, Schofield, C, 'State Practice regarding Straight Baselines in East Asia – Legal, Technical and Political Issues in a Changing Environment' (ABLOS Conference, IHB, Monaco, 16–17 October 2008).
Baumert, K, 'The Outer Limits of the Continental Shelf under Customary International Law' (2018) 111 (4) *AJIL* 827.
Becker, MA, Rose, C, 'Investigating the Value of Site Visits in Inter-State Arbitration and Adjudication' (2017) 8 *JIDS* 219.
Beckett, WE, 'Les questions d'intérêt général au point de vue juridique dans la jurisprudence de la Cour permanente de Justice internationale' (1934) 50 *Recueil des Cours* 189.
Bingham, JW, 'The Continental Shelf and the Marginal Belt' (1946) 40 *AJIL* 173.
Bird, E, *Coastal Geomorphology* (2nd edn, Wiley, 2008).
Bird, E (ed), *Encyclopedia of the World's Coastal Landforms* (Springer, 2010).
Boggs, SW, 'Delimitation of Seaward Areas under National Jurisdiction' (1951) 45 *AJIL* 240.
Bolin, B, *A History of the Science and Politics of Climate Change: The Role of the Intergovernmental Panel on Climate Change* (CUP, 2007).
Bouchez, LJ, 'The Fixing of Boundaries in International Boundary Rivers' (1963) 12 *ICLQ* 789.
Bowditch, N, *The American Practical Navigator* (US NIMA, 2002).

Brownlie, I, *Principles of Public International Law* (7th edn, OUP, 2008).
Brubaker, RD, 'The Legal Status of the Russian Baselines in the Arctic' (1999) 30 (3) *ODIL* 191.
Calder, N, *How to Read a Nautical Chart* (McGraw Hill Professional, 2002).
Carleton, C, 'Problems Relating to Non-natural and Man-made Basepoints under UNCLOS' in Symmons (ed), *Selected Contemporary Issues in the Law of the Sea* (Martinus Nijhoff, 2011) 31.
Carleton, C, Schofield, C, 'Developments in the Technical Determination of Maritime Space: Charts, Datums, Baselines, Maritime Zones and Limits' (2001) 3 *Maritime Briefing* 1.
Caron, D, 'When Law Makes Climate Change Worse: Rethinking Baselines in Light of a Changing Sea Level' (1990) 17 *ELQ* 621.
Caron, D, 'Climate Change, Sea Level Rise and the Coming Uncertainty in Oceanic Boundaries: A Proposal to Avoid Conflict' in Hong and Van Dyke (eds), *Maritime Boundary Disputes, Settlement Processes, and the Law of the Sea* (Martinus Nijhoff, 2009) 1.
Cassella, S, 'Rééquilibrer les effets inéquitables d'une délimitation territoriale' (2009) *AFDI* 253.
Charney, JI, 'Rocks that Cannot Sustain Human Habitation' (1999) 93 (4) *AJIL* 863.
Churchill, R, Lowe, V, *The Law of the Sea* (3rd edn, MUP, 1999).
CLCS, *Scientific and Technical Guidelines* (1999).
Colson, D, 'The Delimitation of the Outer Continental Shelf between Neighboring States' (2003) 97 (1) *AJIL* 91.
Cook, P, Carleton C (eds), *Continental Shelf Limits: The Scientific and Legal Interface* (OUP, 2000).
Corten, O, 'Reasonableness in International Law', MPEPIL Online, accessed 24 April 2018.
Crawford, J, *The Creation of States in International Law* (2nd edn, OUP, 2007).
Crawford, J, *Brownlie's Principles of Public International Law* (8th edn, OUP, 2012).
Cushing, C, 'Arcifinious Boundaries' (1856) 8 *Opinions of the Attorney General of the United States* 175.
D'Amato, A, 'International Law, Intertemporal Problems' in Bernhardt (ed), *Encyclopedia of Public International Law* (2nd edn., North-Holland, 1992) 1234.
Dörr, O, 'Article 31, General Rule of Interpretation' in Dörr and Schmalenbach (eds), *Vienna Convention on the Law of Treaties: A Commentary* (Springer, 2018) 560.
IHO Data Quality Working Group, 'Safe Navigation with Uncertain Hydrographic Data: The Representation of Data Quality in the IHO S-101 Data Model' (6 June 2012) *Hydro International*, <https://www.hydro-international.com/content/article/safe-navigation-with-uncertain-hydrographic-data> accessed 13 February 2017.
Dugard, J, *International Law: The South African Perspective* (3rd edn, Juta, 2005).
Dzurek, D, Schofield, C, 'Parting the Red Sea: Boundaries, Offshore Resources and Transit' (2001) 3 (2) *IBRU Maritime Briefing* 1.
Elden, S, 'Legal Terrain—The Political Materiality of Territory' (2017) 5 (2) *LRIL* 199.
Elias, T, 'The Doctrine of Intertemporal Law' (1980) 74 *AJIL* 285.
Evans, M, *Relevant Circumstances and Maritime Delimitation* (OUP, 1989).
Ferrero, S, Pierozzi, M, Repetti, L, Surace, L, 'An Algorithm for the Unambiguous Determination of the Equidistant Boundary Line between Two (or More) Coastlines' (2009) 1 *Applied Geomatics* 49.
Fietta, S, Cleverly, R, *A Practitioner's Guide to Maritime Boundary Delimitation* (OUP, 2016).
Fisheries and Oceans Canada, 'Tides, Currents, and Water Levels', <http://www.waterlevels.gc.ca>.
Freestone, D, Pethick, JS, 'Sea Level Rise and Maritime Boundaries: International Implications of Impacts and Responses' in Blake (ed), *Maritime Boundaries: World Boundaries*, vol 5 (Routledge, 1994) 73.

Friedman, LM, 'Legal Rules and the Process of Social Change' (1967) 19 *SLR* 786.

Gaja, G, 'General Principles of International Law', MPEPIL Online, accessed 27 June 2017.

Gardiner, R, *Treaty Interpretation* (2nd edn, OUP, 2015).

Geoscience Australia, 'Computing Australia's Maritime Boundaries', <http://www.ga.gov.au/scientific-topics/marine/jurisdiction/maritime-boundaries> accessed 28 March 2016.

Geoscience Australia, 'Australian Ocean Governance and Relevant Legislation', <http://www.ga.gov.au/scientific-topics/marine/jurisdiction/amsis/australian-ocean-governance-and-relevant-legislation> accessed 12 October 2016.

Geoscience Australia, *Seas and Submerged Lands Act 1973: Australian Maritime Boundaries 2014a – Geodatabase*, <http://dx.doi.org/10.4225/25/5539DFE87D895> accessed 12 October 2016.

Gidel, G, *Le plateau continental* (Martinus Nijhoff, 1952).

Grote Stoutenberg, J, *Disappearing Island States in International Law* (Brill, 2015).

Grotius, H, *The Rights of War and Peace* [1646] (Liberty Fund, 2005).

Hart, HLA, *The Concept of Law* (2nd edn, Clarendon, 1994).

Harvard Research, 'The Law of Territorial Waters' (1929) 23 (2) *AJIL Supplement* 241.

Haslett, S, *Coastal Systems* (Routledge, 2008).

Hayashi, M, 'Sea Level Rise and the Law of the Sea: Legal and Policy Options' in *Proceedings of International Symposium on Islands and Oceans* (2009).

Hodgson, RD, Alexander, LM, 'Towards an Objective Analysis of Special Circumstances: Bays, Rivers, Coastal and Oceanic Archipelagos and Atolls' (1972) 13*Law of the Sea Institute University of Rhode Island Occasional Paper* 1.

Houghton, K, Neumann, B, Vafeidis, AT, Alexander, P, 'Maritime Boundaries in a Rising Sea' (2010) 3 *Nature Geoscience* 813.

IDI, *Projet de règlement relatif à la mer territoriale en temps de paix* (Stockholm, 1928).

IDI, *Règles sur la définition et le régime de la mer territorial* (Paris, 1894).

IHO, 'Chart Datum Definition', IHO Resolution 3/1919, as amended 2008.

IHO, *Hydrographic Dictionary* S-32 (5th edn, IHB, 1994).

IHO, *Manual on Hydrography* (1st edn, IHB, 2005, as corrected).

IHO, *Standards for Hydrographic Surveys* S-44 (5th edn, IHB, 2008).

IHO, *Transfer Standard for Digital Hydrographic Data* S-57 (3.1 edn, IHB, 2010).

IHO, *Regulations for International Charts and Chart Specifications* S-4 (4.7.0 edn, July 2017).

IHO, *Status of Hydrographic Surveying and Charting Worldwide* C-55 (IHB, 2011) and (IHB, 2018).

ILA-BC, *Baselines under the International Law of the Sea: Internal Discussion Document* (2010).

ILA-BC, *Baselines under the International Law of the Sea: Final Report* (Sofia Conference, 2012).

ILA Neutrality Committee, Draft Convention on the Laws of Maritime Jurisdiction in Time of Peace (Vienna, 1926).

ILA, *Report of the Forty-Fourth Conference* (Copenhagen, 1950).

ILA, *Report of the Forty-fifth Conference* (Lucerne, 1952).

ILA, *Report of the Forty-Sixth Conference* (Edinburgh, 1954).

ILA Sea Level Rise Committee, *International Law and Sea Level Rise: Conference Report* (2018).

ILC, 'Conclusions Relating to Unilateral Acts of States' (20 July 2006) UN Doc. A/CN.4/L.703.

ILC, 'Guiding Principles Applicable to Unilateral Declarations of States' (2006), UN Doc. A/61/10.

ILC, 'Draft Conclusions on Identification of Customary International Law, with Commentaries' (2018), UN Doc. A/73/10.

ILC, 'Draft Conclusions on Subsequent Agreements and Subsequent Practice in Relation to the Interpretation of Treaties' (2018), UN Doc. A/73/10.

ILC, Yearbooks of the ILC 1951-1956, 1966, <http://untreaty.un.org/ilc/publications/yearbooks/yearbooks.htm>.

Intergovernmental Panel on Climate Change, *Fifth Assessment Report* (IPCC, 2014).

Inventory of Papers of the UN Conferences on the Law of the Sea, MSS 82-6, Special Collections, University of Virginia Law Library).

Jacob, C, *The Sovereign Map: Theoretical Approaches in Cartography throughout History* (UCP, 2006).

Jennings, R, *The Acquisition of Territory in International Law* (MUP, 1963).

Jennings, R, 'A Changing International Law of the Sea' (1972) 31 (1) *CLJ* 32.

Jennings, R, 'Equity and Equitable Principles' (1986) 42 *ASDI* 27.

Jennings, R, Watts, A (eds), *Oppenheim's International Law* (9th edn, OUP, 2008).

Jessup, P, 'The Palmas Island Arbitration' (1928) 22 *AJIL* 735.

Kaikobad, KH, 'Some Observations on the Doctrine of the Continuity and Finality of Boundaries' (1983) 54 *BYIL* 119.

Kaikobad, KH, *Interpretation and Revision of International Boundary Agreements* (CUP, 2007).

Keller, AS, Lissitzyn, OJ, Mann, FJ, *Creation of Rights of Sovereignty through Symbolic Acts, 1400–1800* (Columbia University Press, 1938).

Kennedy, RH, 'Brief Remarks on Median Lines and Lines of Equidistance and the Methods Used in their Construction', provided by the UK delegation to the first United Nations Law of the Sea Conference, 2 April 1958.

Khadem, A, 'Protecting Maritime Zones from the Effects of Sea Level Rise' [1998] *IBRU Boundary and Security Bulletin* 76.

Kittichaisaree, K, *The Law of the Sea and Maritime Boundary Delimitation in South-East Asia* (OUP, 1987).

Klabbers, J, 'Treaties, Amendment and Revision' in MPEPIL Online, accessed 5 December 2018.

Kohen, M, *Lecture on Uti Possidetis and Maritime Delimitations*, UN Audiovisual Library of International Law <http://legal.un.org/avl/ls/Kohen_BD.html>.

Kohen, M, 'Territory, Abandonment' in MPEPIL Online, accessed 22 February 2016.

Kopela, S, *Dependent Archipelagos in the Law of the Sea* (Martinus Nijhoff, 2013).

Koskenniemi, M, Lehto, M, 'Finland and the Law of the Sea' in Treves and Pineschi (eds), *The Law of the Sea: The European Union and its Member States* (Martinus Nijhoff, 1997) 127.

Kwiatkowska, B, Soons, A, 'Entitlement to Maritime Areas of Rocks Which Cannot Sustain Human Habitation or Economic Life of Their Own' (1990) 21 *NYIL* 139.

Lalonde, S, 'The Role of the Uti Possidetis Juris Principle in the Resolution of Maritime Boundary Disputes' in Chinkin and Baetens (eds), *Sovereignty, Statehood and State Responsibility: Essays in Honour of James Crawford* (CUP, 2015) 248.

Land Information New Zealand, <http://www.linz.govt.nz/hydro/tidal-info/tidal-intro/meteorological-effects> accessed 18 September 2013.

Lapradelle, A de, 'Le droit de l'État sur la mer territoriale' (1898) *RGDIP* 264.

Lauterpacht, H, 'Sovereignty over Submarine Areas' (1950) 27 *BYIL* 376.

Legault, L, Hankey B, 'Method, Oppositeness and Adjacency, and Proportionality in Maritime Boundary Delimitation' in Charney and Alexander (eds), *International Maritime Boundaries* (ASIL, 1993) 203.

Linderfalk, U, The Application of International Legal Norms over Time: The Second Branch of Intertemporal Law' (2011) 58 *NILR* 147.

Lloyd Nash, M, *Digest of United States Practice in International Law 1978* (US DOS, 1980).

Malanczuk, P, *Akehurst's Modern Introduction to International Law* (7th edn, Routledge, 1996).

Maling, DH, *Measurements from Maps: Principles and Methods of Cartometry* (Pergamon, 1989).

Marston, G, 'The Stability of Land and Sea Boundary Delimitations in International Law' in Blake (ed), *Maritime Boundaries* (Routledge, 1994) 144.

Marston, G, 'The British Acquisition of the Nicobar Islands, 1869: A Possible Example of Abandonment of Territorial Sovereignty' (1999) 69 (1) *BYIL* 245.

McDonald, S, Prescott, V, 'Baselines along Unstable Coasts: An Interpretation of Article 7(2)' (1989) 8 *Ocean Yearbook* 70.

McDorman, T, 'The Entry into Force of the 1982 Convention and the Article 76 Outer Continental Shelf Regime' (1995) 10 *IJMCL* 165.

McDorman, T, 'The Role of the Commission on the Limits of the Continental Shelf: A Technical Body in a Political World' (2002) 17 *IJMCL* 301.

McDougal, M, Burke W, *The Public Order of the Oceans: A Contemporary International Law of the Sea* (YUP, 1962).

Monmonier, M, *How to Lie with Maps* (2nd edn, UCP, 1991).

Mossop, J, *The Continental Shelf beyond 200 Nautical Miles: Rights and Responsibilities* (OUP, 2016).

Mouton, MW, *The Continental Shelf* (Martinus Nijhoff, 1952).

Nandan, SN, The EEZ: A Historical Perspective' in UNFAO, *Essays in Memory of Jean Carroz: The Law and the Sea* (FAO, 1987).

National Trust for Scotland, 'St Kilda', <http://www.kilda.org.uk> accessed 7 July 2013.

NOAA, *US Coast Pilot*, vol 3 (45th edn, US GPO, 2012).

Nordquist, MH (ed.), *United Nations Convention on the Law of the Sea 1982: A Commentary* (University of Virginia Center for Oceans Law and Policy, Kluwer) (vol 1, 1985) (vol 2, 1993).

Nys, E, *Le droit international: les principes, les theories, les faits*, vol 2 (Castaigne, 1905).

O'Keefe, R, 'Legal Title versus *Effectivités*: Prescription and the Promise and Problems of Private Law Analogies' (2011) 13 *ICLR* 147.

Oppenheim, L, *International Law: A Treatise*, vol 1 (1st edn, Longmans, Green & Co, 1905).

Orakhelashvili, A, 'Natural Law and Customary Law' (2008) 68 *HJIL* 69.

Orrego Vicuña, F, *The Exclusive Economic Zone* (CUP, 1989).

Oude Elferink, A, 'International Law and Negotiated and Adjudicated Maritime Boundaries: A Complex Relationship' (2015) 58 *GYIL* 232.

Oude Elferink, A, 'The Commission on the Limits of the Continental Shelf', MPEPIL Online, accessed 28 February 2018.

Pardo, A 'Who Will Control the Seabed?'(1968) 47 *Foreign Affairs* 124.

Parish, CE, 'Shoreline Mapping' in Yang and Li, *Advances in Mapping from Remote Sensor Imagery* (CRC Press, 2012) 145.

Peter Bernhardt, J, Smith, RW, Greiveldinger, G, *Standard Guidelines for Evaluating Straight Baselines* (US Office of Ocean Law and Policy, 1987).

Phillimore, R, *Commentaries upon International Law*, vol 1 (T & JW Johnson, 1854).

Platzöder, R (ed.), *Third United Nations Conference on the Law of the Sea: Documents* (Oceana) (vol IV, 1983) (vol V, 1984).

Powers, A, Stucko, C, 'Introducing the Law of the Sea and the Legal Implications of Rising Sea Levels' in Gerrard and Wannier (eds), *Threatened Island Nations: Legal Implications of Rising Seas and a Changing Climate* (CUP, 2013) 123.

Prescott, V, *The Gulf of Thailand* (MIM, 1998).

Prescott, V, 'Straight and Archipelagic Baselines' in Blake (ed), *Maritime Boundaries and Ocean Resources* (Routledge, 1987) 44.

Prescott, V, 'Indian Ocean Boundaries' in Colson and Smith (eds), *International Maritime Boundaries*, vol 5 (Martinus Nijhoff, 2005) 3457.

Prescott, V, Bird, E, 'The Influence of Rising Sea Levels on Baselines from which National Maritime Claims Are Measured and an Assessment of the Possibility of Applying Article 7(2) of the 1982 Convention on the Law of the Sea to Offset Any Retreat of the Baseline' in *International Boundaries and Boundary Conflict Resolution: Conference Proceedings 1989* (IBRU, 1990) 279.

Prescott, V, Schofield C, *Maritime Political Boundaries of the World* (2nd edn, Martinus Nijhoff, 2005).

Pufendorf, S, *Of the Law of Nature and Nations* [1729] (Clarendon, 1934).

Pugh, DT, *Changing Sea Levels: Effects of Tides, Weather, and Climate* (CUP, 2004).

Purcell, K, 'Maritime Jurisdiction in a Changing Climate' in Gerrard and Kuh (eds), *The Law of Adaptation to Climate Change: US and International Aspects* (ABA, 2012) 731.

Ranganathan, S, 'Global Commons' (2016) 27 (3) *EJIL* 693.

Rayfuse, R, 'W(h)ither Tuvalu? International Law and Disappearing States' (2009) Paper 9 *UNSWLRS* 1.

Rayfuse, R, 'International Law and Disappearing States: Utilising Maritime Entitlements to Overcome the Statehood Dilemma' (2010) Paper 52 *UNSWLRS* 1.

Rayfuse, R, 'International Law and Disappearing States: Maritime Zones and the Criteria for Statehood' (2011) 41 (6) *EPL* 281.

Rayfuse, R, 'Climate Change and the Law of the Sea' in Rayfuse and Scott (eds), *International Law in the Era of Climate Change* (Edward Elgar, 2012) 147.

Rayfuse, R, 'Sea Level Rise and Maritime Zones: Preserving the Maritime Entitlements of "Disappearing" States' in Gerrard and Wannier (eds), *Threatened Island Nations: Legal Implications of Rising Seas and a Changing Climate* (CUP, 2013) 167.

Redgwell, C, 'UNCLOS and Climate Change' (2012) 106 *ASIL Proceedings* 406.

Reed, MW, *Shore and Sea Boundaries*, vol 3 (US GPO, 2000).

Reisman, WM, Westerman, GS, *Straight Baselines in International Maritime Boundary Delimitation* (Macmillan, 1992).

Roach, JA, Smith, RW, *United States Responses to Excessive Maritime Claims* (2nd edn, Martinus Nijhoff, 1996).

Roach, JA, Smith, RW, 'Straight Baselines: The Need for a Universally Applied Norm' (2000) 31 *ODIL* 47.

Roach, JA, Smith, RW, *Excessive Maritime Claims* (3rd edn, Martinus Nijhoff, 2012).

Roberts, A, 'Comparative International Law? The Role of National Courts in Creating and Enforcing International Law' (2011) 60 *ICLQ* 57.

Rosenne, S (ed), *League of Nations Conference for the Codification of International Law (1930)*, vols 1–4 (Oceana Publications, 1975).

Rosenne, S, *Interpretation, Revision, and Other Recourse from International Judgments and Awards* (Martinus Nijhoff, 2007).

Roth, RE, 'The Rio Grande', MPEPIL Online, accessed 30 January 2018.

Rothwell, D, Stephens, T, *The International Law of the Sea* (Bloomsbury, 2016).

Royal Netherlands Navy, Hydrographic Service, 'Maritime Zones and Boundaries', <https://english.defensie.nl/topics/hydrography/maritime-zones-and-boundaries> accessed 10 January 2015.

Sahlins, P, 'Natural Frontiers Revisited: France's Boundaries since the Seventeenth Century' (1990) 95 (5) *AHR* 1423.

Seabed Committee (Ad Hoc), Report of the Ad Hoc Committee to Study the Peaceful Uses of the Sea-bed (1968) 23 UNGAOR, Doc. A/7230.

Seabed Committee, Report of the Committee on the Peaceful Uses of the Sea-bed and the Ocean Floor beyond the Limits of National Jurisdiction (1970) 25 UN GAOR Supp. 21, UN Doc. A/8021.

Seabed Committee, Report of the Committee on the Peaceful Uses of the Sea-bed and the Ocean Floor beyond the Limits of National Jurisdiction (1971) 26 UN GAOR Supp. 21, UN Doc. A/8421.

Seabed Committee, Report of the Committee on the Peaceful Uses of the Sea-bed and the Ocean Floor beyond the Limits of National Jurisdiction (1972) 27 UN GAOR Supp. 21, UN Doc. A/8721.

Seabed Committee, Report of the Committee on the Peaceful Uses of the Sea-bed and the Ocean Floor beyond the Limits of National Jurisdiction (1973) 28 UNGAOR, Supp. 21, UN Doc. A/9021, Volumes 1–6.

Scheffers, A, Browne, T, 'Egypt—Mediterranean' in Bird (ed), *Encyclopedia of the World's Coastal Landforms* (Springer, 2010) 893.

Schofield, C, 'Against a Rising Tide: Ambulatory Baselines and Shifting Maritime Limits in the Face of Sea Level Rise' in *Proceedings of International Symposium on Islands and Oceans* (Ocean Policy Research Foundation, 2009) 70.

Schofield, C, 'Sea Level Rise and Options to Secure Maritime Jurisdictional Claims' (2009) 4 *CCLR* 405.

Schofield, C, 'Rising Waters, Shrinking States: The Potential Impacts of Sea Level Rise on Claims to Maritime Jurisdiction' (2010) 53 *GYIL* 189.

Schofield, C, Arsana, A, 'Climate Change and the Limits of Maritime Jurisdiction' in Warner and Schofield (eds), *Climate Change and the Oceans: Gauging the Legal and Policy Currents in the Asia Pacific and Beyond* (Edward Elgar, 2012) 127.

Schofield, C, Freestone, D, 'Options to Protect Coastlines and Secure Maritime Jurisdictional Claims in the Face of Global Sea Rise' in Gerrard and Wannier (eds), *Threatened Island Nations: Legal Implications of Rising Seas and a Changing Climate* (CUP, 2013) 141.

Schofield, C, Sas, B, 'Uncovered and Unstable Coasts: Climate Change and Territorial Sea Baselines in the Arctic' in Lalonde and McDorman, *International Law and Politics of the Arctic Ocean: Essays in Honor of Donat Pharand* (Hotei, 2015) 330.

Scovazzi, T, 'Baselines', MPEPIL Online, accessed 24 November 2015.

Selivanov, A, 'The Arctic Coast of Russia' in Bird (ed), *Encyclopedia of the World's Coastal Landforms* (Springer, 2010) 823.

Shaw, M, 'The Heritage of States: The Principle of Uti Possidetis Juris Today' (1996) 67 *BYIL* 75.

Shaw, M, 'Peoples, Territorialism and Boundaries' (1997) 8 *EJIL* 478.

Soons, A, 'The Effects of a Rising Sea Level on Maritime Limits and Boundaries' (1990) 37 *NILR* 207.

Sorel, J, Eveno, V, 'Article 31, General Rule of Interpretation' in Corten and Klein, *The Vienna Conventions on the Law of Treaties: A Commentary*, vol 1 (OUP, 2011).

Steinberg, P, 'Free Sea' in Legg (ed), *Spatiality, Sovereignty and Carl Schmitt: Geographies of the Nomos* (Routledge, 2011) 270.

Steinberg, P, Coddington, K, 'From Ice Law to ICE LAW: Constructing an Interdisciplinary Research Project on the Political-Legal Challenges of Polar Environments' (2015) *Arctic Yearbook* 1.

Stevens, W, 'The Idea of Order at Key West' [1934] in *The Collected Poems of Wallace Stevens* (Vintage Books, 1990) 128.

Tanaka, Y, *Predictability and Flexibility in the Law of Maritime Delimitation* (Hart, 2006).

Thirlway, H, 'The Law and Procedure of the International Court of Justice 1960–1989: Supplement, 2007: Parts Four, Five and Six' (2007) 78 *BYIL* 17.

Treves, T, 'The Development of the Law of the Sea since the Adoption of UNCLOS', paper given at the FNI Conference, 'The World Ocean in Globalization: Challenges for Marine Regions', Oslo, 21–23 August 2008,.

Twiss, T, *Law of Nations Considered as Independent Political Communities - On the Rights and Duties of Nations in Time of Peace* (2nd edn, Clarendon Press, 1884).

UNDOALOS, *Law of the Sea: Current Developments in State Practice* (UN Publications, 1987).

UNCLOS I Official Records, Volumes I to VII, <http://untreaty.un.org/cod/diplomaticconferences/lawofthesea-1958/lawofthesea-1958.html>.

UNCLOS II Official Records, Volumes I and II, <http://untreaty.un.org/cod/diplomaticconferences/lawofthesea-1960/lawofthesea-1960.html>.

UNCLOS III Official Records, Volumes I to XVI, <http://untreaty.un.org/cod/diplomaticconferences/lawofthesea-1982/lawofthesea-1982.html>.

UNGA First Committee, 'Examination of the question of the reservation exclusively for peaceful purposes of the seabed . . . beyond the limits of present national jurisdiction, and the use of their resources in the interests of mankind' (1 November 1967), UN Doc. A/C.1/PV.1515 & 1516.

UNGA First Commiteee, 'Report of the Committee on the Peaceful Uses of the Sea-Bed and the Ocean Floor beyond the Limits of National Jurisdiction' (15 December 1969), UN Doc. A/PV.1833.

UNOLA, *Summary of Practice of the Secretary-General as Depositary of Multilateral Treaties* (UN Publications, 1999).

US Commentary on UNCLOS (1995) 34 *ILM* 1400.

US Commission on Marine Science, Engineering and Resources, *Our Nation and the Sea: A Plan for National Action* (US GPO, 1969).

US DoD, *Maritime Claims Reference Manual* (2014), <https://www.jag.navy.mil/organization/code_10_mcrm.htm>.

US Hydrographic Office, Records 1754–1971, <https://www.archives.gov/research/guide-fed-records/groups/037.html> accessed 31 May 2019.

US NOAA, 'History of Coast Survey', < https://nauticalcharts.noaa.gov/about/history-of-coast-survey.html> accessed 15 October 2019.

US NOAA, 'Chart Updates', <https://nauticalcharts.noaa.gov/charts/chart-updates.html > accessed 12 October 2019.

US NOAA, 'Tides and Currents', <https://tidesandcurrents.noaa.gov/datum_options.html> accessed 6 February 2017.

US NOAA, 'Tides and Water Levels', <http://oceanservice.noaa.gov/education/kits/tides/tides07_cycles.html> accessed 1 July 2012.

US NOAA, *US Coast Pilot*, vol 3 (45th edn, US GPO, 2012).

US DOS, 'Straight Baselines: Venezuela' (1970) 21 *LIS* 1.

US DOS, 'Straight Baselines: Sweden' (1972) 47 *LIS* 1.

US DOS, 'Straight Baselines: Finland' (1972) 48 *LIS* 1.

US DOS, 'Straight Baselines: Germany' (1974) 38 *LIS* 1.

US DOS, 'Straight Baselines: Denmark' (1978) 19 *LIS* 1.

US DOS, 'United States Responses to Excessive Maritime Claims' (1992) 112 *LIS* 1.

US DOS, 'Continental Shelf Boundary: Turkey-USSR and Straight Baselines USSR (Black Sea)' (1988) 109 *LIS* 1.

US DOS, 'Straight Baseline Claims: Albania and Egypt' (1994) 116 *LIS* 1.

US DOS, 'Defining the Limits of the U.S. Continental Shelf', <https://2001-2009.state.gov/g/oes/continentalshelf//index.htm>, accessed 14 August 2011.

US Office of Coast Survey, 'U.S. Maritime Limits and Boundaries', <http://www.nauticalcharts.noaa.gov/csdl/mbound.htm> accessed 11 September, 2013.

US Office of Coast Survey, 'Law of the Sea', <https://web.archive.org/web/20131012232558/http://www.nauticalcharts.noaa.gov/staff/law_of_sea.html>, accessed 12 September 2013.

Vattel, E, *Law of Nations* [1758] (Liberty Fund, 2008).

Versfelt, W, *The Miangas Arbitration* (Kemink, 1933).

Weil, P, *The Law of Maritime Delimitation—Reflections* (Grotius Publications, 1989).

Wheaton, H, *Elements of International Law* (2nd edn, Little, Brown & Company, 1863).

Wolff, C, *The Law of Nations Treated According to a Scientific Method* [1743] (Clarendon, 1934).

Wolfrum, R, 'General International Law (Principles, Rules, Standards)', MPEPIL Online, accessed 30 June 2018.

Yielding, KD, 'The Chamizal Dispute: An Exercise in Arbitration 1845–1945', PhD thesis (Texas Tech University, 1973).

Index

Note: *For the benefit of digital users, indexed terms that span two pages (e.g., 52–53) may, on occasion, appear on only one of those pages.*